TEN YEARS OF UK COMPETITION LAW REFORM

TEN YEARS OF UK COMPETITION LAW REFORM

Edited by
Barry J Rodger

DUNDEE UNIVERSITY PRESS
2010

First published in Great Britain in 2010 by
Dundee University Press
University of Dundee
Dundee DD1 4HN

www.dup.dundee.ac.uk

ISBN 978-1-84586-097-4

No natural forests were destroyed to make this product;
only farmed timber was used and replanted.

British Library Cataloguing-in-Publication Data
A catalogue for this book is available on request from the British Library.

Typeset by Fakenham Photosetting, Norfolk
Printed and bound by the MPG Books Group, Bodmin and King's Lynn

CONTENTS

FOREWORD

A BIRD'S EYE VIEW

Each of the authors of the 11 chapters of this book brings to their subject a level of scholarship that is hard to match. The reader will find not merely a detailed account of competition law in the UK over the last 10 years, in all its many facets, but considerable insight into the strength and weaknesses of the UK system, and some interesting pointers for the future.

As a matter of description, one overriding impression is the extent to which the UK system still differs from its counterparts in the rest of the EU. Thus, as Richard Whish points out in Chapter 1, in his account of the Office of Fair Trading (OFT), the latter has responsibility for both competition and consumer protection, and in any given instance can resort to a "toolkit" of different measures, whether a market study, a reference to the Competition Commission (CC) for a market investigation, or action under statutes other than the Competition Act 1998 (CA 1998) or the Enterprise Act 2002 (EA).[1] These are wider powers than those enjoyed by most European competition authorities. Similarly the CAT, whose early case law is described by David Bailey (Chapter 2), and which is discussed by a number of other authors, is unique within the EU as a specifically created specialised competition court, with a full merits jurisdiction as regards CA 1998 infringements.[2]

As to private litigation, covered in Chapter 3 by Barry Rodger, who has followed this aspect for many years, the UK scene is as lively as any and, despite some teething troubles,[3] may well become the leading European hub for competition litigation.

---

[1] Not always successfully, as shown by the decision of the Supreme Court in *OFT* v *Abbey National plc*, 25 November 2009, [2009] 3 WLR 1215, under the Unfair Terms in Consumer Contracts legislation.

[2] Many Member States, including France, Germany, Sweden, Ireland etc, have designated a particular court to be responsible for dealing with competition law decisions. In Ireland, the High Court is itself the primary decision-maker.

[3] The debate in *Emerald Supplies* v *British Airways* [2009] EWHC 71, as to the scope of a class action under English law, is currently pending before the Court of Appeal. For the procedural questions arising in cases before the CAT, see, eg, *Emerson* [2008] CAT 8. These and other questions are fully discussed in Chapter 3 below.

Turning to administrative enforcement, although consistency with EU law has been largely achieved on substantive matters under s 60 of CA 1998, there are still significant differences of procedure, in particular regarding the lower status accorded to complainants in the UK, as Ben Rayment points out in Chapter 4.[4] Still on the theme of consistency, Renato Nazzini's description, in Chapter 5, of the OFT's determination to maintain a "consumer welfare"-based approach within the constraints of the "structuralist" case law of the Court of Justice is a timely reminder that the monopoly of wisdom does not necessarily reside in the European institutions, and that the flow of ideas between national and European level should ideally be "a two-way street".

In Chapter 6, Giorgio Monti introduces us to the thorny topic of the "concurrent" powers of some six sector regulators to apply the CA 1998, again a relatively unusual situation in European terms. But the contrast with the rest of the EU is perhaps most marked in relation to market investigations carried out by the CC, covered in Chapter 7 by Christian Ahlborn and Daniel Piccinin. This kind of inquiry, which traces its origins to the legislation of 1948, is unique in the EU. Ahlborn and Piccinin perceptively discuss some of the difficulties inherent in exercising the wide-ranging remedial powers the CC enjoys in this context, with no very clear yardstick to go on.

Chapter 7, and the following analysis of UK merger control by Nigel Parr in Chapter 8, again highlight what is perhaps the chief idiosyncracy of the UK system, namely the existence of two competition authorities (the OFT and the CC), the one dependent on references from the other.[5] The need for, and efficiency of, what Nigel Parr describes as a "Rolls-Royce two institution system" is plainly one question that may arise in the next 10 years.

On the other hand, Morten Hviid's study in Chapter 9 of the use of economic (including econometric) analysis under the CA 1998 highlights not the difference between the UK and the EU, but the difference between the UK/EU, on the one hand, and the US on the other. Although the UK is, one would have thought, among the leaders in the EU in this regard, the use of economics in EU competition analysis has not yet reached the sophistication of the US.

Alan Riley's challenging analysis in Chapter 10 of whether, indeed, the European administrative model, on which the CA 1998 is largely based, is itself past its sell-by date, partly reflects, one would suspect,

---

[4] In the French *droit administratif,* the complainant is entitled to a decision on the complaint. EU law too provides for an action for "failure to act" if the European Commission does not respond to a complaint within a reasonable time.

[5] Under the law no 2008-776 of 4 August 2008, the two former French competition authorities were merged into a single Autorité de la concurrence.

an intuition deeply ingrained in the DNA of the common law, that disputes involving complex facts and heavy penalties are more effectively decided by courts rather than administrative bodies. Certainly a court-based approach is virtually uniform in the competition laws of the leading common law economies, with the exception of the UK, but is of course rarer in the EU.[6]

Finally in this *tour d'horizon*, there is of course the issue of criminalisation under s 188 of the EA, discussed by Alan Riley in the light of the *Norris*[7] judgment and analysed in more detail by Angus MacCulloch in Chapter 11, with particular reference to the inclusion of the concept of "dishonesty". Again, like a compass needle swinging naturally to its magnetic pole, it is another common law jurisdiction, that of Australia, with which comparison is made.

One can, I would suggest, fairly draw the conclusion from the detailed and thought-provoking essays in this book that, with some adaptation after 37 years in the EU, the capacity for independence of thought and action in UK competition law is in no way diminished. It is not, perhaps, impossible that the combination of both the European model and the domestic traditions give the UK the best of both worlds in the competition law field.

Against that background, it is perhaps worth re-visiting the historical perspective; assessing where we are; and then identifying, at least briefly, some of the areas of challenge likely to be met over the next 10 years.

A HISTORICAL PERSPECTIVE

In considering competition law in the United Kingdom, it is easy to forget how far we have travelled in only 10 short years. In a nutshell, 10 years ago:

- The substantive law on cartels and other restrictive agreements was to be found in the relatively weak, 40-year-old and largely incomprehensible Restrictive Trade Practices Acts (RTPA), dating from 1956, in which the ultimate yardstick was the various "public interest" gateways.
- The domestic focus was on the possibility of a reference of "a monopoly situation" or "complex monopoly situation" to the

6 Thus in the US, Australia, Canada, South Africa and Ireland, a court or tribunal is the primary decision-maker. In the EU, national procedures tend to be either a full appeal (eg France, Sweden, Germany) or recourse through the administrative court system (eg Italy), following an initial administrative decision.

7 [2008] UKHL 16.

Monopolies and Mergers Commission (the MMC) acting on "public interest" grounds, with the determination of remedies ultimately in the hands of Ministers, under legislation originating in 1948.

- Mergers too were inquired into by the MMC on public interest grounds, with the ultimate decision again being in the hands of Ministers under legislation first introduced in 1965. Although under ministerial policy competition considerations were important, that was a non-statutory position, to which there were exceptions.[8]

This essentially paternalistic, "soft" system, moderately successful by its own lights, involved among other things the absence of penalties;[9] the absence of any effective right of recourse for an individual complainant;[10] and ultimate political control, based on a public interest approach rather than on a framework of more or less clear legally binding rules.

The fact that it took the United Kingdom some time to change was due to a variety of factors. Oversimplifying, the Tory Party favoured competition but was wary of antagonising business interests, and deeply opposed to introducing anything that might smack of "European" influence. The Labour Party, by contrast, was not averse to shaking up the business sector, but the trade union movement feared the threat to jobs implicit in a tougher competition regime. So, apart for some occasional moves in a modern direction, such as the Fair Trading Act of 1973 which created the Director General of Fair Trading (DGFT), and extended the RTPA to the services sector, very little was done about UK competition policy from the mid-1960s, when merger control first came in, to the late 1990s, when reform began to climb the political agenda.

On the other hand, one should not be too critical of the UK decision-makers of the day. On the international scene, it is only in the last 10 years or so that competition law in the modern sense has "taken off" round the world and become a "must have" for over

---

[8] For example, the references in the early 1990s as to whether various acquisitions by bodies ultimately controlled by the French State were in the UK public interest.

[9] The one exception was the application of law of contempt for breach of an order of the Restrictive Practices Court. This led several times to fines being imposed, and could have led to imprisonment, but never did so.

[10] Thus in the 1980s case of *ECS/AKZO*, which led to the seminal decision on predatory pricing by the Court of Justice in *AKZO* v *Commission* [1991] ECR 1-3359 the dispute was an almost entirely domestic matter, between ECS, which was based in Gloucestershire, and AKZO UK, based in Gravesend. Yet in the absence of an effective means of domestic recourse, the only avenue for ECS was to complain to DG IV (as it then was) of the European Commission in Brussels. Fortunately, DG IV took the matter seriously and the Community law on predatory pricing was born.

100 countries. This must be one of the most remarkable examples in modern times of the emergence of an international consensus on a policy issue, almost amounting – like the ancient law of piracy on the high seas – to a sort of modern *ius gentium*.

HOW WE CAME TO WHERE WE ARE

In the last years of the Major Government, the Competition Bill prepared by the DTI proposed the introduction of a regime for agreements and concerted practices based on Art 85 of the Treaty, as it then was, but had no provisions relating to abuse of dominance. After the 1997 election, the in-coming Labour Government took up the Tory Bill, added the provisions on abuse of dominance, and in due course the CA 1998 received the Royal Assent on the same day as the Human Rights Act 1998. One wonders which Act will ultimately be found to have had the more long-lasting effect on British society.

The CA 1998 introduced the Chapter I and II prohibitions, and gave the DGFT powers similar to those of the European Commission, with a merits appeal to the Competition Commission Appeal Tribunal, the newly created judicial arm of the old MMC, which was renamed the CC. The next major step was of course the Enterprise Act 2002 (EA), which followed the 2001 DTI White Paper *Productivity and Enterprise: A World Class Competition Regime*, and came into force in June 2003. That Act essentially removed the powers of Ministers in relation to mergers and what became "market investigations" – a re-vamped version of the old "monopoly" or "complex monopoly" inquiries – although ministerial powers can still be exercised in exceptional circumstances as the recent *LloydsTSB/HBOS* case has demonstrated.[11] Under the EA, the power to initiate a merger reference or a market investigation reference to the CC is in the hands of the OFT, which itself became a corporate body, replacing the DGFT. The CC investigates the matters referred, and takes its own decision, by reference to competition-based tests rather than the old "public interest" yardstick, and also takes its own decision on remedies. The matter, if challenged, then goes on judicial review to the CAT.

The CAT itself was created under the EA out of the old CCAT, it being plainly impossible for the CCAT to remain a part of the CC if it was judicially to review the decisions of the latter. At the same time, the appointment of the President and chairmen of the CAT became a matter for the Lord Chancellor's Department, now the Ministry of

---

[11] [2008] CAT 36.

Justice, whereas the Department of Business, Innovation and Skills, as it now is, remains responsible for appointing the members of the CAT and authorising its budget, as it does for the CC and the OFT. The EA also introduced a right to apply for damages to the CAT, in so-called "follow-on" cases, ie following a finding of infringement by the OFT or the European Commission, including an incohate form of "class action" that can be introduced by specified bodies, the consumer association *Which?* being the only body specified so far. The OFT, for its part, has jurisdiction to enforce both the Chapter I and Chapter II prohibitions under the CA 1998, and Arts 101 and 102 TFEU (ex Arts 81 and 82 EC) as they have now become, renumbered yet again, under the Treaty of Lisbon. From those decisions a full appeal on the merits lies to the CAT.

In terms of the regulated sectors, the Communications Act 2003 set up OFCOM and established an integrated regime for telephony and telecommunications of all kinds, including broadcasting, which is to a large extent based on various European Directives, again with a full merits appeal to the CAT. In other spheres, most sector regulators have concurrent powers to apply the CA 1998 and Arts 101 and 102 TFEU with a merits appeal to the CAT, but may instead use their various regulatory powers. Judicial review of the sectoral regulators' use of their regulatory powers, or of the decisions of the CC under the various regulatory statutes, continues to lie to the High Court.

A MIXTURE OF OLD AND NEW

It is a truism that institutional reform in the UK takes some time: for example, attempts to reform the House of Lords which began in 1911 are still continuing. Old-established institutions have a habit of re-inventing themselves, while reforming statutes sometimes leave in their wake a complex mosaic of different structures. Competition law is no exception, and one may briefly highlight the following features of the present system, "10 years on". For example:

- The central core of the UK system is tripartite, with the OFT acting as prosecutor and decision-maker under Chapters I and II of the CA 1998, and in the initial stages of merger and market investigations; the CC dealing with merger and market investigations referred to it by the OFT; and the CAT hearing merits appeals from OFT decisions under Chapters I and II (and from OFCOM decisions under the Communications Act), and judicial reviews from decisions of the Secretary of State, the OFT and the CC under the mergers and market investigation provisions of the EA.

- The CA 1998 is enforceable by seven regulators, including not only the OFT but the regulators in the gas, electricity, telecoms, water and other sectors, again with a merits appeal to the CAT.
- Side by side with the CA 1998 are the regulatory powers of the various sector regulators, originating under the various privatisation statutes, and often aimed at the same kind of outcomes as the CA 1998. In the main, the mechanism for resolving disputes under these regulatory powers is a reference to the CC by the regulator, made somewhat infrequently in recent years, with judicial review lying ultimately to the High Court.
- There is a certain duality of roles between the CAT and the High Court. Whereas the jurisdiction of the former under the CA 1998 is in respect of "appealable decisions" as there defined, an act or omission by the OFT or other regulator that is not an "appealable decision" is judicially reviewable by the High Court. It is not always easy to tell whether the relevant act or omission is in fact an appealable decision, as the *Cityhook*[12] litigation shows.
- Similarly, while all civil actions can be started before the High Court, and "follow-on" actions before the CAT, the CAT does not have jurisdiction to hear all civil actions where competition points are litigated, pending the bringing into force of s 16 of the EA, which would confer such jurisdiction on the CAT.
- Certain cartel behaviour can be prosecuted criminally under s 188 of the EA.

The overall conclusion must surely be that, despite the very wide-ranging reforms of the last 10 years, the result is still a "somewhat complicated" institutional structure, as Richard Whish puts it. In effect, a great deal of the pre-1998 system is still with us. That is so particularly in relation to the CC, a highly professional and well-respected body, which has survived both the 1998 and 2002 reforms with enhanced powers, despite the transfer to Brussels of jurisdiction to investigate the many mergers falling under the European Merger Regulation. In terms of market investigations, mergers, and regulatory inquiries, the CC operates, in many essential respects, largely as it has for the past 40 years, with the important difference that Ministers have dropped out of the picture and judicial review by the CAT has become an established part of the landscape.

---

12 [2007] CAT 18, and in the judicial review proceedings: [2009] EWHC 204.

THE NEXT 10 YEARS?

If one were thinking of some of the issues that might arise over the next 10 years, one might have on one's list "to think about" the following, among other questions:

- Is the tripartite structure OFT/CC/CAT an optimal solution, and if there are good reasons for retaining it, are there ways of avoiding duplication, and saving time and costs?
- Is the system of market investigations still justifiable and, if so, can it be improved?
- Should the various sector regulators retain CA 1998 powers, or should those be centred on the OFT? One sub-question here might be whether it is a good use of resources to spread the CA 1998 powers over so many regulators?
- In the regulatory field, is the procedure whereby in practice the sole recourse is a reference to the CC at the option of the regulator, with the distant possibility of judicial review by the High Court, the optimal solution in contemporary regulatory practice?
- Should one clarify the relative jurisdictions of the CAT and the High Court, particularly by extending the definition of "appealable decision" under s 47 of the 1998 Act to include, on a judicial review basis, the rejection of a complaint?; and by bringing into force the CAT jurisdiction to hear full infringement actions, not just "follow-on" actions for damages, having regard to s 16 of the EA?
- Is it acceptable that there should be little effective recourse against the refusal of the OFT to intervene?
- Should further steps be taken to facilitate private enforcement? In particular, are there ways of improving ss 47A and 47B of the CA 1998?
- Should the emphasis shift from administrative enforcement to criminal enforcement and/or directors' disqualification in relation to "hard-core" cartels?
- Will the various leniency and settlement programmes of the OFT need overhauling as the years go by?

Important though those questions are from the point of view of streamlining or tidying up the present system, there is perhaps one overarching issue which merits much debate. That is the question of effective enforcement. Whatever its intellectual credentials, one view is that a competition authority is not there primarily to carry out studies and research into markets, but to enforce the law, expeditiously, rigorously and effectively. That means regularly taking and publishing decisions. Stripped of its complexities, it may be said that competition law is above all about two things: the detection and punishment of collusion, and the prevention of exclusion. It may reasonably be asked whether, in those terms, enforcement under the UK regime has been working well over the past 10 years. 2008 passed with no Chapter I decision. Chapter II is rarely enforced. Only two CA 1998 infringements have been found over 10 years in the regulated sector. Certain cartel inquiries have been some years in gestation. While making every allowance for the difficulties of any new regime, and some encouraging signs of improvement, one may reasonably ask whether, over the past 10 years, the UK has had an exemplary record of enforcement of the CA 1998.

In that connection Alan Riley argues that the present system is unduly cumbersome, and would be much streamlined, if the OFT reverted to the role of prosecutor that the DGFT had under the RTPA, bringing its cases before the CAT for decision. Apart from being closer to the common law tradition, that would have the incidental advantage of dealing with any issues that may arise under the European Convention on Human Rights, and perhaps set an example that might in due course be emulated at European level, where the increase in fines in recent years has led to a re-igniting of the debate as to whether the European Commission should continue to combine the roles of prosecutor and decision-maker in competition cases, as it has since 1962.[13] It will be very interesting to see where that debate may lead over the next 10 years.

One final observation: as this book amply demonstrates, a great deal has been done in UK competition law over the last 10 years, at considerable cost in terms of both public and private resources. But the reader may reasonably ask: is the UK now a more dynamic, competitive economy than it was 10 years ago? Has a thriving competition culture become truly embedded in the last 10 years? Let us trust that the second decade, building on the first, will bring further progress in these directions.

Christopher Bellamy
December 2009

[13] See, eg, Hofsetter, "EU Cartel Fining Laws and Policies in Urgent Need of Reform", GCP: *The Antitrust Chronicle*, November 2009.

PREFACE

RATIONALE FOR THE BOOK

Barry Rodger and Angus MacCulloch co-edited a book at the time of the introduction of the Competition Act 1998 (*The UK Competition Act 1998: A New Era for UK Competition Law*, Hart Publishing, 2000) which was designed to consider key aspects of the legislation and the new competition law landscape in the United Kingdom. As outlined in that book, the Competition Act 1998 radically transformed the nature, context, substance and enforcement processes of UK competition law. In particular, it introduced two new prohibitions (Chapter 1 and Chapter 2 prohibitions), modelled on Arts 81 and 82 EC, which came into force as of 1 March 2000. The Act introduced fining powers for the first time, instituted an appeal system, provided for concurrent powers with various regulators and, more broadly, required all businesses to consider the introduction of effective competition law compliance programmes. However, the reform of UK competition law did not stop there and, within 3 years of the passing of the 1998 Act, the DTI published a White Paper, *Productivity and Enterprise: A World Class Competition Regime* (Cm 5223, 2001) which suggested ways to enhance the deterrent effect of UK competition law. The Enterprise Act was subsequently introduced and this further reformed UK competition law, repealing the monopoly and merger provisions of the Fair Trading Act 1973 and making the following changes, *inter alia*: transfer of the functions of the DGFT to a new corporate body, the OFT; reform of UK merger control and the replacement of a public interest test with a new substantial lessening of competition test; introduction of a market investigation scheme to replace the FTA 1973 "monopoly" provisions; enhanced rights for consumer bodies to complain ("super-complaints"); creation of a specialist Competition Appeal Tribunal (CAT); and the creation of a criminal offence for involvement in cartels. As of 1 May 2004, a number of changes were also made to domestic law to mirror the changes introduced following modernisation of EC competition law. Accordingly, UK competition law has undergone a considerable transformation over the last 10 years, and on the tenth anniversary of the landmark date upon which the Chapter 1 and Chapter 2 prohibitions came into force – 1 March 2000 – it is appropriate to reflect on a range of key issues in UK competition law. This book, while not intended to provide comprehensive coverage of every aspect of the development of UK competition law, draws together 11 contributions from a range of eminently-qualified academics and practitioners focusing on various central aspects over the last 10 years (to 8 November 2009) relating to the institutions, processes, substance and enforcement of UK competition law.

REVIEW OF THE CHAPTERS

The Office of Fair Trading plays a central role in UK competition law and policy; it also has numerous powers under various consumer protection laws. The OFT's mission is to make markets work well, and it uses its competition and consumer law powers in a holistic way in order ensure that consumers have the benefit of competitive, efficient and innovative markets. Chapter 1, by Richard Whish, describes the role of the OFT. It begins by reviewing its latest *Annual Plan*, in which the OFT discusses the four main objectives that are contained in a performance framework agreement entered into with HM Treasury in 2007. It then proceeds to describe various aspects of the OFT's work: as an enforcer of the competition rules; as an analyst of markets; as first-phase merger control agency; as an advocate of competition; and as an international partner of organisations such as the ICN and the OECD. The chapter concludes by looking at the key themes that the OFT has identified for the year ahead.

The purpose of Chapter 2, by David Bailey, is to analyse developments of particular significance during the first 9 years of the Competition Appeal Tribunal. The Tribunal was established by the Enterprise Act 2002 to hear appeals against decisions of competition and regulatory authorities, and private damages actions brought by the victims of competition law infringements. The Tribunal has been actively involved in the development of competition law in the UK. In the early years the Tribunal has been vigilant to ensure rigour and expedition in administrative decision-making. The Tribunal has eschewed strict rules on admissibility which would indiscriminately exclude appellants from a judicial consideration of the merits of their arguments. On questions of substance, the Tribunal has had to deal with many legal issues on which there has been little pre-existing authority. The Tribunal has also been concerned that the competition rules are not enforced in "an unduly cautious way". Above all, the Tribunal's case-law has sought to retain flexible procedures in order to deal with cases justly.

Barry Rodger, in Chapter 3, examines the development of private actions following the introduction of the Competition Act 1998.

Although no express provision was made in the Competition Act, it became clear that private action to enforce the new prohibitions was available. The chapter outlines the facilitative provisions in the 1998 Act and in particular the subsequent measures introduced by the Enterprise Act 2002 to provide for follow-on damages actions and representative actions before the Competition Appeal Tribunal. Thereafter the chapter considers the case law development in relation to follow-on actions before the CAT, outlining the important, albeit limited (particularly in relation to representative actions), role the CAT has played to date, in particular with a number of rulings in relation to the limitation periods for bringing a follow-on action. However, the chapter stresses that follow-on actions may still also be raised before the High Court, and there may be important practical reasons, demonstrated by some recent case law, why this is the case. The chapter also looks at the development of stand-alone actions, noting the predominance of abuse cases, considers the availability of interlocutory relief, and stresses the ongoing difficulties in succeeding in an abuse claim or defence. The chapter considers the potential impact of the 2007 OFT proposals for reform and concludes that although private enforcement has played a limited role to date, there are indications that competition law litigation will increase in the coming years.

Chapter 4, by Ben Rayment, considers s 60 of the Competition Act, which introduced a consistency principle designed to ensure as far as possible harmony of interpretation of EU and UK competition law, subject to relevant differences in their provisions. Seen by some as having the potential to give rise to difficult issues, the reality has been that s 60 has been raised infrequently in connection with issues of substantive law in the first 10 years of the Act. Unexpectedly, it has assumed greater significance in relation to questions of procedure, and, specifically, the treatment of third parties by the domestic competition authorities. Over and above the specific legal issues, which are discussed, the explanation for this development must be seen in the context of the concern of the Competition Appeal Tribunal in the early years of the Act that the domestic competition authorities did not, by comparison with the EC Commission, have appropriate procedures in place for involving third parties in their investigations and decision-making.

In Chapter 5, Renato Nazzini reviews the OFT cases in which the Chapter II prohibition and Art 82 EC (now Art 102 TFEU) have been applied or considered and any subsequent judgment on appeal. The discussion focuses on how a welfare-based policy has been applied under a legal framework with significant elements of a structuralist approach. Having identified the key elements of the dominance and abuse tests in the UK, the chapter draws conclusions as to the administrability of welfare-based standards, their compatibility with the case law of the EU courts, and lessons to be learnt about future developments of competition law in the UK and internationally.

Giorgio Monti reviews the application of the Competition Act 1998 by utilities' regulators that have concurrent enforcement powers in Chapter 6, with specific emphasis on three sectors: electronic communications, energy and water. While a detailed procedure governs how cases are allocated, utilities regulators have made little use of competition law. However, in a number of disputes, issues that could have been addressed by competition law have been resolved through the application of sector specific regulation. Accordingly, the chapter calls for the Authorities to work collectively towards establishing criteria to decide when competition law should be applied and when sector-specific regulation would be preferable. This suggestion rejects the view that regulation should be phased out as markets become more competitive and rests instead on the legitimacy of both competition law and regulation as complementary means to address the failures in these markets.

The market investigation regime introduced in the UK in March 2003, discussed in Chapter 7 by Christian Ahlborn and Daniel Piccinin, has turned out to be a flexible competition (and consumer) policy instrument, allowing the OFT and Competition Commission to bridge the gap between competition policy and consumer policy and to introduce competition policy concepts into consumer policy. However, the ambition of the regime in seeking to improve the functioning of competition in markets, combined with the absence of the rigorous analytical framework of "classic" competition policy have posed a dilemma for the OFT and Competition Commission that has played out in the short history of investigations under the regime. In the early years of the regime, it is probably fair to say that the Competition Commission's investigations were not harmful, but even it has expressed doubts as to the effectiveness of the largely transparency and consumer protection based remedies that it imposed. In the later years the Competition Commission seems to have become more aggressive and arguably more error-prone, with the remedies it imposed provoking three judicial review applications in 2008 and 2009. It remains to be seen whether in future the Competition Commission will be able to navigate between the Scylla of non-intrusive but potentially ineffective intervention of early years and the Charybdis of a more robust but also potentially more error-prone policy of recent years.

Nigel Parr, in Chapter 8, considers the impact of the Enterprise Act 2002 (EA) on the assessment of mergers by the Competition Commission (CC). It opens by reviewing the key changes, namely, the removal of ministerial involvement from UK merger control in all but exceptional cases and the introduction of a formal competition-based assessment test. In light of the transition of the CC from an advisory body to a decision maker, it then considers how the standard of proof is applied in the context of a forward-looking assessment process. The intensity of judicial review applied by the Competition Appeal Tribunal is also considered. The chapter then reviews the CC's procedural approach to remedies, which are now explored following publication of the CC's substantive assessment. An unexpected development under the EA is the CC's enhanced concerns in relation to completed mergers and the difficulties of dealing with businesses that have been integrated. The chapter closes by considering areas of potential further reform. First, should the voluntary regime be replaced by a compulsory pre-notification system to remove the perceived problems in dealing with anti-competitive completed mergers? Secondly, is the UK's first-class but expensive bi-institutional regime still justifiable and necessary? The chapter concludes that the reforms introduced by the EA have enhanced the quality of decision-making under the UK merger control regime, but that the case has not been made for further reform.

Chapter 9, by Morten Hviid, considers some of the main developments in economics and in economic tools aimed at addressing competition law issues since the Competition Act 1998 came into force. In doing so it focuses on a few areas to illustrate the different ways in which economics has had an impact. In the area of vertical restraints economics has had a part in shaping our understanding of their pro- and anti-competitive effects and hence on guidelines. In the area of predation, economics has provided some of the theories of harm. In the area of cartels, the design of leniency programmes and the procedural rules surrounding these owes much to game theory. Finally, merger policy and practice offers the area where economics is most actively used in actual decisions.

The Office of Fair Trading has provided a sound basis in the last decade for the further development of the civil anti-cartel regime, as outlined by Alan Riley in Chapter 10. The coming into force of the Competition Act 1998 on 1 March 2000 is the first time the United Kingdom had ever had a domestic statute prohibting price-fixing. Notwithstanding the European prohibition contained in Art 81 EC (now Art 101 TFEU) which had applied in the United Kingdom since January 1973, the notion that price-fixing was more than a weights and measures offence was foreign to many British undertakings. However, in the last decade the OFT has successfully run a major advocacy campaign alerting industry to the dangers of price-fixing; established the law, practice and procedures against price-fixing and made 16 price-fixing infringement decisions with relatively few appeals, all of which have been substantively upheld. Given, in particular, that in the middle of this development the OFT suddenly had a criminal antitrust regime foisted upon it, which required substantial additional changes to practice and procedure the work of the Office in this field is very creditable indeed. This chapter looks forward and argues that by remodelling the leniency programme, introducing an enhanced informants procedure; enhancing individual civil penalties and streamling its contentious procedures, with case originating in the CAT, the OFT can enter its second decade with a very efficient and effective, if not world class civil anti-cartel regime. It further argues that it is far from clear that the criminal antitrust regime introduced in 2003 has much of a future. The ruling of the House of Lords in *Norris* has inflicted significant damage on the operation of the regime; the dishonesty test certainly makes it more difficult to obtain convictions and the requirement for criminal standards of proof creates considerable difficulties for the civil regime. It is argued therefore that a better approach for the future is to enhance the successful civil regime, improve the civil penalties regime against individuals and abandon the criminal regime.

Finally, Angus MacCulloch, in Chapter 11, discusses the first years of the operation of the UK's cartel offence, as introduced by ss 188–189 of the Enterprise Act 2002, and considers its prospects for future success. The pre-history of the offence is examined in order to explain the reasons for its introduction. The only prosecution in relation to the offence, and the subsequent appeal against sentence, is then discussed. This sets out the context for a wider debate as to the future of the offence. The most controversial element of the offence remains the need to prove dishonesty. The difficulty with dishonesty in relation to cartels was highlighted by the judgment of the House of Lords in *Norris* v *USA*. While not directly relevant to the new offence, the potential impact of *Norris* on the development of the offence is considered. The chapter then moves on to consider the recently adopted cartel offences in Australia. These new offences are structured very differently from their UK counterpart; the dishonesty element which was originally proposed being replaced in the eventual legislation with a separate fault element. This alternative model is contrasted with the UK offence. The chapter concludes that while the dishonesty test may make prosecutions in the UK more difficult, it does, however, play an important role in setting out the culpability of cartel behaviour and ensuring that the cartel offence is seen as real crime: rather than a mere regulatory offence.

POSTSCRIPT

Prior to proofs being revised, the remaining EU Member States ratified the Treaty of Lisbon. Accordingly, the Treaty entered into force prior to the publication of this collection of essays and the primary EU competition rules are now found at Arts 101 and 102 of the Treaty on the Functioning of the European Union ("TFEU"). In the text, where appropriate, and as consistently as feasible, references to the Community/EC law/Arts 81 and 82 EC will be confined to quotes and historical references, for instance to practice and decisions prior to the entry into force of the Lisbon Treaty, and otherwise reference will be made to the EU/EU law and the new numbering of the provisions, particularly Arts 101 and 102 TFEU.

LIST OF CONTRIBUTORS

Richard Whish has been Professor of Law at King's College London since January 1991; prior to that, he taught at the University of Bristol. He is a qualified solicitor and was a partner at Watson, Farley and Williams from 1989 to 1998. He acts as a consultant to a variety of companies and regulatory agencies, and was, from April 2003 to March 2009, a non-executive director of the Office of Fair Trading; he is currently a member of the Board of the Singaporean Energy Market Authority. He is the author of or contributor to various books on competition law, including *Competition Law* (6th edn, 2008); volume 47 of *Halsbury's Laws of England* (with Ian Smith); the competition law chapter in *Chitty on Contracts*; the competition law chapter in the *Stair Memorial Encyclopaedia of the Laws of Scotland* (with Ian Flint); *The Competition Act 1998* (with Peter Freeman); and *Merger Cases in the Real World: A Study of Merger Control Procedures* (with Diane Wood). He is co-consultant editor, with Peter Freeman, of *Butterworths Competition Law*.

David Bailey is a Visiting Senior Lecturer at King's College London. He is a qualified solicitor and an attorney-at-law in New York. He is a *référendaire* at the Competition Appeal Tribunal; prior to that, he was an associate at Linklaters LLP. He is the author of Division 1 of *Butterworths Competition Law*, and is the co-editor of the *Competition Law Journal*. He is a member of the UK Association of European Law Committee and the Law Society's Competition Section; he also assists the Association of European Competition Law Judges.

Barry J Rodger has been an academic at Strathclyde University Law School since 1993 and has been a Professor there since 2001. Professor Rodger has published widely in competition law. His co-authored textbook (with A MacCulloch), *Competition Law and Policy in the EC and UK* (Cavendish), is in its fourth edition and he has published numerous articles in journals such as the *European Competition Law Review*, *Columbia Journal of European Law*, *The Common Market Law* Review, the *Juridical Review*, the *Irish Journal of European Law and World Competition*. Many of his recent publications have focused on private enforcement of competition law, including his comprehensive study of all competition-related litigation in the UK courts (2006 ECLR), the Kluwer Law International book *Competition Law and Article 234: An Analysis* (2008) which focuses on all competition law Art 234 preliminary rulings, and an empirical study of competition law litigation settlements in the UK between 2000 and 2005 (2008 ECLR). Professor Rodger is a member of the organising committee of the Scottish Competition Law Forum and is the Vice-Chair of the Competition Law Scholars' Forum (www.clasf.org) and co-editor of the *Competition Law Review*.

Ben Rayment is a barrister at Monckton Chambers, specialising in competition law, utilities regulation and public law, and has appeared in many reported cases in those fields. He was formerly a Legal Secretary at the Competition Appeal Tribunal. He is an editor of the *Competition Law Journal* and of the *Public Procurement Law Review*. He has contributed to a number of works on competition law, including Bellamy & Child's *European Community Law of Competition* (6th edn).

Renato Nazzini is a Reader in Law at the University of Southampton and a Visiting Professor at the University of Turin. He holds doctorates from the University of Milan and the University of London. He is a solicitor of the Supreme Court of England and Wales and a member of the Chartered Institute of Arbitrators. During several years as Assistant Director, Legal and Policy, and then Senior Consultant, at the UK Office of Fair Trading, he has advised on predatory/excess pricing, predatory conduct, margin squeeze, cartels, vertical price and non-price restraints, parallel imports, and competition issues in the financial sector. He has also participated in competition policy projects in the United Kingdom, the European Union and internationally, including the review of Art 82 EC, private enforcement, modernisation, commitments and settlements, and procedural rights of third parties.

Giorgio Monti is Reader in Law at the London School of Economics. He has taught competition law for over 15 years, and is the author of a number of articles on the subject. His book *EC Competition Law* (Cambridge University Press, 2007) was shortlisted for the Peter Birks SLS prize for outstanding legal scholarship in 2008. His research adopts an inter-disciplinary approach to competition law, emphasising the role of economics and political science in explaining legal development.

Christian Ahlborn is a partner in the Competition & Antitrust Group of Linklaters in London. Christian studied law and economics at the Albert Ludwigs Universität, Freiburg, and obtained a *Licence* in

Economics from the Université Paris I and an LL.M. and an M.Sc. in economics from the London School of Economics. He is qualified as a solicitor in England and Wales and as a *Rechtsanwalt* in Germany. Christian specialises in EC competition law, EC state aid control, UK competition law and German competition law. He has worked extensively in network industries, in particular the software industry and electronic financial systems. **Daniel Piccinin** is an associate in the Competition & Antitrust Group of Linklaters in London. Daniel obtained a B.Com. degree in economics and an LL.B. degree from the University of Melbourne. He is qualified as a solicitor in England and Wales and as a lawyer in New South Wales, Australia. Daniel's practice covers both EC and UK competition law.

Nigel Parr leads the competition and EU law practice at Ashurst LLP. He specialises in all aspects of EC and UK competition law, including competition litigation. He has substantial experience in dealing with the EC Commission, UK regulatory authorities, privatised utilities regulators and antitrust authorities in other jurisdictions. He has acted in relation to more than 50 MMC/CC inquiries. He also has extensive experience in handling substantive appeals and judicial review applications on competition law matters before both the specialist Competition Appeal Tribunal and the English High Court. He is ranked as a leading practitioner in the Chambers and Legal 500 directories for competition law and competition litigation. He co-authors *UK Merger Control: Law and Practice* (Sweet & Maxwell, 2005), the leading text on UK merger control. He has LL.B., LL.M. and Ph.D. degrees in Law and EC Law. He has been a partner of Ashurst LLP since 1994.

Morten Hviid was appointed to the Norwich Law School in September 2004 as Professor in Competition Law. Trained as an economist, he has published in both economics and law, including papers in the *Economic Journal*, *European Competition Journal*, *International Journal of Industrial Organization*, *Journal of Law and Economics* and *Oxford Journal of Legal Studies* and a book on merger control with Andrew Scott and Bruce Lyons, *Merger Control in the United Kingdom* (Oxford University Press, 2006). He is a founding member and a principal investigator of the ESRC Centre for Competition Policy at University of East Anglia. He is a former editor of the *Journal of Industrial Economics* and associate editor of the *International Journal of Industrial Organization*. He is also a former member of the Executive Committee of the European Association for Research in Industrial Economics (EARIE). He is currently working on issues relating to cartels and the role of private enforcement in competition law.

Alan Riley is one of the leading competition lawyers in the United Kingdom. He chairs the Competition Law Scholars Forum and is co-editor of the *Competition Law Review*. He is also an Associate Research Fellow of the Centre for European Policy Studies, Brussels, as well as holding a chair at the City Law School, City University, London. He holds a Ph.D. in European Competition Law from the Europa Institute, Edinburgh University, and is a Solictor of the Supreme Court of England & Wales.

Angus MacCulloch first graduated with an LL.B. (Hons) from the University of Dundee (1992), before going on to undertake an LL.M. (European Law) at the University of Strathclyde (1994) and an M.Phil. at the University of Manchester (1997). He took his first academic post as a Lecturer at the School of Law at the University of Manchester in 1996. He joined Lancaster University Law School, as a Senior Lecturer, in September 2006. Much of his recent research has focused on the regulation of cartels through competition law, particularly through criminalisation. He retains a wider interest in all aspects of competition law; co-authoring a popular competition law text book, *Competition Law and Policy in the EC and UK*, with Barry Rodger, and is the Production Editor of the *Competition Law Review*.

TABLE OF CASES

TABLE OF UK STATUTES

TABLE OF UK STATUTORY INSTRUMENTS

TABLE OF EUROPEAN MATERIALS

CHAPTER 1

THE ROLE OF THE OFT IN UK COMPETITION LAW

Richard Whish *

The Office of Fair Trading ("the OFT") plays a central role, and has a variety of functions, in relation to competition law and policy in the UK; it also has significant powers in relation to consumer protection, and endeavours to utilise the various competition and consumer law tools available to it in a holistic way for the benefit of consumers. The OFT is an independent authority;[1] the Enterprise Act 2002 established it as a statutory corporation with effect from 1 April 2003.[2] The OFT is led by a Board consisting of a chairman, a chief executive and (as of June 2009) two executive and six non-executive directors. Section 3 of the Enterprise Act 2002 requires the OFT to publish an annual plan containing a statement of its main objectives and priorities for the year ahead: public consultation on the plan is required by the Act. Section 4 of the Act requires the OFT to publish an annual report, and the report must contain an assessment of the extent to which the OFT has succeeded in meeting the objectives and priorities that it sets itself. A helpful starting point in understanding the OFT's current role is to consider its "Mission", which it first articulated in 2000,[3] and then to look at its *Annual Plan 2009–10*,[4] upon which section 1.2 below is based.

---

* Professor of Law, King's College London; the author was a non-executive director of the OFT from 1 April 2003 to 31 March 2009. Invaluable comments on an earlier draft of this chapter were received from David Bailey, Margaret Bloom and John Fingleton; however all views expressed here are purely personal to the author.

[1] Technically it is a non-ministerial government department.

[2] Prior to that date the OFT provided administrative support to the Director General of Fair Trading, a position created by the Fair Trading Act 1973; that position was abolished by the Enterprise Act 2002.

[3] See the OFT's *Annual Report and Resource Accounts 2000*, HC 419, p 6; see also J Vickers, "Making Markets Work Well for Consumers", 19 June 2001, available at www.oft.gov.uk/news/speeches.

[4] OFT 1036, 2009.

1 THE OFT'S MISSION AND OBJECTIVES

1.1 The OFT's Mission

The OFT's Mission is "to make markets work well for consumers". As it says in its *Annual Plan 2009–10*:

> "Markets work well for consumers and contribute to the health of the wider economy when they are efficient and productive".[5]

The OFT's work is intended to support the development of competitive, efficient and innovative markets. At the heart of successful competitive markets lies consumer choice, and the OFT is vigilant to maximise choice for consumers.

It is important to understand (a point often overlooked by competition lawyers) that the OFT is not only a competition authority with responsibilities under the Competition Act 1998 and the Enterprise Act 2002: it also has a variety of roles – and powers – in relation to consumer laws such as the Estate Agents Act 1979, the Control of Misleading Advertisements Regulations 1988,[6] the Unfair Terms in Consumer Contracts Regulations 1999[7] and the Consumer Protection from Unfair Trading Regulations 2008.[8] This means that, when the OFT discovers markets that appear not to be working well for consumers, and when it seems unlikely that any problems that exist are likely to be corrected by the operation of normal competitive forces, it has a wide variety of tools at its disposal to try to improve the position. At the outset of a case where a market appears not to be working well, it may not be clear whether the most effective solution lies in competition law (for example the prohibition of an anti-competitive agreement or abusive conduct, or the making of a market investigation reference to the Competition Commission) or in consumer law (for example, the removal of unfair contract terms from standard-form agreements or the suppression of deceptive or misleading advertising and mass-marketed scams). In some cases direct enforcement action under competition or consumer law may not be the most effective way of dealing with a problematic market: a better solution might, for example, be competition advocacy on the part of the OFT to the Government, recommending legislative change or some other action to remove "public" restrictions of competition; in other cases the OFT might consider that a market might work better if consumers were better educated as to their rights or available choices – education and communication are an important adjunct to enforcement action.

[5] OFT 1036, 2009, p 9.
[6] SI 1988/915.
[7] SI 1999/2083.
[8] SI 2008/1277.

In principle, therefore, the OFT should remain, throughout an investigation, open-minded and flexible about the best solution to the problems under consideration and about the powers most suitable for use in dealing with a particular market failure. This is why a significant redesign of the structure of the OFT was undertaken in 2006, leading to an end of the formal separation of the Competition Enforcement branch from Consumer Regulation Enforcement and Markets and Policy Initiatives, which had been in place for many years. Since 2006, rather than organising the OFT's work around specific pieces of legislation, matters are arranged quite differently.[9] In particular, within the Markets and Projects area of the OFT groups consider competition and consumer matters across all sectors of the UK economy without any predisposition towards the use of competition law on the one hand or consumer law on the other in a particular case: within Markets and Projects there are groups specialising in each of the goods, services and infrastructure, and knowledge economy sectors; there are also specific teams to deal with each of cartels and the criminal enforcement regime under s 188 of the Enterprise Act 2002 and mergers under the Enterprise Act 2002. The Policy and Strategy area of the OFT is responsible for ensuring that case teams are supported through economic, legal and policy advice, which ensures consistent application and development of the powers available to it; Policy and Strategy also plays an important role in setting the strategic direction and priorities of the OFT and in identifying areas for policy and legislative change.[10]

1.2 Performance framework and objectives

At the time of the Government's Comprehensive Spending Review of 2007, the OFT agreed a performance framework for the years from 2008 to 2011.[11] The framework provides for four main objectives and underpins the OFT's future plans: these are set out in the *Annual Plan 2009–10*.[12] The four objectives of the OFT are: (i) to deliver high-impact outcomes; (ii) to be a centre of intelligence and excellence; (iii) to work in partnership; and (iv) to develop the OFT as an organisation. It is interesting to consider what is involved in each of these four objectives.

---

[9] See the *Annual Report and Resource Accounts 2006-07*, HC 532, p 19.

[10] An organisational diagram of the structure of the OFT is available at www.oft.gov.uk.

[11] See the *OFT–HM Treasury performance framework agreement*, OFT 999 available at www.oft.gov.uk.

[12] OFT 1036, 2009, pp 19–25.

Delivery of high-impact outcomes

The *Annual Plan 2009–10* explains[13] that, within this objective, the OFT has agreed with the Government that it will provide quantitative evidence of how it delivers direct financial benefits to consumers of at least five times that of its cost to the taxpayer across the spending review period. The OFT's budget for 2008–09 was £65.7 million; for 2009–10, £64.1 million; and for 2010–11, £62.6 million: this means that, for that period, the OFT must show a direct return to consumers of at least £962 million. In its *Annual Report and Resource Accounts 2007–08* the OFT estimated that consumer savings as a result of its work that year amounted to £326 million.[14] Further information about the OFT's evaluation work is available on its website;[15] another interesting piece of research was commissioned from Deloitte, *The deterrent effect of competition enforcement by the OFT*.[16]

The provision of evidence of the benefits of the OFT's work is of obvious interest to the Government, which wishes to be assured of a reasonable return on taxpayers' investment in the institution. However, the OFT's evaluation programme has benefits that go beyond meeting the objective of the Comprehensive Spending Review, and the OFT has given a lot of thought to this issue. The OFT's evaluation programme has three particular aims. The first is to meet the need for external accountability, not only in the sense of the Comprehensive Spending Review, but also to other interested scrutineers – for example the Public Accounts Committee of the House of Commons and the National Audit Office. The second aim of the evaluation programme is to improve internal management of the OFT's operations, so that it can learn from the work that it has undertaken in the past and use that learning to target resources towards high-impact work in the future. The third aim is to enable the OFT to evaluate remedies that it has imposed in competition and consumer cases in order to evaluate whether the outcomes achieved matched what was hoped for when the remedy was selected. The Board of the OFT approved the adoption of an evaluation strategy at its meeting in January 2006.[17] In January 2009 it commented on the quality and innovation of the OFT in this area and supported the idea that evaluation should become embedded into all the OFT's projects.[18]

---

13 OFT 1036, p 19.

14 HC 836, p 37; see also *Positive Impact 07/08: Consumer benefits from competition enforcement, merger control, market studies and market investigation references, and scam busting*, OFT 1007, 2008.

15 See www.oft.gov.uk/advice_and_resources/publications/reports/Evaluating.

16 OFT 962, 2007.

17 See www.oft.gov.uk/shared_oft/board/2006.

18 See www.oft.gov.uk/shared_oft/board/2009.

The OFT also agreed, within the first objective of the Comprehensive Spending Review of delivering high-impact outcomes, to publish annual statistics and information on all its enforcement and non-enforcement outcomes, including comparisons with previous years' statistics and, where applicable, those of other leading national competition authorities. The OFT also agreed to publish and develop a framework for prioritising its work, and to report annually on how the framework has been reflected in projects carried out; it also undertook to ensure that its interventions are as swift, efficient and transparent as possible. The OFT's prioritisation principles and enforcement action are discussed in section 2 below.

Being a centre of intelligence and excellence

Under the second objective in the OFT–HM Treasury performance framework agreement the OFT agreed with the Government to monitor markets systematically, with the aim of progressively increasing the impact from market studies, investigations and advocacy; it also agreed to publish objective criteria for undertaking and terminating market studies and to evaluate the impact of at least two market interventions. The OFT's evaluation programme has already been discussed; its work in analysing markets is discussed in section 3 below. Within objective 2, the OFT also undertook to maintain or improve the OFT's rating as one of the top consumer and competition authorities in the world, as measured by the peer review of the Department for Business, Innovation and Skills (formerly Business, Enterprise and Regulatory Reform), the Global Competition Review's annual review (which is based mainly on the views of stakeholders that repeatedly interact with competition authorities in relation to cartel cases and mergers) and other measures.[19] In its 2008 *Rating Enforcement* Global Competition Review, which grades competition authorities as "Elite", "Very good", "Good" or "Fair", placed the OFT in the "Very good" category, maintaining the grade it was awarded in 2007; in 2009, the OFT was again ranked as "Very good", scoring more highly than in 2008.

Working in partnership

Under the third objective of the OFT–HM Treasury performance framework agreement the OFT agreed with the Government that the OFT should work with its various partners, such as the Competition Commission ("the CC"), the UK sectoral regulators

---

[19] For information on peer reviews of competition regimes, see www.berr.gov.uk/whatwedo/businesslaw/competition/policy/reviews/page39860.html.

such as OFCOM, the Gas and Electricity Markets Authority and the Office of Rail Regulation, and the European Commission, in order better to achieve the first and second objectives discussed above. In its *Annual Plan 2009–10* the OFT said that it would work with the CC through working groups and other arrangements as appropriate. Some examples of this include the publication in April 2009 by the OFT and the CC of draft merger guidelines:[20] these will replace, in due course, the distinct guidelines that the OFT and the CC currently have. A further example of working in partnership is the Memorandum of Understanding published in February 2009 to promote greater clarity on the OFT and CC processes for reviewing merger, monopoly and market undertakings and orders.[21]

In April 2009 the OFT issued a Press Release explaining improvements to the market investigation regime under the Enterprise Act 2002 following work by a joint working group of the OFT and CC: this is discussed briefly in section 3 below. The OFT's international activities are discussed in section 6 of this chapter. The OFT's website contains further details of its working in partnership with, for example, the Financial Services Authority and the Department of Health Co-operation and Competition Panel.[22]

A different example of "working in partnership" is the OFT's occasional intervention as a friend of the court (*amicus curiae*) in private litigation as occurred, for example, in *Crehan* v *Inntrepreneur Pub Co*.[23]

Developing the OFT as an organisation

Under the fourth objective agreed between the Government and the OFT the OFT has undertaken to identify the skills required to deliver the OFT's strategic goals and actively shape the staff profile to match; to provide an environment that rewards talent; and to monitor and report on the destination of staff leaving the OFT. In its *Annual Report and Resource Accounts for 2007–08* the OFT reported on its work in connection with this objective. In particular it explained its implementation of its Effective Project Delivery Framework, designed to enable it to work to consistent procedures, to manage and reduce risk and to facilitate staff development and the sharing of skills and capability across the OFT.[24]

---

[20] See *Merger Assessment Guidelines*, A Joint Publication of the Competition Commission and the Office of Fair Trading, available at www.competition-commission.org.uk.

[21] See OFT Press Release 15/09, 17 February 2009.

[22] See www.oft.gov.uk/oft_at_work/partnership_working.

[23] [2006] UKHL 38.

[24] HC 836, pp 61–64.

1.3 Plan of the rest of this chapter

Having considered the OFT's Mission and the objectives set out in its framework agreement with the Government, the rest of this chapter will consider various aspects of its role in UK competition policy. By way of introduction, it should be explained that the institutional design of competition law in the UK is somewhat complicated. In broad terms one can say that, in relation to infringements of competition law (Arts 101 and 102 TFEU (ex Arts 81 and 82 EC) and the Chapter I and Chapter II prohibitions of the Competition Act 1998) the OFT is the enforcer, subject to a full merits appeal to the Competition Appeal Tribunal ("the CAT"); the OFT's enforcement powers are exercised concurrently with the sectoral regulators for gas and electricity, electronic communications, water and rail in their spheres of responsibility. The OFT also has a role in enforcing the "cartel offence" in s 188 of the Enterprise Act 2002. In relation to market investigations and mergers under the Enterprise Act 2002, the OFT is a "phase I" authority with a discretion (in relation to market investigations) and a duty (in the case of some mergers) to make references to the CC in certain circumstances; sectoral regulators enjoy concurrent powers in relation to market investigations, but not in the case of mergers. Decisions of the OFT and the CC on mergers and market investigation references can be appealed to the CAT, though in these cases the CAT conducts a judicial review rather than a full merits appeal.[25] The OFT also has a role as a "competition advocate" in relation to "public" restrictions of competition for which the state bears responsibility; and it also is a representative of the UK in various international fora. The rest of this chapter looks at each of these roles in turn.

2 ENFORCEMENT

The OFT enforces Arts 101 and 102 TFEU and the Chapters I and II prohibitions in the Competition Act 1998, and can impose fines on undertakings that infringe those provisions; the OFT also has a role in relation to the criminal cartel offence in the Enterprise Act.

2.1 Administrative enforcement

The Chapter I and Chapter II prohibitions came into effect in 2000. Since 2004 the OFT has also had the power to apply Arts 101 and 102 TFEU (ex Arts 81 and 82 EC), as a result of EC Council Regulation 1/2003.[26]

---

[25] See D Bailey, Chapter 2 below, on the work of the Competition Appeal Tribunal.

[26] [2004] OJ L1/1; see also the Competition Act 1998 and Other Enactments (Amendment) Regulations 2004, SI 2004/1261.

The OFT conducts an administrative procedure when applying these provisions: it gathers information, initiates proceedings, formulates the case, decides it and determines whether to impose fines and what their amount should be (subject to a statutory maximum of 10 per cent of an undertaking's worldwide turnover in the preceding business year).[27]

Total number of infringements[28]

The OFT has found infringements of the Chapter I prohibition and Art 81 EC on 20 occasions; two of these decisions were set aside on appeal to the CAT – *Attheraces*[29] and *Mastercard*.[30] There are three other cases where undertakings have agreed with the OFT to pay fines for infringements of the Chapter I prohibition and Art 81 EC but where the OFT has not yet adopted a formal infringement decision: these are discussed under "Settlements and early resolution of cases" below. Four individual exemptions were granted before the abolition, in 2004, of the notification of agreements to the OFT for exemption; one of those exemption decisions was suspended on appeal.[31] The OFT has found infringements of the Chapter II prohibition on four occasions. In the case of *Harwood Park Crematorium* the OFT adopted a decision that W Austin and Sons had *not* abused a dominant position by refusing to grant access to a competing firm of funeral directors to its crematorium facilities at Harwood Park in Hertfordshire. The complainant in that case appealed to the CAT against this non-infringement decision, and in *J J Burgess & Sons* v *OFT*[32] the CAT adopted its own decision, on the merits of the case, in which it disagreed with the OFT's analysis and substituted its own finding of an abuse for that of the OFT. This is a good illustration of the fact that appeals to the CAT under the Competition Act are full appeals on the merits. The availability of an appeal on the merits addresses the requirement of the Human Rights Act 1998 that

[27] Competition Act 1998, s 36(8).

[28] For a table of all published decisions up to March 2008, see R Whish, *Competition Law* (6th edn, 2008, OUP, Oxford), pp 367–380. The OFT has adopted one infringement decision since then: *Cardiff Bus* [2009] UKCLR 332; *Construction Recruitment Forum*, 13 November 2009; *Bid rigging in the construction industry in England*, 20 November 2009.

[29] *The Racecourse Association* v *OFT* (Case 1035/1/1/04) and *British Horseracing Board* v *OFT* (Case 1041/2/1/04 [2005] CAT 29.

[30] *Mastercard UK Members Forum Ltd* v *OFT* (Cases 1054–1056/1/1/05) [2006] CAT 14, [2006] CompAR 595.

[31] *Association of British Insurers* v *OFT* (Case 1036/1/1/04), Order of 30 July 2004.

[32] (Case 1044/2/1/04) [2005] CAT 25, [2005] CompAR 1151; the CAT also made a finding of infringement in a case where a third party appealed against a decision by the Water Services Regulation Authority that there had been no infringement of the Chapter II prohibition: see Case 1046/2/4/04 [2006] CAT 36, [2007] CompAR 328, upheld on appeal to the Court of Appeal: *Dŵr Cymru Cyfyngedig* v *Water Services Regulation Authority* [2008] EWCA Civ 536.

undertakings found to have infringed the competition law provisions should have access to a fair and impartial tribunal: the fact that the OFT's administrative procedure means that it acts as prosecutor, judge and jury is tempered by the full merits appeal to the CAT.

Appeals against infringement decisions

Section 46 of the Competition Act provides a list of "appealable decisions" which may be appealed to the CAT. Infringement decisions of the OFT are included in the list, and several of them have been appealed. Nearly all of them were upheld on substance, although the CAT did reduce the level of the fines in some cases (see below). Some of the OFT's findings of infringements were set aside in the *Football Shirts* case;[33] and one finding of abuse was set aside in *Genzyme*.[34] The only infringement decision to have been overturned in its entirety was *Attheraces*.[35] The OFT had concluded that the collective selling by the Racecourse Association of the non-licensed betting office ("non-LBO") media rights to horse racing at 59 racecourses in Great Britain infringed the Chapter I prohibition; and that it did not satisfy the criteria of s 9 of the Competition Act, which provides a defence for restrictive agreements that produce economic efficiencies. The Racecourse Association (and the British Horseracing Board) appealed to the CAT, which disagreed with the OFT's analysis.[36] In the CAT's view the OFT had failed to define the relevant market correctly. The OFT had defined a market for non-LBO media rights, but the CAT considered that this was too narrow: the CAT concluded that this was a sufficient reason in itself to set the decision aside.[37] However, the CAT also went on to consider whether, assuming the OFT had correctly defined the relevant market, the collective selling amounted to an infringement of the Chapter I prohibition.[38] In the CAT's opinion, the collective selling of the media rights in question was objectively necessary:

> "an acquisition via a central negotiation was the only realistic way forward both from the viewpoint of both bidder and sellers [sic] and we regard it as probable that any initial attempt at a self-assembly exercise via individual negotiations would have led quickly to a centrally negotiated one".[39]

---

[33] *JJB* v *OFT* (Case 1021/1/1/03 etc) [2004] CAT 17, [2005] CompAR 29.

[34] *Genzyme* v *Office of Fair Trading* (Case 1016/1/1/03) [2004] CAT 4, [2004] CompAR 358.

[35] OFT decision of 10 May 2004, [2004] UKCLR 995.

[36] *The Racecourse Association* v *Office of Fair Trading* (Cases 1035/1/1/04–1041/2/1/04) [2005] CAT 29, [2006] CompAR 99.

[37] *Ibid*, paras 135–150.

[38] *Ibid*, paras 160–176.

[39] *Ibid*, para 171.

The CAT also concluded that the OFT had failed to demonstrate that collective selling led to an appreciable increase in price;[40] or that it resulted in a loss of non-price competition.[41]

Appeals against non-infringement and case-closure decisions

There have been several appeals to the CAT by third parties disappointed that either the OFT or a sectoral regulator had failed to find an infringement of the Competition Act or of Art 81 or 82 EC. In some cases the OFT or regulator had explicitly decided that there was no infringement. Section 46 of the Competition Act includes, in the list of appealable decisions, a finding of non-infringement, so that there was no doubt that an appeal could be made to the CAT: examples of cases of this kind are the *General Insurance Standards Council* case, where the CAT disagreed with the OFT's finding that the rules of GISC did not infringe the Chapter I prohibition and remitted the matter to the OFT for further consideration;[42] and the *J J Burgess* case, discussed above, where the CAT concluded, contrary to the opinion of the OFT, that there had been an infringement of the Chapter II prohibition.

In some other cases, however, the OFT (or regulator) closed the file without explicitly deciding that there was no infringement: in these cases the CAT has had to decide whether, at least implicitly, a finding of non-infringement had been reached, in which case an appealable decision could be brought before the CAT. If a decision is not an *appealable* one, a third party cannot appeal on the merits to the CAT; at most it can seek a judicial review in the Administrative Court.[43] The case law on the issue of whether a decision involves an implicit finding of non-infringement is fairly extensive and somewhat subtle.[44] The CAT, in its *Claymore* judgment,[45] summarised the law as follows. First, the question of whether an appealable decision has been taken is primarily a question of fact, to be decided in accordance with the particular

---

[40] *The Racecourse Association* v *Office of Fair Trading* [2005] CAT 29, paras 177–202.

[41] *Ibid*, paras 207–211.

[42] See *Institute of Independent Insurance Brokers* v *Director General of Fair Trading* (Cases 1002–1004/2/1/01) [2001] CAT 4, [2001] CompAR 62; as the offending rules were subsequently dropped, the OFT was able to adopt a second non-infringement decision: see *General Insurance Standards Council*, 13 November 2002, [2003] UKCLR 39.

[43] In the case of *Cityhook* v *OFT* (Case 1071/2/1/06) Cityhook not only appealed to the CAT but also sought judicial review in the Administrative Court; Cityhook's subsequent judicial review was largely unsuccessful: see *R* v *OFT on the application of Cityhook*, judgment of the Administrative Court of 20 January 2009, [2009] EWHC 57 (Admin), [2009] UKCLR 255, QBD.

[44] See R Whish, *Competition Law*, pp 429–431.

[45] *Claymore Dairies Ltd and Express Dairies plc* v *Director General of Fair Trading* (Case 1008/2/1/02) [2003] CAT 3, [2004] Comp AR 1, para 122.

circumstances of the case. Second, whether such a decision has been taken is a question of substance, not form, to be determined objectively, taking into account all the circumstances of the case: the test to be applied is whether a decision has been taken on an appealable matter, "either expressly or by necessary implication". Third, there is a distinction between the mere exercise of an administrative discretion not to proceed to the adoption of a decision, and the actual adoption of an appealable decision. At para 148 of the *Claymore* judgment the CAT suggested that it would be useful to pose two questions when deciding whether an appealable decision had been taken: first, did the OFT ask itself whether the Competition Act had been infringed, and, second, if so, what answer did it give to that question? At para 151 of *Claymore* the CAT gave examples of various reasons for the closure of a case file that would not amount to an appealable decision: for example, where the OFT concludes that, as a matter of priority, other cases have a higher importance;[46] or that a market investigation reference should be made to the Competition Commission under the Enterprise Act 2002;[47] or that another competition authority is investigating the matter;[48] or that the case should not be pursued because it might prejudice a criminal investigation under s 188 of the Enterprise Act 2002.[49] A further example was given in the *Freeserve* judgment, of a complaint that was so badly organised that the OFT might decide not to proceed with it;[50] another one not mentioned by the CAT would presumably arise where the matter complained of was the subject of civil litigation in the "normal" courts.[51]

There have been three occasions on which the CAT concluded that the OFT (or sectoral regulator) had adopted an implicit non-infringement decision, despite their protestations to the contrary: *BetterCare Group* v *Director General of Fair Trading*,[52] *Freeserve.com plc* v *Director General of Telecommunications*,[53] and *Claymore Dairies Ltd and Express Dairies*

[46] On this point the CAT specifically referred to the judgment of the CFI in *Automec* v *Commission (No 2)* (Case T–24/90) [1992] ECR II–2223, [1992] 5 CMLR 431.

[47] On market investigations under the Enterprise Act 2002, see R Whish, *Competition Law*, n 28 above, at Chap 11.

[48] Presumably this could refer to a competition authority in another jurisdiction or, in the specific context of UK law, to an authority with concurrent powers to enforce the Competition Act.

[49] On the criminal cartel offence, see R Whish, *Competition Law*, pp 415–422.

[50] *Freeserve.com plc* v *Director General of Telecommunications* (Case 1007/2/3/02) [2002] CAT 8, [2003] CompAR 1, para 101.

[51] Note that this was a reason for the Commission's closure of the file in the *Automec* case, n 46 above.

[52] (Case 1006/2/1/01) [2002] CAT 6, [2002] CompAR 226.

[53] (Case 1007/2/3/02) [2002] CAT 8, [2003] CompAR 1.

plc v *Director General of Fair Trading*.[54] In five cases the CAT reached the opposite conclusion, that there had not been an implicit finding of non-infringement, but instead an administrative decision to close the file: *Aquavitae (UK) Ltd* v *Director General of Water Services*,[55] *Independent Water Company* v *Ofwat*,[56] *Casting Book Ltd* v *OFT*,[57] *Cityhook Ltd* v *OFT*,[58] and *Independent Media Support Ltd* v *Ofcom*.[59] In *Cityhook Ltd* v *OFT* the CAT concluded that the OFT, when closing its file, had not adopted an appealable decision, but said that it had not found the case an easy one to decide;[60] the CAT also noted the "incongruous" result that this meant that Cityhook did not have a right to appeal on the merits to the CAT.[61] The former President of the CAT drew attention to this situation in the CAT's Annual Report for 2006–07, saying that the "invidious" position of complainants having to choose whether to apply to the CAT or to the Administrative Court for a judicial review, depending on whether a decision was appealable or not, "should have no place in a modern legal system".[62] In *Independent Media Support Ltd* v *OFCOM*, the CAT drew attention to the same problem. In that case the CAT was satisfied that, when OFCOM decided to close its file, it had "genuinely abstained from expressing a firm view, one way or the other, on the question of infringement";[63] however, it considered that the position of the complainant was therefore an unsatisfactory one, but one that could be remedied only by legislation.[64]

Total value of fines

The total amount of the fines imposed in the UK under the Competition Act (and Arts 81 and 82 EC) by November 2009 was £920,052,194 before reductions for leniency and £692,120,507 after leniency:[65] these figures include fines that undertakings have agreed to pay in the *British Airways*, *Dairy Products* and *Tobacco*

---

[54] (Case 1008/2/1/02) [2003] CAT 3, [2004] CompAR 1.

[55] (Case 1012/2/3/03) [2003] CAT 17, [2004] CompAR 117.

[56] *Independent Water Company Ltd* v *Ofwat* (Case 1058/2/4/06) [2007] CAT 6, [2007] CompAR 614.

[57] *Casting Book Ltd* v *OFT* (Case 1068/2/1/06) [2006] CAT 35, [2007] CompAR 446.

[58] *Cityhook Ltd* v *OFT* (Case 1071/2/1/06) [2007] CAT 18, [2007] CompAR 813.

[59] (Case 1087/2/3/07) [2007] CAT 29, [2008] CompAR 48.

[60] *Ibid*, para 296.

[61] *Ibid*, para 299.

[62] See the CAT's *Annual Review and Accounts 2006/2007*, p 4.

[63] [2007] CAT 29, [2008] CompAR 48, para 42.

[64] *Ibid*, para 56.

[65] This figure includes the fines imposed by the Office of Rail Regulation in the *English, Welsh and Scottish Railway* decision (£4.1 million) and the fine imposed by the Gas and Electricity Markets Authority in the *National Grid* decision (£41 million, reduced on appeal to £30 million in *National Grid plc* v *The Gas and Electricity Markets Authority* (Case 1099/1/2/08) [2009] CAT 14).

cases, but where the OFT has yet to adopt formal decisions to that effect (see below). On appeal to the CAT some of the fines were reduced: after making allowance for those reductions the total figure after leniency should be reduced to £614,481,389. The fine that British Airways agreed to pay, of £121.5 million, represented a major landmark in the development of competition policy in the UK since it was considerably higher than in any previous case.

Settlements and early resolution of cases

Step 3 of the OFT's *Guidance on penalties*[66] gives as one of the mitigating factors that can lead to a reduction in a fine co-operation which enables the OFT's enforcement process to be concluded more effectively and/or speedily. On seven occasions the OFT (in *Independent Fee Paying Schools, British Airways, Dairy Products, Tobacco, Construction Recruitment Forum and Construction bid rigging*) and the Office of Rail Regulation (in *English*, *Welsh* and *Scottish Railway Ltd*) have adopted, or are in the process of adopting, decisions in which the penalty was reduced in return for co-operation. In the case of *British Airways*, British Airways agreed to pay a fine of £121.5 million after admitting collusion over the price of long-haul passenger fuel surcharges;[67] as Virgin Atlantic had "blown the whistle" in this case it is anticipated that it will not have to pay a fine. There is no formal decision in this case yet since a separate criminal action against a number of individuals is being conducted under s 188 of the Enterprise Act 2002: it is understood that the OFT will not publish a decision in the administrative case against British Airways until the criminal proceedings have been concluded. In the *Dairy Products* case seven undertakings have agreed to pay fines of more than £120 million after admitting their participation in collusion on the retail prices of liquid milk, butter and UK-produced cheese: no formal decision has been adopted in this case since administrative proceedings are continuing against certain undertakings that have not admitted to participation in unlawful conduct.[68] In the *Tobacco* case six undertakings have admitted to unlawful conduct and have agreed to pay fines of £132.3 million: again, there is no OFT decision yet because proceedings are continuing against undertakings that have not admitted to unlawful behaviour.[69] In the *Construction bid rigging* case[70] 86 out of 103 undertakings received reductions in their penalties

---

66 Available at www.oft.gov.uk.

67 OFT Press Release 113/07, 1 August 2007.

68 OFT Press Releases 170/07, 7 December 2007 and 22/08, 15 February 2008.

69 OFT Press Release 82/08, 11 July 2008.

70 *Bid rigging in the construction industry in England,* 20 November 2009.

because they admitted their involvement prior to the OFT's decision. In *Construction Recruitment Forum* seven out of eight undertakings received reductions as a result of their co-operation with the OFT, the fines amounting to approximately £39 million. Had it not been for their co-operation the fines would have amounted to £173 million.[71]

The process of paying a reduced fine in return for co-operation with the OFT is sometimes referred to as one of "settlement" or "early resolution"; it should be distinguished from applications for leniency whereby full immunity or a reduced penalty is allowed in return for the provision of information to the OFT that enables it to investigate a case. It is possible that at some point in the future the OFT may, in the light of its own experience and that of the European Commission,[72] publish guidance on its approach to the early resolution of cases.

Comment and criticism

As noted earlier, the OFT has adopted a total of 22 infringement decisions under the Competition Act and Arts 81 and 82 EC, two of which were annulled on appeal to the CAT. Some critics of the OFT consider that the number of findings of infringement is unacceptably low; and there have also been concerns about the long duration of some of its investigations.

In 2005 the National Audit Office conducted an examination of the OFT's competition enforcement work;[73] in particular it looked at the OFT's approach to competition enforcement and its management of cases. This was followed in 2006 by an examination and report by the House of Commons Committee of Public Accounts,[74] which made various recommendations: a Treasury Minute accepted the Committee's recommendations. The recommendations were far-ranging, including that the OFT should be less reliant on complaints as a source for its competition enforcement work; that it should employ larger case teams for its investigations, so that the risk of important staff members leaving would be reduced and so that a broader range of skills and experience could be brought to cases; that the OFT should set clear and realistic timescales for its investigations; and that the OFT should share its analysis of markets with the undertakings under scrutiny earlier in its investigations than was then the case. In 2009 the National Audit Office published a

---

[71] OFT decision of 13 November 2009.

[72] Note that on 30 June 2008 the European Commission introduced a settlements procedure: see its *Notice on the conduct of settlement procedures in view of the adoption of Decisions pursuant to Article 7 and Article 23 of Council Regulation (EC) No 1/2003 in cartel cases* [2008] OJ C167/1.

[73] *Enforcing competition in markets*, HC 593, Session 2005–06.

[74] *Enforcing competition in markets*, HC 841, Session 2005–06.

further report in which it examined the progress that the OFT had made in responding to the Committee's recommendations.[75] The 2009 Report was broadly positive for the OFT. It noted that the OFT had created a system of prioritisation to direct its resources to areas where it can have the most impact; and that it had improved the quality of its project management, enabling it to deliver higher impact cases more quickly. Among the NAO's recommendations were that the OFT should focus particularly on strengthening the skills and experience of its staff at key grades; and that it should do more to set indicative timescales and to report its performance against them.

In October 2008 the OFT published its *OFT Prioritisation Principles*.[76] In this document the OFT explains the principles that it applies when prioritising its work: in particular it will consider the impact on consumer welfare (direct and indirect) that intervention in a particular case is likely to have; whether action on the OFT's part fits with its strategy as set out in its Annual Plan and/or with other objectives of the OFT; the risks associated with any planned action; and the resource implications of taking on a particular piece of work.

The early resolution of the *British Airways*, *Dairy Products* and *Tobacco* cases in 2007 and early 2008 was a very important development for the OFT in its role as enforcer of the competition rules: the fines agreed to be paid were very large, and the markets affected were large ones of direct significance to consumers. The NAO'S 2009 report was largely positive in its analysis of the OFT's enforcement work, and the adoption of the OFT's *Prioritisation Principles* responded directly to recommendations that had been made by the Public Accounts Committee. However, it is somewhat disappointing that, in the course of 2008, the OFT adopted only one infringement decision – *Cardiff Bus* – and that no fine could be imposed in that case since Cardiff Bus' turnover was below £50 million;[77] and that, by June 2009, the OFT had not adopted any decisions at all during that calendar year. The OFT's reputation as an enforcer of competition law depends, among other things, on a steady flow of infringement decisions. The position was considerably improved by the adoption in the autumn of 2009 of the decisions in the *Construction bid rigging* and *Construction Recruitment Forum* cases. In November 2009 the OFT's website disclosed that there were five current Competition Act investigations.[78]

---

[75] *Progress Report on Maintaining Competition in Markets*, HC 127, Session 2008–09.

[76] OFT 953, 2008, available at www.oft.gov.uk.

[77] Section 40 of the Competition Act provides immunity from fines for "conduct of minor significance", and SI 2000/262 provides that conduct is of minor significance where the perpetrator's worldwide turnover in the previous year was below £50 million.

[78] See www.oft.gov.uk/oft_at_work/current-cases.

2.2 Criminal enforcement

An important supplement to the competition rules applicable to undertakings in the Competition Act, Arts 81 and 82 EC and the market investigation provisions is the criminal offence in s 188 of the Enterprise Act 2002. Individuals who participate in "dishonest" cartelisation of markets can be sentenced to terms of imprisonment of up to five years and fined an unlimited amount of money. The first convictions under the Enterprise Act were secured in the *Marine Hose* case where sentences were imposed on three UK businessmen, the longest of which was for 3 years;[79] the sentences were slightly reduced on appeal to the Court of Appeal.[80] This was an important case in which the OFT worked closely with the relevant authorities in the US: among the individuals arrested in Houston, Texas were the three UK businessmen who were allowed to return to the UK to face charges there as part of plea bargain agreements between them and the US Department of Justice. The OFT is currently involved in court proceedings involving four former or current executives at British Airways for their alleged participation in the air passenger fuel surcharge cartel: this case may go to trial in the course of 2010.

3 ANALYSING MARKETS

As noted at the outset of this chapter, the OFT has a variety of tools to deal with markets that are not working well for consumers. In some cases it may be clear that the OFT should take enforcement action under the competition rules: for example, where it discovers a secret cartel or predatory behaviour on the part of a dominant firm. However, there may be other reasons why a market is not working well: for example, the lack of adequate information for consumers to enable them to make rational choices, governmental distortions of competition or an oligopolistic market structure that leads to economic inefficiency. The OFT analyses markets that are not working well, in particular by conducting market studies; market studies sometimes lead to market investigation references to the Competition Commission, though, as explained below, there are several other possible outcomes of a market study. It should be added that a market investigation reference can be made without a prior market study having been conducted.

---

[79] See OFT Press Release 72/08, 11 June 2008; the individuals were also disqualified from acting as company directors, and confiscation orders totalling just over £1 million were also made against them.

[80] See *R* v *Whittle* [2008] EWCA Crim 2560 (14 November 2008), [2009] UKCLR 247.

3.1 Market studies

Section 5 of the Enterprise Act provides that one of the general functions of the OFT is to obtain, compile and keep under review information about matters relating to the carrying out of its functions. One of the ways in which the OFT carries out this general function is by conducting market studies of markets which appear not to be working well for consumers but where enforcement action under competition or consumer law does not, at first sight, appear to be the most appropriate response.[81] The general function contained in s 5 is the only legal basis for OFT market studies; there are no further provisions, and therefore no specific legal framework. The OFT can *request* information under s 5(1) of the Enterprise Act 2002 when conducting a market study; however, it has formal powers to *demand* information under s 174 of the Act only where the prospect of making a market investigation reference arises. It follows that undertakings, should they so wish, could decide not to co-operate with an OFT market study if there is no possibility of a reference to the CC.

Market studies are usually carried out by the Markets and Projects division of the OFT; they are intended to enable the OFT to understand as well as possible how markets are working and whether the needs of consumers are being met. An important feature of the OFT's market studies is that they are a way of scrutinising the extent to which governmental behaviour and legislation might have a harmful effect on the way in which markets work. The market studies into, for example, *Pharmacies*, *Taxi Services*, *Public Sector Procurement*, *Property Searches*, *European State Aid Control*, *Public Subsidies*, *Commercial Use of Public Information* and *Pharmaceutical Price Regulation Scheme* were all concerned with what might be termed "public" as opposed to private distortions of competition: several of these cases ended with the OFT providing advice to the Government in its role as an "advocate" of competition (see further section 5 below). The Government gave a commitment in 2001 that it would respond to OFT reports on public restrictions of competition within 90 days.[82]

---

[81] The sectoral regulators also conduct market studies: see, eg, the Office of Rail Regulation's *Approach to reviewing markets* (April 2006) and *The Leasing of Rolling Stock for Franchised Passenger Services* (November 2006) (both available at www.rail-reg.gov.uk). The market study led to a market investigation reference to the CC: *Rolling stock*. See also the study launched by GEMA into energy supply markets in February 2008 (details can be found at www.ofgem.org.uk) and Ofcom's investigation of the Pay TV market launched in March 2007 (details can be found at www.ofcom.org.uk).

[82] See the Government's White Paper, *Productivity and Enterprise – A World Class Competition Regime* (Cm 5233, 2001), paras 4.15 and 6.37.

There is an obvious similarity between the market studies carried out by the OFT and the sectoral investigations that the European Commission is able to conduct under Art 17 of EC Regulation 1/2003. The OFT has published *Market studies: Guidance on the OFT approach*[83] on the procedure that it normally follows when selecting a market for study and when carrying out such a study.[84] In the course of 2008 the OFT conducted a review of the market studies regime: this led to a consultation on revised *Guidance* which was launched in May 2009.[85]

Market studies may be triggered in various ways: for example, the OFT might commence one on its own initiative, trading standards officers might bring problems to the OFT's attention, or a market study might be prompted by a "super-complaint" from a designated consumer body;[86] any other interested stakeholders may request the OFT to conduct a market study (the study of *Isle of Wight Ferries* was prompted by a complaint from the local Member of Parliament with the support of 8,000 inhabitants of the island). Market studies are distinct from market investigation references under Part 4 of the Enterprise Act,[87] although it is possible that a market study might lead to a market investigation reference. This occurred, for example, in the cases of *Store Card Credit Services*, *Payment Protection Insurance* and *Airports*: the possibility that an OFT market study might be followed by a market investigation can lead to a somewhat prolonged scrutiny of some markets.[88] The desirability of avoiding unnecessary duplication of work is a factor that the OFT takes into account when deciding whether to launch a market study. Sometimes the OFT outsources a market study or part of it to an external consultancy: for example, OXERA, an economics consultancy, carried out the research for the market study on the Financial Services and Markets Act 2000.[89] An account of the OFT's work in studying markets can be found in its Annual Report and Resource Accounts;[90] a very helpful document on the OFT's website provides a summary of the findings, recommendations and outcomes of its market studies.[91]

---

[83] OFT 519, November 2004.

[84] The OFT's guidance on *Market studies* does not apply to the sectoral regulators.

[85] *Market studies guidance: consultation*, OFT 1080con, available at www.oft.gov.uk/shared_oft/consultation.

[86] On super-complaints see R Whish, *Competition Law*, pp 442–445.

[87] See *Market studies: Guidance on the OFT approach*, para 1.12.

[88] On this point, see J Pickering, "UK Market Investigations: An Economic Perspective" (2006) 5 Competition Law Journal 215.

[89] Enterprise Act, s 5(3) provides a statutory basis for the OFT to do this.

[90] See, eg, the *Annual Report 2005–06*, pp 59–61; the *Annual Report 2006–07*, pp 53–58.

[91] Available at www.oft.gov.uk/investigations/marketstudiessummary.

Sometimes the OFT conducts a "short" market study, of 3–6 months or so, often limited to fact-finding; other market studies may be "full", and may last a year or even more.[92] A decision to launch a full market study is usually taken by the Board of the OFT. Commencement of a market study is announced by a Press Release.[93] There will follow a period of investigation, culminating in the publication of a report.[94]

The OFT welcomes reasoned suggestions of UK markets to be considered for market studies, and has produced an electronic suggestions form which can be accessed on its website.[95] The OFT's *Annual Plan for 2007–08* stated that it would publish performance monitoring arrangements for market studies and report on success against the targets in its Annual Report.[96]

Various outcomes may follow a market study by the OFT. The following possibilities are set out in the OFT's guidance:

- a clean bill of health for the market in question;
- the publication of better information for consumers;
- encouraging firms to take voluntary action;
- encouraging a consumer code of practice;
- making recommendations to the Government or regulators;
- investigation or enforcement action under consumer or competition law;
- a market investigation reference to the CC under Part 4 of the Enterprise Act.[97]

3.2 Market investigation references

Chapter 1 of Part 4 of the Enterprise Act establishes the system of market investigation references. Sections 131–133 deal with the making of references and ss 134–138 with their determination. The OFT's *Market investigation references: Guidance about the making of references under Part 4 of the Enterprise Act* ("the *OFT Guidance*")[98] and the CC's *Market Investigation References: Competition Commission Guidelines* ("the *CC Guidance*")[99] provide helpful guidance on market investigation references. The market investigation regime is a notable feature of the UK system of competition law, and recognises that not every market failure can be cured through the

---

[92] See *Market studies: Guidance on the OFT approach*, paras 1.13 and 3.1–3.3.
[93] *Ibid*, para 3.4.
[94] *Ibid*, paras 3.5–3.13.
[95] See www.oft.gov.uk/shared_oft/investigations/marketstudiesideas.doc.
[96] HC 339, p 19, available at www.oft.gov.uk.
[97] *Market studies: Guidance on the OFT approach*, paras 1.10 and 3.18–3.41.
[98] OFT 511, March 2006, available at www.oft.gov.uk.
[99] CC3, June 2003.

application of the "conventional" tools of competition law, Arts 101 and 102 TFEU (ex Arts 81 and 82 EC), and their domestic analogues. The market investigation regime focuses on markets rather than on the behaviour of individual firms, and enables the CC to investigate whether features of the market such as economies of scale, network effects, switching costs, and other barriers to entry, or market imperfections, such as informational asymmetries, have an adverse effect on competition. A wide range of remedies is available to eliminate, as far as possible, such adverse effects and any detrimental effects on customers that the CC identifies.

The OFT plays a crucial role in the market investigation system. Although the CC conducts the actual investigation, it does not have any original jurisdiction: rather it receives references from the OFT (or the sectoral regulators).[100] The OFT (or a regulator) may make a market investigation reference to the CC when it has "reasonable grounds for suspecting"[101] that one or more "features" of a market prevent, restrict or distort competition in the supply or acquisition of goods or services in the UK or in a part thereof.[102] A decision to make a market investigation reference is made by the Board of the OFT. The CAT has made clear that the "reasonable grounds for suspecting" test does not impose a particularly high burden on the OFT: the scheme of the Act is that the full investigation of a market is to be carried out by the CC, not the OFT.[103] At the same time the CAT stressed that the first-stage investigation by the OFT should not be unduly protracted,[104] and suggested that it was at least arguable that, if the OFT were to delay unreasonably the making of a decision whether to refer or not, an aggrieved person might be able to seek a review of that fact by virtue of s 179(2) of the Act.[105]

By November 2009 the OFT had made eight market investigation references to the CC, three of which originated as super-complaints to the OFT; there had also been one reference from the Office of Rail Regulation, *Rolling Stock*. As noted above, some of the market investigation references followed market studies by the OFT; other cases, such as *Classified Directory Advertising Services* and *Groceries*,

---

[100] The sectoral regulators with concurrent powers are listed in para 1.2 of the *OFT Guidance*; on the powers of the sectoral regulators in relation to market investigation references, see the Enterprise Act 2002, Sch 9, Part 2 and *OFT Guidance*, paras 3.15–3.16.

[101] Note that the Government resisted a proposed amendment to the Enterprise Bill that would have required the OFT to have reasonable grounds for believing rather than for *suspecting* there to be a problem: see Lord Sainsbury of Turville, *Hansard*, HL, vol 637, col 1511 (18 July 2002), available at www.publications.parliament.uk.

[102] Enterprise Act 2002, s 131(1).

[103] *The Association of Convenience Stores* v *OFT (Ruling Setting Aside of Decision)* (Case 1054/6/1/05) [2005] CAT 36, [2006] CompAR 183, para 7.

[104] *Ibid*, para 8.

[105] *Ibid*, para 12.

concerned markets that have been the subject of investigation by the OFT and CC over many years.

The OFT and CC established a joint working group in 2008 to consider how well the market investigation regime is operating and how it could be improved, particularly in relation to the timescale of references to the CC and the sharing of information and closer partnership working. In April 2009 it was announced that in market studies where a reference to the CC is one of the outcomes being considered at launch, the OFT will aim to consult on a reference within 6 months of launch; in addition, the CC announced that it is looking to complete future market investigations in 18 months instead of the statutory maximum of 24 months, and in a shorter time in the case of smaller markets.[106]

4 INVESTIGATING MERGERS

The OFT plays an important role in relation to mergers: this is clearly set out in the Enterprise Act 2002. In essence, the system of control for "ordinary" mergers (as opposed to public interest[107] or other special cases) contained in the Act is as follows. The OFT has a duty to refer certain mergers to the CC; in some circumstances it has a discretion not to refer, and some mergers cannot be referred at all. There is no obligation on undertakings to pre-notify mergers to the OFT, although provision is made for them to do so on a voluntary basis either by making an informal submission or by submitting a more formal "merger notice" for which there is a legislative basis: the difference between the two lies in the timetable that each triggers. In practice, many firms voluntarily have pre-merger discussions with the OFT, not least because power exists to refer a merger to the CC even after it has been consummated and, where appropriate, to require a merger to be reversed: a highly undesirable outcome for the firms concerned. Provision is made for the OFT to accept legally binding undertakings to modify a merger in lieu of a reference to the CC, and the OFT has been able to dispose of many cases on this basis.[108]

---

[106] See OFT Press Release 41/09, 8 April 2009.

[107] A high-profile "public interest" case arose in *Lloyds TSB Group plc/HBOS*, where the OFT reported to the Secretary of State, as required by the Enterprise Act, on the competition aspects of the transaction (OFT report of 24 October 2008, available at www.oft.gov.uk); the Secretary of State chose not to refer the case to the CC on public interest grounds, as permitted by the Act: his decision was unsuccessfully challenged in *Merger Action Group* v *Secretary of State for Business, Enterprise and Regulatory Reform* (Case 1107/4/10/08) [2008] CAT 36, [2009] CompAR 167.

[108] See, eg, the *Co-operative Group Ltd/Somerfield Ltd* case in May 2009: the undertakings will be found at www.oft.gov.uk/advice_and_resources/resource_base/Mergers_home/register/undertakings-in-lieu/cooperative3.

In cases where the OFT is concerned that there is a realistic prospect of a substantial lessening of competition ("SLC") and where it is not possible to agree a remedy, the matter will be referred to the CC: there is an obvious analogy here with the procedure under the EU Merger Regulation, where cases that raise "serious doubts" as to the compatibility of a merger with the common market are taken to an in-depth Phase II investigation; however, a significant difference is that, in the UK system, Phase II is conducted by a separate body from Phase I. The CC, when conducting an investigation under the Act, must determine whether the merger would lead to an SLC within any market or markets in the UK for goods or services; it must also decide on appropriate remedies, having regard to the need to achieve as comprehensive a solution as is reasonable and practicable to any SLC and any adverse effects resulting from it. In framing remedies, the CC may also take into account any "relevant customer benefits", as defined in the legislation. The CC has available to it a number of final powers following its investigation including, where necessary, the power to prohibit a merger outright and to require the reversal of a merger that has already been consummated.

Early in the life of the merger regime under the Enterprise Act the CAT and the Court of Appeal were called upon to examine the precise nature of the "duty" of the OFT to make merger references to the CC. Section 22 (for completed mergers) and s 33 (for anticipated mergers) of the Enterprise Act require the OFT to refer a merger to the CC if "it is or *may be*" the case that a merger "*may be* expected to result" in an SLC (emphasis added). In the CAT's view,[109] this formulation meant that if the OFT itself did not consider that a merger would result in an SLC, but if it was possible that the CC might credibly have that view, the OFT was obliged to refer:

> "If there is room for two views, the statutory duty of the OFT is to refer the matter."[110]

On appeal, the Court of Appeal concluded that the CAT's formulation of the duty on the OFT was incorrect.[111] The Vice-Chancellor (as he then was) was of the opinion that the CAT's "two-part" test was wrong and that it would make various provisions in the Act unworkable:

---

[109] *IBA Health Ltd* v *OFT* (Case 1023/4/1/03) [2003] CAT 27, [2004] CompAR 235.

[110] *Ibid*, para 192.

[111] *OFT* v *IBA Health Ltd* [2004] EWCA Civ 142, [2004] UKCLR 683; for comment, see N Parr, "Merger Control in the Wake of *IBA Health*" (2007) 6 Competition Law Journal 282.

> "the relevant belief is that the merger may be expected to result in a substantial lessening of competition, not that the Commission may in due course decide that the merger may be expected to result in a substantial lessening of competition. Further, the body which is to hold that belief is the OFT not the Commission."[112]

The Vice-Chancellor went on to say that the words in ss 22 and 33 should be applied in accordance with their ordinary meaning.

A wealth of information about past and current merger cases is available on the OFT's website, including the sector affected by a particular transaction, the contact person at the OFT dealing with it, the expected decision date for the case and whether the case might be dealt with on the basis of undertakings in lieu of a reference.[113] This information is regularly updated.

5 COMPETITION ADVOCACY

An important role of the OFT is to act as an advocate of competition. The Government's 2001 White Paper stated that:

> "In future, the Government would like our competition authorities to take on a high profile advocacy role, both by advising on the impact of the Government's own laws and regulations on competition; and more widely acting to promote competition in the economy in a variety of ways."[114]

Section 6 of the Enterprise Act 2002 specifically provides that the OFT has the function of making the public aware of the ways in which competition may benefit consumers in, and the economy of, the UK; and s 7 provides that the OFT has the function of making proposals and giving information or advice on matters such as competition policy to any Minister of the Crown or other public authority. In its *Annual Plan 2009–10* the OFT emphasised the importance of advocacy:

> "the OFT's competition and consumer advocacy role has never been more important. We are focussing our policy and strategy work on ensuring that the benefits of the UK competition and consumer regimes, and the role and functioning of markets, are properly understood and that market failure is addressed by regulation that does not unnecessarily or disproportionately restrict competition or consumer benefits."[115]

In its *Annual Plan* the OFT also said that it is prioritising resources for its advocacy function, so that it can provide positive inputs to

---

112 *OFT* v *IBA Health*, para 38.

113 See www.oft.gov.uk/advice_and_resources/resource_base/Mergers_home.

114 *Productivity and Enterprise – A World Class Competition Regime* (Cm 5233).

115 OFT 1036, 2009 p 8.

government policy on individual issues as well as helping to allow competition to deliver other government aims.[116]

The office of the Chief Economist of the OFT takes the lead role in relation to competition (and consumer) advocacy, but the strategy of promoting competition is one that applies throughout the organisation. Clearly competition advocacy becomes even more important at times of economic crisis, when both businesses and government might be tempted to subordinate competition policy to others: in such circumstances the role of the OFT is to articulate the case for maintaining competitive markets for the benefit of consumers.[117] The OFT engages in "issues advocacy": that is to say, it advises and comments upon particular matters as they arise, such as the public restrictions of competition that came to light in many of the market studies discussed above. The OFT is also increasingly involved in "framework advocacy", where it emphasises the importance for long-term business investment of a consistent and clear framework of competition and consumer enforcement.

6 INTERNATIONAL ACTIVITIES

Competition law has spread around the world with remarkable speed in the last 20 years, and there are now more than 100 systems of law in existence. In 2008 and 2009 China and India implemented competition laws, hopefully bringing the benefits of competitive markets to a further 2 billion of the world's citizens. The OFT plays an active role, both within the European Union (as a member of the European Competition Network) and beyond, in engaging with competition authorities and other international agencies, such as the International Competition Network and the Organisation for Economic Co-operation and Development, in the development of competition policy. The Chief Executive of the OFT, John Fingleton, was appointed as the Chair of the ICN's Steering Group in June 2009. International engagement is particularly important at a time of economic crisis of the kind experienced in 2009. As the OFT's *Annual Plan 2009–10* says:

> "A fragmented European or international response would hamper the UK's and other countries' recovery from the crisis as well as leading to the risk of increasing protectionism and growing friction in world trade."[118]

---

[116] OFT 1036, p 15.

[117] See J Fingleton, "Competition policy in troubled times", 20 January 2009, available at www.oft/gov.uk/news/speeches.

[118] OFT 1036, p 8.

The international work of the OFT is conducted by a team of six people within the OFT, with a dedicated focus on the strategy, co-ordination and consistency of approach across all the operations of the OFT on international consumer and competition work. The team works within the Executive Office of the OFT.

7 CONCLUSION

This chapter has outlined the central role that the OFT plays in UK competition policy; it has also explained that the OFT has a variety of tools at its disposal to deal with markets that are not working well for consumers, including consumer, as well as competition, law powers. In its *Annual Plan 2009–10* the OFT says that its key themes for the year will be to maintain its record of high-impact enforcement and interventions; to respond flexibly to changing circumstances and events; to influence the debate around competition and consumer issues; and to work effectively with its local, national and international partners. It adds that, at a time of economic downturn, it is vital that a strong competition regime should be maintained to protect consumers and legitimate businesses.[119]

---

[119] OFT 1036, pp 14–16.

CHAPTER 2

THE EARLY CASE LAW OF THE COMPETITION APPEAL TRIBUNAL

*David Bailey**

This chapter reviews developments of particular significance during the first 9 years of the Competition Appeal Tribunal ("the CAT", or "the Tribunal"). The Tribunal was established by s 12 of and Sch 2 to the Enterprise Act 2002, which came into force on 1 April 2003. Like a butterfly that is not completely out of the chrysalis, the Tribunal was already in existence, its forerunner having been operating under a slightly different name since 1 March 2000.[1] With multi-disciplinary membership and bespoke procedures for managing competition cases, the Tribunal has a number of functions under various statutory provisions. As of 8 November 2009 some 248 judgments and rulings had been handed down in a total of 111 cases.

Since its inception the CAT has had the task of hearing appeals under the Competition Act 1998.[2] Further functions have been conferred on the CAT by the Enterprise Act 2002, the Communications Act 2003 and secondary legislation.[3] Applications to the CAT for a review of decisions in mergers and market investigations may be brought under

---

* Référendaire of the Competition Appeal Tribunal, Visiting Senior Lecturer at King's College London. All views expressed in this chapter are strictly personal, and should not be construed as reflecting the opinion of the Competition Appeal Tribunal. The author gratefully acknowledges comments received from Bill Allan, Steven Cottrell, Charles Dhanowa, Stephen Hurley, Barry Rodger, Vivien Rose, Robert Wells, Richard Whish, and Wouter Wils.

[1] The CAT is the successor body of the Competition Commission Appeal Tribunals, on which see the fourth edition of R Whish, *Competition Law* (2001, Butterworths), p 358.

[2] CA 1998, ss 46–47.

[3] Eg Competition Act 1998 and Other Enactments (Amendment) Regulations 2004, SI 2004/1261; Electricity (Single Wholesale Market) (Northern Ireland) Order 2007, SI 2007/913, Sch 1, para 10; Mobile Roaming (European Communities) Regulations 2007, SI 2007/1933, reg 14; Payment Services Regulations 2009, SI 2009/209.

the Enterprise Act.[4] The CAT also has an important role in relation to monetary claims which rely on a pre-existing decision finding an infringement of EC or UK competition law.[5] Separately, the CAT has an appellate function under the Communications Act 2003[6] which implements the European Common Regulatory Framework on electronic communications. The Tribunal's jurisdictions extend to the whole UK.[7] Section 1 below explains the constitution and functions of the CAT in more detail and considers the implications of its role as a *specialist* tribunal.

Section 2 reviews the way in which the CAT has approached its jurisdiction to hear appeals on the merits, applications for review and monetary claims. As with any new legal system, there have been controversial moments. A particularly contentious case was *IBA Health* where the Tribunal considered the appropriate balance between the first and second phases of merger control under the Enterprise Act.[8] On appeal, the Court of Appeal upheld the CAT's decision but disagreed with aspects of its reasoning.[9] Section 3 examines the powers of the Tribunal under the Competition Act and considers the important judgments of the Court of Appeal in *Floe I* and *Albion*.[10] Section 4 provides a short overview of the Tribunal's contribution to the development of domestic competition law,[11] and the concluding comments are contained in section 5.

1 THE CONSTITUTION AND FUNCTIONS OF THE TRIBUNAL

1.1 Constitution of the CAT – a specialist court

The Tribunal is a specialist court presided over by the President, who must be a senior legally qualified person with appropriate experience and knowledge.[12] The Tribunal is not a "superior court of

---

4 EA 2002, ss 120 and 179. The CAT may also hear appeals against penalties imposed by the Competition Commission in certain circumstances: EA 2002, s 114.

5 CA 1998, ss 47A–47B; see further sections 1.2 and 2.4 below.

6 CA 2003, s 192.

7 The CAT sits in, and applies the laws of, England and Wales, Scotland or Northern Ireland.

8 *IBA Health Ltd* v *OFT* [2003] CAT 27, [2004] CompAR 235.

9 *IBA* [2004] EWCA Civ 142, [2006] 4 All ER 688.

10 [2008] EWCA Civ 536, [2009] 2 All ER 279.

11 See further, C Bellamy, "The Work of the Competition Appeal Tribunal", the Beesley Lectures on Regulation (Series XIII, 2004); P Collins, "Some Reflections on the First 7 Years of the Competition Appeal Tribunal" [2007] Comp Law 307.

12 EA 2002, Sch 2, para 1(1); on specialist tribunals see Carnwath LJ, "Tribunal Justice – A New Start" 18 November 2008, at http://www.judiciary.gov.uk/docs/speeches/spt-ajtc-new-start-191108.pdf.

record".[13] The Competition Service, an executive non-departmental public body, was set up under the Enterprise Act 2002 to provide the support staff, finance and accommodation required by the Tribunal. In addition, the Tribunal has a panel of chairmen (who must also be senior lawyers)[14] and a panel of ordinary members. Each case is heard by a panel consisting of the President or a Chairman and two members. Judges of the Chancery Division of the High Court are also members of the panel of Chairmen. Decisions of the Tribunal must state the reasons for the decision and whether it was unanimous or taken by a majority.[15] There have been two dissenting opinions as at 8 November 2009:[16] the first concerned the level of the penalty to be imposed for collusive tendering[17] and the second related to the scope of the Tribunal's powers to dispose of BT's appeal under the Communications Act 2003.[18]

Ordinary members of the Tribunal need not be lawyers. The current members of the Tribunal come from a variety of backgrounds, including economics, accountancy, business and public service. This enables the Tribunal to appoint specialist panels encompassing a wide a range of expertise. In *Sky* the Tribunal explained that cases may require complex economic assessments to be made and so "the Tribunal's composition is required by statute to contain competition expertise, and its members are selected for their relevant knowledge and experience".[19]

The advantage of a specialist body equipped with appropriate expertise and flexible powers was noted by Buxton LJ in *Napp*[20] and by Mummery LJ in *Attheraces*,[21] both cases concerning the complex question of determining the appropriate control of excessive pricing. Unsurprisingly, the Tribunal has also referred to its specialist expertise. In *BetterCare*[22] the Tribunal noted that the question at

---

[13] See *Halsbury's Laws* (4th edn, paras 308–309).

[14] EA 2002, Sch 2, para 1(2); para 8 imposes an obligation on the President to arrange training for the members.

[15] EA 2002, Sch 4, para 1(1).

[16] See J Ginsburg "The Role of Dissenting Opinions", 21 October 2007, at http://www.supremecourtus.gov/publicinfo/speeches/sp_10-21-07.html.

[17] *Makers UK Ltd* v *OFT* [2007] CAT 11, [2007] CompAR 699, paras 172–173.

[18] *British Telecommunications plc* v *OFCOM* [2009] CAT 1, paras 91–107.

[19] *Sky* [2008] CAT 25, [2008] CompAR 223, para 60.

[20] *Napp Pharmaceutical Holdings Ltd* v *Director General of Fair Trading* [2002] EWCA Civ 796, para 34; see, similarly, *Revenue & Customs* v *Procter & Gamble UK* [2009] EWCA Civ 407, paras 11 and 48.

[21] *Attheraces Ltd* v *The British Horseracing Board Ltd* [2007] EWCA Civ 38, [2007] UKCLR 309, para 7; cf House of Lords Select Committee Report, *An EU Competition Court*, HL Paper 75, 23 April 2007, para 113.

[22] *BetterCare Group Ltd* v *Director General of Fair Trading* [2002] CAT 6, [2002] CompAR 226, para 91.

issue concerned a competition law point – whether a health care trust was acting as an undertaking – which the Tribunal is supposed to be equipped to deal with, hence the statutory requirements governing the appointment of chairmen,[23] the process of appointment of appeal panel members and the training of appeal panel members.[24] However, in *T-Mobile & O2* v *Ofcom*[25] the Tribunal declined the invitation to use its specialist expertise as a basis for asserting jurisdiction under the Communications Act. The appeals challenged decisions made by the Office of Communications ("Ofcom") as to how and when they intended to go about licensing the use of digital spectrum for telecommunications purposes. The Tribunal considered points of Community law on electronic communications, namely whether the appellants had a directly effective right to challenge Ofcom's decisions before the Tribunal. The Tribunal held that it did not have jurisdiction (under domestic or EC law) to hear the appeals. T-Mobile and O2 appealed to the Court of Appeal partly on the question whether *only* a specialist tribunal satisfied the "appropriate expertise" requirement in the relevant European legislation.[26] The Court of Appeal upheld the CAT's decision. In the opinion of Jacob LJ:

> "[Counsel for O2] emphasised that the CAT has lay members whereas the [Administrative] court does not. But the CAT's lay members may well not have any experience of the particular subject-matter, so that point goes nowhere. And besides the [Administrative] court itself, if it felt expertise were necessary (which would be a rare case) could sit with assessors ... Also, [counsel] did not identify with particularity any expertise which would be unavailable to [the Administrative] court so far as this case is concerned."

The way in which the Tribunal uses its specialist composition varies according to the specific context. The relevance of its expertise to the standard of review in merger cases has been raised in several cases, notably *IBA Health* and *Sky*.[27] In such cases the Tribunal is required to apply the principles which would be applied "by a court on an application for judicial review".[28] This is clear on the face of the Enterprise Act, and any lingering uncertainty was dispelled by the judgment of Carnwath LJ in *IBA Health*.[29] In *Sky* the Tribunal

---

[23] See n 14 above.

[24] EA 2002, Sch 2, para 8.

[25] [2008] CAT 15, upheld on appeal [2008] EWCA Civ 1373.

[26] Directive 2002/21/EC on the common regulatory framework for electronic communications networks and services [2002] OJ L108/33, Art 4.

[27] See section below.

[28] EA 2002, s 120(4).

[29] *IBA* [2004] EWCA Civ 142, [2006] 4 All ER 688, para 88.

rejected a submission by Sky that the Tribunal should apply judicial principles with a greater intensity of review because it is a specialist judicial body. The Tribunal's multi-disciplinary expertise enables it to bring to bear "a degree of familiarity with the statutory regime, the relevant case-law and some of the legal and economic concepts which arise".[30] However, these attributes do not mean "that the Tribunal is applying judicial review principles in a different way or is exercising a higher intensity of review than would be the case if the matter were before the Administrative Court".[31] Sky has appealed this point to the Court of Appeal, submitting that the intensity of the Tribunal's review should be stricter.[32]

In *Floe II*[33] the Court of Appeal made a more general point about specialist tribunals. The Tribunal dismissed an appeal by Floe against a decision by Ofcom that Vodafone had not infringed the Chapter II prohibition by disconnecting Floe's use of certain mobile phone services. Rather unusually, Ofcom, which had been the successful party in the CAT, nevertheless appealed against the judgment since it contained statements of law, unnecessary for the result, with which Ofcom disagreed but which were of major significance for other aspects of their work. Mummery LJ, with whom Lawrence Collins LJ and Sir John Chadwick agreed, observed:

> "Specialist tribunals seem to be more prone than ordinary courts to yield to the temptation of generous general advice and guidance. The wish to be helpful to users is understandable. It may even be commendable. But bodies established to adjudicate on disputes are not in the business of giving advisory opinions to litigants or potential litigants. They should take care not to be, or to feel, pressured by the parties or by interveners or by critics to do things which they are not intended, qualified or equipped to do. In general, more harm than good is likely to be done by deciding more than is necessary for the adjudication of the actual dispute."[34]

The Tribunal has often given general advice and guidance in the early years of the Competition Act. In *Napp* the Tribunal set out its approach to the standard of proof, although the issue was academic in that case.[35] The Tribunal also considered this issue in *Claymore* and

---

[30] *IBA* [2004] EWCA Civ 142, para 61.

[31] *Ibid*, para 62.

[32] Order of Carnwath LJ of 17 March 2009 granting permission to appeal; not yet decided.

[33] *Ofcom and T-Mobile (UK) Ltd* v *Floe Telecom Ltd* [2009] EWCA Civ 47. *Floe I* is discussed in section 3.4 below.

[34] *Ibid*, para 21; cf T Buck, "Precedent in Tribunals and the Development of Principles" (2006) 25 CJQ 458.

[35] *Napp* [2002] CAT 1, [2002] CompAR 13, para 113.

was concerned that the requisite standard should not inhibit public enforcement.[36] In *Freeserve* the Tribunal adumbrated its approach to third party appeals[37] and, at a later stage, made observations on the regime for the acceptance of commitments.[38] The Tribunal's observations were *obiter dicta* (since they were not necessary for the Tribunal's decision). Still, they were not throw-away lines either. They formed part of carefully prepared, reserved judgments. They helpfully filled the vacuum of authority that exists in any new system of law. They were (and remain) immensely valuable from a legal and practical point of view. However, as the regime evolves, it may be anticipated that the Tribunal will decide no more than is necessary to dispose of appeals.[39] As Mummery LJ pointed out in *Floe II*, avoiding advisory rulings may "be described as an unimaginative, unadventurous, inactive, conservative or restrictive approach to the judicial function" but "the lessons of practical experience are that unnecessary opinions and findings of courts are fraught with danger."[40]

1.2 Functions of the Tribunal

The caseload of the Tribunal has steadily grown since 2000, as has its statutory jurisdiction. While the Tribunal has not been involved in shaping the trajectory of this legislative change, it has certainly been the subject of various reforms as part of the "Ten years of UK competition law reform". The Enterprise Act gave effect to the Government's intention to establish a world-class competition regime in the UK.[41] Originally established to hear appeals under the Competition Act,[42] the Enterprise Act broadened the Tribunal's function to include determining applications for judicial review of decisions in merger and market investigation references.[43] The Enterprise Act also amended the Competition Act – inserting ss 47A and 47B and enabling certain damages actions to be brought before

---

[36] [2003] CAT 18, [2004] CompAR 177.

[37] *Freeserve.com plc* v *Director General of Telecommunications* [2003] CAT 5, [2003] CompAR 202, paras 92–122.

[38] [2004] CAT 20, [2005] CompAR 430; CA 1998, s 31A.

[39] *Sky* [2008] CAT 7, [2008] CompAR 143, para 37 (disclosure); cf *T-Mobile (UK) Ltd* v *Ofcom* [2008] CAT 12, paras 175–189 (the parties specifically requested guidance from the Tribunal).

[40] *Floe* [2009] EWCA Civ 47, para 20; *Albion* [2009] CAT 12, para 4; cf *Kay* v *Commissioner of Police of the Metropolis* [2008] UKHL 69, [2008] 1 WLR 2723, para 1.

[41] See Government's White Paper, *Productivity and Enterprise – A World Class Competition Regime* (Cm 5233, 2001).

[42] See section 2.2 below.

[43] See section 2.3 below.

the CAT. Broadly, there are two types of damages action. First, there are "follow-on" actions where a claimant seeks damages following a pre-existing decision finding an infringement of EU or UK competition law. Second, there are "stand-alone" actions pursuant to which a claimant must establish both liability and relief. At 8 November 2009 follow-on actions may be brought in either the CAT[44] or the High Court[45] but stand-alone actions may only be brought in the High Court.[46] Section 47B is a potentially important companion of s 47A. Section 47B provides for a specified consumer body[47] to bring a "representative" follow-on action for damages on behalf of named consumers;[48] claims on behalf of businesses are expressly excluded.[49]

With effect from 25 July 2003 the CAT's jurisdiction was further extended by the Communications Act. The CAT hears appeals on the merits from certain decisions of Ofcom, mainly relating to the exercise of its powers to regulate electronic communications networks and services. Appeals under the Communications Act are an increasingly important part of the Tribunal's case docket, but lack of space prevents a detailed discussion of them here.[50]

Still further changes occurred as a result of the entry into force of Regulation 1/2003.[51] These changes were effected by statutory instrument on 1 May 2004: the Competition Act 1998 and Other Enactments (Amendment) Regulations 2004.[52] Of particular importance is the Tribunal's jurisdiction to hear appeals from decisions taken by the OFT and sectoral regulators[53] under Arts 101 and 102 TFEU as well as appeals against a refusal to order interim measures. An important additional change is the possibility of applying to the CAT for judicial review of a decision to accept, vary or release binding commitments to address the competition concerns identified by the relevant authority.[54]

Finally, the jurisdiction of the CAT may be expanded by regulations made under s 16 of the Enterprise Act. Those regulations

---

[44] CA 1998, ss 47A–47B; see further section 2.4 below.

[45] CA 1998, s 47A(10).

[46] Cf EA 2002, s 16.

[47] The Consumers' Association has been specified: the Specified Body (Consumer Claims) Order 2005, SI 2005/2365; see further R Wells, "Collective Actions in the UK" [2008] Comp Law 57.

[48] To date, there has only been one case brought under s 47B: *The Consumers' Association v JJB Sports Plc* [2009] CAT 2.

[49] CA 1998, s 47B(7). For further discussion of the Enterprise Act provisions on damages actions and the subsequent case law, see B Rodger, Chapter 3 below.

[50] See, eg, *Hutchison 3G (UK) Ltd* v *Ofcom* [2008] CAT 11; affirmed on appeal: [2009] EWCA Civ 683.

[51] [2003] OJ L1/1, [2003] 4 CMLR 551.

[52] SI 2004/1261.

[53] CA 1998, s 54.

[54] CA 1998, s 47(1)(c).

would give the High Court the power to transfer to the CAT matters arising in civil litigation that require a determination of any question relating to whether or not there has been an infringement of the prohibitions in the EC Treaty and/or in the Competition Act. The President of the Tribunal has noted, extra-judicially, that the fact that the CAT is only empowered to deal with follow-on claims "is beginning to look anomalous and out of harmony with the current drive for more effective private enforcement of competition law".[55] At the time of writing the issue remains under discussion.

2 THE JURISDICTION OF THE TRIBUNAL

The Tribunal has jurisdiction to hear appeals on the merits under the Competition Act 1998, applications for judicial review under the Enterprise Act 2002 and "follow-on" damages actions. Before discussing the *way* in which the Tribunal has exercised each jurisdiction, this section considers what decisions can be appealed to the Tribunal under the Competition Act. The answer to that question determines whether the Tribunal has jurisdiction to hear appeals on the merits and has been raised by numerous cases to date.

2.1 Appealable decisions

The question whether the OFT (or a sectoral regulator) had taken a decision that could be appealed to the Tribunal proved to be important during the early years of the Competition Act 1998. It was unexpected because ss 46(3) and 47(1) list, in the interests of certainty, the kinds of decision in respect of which an appeal may be made to the Tribunal. The question is important because it affects the institutional balance between the Tribunal and the domestic competition authorities.[56] If a decision does not fall within s 46 or s 47, then it may be amenable to an application for judicial review in the Administrative Court. The "fault line" between the Tribunal and the Administrative Court "is a result of the legislation which limits the Tribunal's jurisdiction to certain kinds of decision only. It cannot be cured by the Tribunal seeking to extend its jurisdiction beyond the scope provided for in the legislation."[57]

The "appealable decision" issue has arisen in several cases where the authority rejected a complaint, closed the file and the

---

[55] G Barling, "Change and the CAT" (2009) European Advocate 2; see also C Brown, "Section 16 Enterprise Act 2002 – Time for Activation" (2007) 28 ECLR 488.

[56] *BetterCare* [2002] CAT 6, [2002] CompAR 226, paras 90–94.

[57] [2007] CAT 29, [2008] CompAR 48, para 56; see also the (former) President's Statement in the CAT *Annual Review and Accounts 2006/2007*, p 4.

complainant appealed from that "decision". The complainant can be placed in an awkward position in these cases in having to argue that the authority took an (appealable) non-infringement decision in order to then be able to go on to argue that the decision was wrong. The CAT has considered this question in ten cases: five decisions were found to be appealable and five appeals were held to be inadmissible. The overall position reached by the Tribunal's jurisprudence is that express *and* implicit substantive decisions, whether finding an infringement or no infringement, are appealable to the Tribunal.[58] Whether an appealable decision has been taken is a question of substance, not form, and is to be determined objectively on the facts of each case.[59]

In *BetterCare*, in deciding that the North and West Belfast Health and Social Services Trust was not "an undertaking", the Tribunal held that the OFT had not only rejected the subject-matter of BetterCare's complaint but also had made a decision that was appealable to the Tribunal. If the healthcare trust was not acting as an undertaking when purchasing social care then, by definition, its behaviour was not caught by the Competition Act. The OFT's decision had necessarily been that the Chapter II prohibition had not been infringed and therefore the OFT had made an appealable decision.[60] The Tribunal reached similar conclusions in *Freeserve*,[61] *Claymore*,[62] *Pernod*,[63] and *Brannigan*.[64]

This issue presents a sharp clash between two competing assertions of the public interest.[65] The complainant asserts the public interest in effective enforcement and the role played by third parties. The competition authority asserts the public interest in protecting its prosecutorial discretion from undue judicial intervention. Each side acknowledges the public interest asserted by the other, but each argues that the public interest which it asserts should prevail in the instant case. The Tribunal has recognised the importance of both conceptions of the public interest.[66] It has specifically noted that third parties act as "catalysts for public enforcement"[67] and can

---

[58] See R Whish, *Competition Law* (6th edn, 2008, OUP, Oxford), pp 427–428.

[59] *BetterCare* [2002] CAT 6, [2002] CompAR 226, paras 24 and 62.

[60] [2002] CAT 6, [2002] CompAR 226.

[61] [2002] CAT 8, [2003] CompAR 1; see D Bailey, "When are decisions appealable under the Competition Act 1998?" (2003) 2 Comp Law 41.

[62] [2003] CAT 3, [2004] CompAR 1.

[63] [2004] CAT 10, [2004] CompAR 707.

[64] [2006] CAT 28, [2007] CompAR 420, paras 63–78.

[65] *A-G* v *Observer Ltd* [1990] 1 AC 109, at 213.

[66] *Claymore* [2003] CAT 3, [2004] CompAR 1, para 184.

[67] *Cityhook* [2007] CAT 18, [2007] CompAR 813, para 203.

be an "important source of information"[68] for investigations. The Tribunal accordingly expounded the scheme of the Competition Act as giving third parties a right of appeal to the Tribunal where the OFT takes a decision to close an investigation and communicates its view on the merits of their complaint.[69]

The second, but no less important, aspect of the public interest concerns the discretion of the competition authorities under the Competition Act whether or not to conduct an investigation and whether or not to proceed to a final decision. This discretion was first recognised by the Tribunal in *BetterCare*[70] and affirmed recently by the Administrative Court in *Cityhook*.[71] Thus a competition authority may genuinely abstain from expressing a firm view, one way or the other, on the question of infringement and refrain from taking an appealable decision. This has occurred in several cases to date,[72] including Ofcom's decision to close its 2-year investigation into a contract for the provision of access services (viz subtitling) by BBCB to the BBC in *Independent Media*.[73]

In *Cityhook* the OFT closed a 4-year investigation into a complaint by a small company which had revealed, in the OFT's view, evidence of a potential infringement of the Chapter I prohibition, but which was no longer an administrative priority. The Tribunal held that the OFT had not taken an appealable decision.[74] Cityhook subsequently brought an application for judicial review of the OFT's case closure decision. Foskett J rejected Cityhook's submission that the Competition Act distinguishes between the nature and extent of the OFT's discretion to continue or discontinue an investigation depending upon the stage at which its processes have reached. The Judge noted:

> "... I do not consider that the ambit of the discretion conferred by section 25 of the Competition Act becomes any more circumscribed once a decision to investigate has been taken and the investigation embarked upon. As with any discretion, it may only be exercised rationally by reference to the factors relevant at the time it is exercised

---

[68] *Pernod-Ricard SA* v *OFT* [2004] CAT 10, [2004] CompAR 707, para 197.

[69] The right of appeal does not prejudge the way in which the Tribunal may exercise its jurisdiction in such appeals: see *Claymore* [2003] CAT 3, [2004] CompAR 1, paras 184 and 205.

[70] [2002] CAT 6, [2002] CompAR 226, para 80.

[71] [2009] EWHC 204 (Admin), para 97; see also *Crest Nicholson plc* v *OFT* [2009] EWHC 1875 (Admin), para 45 per Cranston J.

[72] See *Aquavitae (UK) Ltd* v *Director General of Water Services* [2003] CAT 17, [2004] CompAR 117; *Casting Book Ltd* v *OFT* [2006] CAT 35, [2007] CompAR 446; *Independent Water Co Ltd* v *Water Services Regulation Authority* [2007] CAT 6, [2007] CompAR 614.

[73] *IMS* v *OFCOM* [2007] CAT 29, [2008] CompAR 48.

[74] [2007] CAT 18, [2007] CompAR 813.

> and the importance of a particular factor may increase or diminish with the passage of time and any changes of circumstances that may have taken place."[75]

Looking to the future, as the Tribunal observed in *Freeserve*, the test for what is an "appealable decision" should be as straightforward as possible, notably so that complainants may know what their rights are and interlocutory skirmishes are avoided.[76] Whilst the list approach adopted by ss 46 and 47 may appear straightforward, it has given rise to numerous skirmishes and procedural difficulties. One solution might be to prescribe additional decisions as appealable decisions subject, of course, to an appropriate standard of review.[77] A better solution would be to enable any person aggrieved by a decision taken by the OFT or sectoral regulator under the Competition Act to have standing before the Tribunal. Some decisions, such as infringement decisions, could be appealed on the merits; other decisions, such as case closure decisions, could be subject to judicial review, as is already the case when the OFT accepts commitments.[78] This would mirror the approach to standing under the Enterprise Act, under which any person aggrieved by a decision in connection with a (possible) merger or market investigation reference may apply for judicial review by the Tribunal.[79]

2.2 Appeal on the merits

Before summarising the flexible approach adopted by the Tribunal to appeals under the Competition Act it is important to understand why it hears appeals *on the merits*. The OFT has extensive powers to uncover and investigate possible infringements of the Chapter I and II prohibitions and/or Arts 101 and 102 TFEU. The Act also empowers the OFT to impose severe penalties for infringements of competition law. At the time of passing the Competition Act, and the Human Rights Act 1998, there was a concern that the combination of these roles might be incompatible with Art 6(1) of the European Convention on Fundamental Rights and Freedoms ("ECHR").[80] To

---

75 [2009] EWHC 204 (Admin), para 97.

76 *Freeserve* [2002] CAT 8, [2003] CompAR 1, para 91; see also *National Grid plc* v *Gas and Electricity Markets Authority* [2008] CAT 26, [2008] CompAR 305, para 3.

77 CA 1998, ss 46(3) and 47(1)(f); the list may extend to "such other decision as may be prescribed".

78 CA 1998, s 46(3)(g)–(h), s 47(1)(c) and Sch 8, para 3A.

79 EA 2002, ss 120 and 179; see similarly Art 230 EC and the Communications Act 2003, which respectively adopt a broad approach to reviewable "acts" and decisions.

80 The same concern has been raised by one of the appeals against the European Commission's *Car Glass* decision: *Saint-Gobain Glass France* v *Commission* (Case T–56/09).

alleviate this concern, the Act provides for a full judicial determination of the merits of the OFT's decision,[81] with the Tribunal being vested, notably, with the power to take any decision the OFT could have taken. During the passage of the Competition Bill the Minister for Competition and Consumer Affairs, Mr Griffiths, stated that it was the Government's intention that:

> "the tribunal should be primarily concerned with the correctness or otherwise of the conclusions contained in the appealed decision and not with how the decision was reached or the reasoning expressed in it... The Bill provides for a full appeal on the merits of the case, which is an essential part of ensuring the fairness and transparency of the new regime."[82]

In *Napp* the Tribunal considered the systemic importance of access to an independent tribunal. Napp claimed that the OFT's conduct of the investigation had been intrinsically unfair and that it failed to comply with the requirements contained in Art 6(1) of the ECHR.[83] This is a familiar objection and one that has been raised in respect of the European Commission's procedure from time to time.[84] Nonetheless, Napp's argument called into question the administrative system of enforcement of competition law. The Tribunal gave the argument short shrift and held that the OFT's procedure involves no breach of Art 6 since the OFT's decision is subject to judicial control on the merits by an independent and impartial tribunal.[85] In fact the House of Lords has since recognised that sufficient judicial control for this purpose does not always *require* an appeal on the merits; in some cases it may be sufficient for there to be a review of the legality of the decision and of the procedures followed.[86]

The Tribunal considered, in general terms, the approach it should follow in appeals under the Competition Act in *Freeserve*, since

---

[81] CA 1998, Sch 8, para 3(1).

[82] *Hansard*, HC, vol 333, col 496 (18 June 1998); cited in *Floe* [2005] CAT 14, para 65.

[83] *Napp* [2001] CAT 3, [2001] CompAR 33, para 74; *Napp* [2002] CAT 1, [2002] CompAR 13, paras 136–137; see similarly *Argos* [2003] CAT 16, [2004] CompAR 80, para 76.

[84] C D Ehlermann, "Reflections on a European Cartel Office" (1995) 32 CMLRev 471; W Wils, "The Combination of the Investigative and Prosecutorial Function and the Adjudicative Function in EC Antitrust Enforcement: A Legal and Economic Analysis" (2004) 27 World Competition 201.

[85] [2002] CAT 1, [2002] CompAR 13, para 137; see also *Kingsley* v *United Kingdom* (2002) 35 EHRR 10, para 51.

[86] *R* v *Secretary of State for the Environment, ex p Holding and Barnes, Alconbury Developments Ltd* [2001] UKHL 23, [2003] 2 AC 29, para 49; *Magill* v *Weeks* [2001] UKHL 67, [2002] 2 AC 357, paras 87–94; but see *Tsfayo* v *United Kingdom* (2009) 48 EHRR 18.

confirmed in *Burgess*[87] and other cases.[88] Unlike applications for judicial review,[89] in which a decision can be called into question on certain well-established grounds,[90] appeals on the merits mean "that the Tribunal has a full jurisdiction to find facts, make its own appraisals of economic issues, apply the law to those facts and appraisals, and determine the amount of any penalty".[91] In *Freeserve* the Tribunal acknowledged that "the way in which the Tribunal *exercises* its jurisdiction is ... likely to be affected by the particular circumstances".[92] This proposition has an obvious attraction. It sensibly reflects the fact that the way in which the Tribunal will exercise its jurisdiction will depend on the "infinite variety" of cases brought before it. The Tribunal went on to formulate a "convenient checklist of matters" for the guidance of future panels hearing third party appeals. Third party appellants will normally bear the burden of persuading the Tribunal that:

> "the decision is incorrect or, at the least, insufficient, from the point of view of (i) the reasons given; (ii) the facts and analysis relied on; (iii) the law applied; (iv) the investigation undertaken; or (v) the procedure followed."[93]

These grounds of challenge are partly based on the need to avoid the Tribunal converting itself from an appellate tribunal to a first instance decision-maker.[94] While the complainant is not limited to the evidence that was before the authority, the grounds set out in *Freeserve* recognise that "an appeal is not an occasion to launch what is in effect a new complaint".[95] The checklist may be straightforward to apply to infringement decisions.[96] In the more "choppy waters" of third party appeals against non-infringement decisions the Tribunal's task depends on the authority's reason for finding no infringement and on the extent of its investigation before coming to

---

[87] *Burgess* [2005] CAT 25, [2005] CompAR 1151, paras 125–126.

[88] *Claymore* v *OFT* [2005] CAT 30, [2006] CompAR 1, paras 167–170; *Albion* [2006] CAT 23, [2007] CompAR 22, paras 287–291; *Brannigan* v *OFT* [2007] CAT 23, [2007] CompAR 956, paras 39–50; *IMS* v *Ofcom* [2008] CAT 13, [2008] CompAR 161, para 24.

[89] *Albion* [2008] CAT 31, [2009] CompAR 28, paras 64–72 (rejecting an argument that the Tribunal should apply the principles of judicial review when reviewing a report prepared by the Authority pursuant to the Tribunal's case management powers).

[90] See section 2.3.

[91] *Freeserve* [2003] CAT 5, [2003] CompAR 202, paras 107–110.

[92] *Ibid*, para 111.

[93] *Ibid*, para 114.

[94] *Ibid*, paras 112–13; citing *Aberdeen Journals I* [2002] CAT 4, [2002] CompAR 167, para 177.

[95] [2003] CAT 5, [2003] CompAR 202, paras 116–118.

[96] Eg *British Horseracing Board* v *OFT* [2005] CAT 29, [2006] CompAR 99; *E.ON UK plc* v *Office of Rail Regulation*.

that conclusion. In cases where there has been a limited investigation of the facts, it may be difficult for the Tribunal to determine whether the OFT has made a material error of fact or has failed to investigate the matter sufficiently.[97] However, it would be wrong to suppose that the Tribunal will never make findings of fact in third party appeals. In *Burgess* and *Albion* the Tribunal not only made findings of fact and set aside the non-infringement decision, but also made its own finding that there had been an infringement of the Chapter II prohibition in each case.[98] As befits the common law, the CAT's approach to appeals will no doubt be further refined in the particular circumstances of future cases.

2.3 Applications for review

Unlike the unitary administrative system of enforcement under the Competition Act, the Enterprise Act continued the two-tier approach created by earlier legislation. In essence the OFT (the first tier) must refer mergers or may refer markets to the Competition Commission ("CC") (the second tier) where it reasonably believes that a relevant merger situation may substantially lessen competition or a feature of the market[99] may have an adverse effect on competition. The CC will then consider in detail the impact upon competition of the merger or feature of the market and decide what action (if any) should be taken to remedy or prevent any resulting adverse effects. The Tribunal has jurisdiction to decide applications on a judicial review basis in respect of decisions taken by the OFT, the CC or the Secretary of State in relation to the provisions for merger and market investigations.

The Enterprise Act provides that the Tribunal "shall apply the same principles as would be applied by a court on an application for judicial review".[100] The grounds of judicial review are well established, although "the intensity of review in a public law case will depend on the subject matter in hand".[101] The Tribunal can review, essentially, whether the decision-maker has properly applied the relevant statutory provisions and acted fairly and rationally. In *Tesco* the Tribunal said that these grounds "clearly reflect the fact that

---

[97] *Brannigan* v *OFT* [2007] CAT 23, [2007] CompAR 956, paras 46–50.

[98] *J J Burgess* v *OFT* [2005] CAT 25, [2005] CompAR 1151; *Albion* v *WSRA* [2006] CAT 23, [2007] CompAR 22 (6 October 2006); [2006] CAT 36, [2007] CompAR 328 (18 December 2006); [2008] CAT 31, [2009] CompAR 28 (7 November 2008).

[99] EA 2002, s 131(2).

[100] EA 2002, ss 120(4) and 179(4).

[101] *R (Daly)* v *Secretary of State for the Home Department* [2001] 2 AC 532, [2001] 2 WLR 1622, para 28.

judicial review is in general about legality and the decision-making process rather than the merits of a decision".[102]

By 8 November 2009 there had been six (at least partially) successful applications for review:[103] three under s 120 – *IBA Health*, *Unichem* and *Virgin* – and two under s 179 – *Association of Convenience Stores, Tesco* and *Barclays*. A notable unsuccessful application under s 120 was brought in December 2008 by the *Merger Action Group* against the Secretary of State's decision not to refer the merger between Lloyds TSB and HBOS to the CC.[104] Apart from the speed of the proceedings, the case is of particular interest on the question of standing to bring applications. The CAT found that the applicants had "failed to establish any specific concern that differentiates them from the general body of consumers of banking services".[105] It nonetheless concluded that "in the wholly exceptional circumstances of this case, and particularly in view of the specific interest and strong feeling which the Merger has aroused in Scotland",[106] they were "persons aggrieved" by the decision and accordingly had standing. It remains to be seen whether the same conclusion would be reached in different circumstances.

The successful applications in *IBA Health* and *Unichem* were brought by disappointed competitors against decisions by the OFT not to refer the mergers to the CC. The *IBA Health* case concerned the OFT's decision not to refer an anticipated merger between two leading companies supplying software in the health sector to the CC. On appeal the CAT allowed the application since it was clear that the CC could reach an alternative view of the iSOFT/Torex merger. The CAT held that "if there is room for two views" about whether a merger may be expected to lead to a substantial lessening of competition "the statutory duty of the OFT is to refer the matter to the [CC]".[107] The Court of Appeal agreed with the CAT that the OFT had failed adequately to explain or justify its conclusion in accordance with the statutory test, but disagreed with the CAT's interpretation of that test.[108] In *Unichem*, a case concerning the acquisition of a pharmaceutical wholesaler in East Anglia, the CAT held

[102] [2009] CAT 6, para 77; see A Robertson, M Lester and S Love, "Judicial Review in the UK of Competition and State Aid Decisions: Part 1" (2007) 28 ECLR 553.

[103] There have been several unsuccessful applications: eg *Celesio* v *OFT* [2006] CAT 9, [2006] CompAR 515; *Somerfield plc* v *Competition Commission* [2006] CAT 4, [2006] CompAR 390.

[104] *Merger Action Group* v *Secretary of State for Business, Enterprise and Regulatory Reform* [2008] CAT 36, 2009 SLT 10.

[105] *Ibid*, para 45(b).

[106] *Ibid*, para 47.

[107] [2003] CAT 27, [2004] CompAR 235, paras 191–198.

[108] [2004] EWCA Civ 142, [2006] 4 All ER 688.

that the OFT had not verified salient facts with Unichem, an interested third party, before deciding not to refer the merger to the CC. In *Virgin Media* the CAT was asked to review the CC's report and the Secretary of State's decision on the acquisition by Sky of a 17.9 per cent interest in ITV. The CAT agreed with Virgin that the CC had misdirected itself as to the meaning and effect of the legislation on the specified media public interest consideration,[109] but refused to remit the matter because that would serve no useful purpose.[110]

There have been four applications for review under the market investigation provisions as at 1 June 2009.[111] In *Association of Convenience Stores* v *OFT* an association of small shopkeepers challenged the OFT's decision not to refer the groceries market to the CC, whereupon the OFT indicated that it would reconsider the matter. The CAT quashed the decision and remitted the matter to the OFT.[112] The OFT subsequently referred the supply of groceries by retailers in the UK to the CC.[113] After the ensuing groceries market investigation,[114] in *Tesco* the Tribunal granted an application that the CC had not considered certain matters which were relevant to the cost and proportionality of its recommendation that a competition test be introduced into land planning procedures applicable to proposals to build large grocery stores.[115] The Tribunal made an order quashing the relevant part of the Commission's decision and ultimately decided to refer the matter back to the CC for reconsideration.[116] In *Barclays* the Tribunal dismissed most of the grounds of review but concluded that the CC had failed to take account of the loss of convenience that would ensue from the imposition of a remedy prohibiting the sale of payment protection insurance at the point of sale of credit products. This constituted a failure by the CC to take into account a material consideration and the question of whether to impose the "point of sale prohibition" remedy was remitted to the CC for reconsideration.

2.4 Monetary claims

An increasingly important function of the Tribunal is to hear so-called "follow-on" actions for damages, or other sums of money, under

---

[109] EA 2002, ss 58(2C)(a) and 58A(4)–(5); *Virgin* [2008] CAT 25, [2008] CompAR 223, paras 249–268.

[110] [2008] CAT 32, [2009] CompAR 98.

[111] One application is pending: *BAA Ltd* v *Competition Commission.*

[112] [2005] CAT 36, [2006] CompAR 183.

[113] "The grocery market" (OFT 845, 9 May 2006).

[114] Final Report, "The supply of groceries in the UK: market investigation", 30 April 2008.

[115] *Tesco* [2009] CAT 6.

[116] *Tesco* [2009] CAT 9.

ss 47A and 47B of the Competition Act, as discussed more fully in Chapter 3.[117] In determining any such claim the Tribunal is bound by the decision (once definitive) which establishes the infringement.[118] It is often assumed that so-called follow-on actions are straightforward. While the finding of infringement certainly provides a valuable springboard for claimants, it is by no means an automatic entitlement to an award of damages. In the 11 actions to date, various questions of a procedural nature have arisen before the Tribunal. They have ranged from applications for security for costs (*BCL I*[119]) or for summary disposal (*Enron*[120]) to preliminary issues as to whether claims were premature (*Emerson*[121]) or time-barred (*BCL II*[122]).

Monetary claims so far commenced have settled before the legal issues have been adjudicated by the Tribunal. Many factors influence case resolution including the parties' beliefs about their chances of success if the case is fully litigated, the relationship of the claimant to the defendant, the availability of funding, the probable size of the award of damages, to name but a few. The judgment delivered in *Healthcare-at-home* v *Genzyme* is amongst the most important to date since, for the first time in a competition case in the UK, an award of interim damages of £2 million was made.[123]

The first trial of a damages claim took place in September 2009. Enron is claiming £19.1 million for loss and damage caused by English, Welsh and Scottish Railway, who the Office of Rail Regulation had found to have abused its dominant position in the market for haulage of coal by rail in Great Britain.

3 THE POWERS OF THE TRIBUNAL[124]

3.1 Introduction

Unlike the High Court, the Tribunal has no inherent jurisdiction. The Tribunal's jurisdiction is statutory. The procedures to be followed in proceedings before the Tribunal are set out in the Competition Appeal Tribunal Rules 2003.[125] The Tribunal has generally eschewed

---

[117] On the proposals for reform of private enforcement, see R Whish, *Competition Law* 6th edn, 2008 (OUP, Oxford), pp 319–322.

[118] CA 1998, ss 47A(9) and 47B(5).

[119] [2005] CAT 2, [2005] CompAR 485.

[120] [2009] CAT 7.

[121] [2007] CAT 28, [2008] CompAR 9; [2007] CAT 30, [2008] CompAR 37; and [2008] CAT 8, [2008] CompAR 118.

[122] [2008] CAT 24, [2008] CompAR 210, reversed on appeal: *BCL Old Co Ltd* v *BASF SE* [2009] EWCA Civ 434; Enron has applied for permission to appeal to the Supreme Court.

[123] [2006] CAT 29, [2007] CompAR 474.

[124] See R Rayment, "Powers of the Competition Appeal Tribunal" [2005] Comp Law 273.

[125] SI 2003/1372.

legalistic and technical arguments about the scope of its statutory and case management powers.[126] In *Argos*, for example, the Tribunal observed that its power to award costs is *not* subject to the need for any application for costs to have been made, nor can it be ousted by an agreement between the parties.[127] The Tribunal has also emphasised the need to maintain the flexibility of its procedures[128] and to deal with cases justly.[129] In *BCL I* the Tribunal said that it:

> "should be extremely slow to adopt a construction of the Tribunal's Rules which gives rise to a risk of injustice or procedural difficulty unless such a construction was the only possible construction of the Tribunal's Rules."[130]

Three issues have been selected for this section to illustrate briefly how the Tribunal has approached its powers in different contexts: case management, penalties and disposal of appeals.

3.2 Case management

The Tribunal may give directions to secure the just, expeditious and economical conduct of its proceedings.[131] The Tribunal has significant powers of case management, which include powers to regulate the manner in which proceedings are conducted. Procedural issues were a major preoccupation of the Tribunal's early case work under the Competition Act, but constraints of space preclude a detailed discussion here.[132] A matter of major importance for the Tribunal has been to deal with appeals as expeditiously and fairly as possible. The Tribunal Rules lay down strict limits for appellants who have to lodge appeals under the Competition Act within 2 months (with little possibility of extension).[133] The use of strict timetables is emphasised

---

[126] *Pernod* [2004] CAT 10, [2004] CompAR 707, para 185 (rejecting a narrow literal construction of the words "has been" in CA 1998, s 46(3); see further n 156 below).

[127] [2005] CAT 15, [2005] CompAR 996, para 4; see also *Animatrix Ltd* v *O'Kelly* [2008] EWCA Civ 1415, paras 50–57.

[128] *Allsports Ltd* v *OFT* [2004] CAT 1, [2004] CompAR 323, paras 58–61.

[129] *Emerson Electric Co* v *Morgan Crucible Co plc* [2008] CAT 8, [2008] CompAR 118, para 79.

[130] [2005] CAT 1, [2005] CompAR 470, para 42; *Emerson* [2008] CAT 28, [2009] CompAR 7, para 36.

[131] Competition Appeal Tribunal Rules 2003, r 19.

[132] See, for further discussion, B Rayment, "Practice and Procedure before the Competition Appeal Tribunal" in T Ward, and K Smith (eds), *Competition Litigation in the UK* (2005, Sweet & Maxwell, London) and N Green and M Brealey (eds), *Competition Litigation: UK Practice and Procedure 2009/2010* (OUP, 2009).

[133] CAT Rules, r 8; see Order in *Prater* v *OFT* [2006] CAT 11, [2006] CompAR 624. The same applies to appeals under CA 2003, s 192.

by both the Tribunal's *Guide to Proceedings*[134] and its rulings.[135] In *Hasbro* the former President said that "respect for the deadline in commencing proceedings is, in many ways, the keystone of the whole procedure".[136] It is therefore of no surprise that in very urgent cases, notably *IBA Health* and *Merger Action Group*, the Tribunal applied an extremely expedited procedure. It is equally true, however, that a handful of appeals before the CAT, such as *Albion*,[137] have raised complex matters which have taken several years to determine.

3.3 Penalties

The Tribunal is entitled to make its own assessment of the level of the penalty on the basis of a "broad brush" approach[138] and has done so in some cases.[139] In *National Grid* the Tribunal substantially reduced the penalty because of different findings of fact on the presence of mitigating factor arising from the regulator's involvement in the development of the abusive contracts.[140] In several cases, however, the Tribunal has decided not to interfere with the OFT's assessment.[141] The OFT enjoys a "margin of appreciation" both as to the interpretation and as to the application of the *Guidance on penalties* in a particular case.[142] In *Football Replica Kits* the Tribunal held that it had the power to increase the penalty imposed by the OFT,[143] albeit it "should not be exercised lightly".[144] The Tribunal increased the penalty imposed on Allsports by revoking a 5 per cent discount that had been given for co-operation with the OFT. Allsports's evidence before the Tribunal showed that its conduct could not reasonably be regarded as co-operation giving rise to any mitigation of penalty.

---

134 *Guide to Proceedings* (October 2005), para 3.4.

135 *Napp* [2001] CAT 2, [2001] CompAR 21; *Freeserve* [2002] CAT 9, [2003] CompAR 57.

136 *Hasbro UK Ltd* v *Director General of Fair Trading* [2003] CAT 1, [2003] CompAR 47.

137 See n 98 above.

138 *Napp* [2002] CAT 1, [2002] CompAR 13, paras 497–503, approved in *JJB* [2006] EWCA Civ 1318, [2006] UKCLR 1135, para 163.

139 *Aberdeen Journals I* [2003] CAT 11, [2003] CompAR 67, paras 476–499.

140 *National Grid plc* v *The Gas and Electricity Markets Authority* [2009] CAT 14, paras 201–220.

141 *Apex* [2005] CAT 4, [2005] CompAR 507; *Achilles Paper Group Ltd* v *OFT* [2006] CAT 24, [2007] CompAR 1; *Makers UK Ltd* v *OFT* [2007] CAT 11, [2007] CompAR 699; *Sepia Logistics Ltd* v *OFT* [2007] CAT 13, [2007] CompAR 747.

142 *Argos* [2005] CAT 13, [2005] CompAR 834, para 168; see V Rose, "Margins of appreciation: changing contours in Community and domestic case law" (2009) 5(1) Competition Policy International 3.

143 [2005] CAT 22, [2005] CompAR 1060, paras 208–235.

144 *Ibid*, para 218.

3.4 Powers on disposal of the appeal

The powers of the Tribunal when disposing of appeals under the Competition Act 1998 were considered by the Tribunal and the Court of Appeal in *Floe* and *Albion*. Each case will be discussed in turn. The administrators of Floe successfully challenged a decision by Ofcom that Vodafone was not acting in breach of the Chapter II prohibition by disconnecting the telecommunications services it was providing to Floe.[145] The Tribunal set aside the decision and remitted the matter to Ofcom by Order dated 1 December 2004. Ofcom had offered an undertaking to re-investigate, but the Tribunal disagreed with Ofcom as to the time period within which this could or should be done. This disagreement raised the question whether the Tribunal had the power to set a time limit for a re-investigation. The Tribunal held that it did have such a power. Referring to its "overriding function" to decide points taken in a notice of appeal on the merits, its extensive powers in Sch 8 to the Competition Act, its past practice[146] and the concern that administrative proceedings should be completed within a reasonable time, the Tribunal took a broad view of its statutory powers. The Tribunal concluded by noting that a power to give directions as to the time period in which a further investigation should be carried out:

> "enables the Tribunal to ensure that investigations are completed within a reasonable time period so that the party being investigated is not exposed to being under investigation for an indeterminate and unreasonable period of time as well as to ensure that complaints are dealt with within a reasonable time."[147]

The Court of Appeal disagreed and held that the Tribunal did not have the power to direct the time within which a new investigation should be carried out. Having set aside the decision and remitted the matter, there was no subsisting appeal. The Tribunal was therefore unable to use its case management powers.[148] While it could express its own view as to the urgency of the matter remitted, the Tribunal does not have the power to give such a direction under para 3 of Sch 8. This is correct as a matter of statutory construction, institutional balance, and practicality. The statutory scheme is based on a clear distinction between the internal management of an investigation and the external directions that an authority may give to third parties. Underlying that scheme is the proper institutional balance

---

[145] [2004] CAT 18, [2005] CompAR 290.

[146] The Tribunal emphasised the importance of the speedy resolution of matters remitted by it to the authorities: *Freeserve* [2003] CAT 15, [2004] CompAR 75, para 11; *Association of Convenience Stores* v *OFT* [2005] CAT 36, [2006] CompAR 183, para 8.

[147] [2005] CAT 14, [2005] CompAR 1004, para 142.

[148] Cf *Albion* [2006] CAT 36, [2007] CompAR 328, paras 275–281.

between the Tribunal and the regulators. Lloyd LJ described the Tribunal's function as follows:

> "the Tribunal has the task of deciding such appeals as are brought to it in accordance with the provisions of the [Competition] Act and the rules, but it does not have a more general statutory function, of supervising regulators."[149]

It follows that the Tribunal had fulfilled that task when it allowed the appeal and remitted the whole of the decision to Ofcom. There is, further, a good reason why the Tribunal has not been given some general supervisory function: as Lloyd LJ noted, the Tribunal "cannot know what are the competing demands on the resources of the particular regulator" at any given moment.[150] The CFI has made the same point in respect of the European Commission.[151] It does not follow that, once remission has been ordered, parties are at the mercy of the competition authority in respect of time. As Sedley and Chadwick LJJ noted, any undue delay falls within the supervisory jurisdiction of the High Court.[152]

The litigation in *Albion* concerned the lawfulness of the price offered by Dŵr Cyrmu for the partial treatment and transmission of non-potable water through a pipeline to a large paper factory on the North Wales coast. Dŵr Cyrmu, an intervener in Albion's appeal, the owner of the pipeline and the dominant undertaking in question, challenged the Tribunal's jurisdiction to take its own decision. Dŵr Cyrmu submitted that the Tribunal may only take a decision in respect of a matter forming part of the decision under appeal if the authority could have done so at the time it took its decision. Dŵr Cyrmu referred to the statutory scheme comprising a two-stage process: the first stage is an administrative procedure that may culminate in a decision; and, if there is an appeal, there is a second judicial stage before the CAT. To elide these two stages into one, Dŵr Cyrmu argued, would undermine the procedural safeguards under the Competition Act. The Tribunal and the Court of Appeal both rejected this argument.[153] The Act clearly provides the Tribunal with jurisdiction to "make any other decision which the OFT could itself have made". The Tribunal must, of course, act fairly when reaching its own decision. It will be of interest to see when (as opposed to whether) the Tribunal makes its own decision in future cases.

---

149 [2006] EWCA Civ 768, [2006] 4 All ER 688, para 34; see also Chadwick LJ at para 57.
150 *Ibid*, paras 37–38.
151 *Automec* v *Commission* (Case T–24/90) [1992] ECR II-2223, para 77; *Scippacercola* v *Commission* (Case T–306/05) [2008] 4 CMLR 1418, para 92.
152 [2006] EWCA Civ 768, [2006] 4 All ER 688, paras 53 and 58; see also *Tesco* [2009] CAT 9, paras 39–44.
153 [2006] CAT 36, [2007] CompAR 328, paras 191–198, upheld in [2008] EWCA Civ 536, [2009] 2 All ER 279, paras 112–128.

4 THEMES IN THE TRIBUNAL'S SUBSTANTIVE CASE LAW

The Tribunal's contribution to the development of competition law has been significant and wide-ranging. The following snapshot does not do justice to the wealth of jurisprudence that has built up over the years since 2000: naturally there are many other decisions as well. This section focuses on three themes of the Tribunal's jurisprudence: consistency with EC law, deciding new points of law and deciding cases on their specific facts.

4.1 Consistency with the Community regime

Section 60 is a lodestar for the interpretation of the Competition Act 1998.[154] It is therefore not surprising that the Tribunal has invariably taken its cue from the jurisprudence of the Community Courts. In *BetterCare* the Tribunal conceived its duty under s 60 to approach the "undertaking" question in the manner in which the ECJ would approach it.[155] The Tribunal's ruling in *Pernod* exemplifies this approach.[156] There, the Tribunal considered the application of s 60 to the procedural principles that apply to the public enforcement of domestic competition law.[157] Apart from the right of appeal under s 47, the Competition Act (unlike EU law) is silent on the procedure for dealing with complaints.[158] The Tribunal held that, in the circumstances of that case, the complainant should have been given an opportunity to be heard by the OFT before certain decisions were taken, in particular when it decided to discontinue its investigation of the complaint. The unanswered question whether s 60 requires the authority to consult a complainant on its decision not to proceed on a complaint in different circumstances from *Pernod*[159] may now have been overtaken by the OFT's guidelines on *Involving Third Parties in Competition Act Investigations*.[160]

---

[154] Section 60 provides, broadly speaking, that questions arising under Pt 1 of the Competition Act in relation to competition within the UK are to be dealt with, so far as possible, and having regard to any relevant differences, in a manner consistent with Community law.

[155] [2002] CAT 7, [2002] CompAR 299, para 32.

[156] [2004] CAT 10, [2004] CompAR 707. In *Pernod*, the Tribunal held that, notwithstanding the literal wording of s 46(3)(b) of the Competition Act, the OFT, like the European Commission, should not be limited to taking decisions regarding matters in the past: *ibid*, paras 185–187.

[157] D Bailey, "The impact of Pernod v OFT on Section 60 and the enforcement of UK competition law" (2004) 3 Comp Law 153.

[158] [2004] CAT 10, [2004] CompAR 707, para 197.

[159] OFT Press Statement, 1 July 2004.

[160] OFT 451, April 2006.

4.2 Anticipating the development of Community law

The Tribunal has been confronted with points of law that have yet to be determined by the Community Courts on three notable occasions. The first occasion was *BetterCare*. The issue was whether a healthcare trust was acting as an "undertaking" when procuring contracted-out residential and nursing care for elderly people who lacked means of their own. The OFT concluded that the trust was not an undertaking. In the OFT's view, the relevant activity could not be carried on (potentially) for profit by a private entity. The CAT disagreed and held that the purchase of nursing and residential care from the private sector by the NHS was, in itself, economic activity.[161] The ECJ subsequently considered the characterisation of purchasing in *FENIN* and *SELEX*, and has emphasised that "the nature of the purchasing activity must be determined according to whether or not the subsequent use of the purchased goods amounts to an economic activity".[162]

In *Apex* the Tribunal was asked to consider whether the OFT had demonstrated that Apex, a roofing contractor, had infringed the Chapter I prohibition by collusive tendering for flat roofing contracts in the West Midlands. The issue of collusive tendering had never been the subject of Community case law. The Tribunal upheld the OFT's decision that the concept of concerted practice applied to cover bidding, ie a tendering process where bidders submit a price for a contract that is not intended to win. The judgment contains a useful summary of the principles of law applicable to concerted practices.[163] The Tribunal concluded that "concertation the object of which is to deceive the tenderee into thinking that a bid is genuine when it is not, plainly forms part of the mischief which section 2 of the Act is seeking to prevent".[164]

The appeals in *Football Replica Kits* and *Toys and Games* provided another occasion for the CAT and the Court of Appeal to break new ground. The issue was the circumstances in which discussions between a supplier and its retailers may give rise to collusion between them. The Court of Appeal indicated that a tripartite agreement or concerted practice may be established where a competitor discloses confidential pricing intentions to a supplier in circumstances where it is known that that information will be disclosed to another competitor.[165]

---

[161] The healthcare trust was, notably, acting as a supplier as well as a purchaser of social care.

[162] *FENIN* v *Commission* (Case C–205/03P) [2006] ECR I–6295, [2006] 5 CMLR 559, para 26; *SELEX* v *Commission* (Case C–113/07P) judgment of 26 March 2009, para 102.

[163] [2005] CAT 4, [2005] CompAR 507, para 206.

[164] *Ibid*, para 250.

[165] [2006] EWCA Civ 1318, [2006] UKCLR 1135, paras 91 and 141; see D Bailey, "Contours of Collusion: Football Shirts and Toys and Games" [2006] Comp Law 236.

4.3 Each case turns on its own facts

"Precedent should act as a guide not a cage."[166] As so often, all will depend on the circumstances. The jurisprudence of the CAT under the Chapter II prohibition epitomises this point.[167] In *Napp* the Tribunal recognised and applied the concept of so-called "super-dominance"[168] in support of its finding that Napp had engaged in abusive predatory and excessive pricing of sustained release morphine tablets. In *Aberdeen Journals II* the Tribunal upheld the OFT's finding of predatory pricing in relation to advertising space in local newspapers in the Aberdeen area. The Tribunal held that there was no need for the OFT to prove that Aberdeen Journals, the dominant undertaking, had the ability to recoup its losses since there was a risk that its principal competitor would be eliminated.[169] The ECJ has since held in *France Télécom* that proof of the possibility of recoupment of losses is not a precondition for a finding of predatory pricing.[170] A different point is that the facts of *Aberdeen Journals II* also influenced the Tribunal's ruling that the OFT did not need to show that there was an appreciable effect on trade within the UK.[171]

The CAT focused on the individual circumstances in *Genzyme* when it rejected various justifications advanced in support of pricing one of its drugs at such a level as to jeopardise the viability of an efficient distributor. The CAT held that Genzyme's insistence upon supplying the drug at the NHS list price to independent distributors imposed an abusive margin squeeze.[172] The case-by-case approach was slightly moderated in *Burgess* when the Tribunal helpfully set out three (non-exhaustive) propositions on refusal to supply, drawn from the Community jurisprudence.[173] The CAT held that, by refusing access to a local crematorium to a competing funeral director, the owner had abused its dominant position in the supply of crematoria services in the Stevenage/Knebworth area. The Tribunal in *National Grid* similarly emphasised the facts of the case when confirming the Gas and Electricity Market Authority's finding that particular provisions of National Grid's long-term contracts with

---

166 *R* v *Inland Revenue Commissioners, ex p Unilever plc* [1996] STC 681, at 690f.

167 B Allan, "The Control of Dominant Firms in the UK: The Jurisprudence of the CAT" [2007] Comp Law 265.

168 [2002] CAT 1, [2002] CompAR 13, para 219.

169 [2003] CAT 11, [2003] CompAR 67, paras 436–446.

170 Case C–202/07P, judgment of 2 April 2009, para 110.

171 [2003] CAT 11, [2003] CompAR 67, paras 456–62; for an alternative view see *P&S Amusements Ltd* v *Valley House Leisure Ltd* [2006] EWHC 1510 (ChD); [2006] UKCLR 876, para 22.

172 [2004] CAT 4, [2004] CompAR 358.

173 [2005] CAT 25, [2005] CompAR 1151, para 311.

gas suppliers constituted an abuse of its dominant position in the market for provision of installed domestic-sized gas meters in Great Britain.[174] The Tribunal held that the anti-competitive effect of the contracts was too severe to be justified by their legitimate aim to recover the sunk costs of installing the meters.[175]

A common theme of the Tribunal's case law is the emphasis on the circumstances in which effective competition can be protected only by imposing on the dominant firm a "special responsibility" not to behave in certain ways vis-à-vis its remaining competitors. As the Tribunal put it, while a competitor "is not entitled to be protected against normal market forces", it is entitled "not to be eliminated as an efficient operator in the market by the abusive practices of a dominant firm".[176]

5 CONCLUSION

The CAT has been actively involved in the development of UK law. In the early years the Tribunal was vigilant to ensure rigour and expedition in administrative decision-making. The Tribunal has eschewed strict rules on admissibility which would indiscriminately exclude appellants from a judicial consideration of the merits of their arguments. On questions of substance, the Tribunal has had to deal with many legal issues on which there has been little pre-existing authority. The Tribunal has also been concerned that the competition rules are not enforced in "an unduly cautious way".[177] Above all, a golden thread running through the Tribunal's case law has been to retain flexible procedures in order to deal with cases justly. As Sir Thomas Bingham MR (as he then was) put it, "while the court must properly defer to the expertise of responsible decision-makers, it must not shrink from its fundamental duty to 'do right to all manner of people'".[178] It will be fascinating to see how the Tribunal's approach evolves.

---

[174] [2009] CAT 14.

[175] *Ibid*, para 200.

[176] See n 173 above, para 332.

[177] *JJB Sports plc* v *OFT* [2004] CAT 17, [2005] CompAR 29, para 205.

[178] R v *Ministry of Defence, ex p Smith* [1996] QB 517, at 556D–E.

CHAPTER 3

UK COMPETITION LAW AND PRIVATE LITIGATION

Barry J Rodger *

The Competition Act 1998 ("the Competition Act") introduced dramatic changes to UK domestic competition law in relation to both substantive law and its enforcement.[1] The 1998 Act introduced a system based on the rules set out in Arts 81 and 82 EC Treaty, known as the Chapter I and Chapter II prohibitions.[2] These are expressed in virtually identical terms to Arts 81 and 82 EC (and now Arts 101 and 102 TFEU) and there is also provision in s 60 of the Act designed to ensure that the domestic prohibitions are interpreted by the authorities and courts consistently with the interpretation afforded to the Community provisions. The Act placed the Office of Fair Trading ("the OFT") at the apex of the enforcement system with similar powers and sanctions as provided to the Commission by Regulation 17 (now Regulation 1/2003).[3] This was the first time that any real, effective direct sanction could be imposed under UK competition law.[4] Moreover, it was clearly intended that the prohibitions introduced by the Competition Act should be enforceable by means

---

* Professor of Law, University of Strathclyde, Glasgow. The author would like to thank Richard Whish and Angus MacCulloch for their helpful comments on the draft of this chapter; the errors, of course, remain entirely the author's.

1 See B J Rodger and A MacCulloch (eds), *The UK Competition Act: A New Era for UK Competition Law* (2000 Hart, Oxford).

2 Sections 2 and 18 of the Act respectively.

3 See R Whish, Chapter 1 above and the discussion re the transfer of functions to the OFT from the DGFT following the Enterprise Act 2002.

4 See B J Rodger and A MacCulloch, above and see also B J Rodger, "The Competition Act and Enterprise Act Reforms: Sanctions and Deterrence in UK Competition Law" in G Dannecker and O Jansen (eds), *Competition Law Sanctioning in the European Union* (2004 Kluwer, The Hague), at pp 101–132.

of private law actions through normal court processes.[5] Previously, the only provision which could have been directly enforced by individuals was s 35(2) of the Restrictive Trade Practices Act 1976, although no damages were awarded under this provision.[6] This chapter will consider the developments in private enforcement in the UK in the last 10 years following the introduction of the Competition Act. Section 1 of this chapter will outline the legislative framework introduced by the Competition Act, and enhanced by the Enterprise Act 2002 ("the Enterprise Act"), to facilitate competition law litigation. Section 2 will assess the practical impact of the Enterprise Act provisions designed for follow-on actions. Section 3 will consider the key case law in the courts in stand-alone actions and particularly focus on emerging trends in the case law in terms of substance and remedies. Section 4 will consider further recent and ongoing reform developments before concluding remarks in section 5.

It is important to stress at the outset that this chapter is focusing on developments in relation to private litigation involving UK competition law. Accordingly, the focus will not be on the ongoing developments at the European level; notably the Green and White Papers of 2006 and 2008 respectively.[7] Nonetheless, it is difficult to separate the development of private enforcement of UK competition law from the wider European context, for a number of reasons. First, much of the case law reflects the potential for parties to bring proceedings, or defend an action, on the basis of domestic and/or EU competition law. Second, the Enterprise Act provisions, discussed further below, make provision for follow-on actions in relation to prior infringements of both the domestic Competition Act prohibitions and Arts 101 and 102 TFEU. Furthermore, the 2007 OFT reform proposals, discussed in section 4, seek to establish the UK courts, particularly the CAT, as a hub for European competition law litigation, and are therefore not limited solely to facilitating

---

[5] See *A Prohibition Approach to Anti-Competitive Agreements and Abuse of a Dominant Position: Draft Bill.* (DTI, August 1997).

[6] There were a number of non-publicised settled claims for damages under the Act. Note that there was also the possibility of a private action under the FTA 1973 for breach of an undertaking or order, as discussed by B Rodger, "Mid Kent Holdings plc v General Utilities plc: Remedies under the Fair Trading Act 1973" [1997] European Competition Law Review 273.

[7] See Green Paper at COM (2005) 672, 19 December 2005, and associated staff working document; White Paper on damages actions for breach of the EC antitrust rules and associated Commission staff working paper, and also the detailed consideration in "Making Antitrust damages more effective in the EU: welfare impact and potential scenarios" – all available at http://ec.europa.eu/competition/antitrust/actionsdamages/documents.html#link1. Also, a draft Directive was circulated during the summer of 2009, although this was subsequently withdrawn.

actions based on the domestic competition litigation framework.[8] Finally, the litigative context in which EC or UK competition law may be applied before the UK courts is to all intents and purposes identical, in terms of substantive law,[9] procedural law,[10] and more general issues such as collective redress, financing of actions and cost recovery rules. Nonetheless, this chapter sets out to consider private enforcement within the focused context of "Ten Years of UK Competition Law Reform". The direct effect doctrine under EU law had ensured that Arts 81 and 82 EC could be used as a sword or a shield in private litigation long before the introduction of the Competition Act, and there has been considerable academic literature considering the use of EC competition law before the courts,[11] the obstacles to effectiveness[12] and suggestions for reform to facilitate private litigation.[13] Private litigation involving domestic UK competition law was, however, completely uncharted territory. Indeed, prior to the introduction of the Competition Act, UK competition law, predicated on the "public interest" and with the Fair Trading Act 1973 as its cornerstone, was enforceable by administrative action and could not be described as competition "law" in that it did not create rights and obligations nor were there any effective

[8] This latter point is reinforced by the introduction of the Rome II Regulation ([2007] OJ L299/40) which provides rules for the courts of the EU Member States, including the UK, to determine the applicable law in a delictual action, and contains specific rules to ascertain the applicable law in an action based on competition law.

[9] See s 60 of the Competition Act.

[10] For instance, in relation to issues such as limitation periods and interlocutory relief, as discussed further below.

[11] See, for instance, S F Hall, "Enforcement of EC Competition Law by National Courts" in P Jan Slot and A McDonnell (eds), *Procedure and Enforcement in EC and US Competition Law* (Sweet & Maxwell, London, 1993); J H J Bourgeois, "EC Competition Law and Member States' Courts" (1994) 17 Fordham International Law Journal 332; Behrens (ed) *EEC Competition Rules in National Courts, I and II* (Nomos Verlasgesellschaft, 1992 and 1994); N. Reich, "The 'Courage' Doctrine: encouraging or discouraging compensation for antitrust injuries?" (2005) 42 CML Rev 35.

[12] See, for example, the Ashurst Report: Study on the conditions of claims for damages in case of infringement of EC competition rules, available at http://ec.europa.eu/comm/competition/antitrust/others/actions_for_damages/study.html.; S Kon and Maxwell, "Enforcement in National Courts of the EC and New UK Competition Rules: Obstacles to Effective Enforcement" [1998] 7 ECLR 443.

[13] The Commission White Paper on damages actions for breach of EC antitrust rules, available at http://ec.europa.eu/competition/antitrust/actionsdamages/documents.html#link1. The White Paper is currently before the European Parliament. "A Little more Action please! The White paper on damages actions for breach of the EC antitrust rules" (2008) CML Rev 609; F Bulst, "Of Arms and Armour – The European Commission's White Paper on Damages Actions for Breach of EC Antitrust Law" [2008] Bucerius Law Journal 81. See also the earlier Green Paper at COM (2005) 672, 19 December 2005, and associated staff working document, SEC (2005) 1732, both available at http://ec.europa.eu/comm/competition/antitrust/actionsdamages/documents.html#greenpaper.

sanctions. Therefore, it will be interesting in this chapter to chart the development of private competition litigation involving the UK prohibitions and identify key trends and themes in the case law. The focus will be on litigation in which the domestic prohibitions have been relied on,[14] although cases solely involving EC competition law may also raise more generic issues about the availability of remedies and the procedural framework and will be considered to the extent that they impact on the development of private enforcement in a domestic context.

1 THE LEGISLATIVE FRAMEWORK

UK competition law underwent a fairly dramatic overhaul within the space of 4 years following a period of 25 years of relative stability,[15] albeit there was considerable debate during the 1990s about reform to introduce a system modelled on EC competition law.[16] The Competition Act and the Enterprise Act transformed the landscape. The former introduced prohibitions modelled on Arts 81 and 82 EC, but, more importantly in this context, set out to overhaul the system of enforcement, to introduce effective administrative sanctions and, mirroring EC law, to encourage private parties to protect their rights created by the new legislative provisions. The Enterprise Act sought to further encourage the latter development.

1.1 The Competition Act 1998 – a new system for private enforcement

The Competition Act facilitated claims by providing, in s 58, that those findings of fact by the OFT, which are relevant to an issue arising in a court action, are binding on the parties if that decision in which the findings of fact were made is no longer subject to appeal, or have been confirmed on appeal. In addition, s 55 enables the OFT to disclose information to third parties, subject to the limitations under s 56 relating to, *inter alia*, the public interest and certain

---

[14] Note that it is impossible to undertake a comprehensive analysis in this chapter, and further reference should be made to B Rodger, "Competition Law Litigation in the UK Courts: A Study of All Cases to 2004" (Parts I–III) [2006] European Competition Law Review 241, 279 and 341 respectively; and B Rodger, "Competition Law Litigation in the UK Courts: A Study of all cases 2005–2008" (Parts I and II) [2009] Global Competition Litigation Review 92 and 136 respectively. More generally, see M Brealey and N Green, *Competition Litigation: UK Practice and Procedure* (OUP, 2009).

[15] The Restrictive Trade Practices Act 1976 consolidated earlier restrictive practices legislation and the Competition Act 1980 was introduced but had minimal impact.

[16] See, for instance, R Whish, "The Competition Act 1998 and the prior debate on reform" in B J Rodger and A MacCulloch (eds) *The UK Competition Act*, n 1 above, at Chap 1.

confidential information. Nonetheless, the Competition Act contains no express provision stating that the prohibitions can be enforced by private civil law action. Where statutes do not state specifically that private law remedies are available, it is a matter of construction of the particular statute as to whether Parliament intended to create such remedies.[17] In any event, in the first case on the substance of the Chapter II prohibition, *Claritas (UK) Ltd* v *The Post Office and Postal Preference Service Ltd*,[18] the matter was not raised and the case proceeded on the assumption that the new prohibitions could be enforced in private litigation. Furthermore, there have been a number of more recent examples of private litigation in which claims have been made on the basis of infringement of the prohibitions.[19]

1.2 The Enterprise Act 2002 – follow-on actions and the CAT

The Enterprise Act made further provision for encouraging private actions in relation to breaches of the Competition Act prohibitions. Under s 47A of the Competition Act, as introduced by s 18 of the Enterprise Act, the CAT,[20] in addition to its role as an appeal tribunal, is able to award damages and other monetary awards where there has already been a finding by the relevant authorities of an infringement of the Chapters I and II prohibitions, or Arts 101 and 102 TFEU.[21] During the passage of the Competition Act, the issue of a possible role for the CAT in damages actions was debated but ultimately rejected. The original version of the Enterprise Bill provided only for damages awards but this was revised to recognise the possibility of other forms of claims consequent upon competition law infringements.[22] Section 47A(10) makes it clear that a unitary system for dealing with damages claims under UK or EC law has not been instituted, by providing that this section does not affect the right to commence ordinary civil proceedings in respect of any of the infringements. Accordingly, follow-on actions may, but are

---

[17] See A MacCulloch, "Private enforcement of the Competition Act prohibitions" in B J Rodger and A MacCulloch (eds), *The UK Competition Act*, n 1 above, at Chap 5.

[18] [2001] UKCLR 2.

[19] See B Rodger [2009] Global Competition Litigation Review 92, n 14 above.

[20] For a fuller discussion of the CAT, its role, functions and caseload, see D Bailey, Chapter 2 above.

[21] See, for instance, *HealthCare at Home Ltd* v *Genzyme Ltd* [2006] CAT 29, a judgment for interim relief by the CAT, discussed further below.

[22] As Lord McIntosh of Haringey indicated at Committee Stage in the Lords, 16 July 2002, col 1437: "This could conceivably include claims for the restitution of profits unlawfully made by the infringing company as well as in respect of loss caused to the injured party, although the scope for these will depend on the evolving jurisprudence of the courts."

not required to, be brought before the CAT, as demonstrated, for example, in *Devenish*.[23] Of course, the key issue in s 47A concerns the periods within which an action must be raised before the CAT, as demonstrated by the follow-on damages actions case law to date. In fact, there are two related but apparently contradictory sets of requirements relating to the period within which an action may be brought before the CAT – suspensive and definitive periods – as discussed further below.[24]

Section 19 added s 47B to the Competition Act, allowing damages claims to be brought before the CAT by a specified body on behalf of two or more consumers who have claims in respect of the same infringement[25] – a form of "consumer representative action".[26] The representative body requires the consent of the individuals to pursue their claims.[27] Section 47B(6) sets out who constitute consumers for these purposes, and states that a consumer is an individual who received goods or services, or sought to receive them, otherwise than in the course of a business, notwithstanding that this was with a view to carrying on a business. In addition, the goods or services must be supplied to the individual in the course of a business.[28] This is a fairly wide definition of consumer for these purposes and reading subss (2) and (7) together makes clear that this procedure may be utilised in respect of indirect purchasers. Section 47B was inserted to support an underlying aim of the Enterprise Act to reinforce the links between competition law and consumers. Nonetheless, the only specified body to date is Which? (the Consumers' Association),[29] and there has only been one, albeit high-profile, s 47B claim, in *The Consumers' Association* v *JJB Sports plc*.[30]

In order for the follow-on provision to have greatest success in facilitating litigation, it was considered necessary to include provision regarding the binding nature of prior enforcement authority

---

[23] *Devenish Nutrition Ltd* v *Sanofi-Aventis SA (France)* [2007] EWHC 2394 (Ch) and [2008] EWCA Civ 1086 (CA), discussed further below.

[24] See section 2 below.

[25] Section 47B(1) and (4). Subsections (9)–(10) make provision regarding the specification of a body by the Secretary of State.

[26] For instance, *The Consumers' Association* v *JJB Sports plc* (CAT Case 1078/7/9/07), a follow-on consumer representative action under these provisions before the CAT in relation to Replica Kits, although this case was settled out of court in January 2008 following an agreement by JJB to pay consumers who were unlawfully overcharged £20 each (see CAT Order of 14 January 2008).

[27] Section 47B(3), ie it is an opt-in form of representative action.

[28] In this context, business is defined in subs (8) as including: (a) a professional practice; (b) any other undertaking carried on for gain or reward; (c) any other undertaking in the course of which goods or services are supplied otherwise than free of charge.

[29] Pursuant to Specified Body (Consumer Claims) Order 2005, SI 2005/2365.

[30] Case 1078/7/9/07.

decisions. Section 20 added s 58A to the Competition Act, which provides that, in any action for damages for an infringement of the 1998 Act prohibitions or Arts 101(1) or 102 TFEU, a court will be bound by a decision of the OFT or CAT that any of the prohibitions have been infringed,[31] if the requisite appeal process has taken place or the period for appeal lapsed.[32] Nonetheless, despite this supporting provision, there have been difficulties, outlined below, in determining the scope of the effect of a prior binding decision.[33]

The next section will focus on the follow-on damages actions case law under ss 47A and 47B of the Competition Act before the CAT. A particular advantage of claims raised before the CAT is that they leave a "footprint" even where the case settles before any judicial determination of the issues arising in the claim. On the other hand, with actions before the normal civil courts, primarily stand-alone actions,[34] one must always be aware of the "hidden story" of competition litigation settlements which means that the visible litigation practice is effectively the "tip of the iceberg",[35] such that we can only consider litigation practice through analysis of case law judgments. Before we proceed to a more detailed consideration of the case law under the follow-on actions provisions introduced by the Enterprise Act, it should be noted that the figures for cases registered at the CAT under these provisions, as outlined in the CAT annual review,[36] are limited. Of 19 new cases (appeals, applications and claims) received in the year prior to 31 March 2008 in relation to the various functions of the CAT, only two were monetary claims under s 47A of the Competition Act. The figures were similarly low in the previous 3 years, although there has been a notable, if limited, increase to March 2009 with four of 11 new eases involving monetary claims.

2 FOLLOW-ON ACTIONS

Since the introduction of the Enterprise Act provisions, three follow-on actions have been raised and dealt with at the High Court (and Court of Appeal in one – *Devenish*) in *English, Welsh and Scottish Railway Ltd* v *E.ON UK plc*[37] ("*EWS*"), *Devenish Nutrition Ltd* v *Sanofi-Aventis SA (France)*,[38] ("*Devenish*") and *National Grid Electricity Submission plc* v

[31] Section 58A(2).

[32] Section 58A(3). See also Art 16 of Regulation 1/2003 re decisions of the Commission.

[33] See further below re *Enron Coal Services Ltd (in Liquidation)* v *English, Welsh and Scottish Railway Ltd* [2009] CAT 7 and on appeal to the Court of Appeal [2009] EWCA Civ 647.

[34] See further re follow-on actions in section 2 below.

[35] See B Rodger, "Private Enforcement of Competition Law The Hidden Story: Competition Litigation Settlements in the UK 2000–2005" [2008] ECLR 96.

[36] http://www.catribunal.org.uk/files/AnnualReview08_09.pdf.

[37] [2007] EWHC 599 (Comm).

[38] [2007] EWHC 2394 (Ch) and [2008] EWCA Civ 1086 (CA).

ABB Ltd ("*National Grid*").[39] As at 8 November 2009, there have been a total of five follow-on actions which have resulted in judgments by the CAT, including *Enron Coal Services*,[40] although none of these have been final judgments on the merits.[41] There have been multiple judgments in some cases where the CAT has determined a number of interim process issues, notably in relation to time-bar, as discussed further below.[42] Overall, there appears to be a limited number of follow-on claims before the CAT, 11 in total, when one assesses the decision-making activities of the OFT alone.[43] Given that follow-on actions may be raised at the CAT in relation to OFT (and sectoral regulators) and Commission infringement decisions,[44] the results certainly appear disappointing at first glance. In fact, one of the actions before the High Court, *Devenish*, was raised following the Commission's *Vitamins* decision,[45] as were the two *BCL Old Co* cases,[46] and the protracted *Emerson* litigation follows the *Electrical and Mechanical Carbon and Graphite Products* Commission decision.[47] The other two cases, *Deans Foods Ltd* v *Roche*, which settled,[48] and the ongoing *Grampian Country Food Group Ltd* v *Sanofi-Aventis* claim,[49] both also derived from the Commission *Vitamins* decision. The *National Grid* case, raised at the High Court, is a follow-on action to the Commission decision in *Gas Insulated Switchgear*.[50] The only judgments following UK authority decisions were in *EWS* (an infringement finding by the ORR),[51] *Healthcare at Home Ltd* v *Genzyme Ltd*,[52] and the *Enron Coal Services*

---

[39] [2009] EWHC 1326.

[40] [2009] CAT 7 and [2009] CAT 18; see also CA [2009] EWCA Civ 647. See also *BCL Old Ltd* v *Aventis SA*; *BCL Old Co Ltd* v *BASF SE*; *Emerson Electric Co* v *Morgan Crucible Co plc* and *Healthcare at Home Ltd* v *Genzyme Ltd*.

[41] Although in *Healthcare at Home Ltd*, the CAT awarded an interim damages payment of £2 million prior to the case settling.

[42] See, for instance, *Emerson I, II, III and IV* and both cases involving *BCL Old Co Ltd* which have involved two judgments each.

[43] See http://www.oft.gov.uk/advice_and_resources/resource_base/ca98/decisions/. See the discussion by R Whish, Chapter 1 at p. 8–15 above.

[44] In addition to the decisions of various sectoral regulators (see R Whish, Chapter 1 above, and also G Monti, Chapter 6 below) and also indeed following infringement decisions by the CAT itself, as in *Burgess* v *W Austin & Sons (Stevenage) Ltd and Harwood Park Crematorium Ltd*, following *Burgess* v *OFT* [2005] CAT 25.

[45] Commission Decision 2003/3/EC [2003] OJ L6/1.

[46] *BCL Old Ltd* v *Aventis SA*; *BCL Old Co Ltd* v *BASF SE*.

[47] Commission Decision 2004/420/EC [2004] OJ L125/45.

[48] Case 1029/5/7/04.

[49] Case 1101/5/7/08. At the time of writing, judgment was awaited in relation to an application under r 19 of the Tribunal's rules to extend the time to bring the respective claims before the Tribunal.

[50] Case COMP/F/38/899.

[51] [2007] EWHC 599 (Comm).

[52] [2006] CAT 29.

Ltd case (involving the same ORR infringement finding).[53] The related *Freightliner Ltd* case settled at an early stage,[54] and there have been two other cases following UK infringement findings. The most recent claim which has already settled, *Wilson* v *Lancing College Ltd*,[55] followed the OFT decision taken in the first innovative "early resolution" decision taken by the OFT in relation to independent school fees.[56] More interesting is the *Burgess* case,[57] which was a follow-on action subsequent to an infringement finding by the CAT itself, acting in its appeal capacity where it overruled an earlier rejection of a complaint to the OFT.[58] There have been very few cases to date, and, with the exception of the *Independent School Fees* case,[59] all cases have either been claims by legal persons as direct or indirect purchasers from a cartel, or by competitor companies in relation to a Chapter II/Art 82 abuse finding. Moreover, there have been no judgments in any s 47B representative action proceedings by the CAT. However, there has been one high-profile s 47B claim, in *The Consumers' Association* v *JJB Sports plc*.[60] Ultimately, this action, with only 144 consumers party to the action, was settled on the basis of compensation up to a maximum of £20 per individual consumer.[61] The paucity of s 47B claims is disappointing but the difficulties in bringing collective actions under existing mechanisms before the courts was demonstrated recently by *Emerald Supplies Ltd* v *British Airways plc*.[62] That case related to alleged overcharges in relation to transatlantic air freight brought by the claimants, who import cut flowers from Columbia and Kenya, against BA, on their own behalf and on behalf of all other direct and indirect purchasers of air freight services. The action was raised in the High Court and BA were successful in an application to strike out the purported representative element of the claim on the basis that the other persons did not have "the same interest" under the relevant court rules to bring such a

---

[53] *Enron Coal Services Ltd (in liquidation)* v *English, Welsh and Scottish Railways Ltd* [2009] CAT 7.

[54] Case 1005/5/7/08 *Freightliner Ltd and Freightlines Heavy Haul Ltd* v *English, Welsh and Scottish Railways Ltd.*

[55] Case 1008/5/7/08.

[56] See OFT Press Release 166/06, 23 November 2006, http://www.oft.gov.uk/news/press/2006/166-06 in relation to the early resolution procedure in the *Independent School Fees* case.

[57] *Burgess* v *W Austin & Sons (Stevenage) Ltd and Harwood Park Crematorium Ltd* (Case 1088/5/7/07).

[58] *Burgess* v *OFT* [2005] CAT 25.

[59] Case 1108/5/7/08.

[60] Case 1078/7/9/07.

[61] If receipts had been retained: see http://www.which.co.uk/news/2008/01/jjb-to-pay-fans-over-football-shirt-rip-off-128985.jsp.

[62] [2009] EWHC 741 (Ch). Note that an appeal in this case was due to be heard before the Court of Appeal in December 2009.

representative action,[63] partly as there would be an inevitable conflict between the claims of different members of the class. This was a disappointing and narrow interpretation of the particular court rules. More generally there have been a very limited number of follow-on claims raised before the CAT, although there are signs of a recent increase in this context.

Of course, as emphasised earlier, claimants are not required to bring claims before the CAT, and non-monetary claims are specifically excluded from the ambit of the CAT's jurisdiction. This explains why the action in *EWS* was raised before the High Court.[64] In *EWS*,[65] the claimant, an operator of bulk freight services, entered into a coal carriage agreement ("CCA") in 1997 with the defendant which was in the business of electricity generation. In 2006, the ORR found that EWS had foreclosed the Great Britain coal haulage by rail market, abusing its dominant position by *inter alia* the exclusionary terms of the CCA. They were fined £4.1 million, and EWS and E.ON then disputed the CCA. EWS applied for a declaration to the effect that the ORR Directions rendered the CCA void. It was held that the exclusionary terms were illegal and void *ab initio* in terms of Art 82, and also subsequently in relation to Chapter II, that there could be no severance of the exclusionary term and the whole contract was void and unenforceable.[66] *Devenish*[67] was a post-*Vitamins* follow-on action in the High Court and concerned the preliminary issue of whether the claimant would be entitled to restitution of unjust enrichment and exemplary damages, although only the former issue was considered on appeal, unsuccessfully.[68] This may be explained by the 6-year limitation period for bringing damages claims to the High Court, compared to the 2-year period from infringement decision (including appeal process) to raise monetary claims before the CAT. Another rationale for a claim being raised before the High Court relates to the suspensive requirements contained in s 47A for an action to be raised before the CAT, as demonstrated by *Emerson III*.[69] In that case before the CAT, the claimants made applications for permission to make a claim for damages pursuant to s 47A(5)(b) and r 31(3) of the Tribunal Rules against parties who had made appeals to the CFI. Section 47A(5)(b) of the 1998 Act provides that no claim may be made before

63 CPR, r 19.6.

64 [2007] EWHC 599 (Comm). This case was raised in the Commercial Court rather than the Chancery Division as it was a matter of contract law rather than competition law.

65 [2007] EWHC 599 (Comm).

66 The courts are required to apply the doctrine of severance and the same approach was held to apply where a contract is void by reason of Art 82 and the Chapter II prohibition.

67 [2008] EWCA Civ 1086 (CA).

68 See J Skilbeck, "Cartel damages: the Court of Appeal rejects a gain-based remedy" [2009] European Competition Law Review 105.

69 [2008] CAT 8.

the CAT except with permission during any period specified in subss (7) and (8), ie during the period in which an appeal may be instituted or, if so, prior to its determination. The claimants contended that the claims against those parties were so interrelated with other claims that had been raised that it would be expeditious and fair to grant permission against the proposed defendant. The CAT confirmed that permission in these circumstances would be "exceptional" and the overriding consideration would be whether it enabled a case to be dealt with justly. The CAT was not satisfied that justice would not be done if the claimants waited, and, furthermore, the European Courts' appeal process may be relevant to quantification of a claim. In any event, the CAT stressed that stand-alone actions could be raised before the civil courts. These restrictions on the jurisdiction of the CAT, and the concomitant advantages of proceeding with a follow-on action before the High Court, were exemplified by *National Grid*, a follow-on claim seeking damages in the sum of £249 million. The particular proceedings and ruling concerned an application by the defendants to stay the proceedings, and the appropriate test for determining when a stay should be granted in the light of *Masterfoods*[70] and Art 3 of Regulation 1/2003.[71] Nonetheless, it was clear that proceedings were raised in the High Court because a number of parties to the Commission *Switchgear* decision had appealed to the Court of First Instance, and the claimants ran the risk of an "Italian torpedo" involving a negative declaratory action being raised in an alternative jurisdiction should they be required to wait until appeal proceedings had been completed and an action could be raised before the CAT.[72] Furthermore, by kick-starting the action with immediate effect, *National Grid* also demonstrated that claimants could benefit from immediate disclosure of documents by the defendants.

In particular, the CAT has been required to consider two key aspects related to the scope of its follow-on jurisdiction. The first relates to the limitation rules before the CAT, distinctive from the 6-year limitation period for High Court claims and dependent on the post-infringement finding appeal process as discussed below. There have been two CAT judgments focused directly on time-bar issues.[73] In *Emerson I*,[74] the Emerson claimants were seeking damages following the Commission decision in *Electrical and Mechanical Carbon and Graphite Products*. In addition, r 31 of the Tribunal

[70] *Masterfoods* v *HB Icecream Ltd* (Case C–344/98) [2000] ECR I–11369.

[71] The High Court allowed the action to proceed in the interim until close of pleadings.

[72] See also F M Moretti and L Nascimbene, "No Scent of 'Torpedo'" [2009] Global Competition Litigation Review 67.

[73] See also *Emerson III* [2008] CAT 8.

[74] [2007] CAT 28.

Rules[75] provides that a claim must be made within 2 years of the relevant date, which is the later of the following: (a) the end of the period specified in s 47A(7) or (8) of the Competition Act in relation to the decision on the basis of which the claim is made; (b) the date on which the cause of action accrued. The claimants were direct purchasers of mechanical carbon and graphite products and sought exemplary damages. Morgan Crucible was a successful leniency applicant and did not bring an action for annulment of the relevant Commission decision, although other parties to the decision brought annulment applications before the CFI. The CAT emphasised that s 47A refers to any such appellate proceedings and therefore, although Morgan Crucible did not appeal, the time limit for raising an action would not start to run until the appeal process had been completed, and accordingly the action against Morgan Crucible was not time-barred. A similar issue arose in *BCL Old Co Ltd* v *BASF I*,[76] a post-*Vitamins* indirect purchasers' claim. BASF appealed against the Commission decision to the CFI but did not appeal against the infringement, and thereby claimed that the possibility of appeal against infringement ended in January 2002. The CFI determined the appeal on 15 March 2006 and the CAT claim was commenced on 13 March 2008. The CAT considered in detail the earlier *Emerson I and III* rulings and held that the claim was not time-barred:

> "The findings made by a competition authority in deciding to impose, and calculating the level of, a penalty may well be relevant to, and be determined by, the nature and extent of the infringement which is being penalised. For example, the gravity, duration and scope of the infringement ... may well be factors relevant, not only to the size of the penalty imposed, but also to liability in damages."[77]

This is the only follow-on case to date where the subsequent appeal mechanism under s 49 has been utilised. The Court of Appeal overturned the CAT's decision,[78] emphasising the distinction between a decision that a relevant prohibition has been infringed and a decision imposing a penalty, which was made clear in s 47A. In particular, s 47A(5)(a) refers only to infringement decisions,[79] even where, as here, the Commission

---

[75] Competition Appeal Tribunal Rules 2003, SI 2003/1372, adopted pursuant to Pt 2 of Sch 4 to the 2002 Act.

[76] [2008] CAT 24.

[77] At para 34.

[78] [2009] EWCA Civ 434 (CA). Enron has applied for permission to appeal to the Supreme Court.

[79] No claim can be made until "a decision mentioned in subsection (6) has established that the relevant prohibition in question has been infringed". This was a Commission decision but the Court of Appeal emphasised that the distinction appeared elsewhere in the Act, for instance in ss 31 and 36 in relation to OFT decisions.

had issued a single decision containing findings on infringement and fines in different articles thereof.[80] Accordingly, the application for annulment of the fine did not extend the period within which a claim could be made, and the claim was accordingly time-barred. Nonetheless, an application could be made to the CAT under r 31(3) to extend the time period, and the Court of Appeal indeed noted that the restricted period between publication of the decision of the Commission in the Official Journal and expiry of the time period may be relevant in the context of an application to extend the time limit.

The second issue concerns the precise nature of the competition authority's findings and the consequences of those findings, and this may involve factually complicated determinations by the CAT, as evidenced by *Enron Coal Services Ltd (in Liquidation)* v *EWS Ltd*.[81] This was a follow-on claim to an ORR decision that EWS had infringed the Chapter II prohibition and Art 82, finding that it had abused its dominant position by: (a) making agreements with industrial coal users for the haulage of coal which had an exclusionary effect between 1996 and 2005; and (b) engaging in certain unlawful price discrimination practices. The claimant contended that this resulted in an unlawful overcharge and also put the claimant at a competitive disadvantage in seeking to renew coal supply agreements with existing customers. The claimant sought various remedies including damages and lost profit. The defendant made a r 40 application, effectively to strike out certain aspects of the claim, involving the scope of the follow-on jurisdiction of the CAT. The claimants also made a "lost opportunity" claim for £77 million, but the disputed issue here concerned whether they could claim an overcharge before the CAT. It was stressed throughout the proceedings that establishing liability is not an issue for the CAT under s 47A, which is concerned with causation and quantum. The defendants noted that the ORR decision established liability but that there was a relevant market limitation, a geographical limitation and also necessarily a temporal limitation to the scope of the decision. The claimants noted the different limitation periods in the High Court and emphasised the importance of all matters related to an infringement decision being considered in one forum, meeting the needs of efficiency and public policy, and thereby affording claimants the right to come to a specialist tribunal with its expertise and allowing them to benefit from the special limitation periods. In relation to one particular

---

[80] This was also consistent with Community law: see *Sumitomo Chemical Co Ltd* v *European Commission* (Cases T–22 & 23/02) [2005] ECR II–4065.

[81] Case 1106/5/7/08. See also the earlier case of *Deans Foods Ltd* v *Roche Products Ltd* (Case 1029/5/7/04), where one issue was whether the prior decision allowed claims in relation to yellow carophyll in addition to red carophyll.

overcharge claim,[82] the CAT held that the ORR decision had stated that unlawful price discrimination had taken place between May and November 2000, and therefore the consequential effects of the price discrimination were limited to periods beyond May 2000.[83] Moreover, on appeal, the Court of Appeal overturned the CAT in relation to the overcharge case which was allowed to proceed to trial, illustrating "the dangers of not taking a sufficiently strict approach as to what finding of infringement the regulator has in fact made".[84] This case and particular dispute, involving a decision over 400 pages in length, which was described by the CAT as an "extraordinarily long and complex" document,[85] demonstrates the difficulties in ascertaining exactly what support the enforcement authority decision provides for subsequent claims. This may also create a backward pressure on regulatory authorities to be even more precise in terms of their findings,[86] a task which may be difficult, particularly in early resolution decisions.[87] The problems in this context are likely to be exacerbated by linguistic difficulties should the EU adopt the European Commission's White Paper proposal that national courts and tribunals should be similarly bound by the Art 81 and 82 infringement decisions by other Member States' NCAs.[88]

Finally, *Healthcare at Home Ltd* v *Genzyme Ltd*[89] comes as close to a final ruling awarding damages as there has been in the UK. This was an action under s 47A of the Competition Act following an earlier OFT decision[90] that the defendant had a dominant position in the upstream market for the supply of drugs for the treatment of Gaucher disease and had abused it by a margin squeeze abuse.[91] The defendant

---

[82] The so-called "EME" overcharge in relation to coal hauled to two power stations owned by Edison Mission Energy.

[83] [2009] CAT 7.

[84] *EWS Ltd* v *Enron Coal Services Ltd (in Liquidation)* [2009] EWCA Civ 647, per Patten LJ at para. 59. He also stressed at para 60 that the task for the CAT in this context is the same as the r 40 hearing and a trial and the CAT "should have decided whether it was clear from the Decision that a finding of infringement had been made which covered the pleaded claims".

[85] At para 14.

[86] As Carnwath LJ noted, at para 64, "in drafting such a decision the regulator should leave no doubt as to the nature of the infringement (if any) which has been found".

[87] See R Whish, Chapter 1 above.

[88] See Commission White Paper on *Damages actions for breach of the EC antitrust rules*, http://ec.europa.eu/competition/antitrust/actionsdamages/files_white_paper/whitepaper_en.pdf, April 2008, at para 3.2, and see also Art 12 of the proposed Council Directive on rules governing damages actions for infringements of Arts 81 and 82 of the Treaty.

[89] [2006] CAT 29.

[90] Decision CA 98/3/03.

[91] See D Ridyard, "The Genzyme Case and the OFT's Margin Squeeze Muddle", RBB Brief, 10 July 2003; B Allan, "The Control of Dominant Firms in the UK – the Jurisprudence of the CAT" (2007) 6 Comp Law Journal 265.

admitted that the claimant was entitled to rely on the Tribunal finding and the claimant sought an order for an interim payment. The Tribunal stressed that it "may make an interim payment order if it is satisfied that if the claim were to be heard the Claimant would obtain judgment for a substantial amount of money".[92] The Tribunal awarded £2 million as an interim payment, on the basis of the lowest estimated loss of revenue at £2,866,490, and the action was subsequently settled. Nonetheless, it remains the case that there have been no final damages awards in the courts in the UK, and the important questions as to the nature and extent of the passing-on defence, the scope for indirect purchasers to sue, and the process of quantification of damages, have yet to be tackled in any detail by the courts and/or CAT. The first trial before the CAT, in *Enron Coal Services Ltd* v *EWS*, took place in September 2009, and the outcome is awaited with interest.

3 STAND-ALONE ACTIONS

The existence of a dedicated scheme for follow-on actions, albeit with limitations, is evidently important, particularly in the early phase of development of a private competition litigation culture. However, given the prioritisation policy by the OFT[93] (and European Commission), and the delays involved in a lengthy competition authority investigation, and subsequent appeal process, parties may need to take independent action where necessary. This section will consider the case law in relation to stand-alone actions since the introduction of the Competition Act prohibitions, and will also outline briefly the role of the prohibitions as defences. Of course, such stand-alone actions (and follow-on actions, without the support of the mechanisms now contained in the Competition Act), have been available in relation to Arts 81 and 82 since before the introduction of the Competition Act.[94] Moreover, as noted earlier, there have been a number of cases in the last 10 years in the UK courts dealing with Arts 81 and 82 alone,[95] including some important contributions to the ongoing development of private enforcement and the application of the substantive competition law prohibitions between private parties;[96] the focus in this section will be on

---

[92] At para 66.

[93] See R Whish, Chapter 1 above, and OFT Prioritisation Principles, OFT 953 (2008), available at www.oft.gov.uk.

[94] See B Rodger, "Competition Law Litigation in the UK Courts: A Study of All Cases to 2004" and "Competition Law Litigation in the UK Courts: A Study of all cases 2005–2008", n 14 above.

[95] *Ibid.*

[96] The Crehan saga, which ended in the House of Lords, *Crehan* v *Inntrepreneur* [2007] 1 AC 333, is notable in this context. See, for instance, A Komninos, "New Prospects for

stand-alone actions where UK competition law was raised alone,[97] or in combination with EC law.[98] There has been a steady stream of litigation over the years, although there has not been a dramatic increase as may have been anticipated,[99] partly because we may only be witnessing the "tip of the iceberg" of competition litigation due to prevailing settlement practice.[100] In relation to the number of competition law claims and defences each year, the preponderance of competition law defences, in the 1970s, 1980s and early to mid 1990s was notable. The position has changed in recent years, as demonstrated by the case law in relation to the prohibitions, with the majority of cases being sword-type actions[101] as opposed to defensive shields.[102] In terms of the substantive classification of the case law, the vast majority of the stand-alone actions have been abuse cases, in contrast with follow-on actions before the CAT, partly because it would be incredibly complex for a claimant to prove the existence of a cartel in a stand-alone action due to the evidential difficulties. Nonetheless, there have also been a number of actions based on the Chapter I prohibition alone or in combination with Art 81 or the abuse-based prohibition(s), and these have tended to be brought in relation to explicit agreements, as in BAGS, rather than covert cartels.

---

private enforcement of EC Competition Law: Courage v Crehan and the Community right to damages" (2002) 39 CMLRev 447; B Rodger, "The Interface Between Competition Law and Private Law: Article 81, Illegality and Unjustified Enrichment" (2002) 6 Edin LR 217, particularly at 217–226 and 232–233; T Petch, "Relying on Commission Decisions" (2007) 123 LQR 186; B Rodger (ed), *Article 234 and Competition Law: An Analysis* (2008 Kluwer, The Hague), at pp 545–552. See also, for instance, *Devenish*, discussed above; *Arkin* v *Borchard Lines* Ltd [2003] 2 Lloyd's Rep 225; *HMSO* v *AA* [2001] ECC 34; and *Calor Gas Ltd* v *Express Fuels (Scotland) Ltd* [2008] CSOH 13.

[97] See, for example, *Synstar Computer Sevices (UK) Ltd* v *ICL (Sorbus) Ltd* [2001] UKCLR 585; *Land Rover Group Ltd* v *UPF (UK) Ltd (in administrative receivership)* [2002] EWHC 3183; *Getmapping* v *Ordnance Survey* [2002] EWHC 1089 (Pat) and *Chester City Council* v *Arriva plc* [2007] EWHC 1373 (Ch).

[98] See, for example, *Claritas (UK) Ltd* v *Post Office* [2001] ECC 12; *Hendry* v *World Professional Billiards & Snooker Association Ltd* [2002] ECC 8; *Attheraces* v *British Horseracing Board Ltd* [2005] EWHC 3015 (Ch) and [2007] EWCA Civ 38; and *BAGS* v *Amalgamated Racing Ltd* [2008] EWHC 1978 (Ch); [2009] EWCA Civ 750 (CA).

[99] See B Rodger, "Competition Law Litigation in the UK Courts: A Study of all cases 2005–2008", n 14 above.

[100] See B Rodger, " The Hidden Story ..." [2008] ECLR 96, n 35 above.

[101] See, for instance, *Synstar*, *Land Rover*, *Getmapping*, *Chester*, *Claritas*, *Hendry*, *Attheraces* and *BAGS*, all above, nn 97 and 98; and also, for example, *Leeds City Council* v *Watkins and Whiteley* [2003] EWHC 598 (Ch).

[102] See, for instance, *Microsoft* v *Ling* [2006] EWHC 1619 (Ch); *Intel* v *Via Technologies* [2002] EWCA Civ 1905 (CA); *PIK Facilities Ltd* v *Watson's Ayr Park Ltd* [2005] CSOH 32.

3.1 Anti-competitive agreements cases

As discussed above, there have been a limited number of cartel-related follow-on actions,[103] and also some stand-alone actions relating to vertical agreements, before the High Court involving the application of Art 81.[104] *Hendry* was a noteworthy stand-alone action involving a combination of the four UK and EC prohibitions in relation to the rules of the governing organisation for snooker, which was partially successful, and *Synstar*[105] was also an interesting case involving an alleged breach of the Chapter I and II prohibitions by the claimant where the defender was granted a stay.[106] There is very limited evidence of stand-alone actions being raised in hard-core cartel cases, one case being *Secretary of State for Health* v *Norton Healthcare Ltd.*[107] The most significant of the Chapter I related claims is probably *Bookmakers' Afternoon Greyhound Services Ltd* v *Amalgamated Racing Ltd*, which involved two judgments on the merits.[108] BAGS, a not-for-profit organisation, promoted the interests of bookmakers in licensed betting offices ("LBOs"). The other claimants were three large bookmakers. The defendants included AMRAC, which provided, to subscribing LBOs, live images and sound in respect of horse races at various courses in Great Britain. The other defendants were operators of 30 racecourses in this dispute which alleged a breach of Art 81 and the Chapter I prohibition. The claimants sought: a declaration that collective exclusive licensing on a closed basis of the rights necessary for the supply to LBOs in UK and Ireland of images, sound and data in respect of horse races was prohibited; an injunction to prevent the defendants from giving effect to or providing for collective exclusive

---

[103] See *Devenish* and *National Grid*, discussed above, in addition to *Emerald Supplies Ltd* v *British Airways plc*, albeit the latter was formally a stand-alone action.

[104] See notably *Crehan* in this regard. *Calor Gas Ltd* v *Express Fuels (Scotland) Ltd* was an action before the Court of Session in Scotland. Calor, the market leaders in the distribution and supply of bulk and cylinder LPG in Great Britain distributed its products through a network of independent dealers and retailers. The defender terminated its agreement and entered a dealership with a competitor. Calor sought damages and interdict, but the action was defended successfully on the basis that the single branding obligation for 5 years and the post-termination restriction in the agreements were null and void in accordance with Art 81. See also *Murphy* v *Media Protection Services Ltd* and *Football Association Premier League Ltd* v *QC Leisure*, which were both referred to the ECJ for a preliminary ruling in relation to Art 81 and the prohibition on export bans.

[105] *Synstar Computer Sevices (UK) Ltd* v *ICL (Sorbus) Ltd* [2001] UKCLR 585.

[106] See also *Suretrack Rail Services Ltd* v *Infraco JNP Ltd* [2002] EWHC 1316 (Ch).

[107] [2004] EWHC 609 (Ch) and [2003] EWHC 1905 (Ch). In that case the Secretary of State for Health and other health bodies were suing over alleged participation in a warfarin cartel involving elements of price-fixing, supply fixing and market sharing. The claimant's case was based on a combination of the Chapter I and Art 81 and the claimant was successful in having the application by the defendant to strike out dismissed.

[108] [2008] EWHC 1978 (Ch) and [2008] EWHC 2688 (Ch).

licensing of the rights on a closed basis; and damages. Following trial, in a 77-page judgment of 523 paragraphs, it was held that the relevant concerted practice between racecourses did not have the object of fixing prices, and that foreclosure was "hypothetical". In relation to collective selling, the claimants had not shown that the collective negotiation was likely to result in a higher price being paid, and, accordingly, the claim fell and was dismissed. Subsequently, the court also dismissed counterclaims relating to collusive behaviour by certain bookmakers which had allegedly formed an unlawful concerted practice to boycott Turf TV, and to withdraw sponsorship from certain racecourses which had licensed their LBO rights to AMRAC. A subsequent appeal to the Court of Appeal was dismissed. Competition was not restricted and there was no breach of Art 81(1) where co-operation was the only commercially justifiable way to enter a new market or launch a new product.[109] Overall, there has been very little reported case law on the application of Chapter I in a stand-alone context.

3.2 Abuse cases

Unsurprisingly, the majority of stand-alone actions have been abuse cases, and we can identify some trends in the types of case that have been raised, which, to an extent, have mirrored the preoccupations of Community law over the years.[110] Accordingly, a number of claims have concerned refusals to supply or the essential facilities doctrine, despite the apparent reining in of the doctrine by the ECJ in *Oscar Bronner*.[111] This is reflected by the lack of success in *Getmapping plc* v *Ordnance Survey*[112] and *Suretrack*,[113] and the more conventional refusal to supply case of *Land Rover Group Ltd* v *UPF (UK) Ltd (in administrative receivership)*,[114] where the claimant unsuccessfully sought an interlocutory order for specific performance. Although not

---

[109] [2009] EWCA Civ 750 (CA), at paras 101–110 in particular.

[110] See, for instance, R Whish, *Competition Law* (6th edn, 2008, OUP, Oxford; B Rodger and A MacCulloch, *Competition Law and Policy in the EC and UK* (4th edn, 2008, Cavendish, London), at pp 117–136.

[111] (Case C–7/97) [1998] ECR I–7791.

[112] Above, n 97.

[113] Above, n 106. See also *Attheraces Ltd* v *British Horseracing Board* [2005] EWHC 3015 (Ch) and [2007] EWCA Civ 38; *The Wireless Group plc* v *Radio Joint Audience Research Ltd* [2004] EWHC 2925 (Ch); and the Scottish case of *PIK Facilities Ltd* v *Watson's Ayr Park Ltd* [2005] CSOH 32. The pursuers were proprietors of Glasgow Prestwick International Airport and sought interdict against the defenders from trespassing on airport roads, by buses and taxis, to collect and drop off passengers being conveyed by them from their off-airport car parking facilities. A defence, based on infringement of Chapter II of the Competition Act 1998, relying on the "essential facilities" doctrine as developed under Community jurisprudence, failed at the first hurdle of establishing the relevant market.

[114] Above, n 97.

strictly speaking an essential facilities case, *Software Cellular Network* v *T-Mobile (UK) Ltd*[115] concerned the provision of mobile telephony services and the launch of a new service – Voice over Internet Protocol ("VoIP") technology. T-Mobile refused to activate numbers associated with Truphone, the trading name of the claimant, who contended that this amounted to an unlawful abuse of a dominant position. Crucially, in relation to the adequacy of damages as a remedy, the claimant argued that its commercial survival would be in doubt if it would be required to await trial, even speedy trial, before launching a full service. On the balance of convenience, and taking into account the cross-undertaking in damages, the potential impact on Truphone favoured the grant of interim remedies. Surprisingly, there has only been one case related to predatory pricing, in *Chester City Council* v *Arriva plc*,[116] where the predatory pricing claim was unsuccessful after a trial.

Despite the focus on exclusionary abuses by the European Commission, there is evidence that the UK authorities will pay greater attention to exploitative abuses, particularly excessive pricing.[117] There has also been a relatively high number of private law claims involving allegations of excessive pricing.[118] Nonetheless, the difficulties in establishing an excessive pricing case have been made clear in the two cases which proceeded to trial. In *Ineos Vinyls Ltd* v *Huntsman Petrochemicals (UK) Ltd*,[119] the claimants sought declarations that clauses of various supply agreements were void and unenforceable as the defendant had abused a dominant position by charging prices and delivery charges which were unfair under the Chapter II prohibition and Art 82. The claim failed on the basis that the claimant had not analysed the costs incurred in producing the product or compared costs with the price charged and had accordingly failed to satisfy the test set out in *United Brands*.[120] The clear difficulties, and reticence of the judiciary to become involved in commercial pricing decisions, are demonstrated even more clearly by the Court of Appeal in *Attheraces Ltd* v *British Horseracing Board*.[121] The claimant, which supplied websites, TV channels, and other media relating to British horse racing, alleged that the defendant, which had a central role in the organisation and promoting of British horse racing

[115] [2007] EWHC 1790 (Ch).

[116] [2007] EWHC 1373 (Ch).

[117] See, for instance, *Napp Pharmaceuticals Holdings Ltd and Subsidiaries ("Napp")* (DGFT decision CA98/2/2001) [2001] CAT 1; *Albion Water Ltd* v *Water Services Regulation Authority ("Dŵr Cymru/Shotton Paper")* [2008] CAT 31.

[118] See, for instance, the follow-on action raised by *EWS* discussed above, and also the unsuccessful defence on this basis in *BHB* v *Chandler*, n 135 below.

[119] [2006] EWHC 1241 (Ch).

[120] *United Brands* v *Commission* (Case 27/76) [1978] ECR 207.

[121] [2005] EWHC 3015 (Ch) and [2007] EWCA Civ 38.

and which kept a computerised database of data including pre-race data, had abused a dominant position and thereby infringed both Art 82 and the Chapter II prohibition. BHB effectively held a monopoly in the provision of the pre-race data and it was held in the High Court that it had abused its dominant position by excessive, unfair and discriminatory pricing. Referring to European Court case law on excessive and discriminatory pricing, it was held that the price was excessive in comparison to the cost to BHB plus a reasonable return, and discriminatory in being markedly higher than the sum normally charged to other broadcasters. On appeal, this ruling was overturned by the Court of Appeal, which was sceptical about Art 82/Chapter II becoming a general provision for the regulation of prices.[122] The court stated that exceeding cost was a necessary but not a sufficient test for abuse of dominance; there was little evidence that competition on the market was being distorted by BHB's demands and that the value to ATR of the pre-race data was relevant in determining whether the price was excessive. Furthermore, differential pricing was not necessarily abusive, and prices essentially were dependent on market forces. Accordingly, BHB's pricing strategy was not abusive, and the Court of Appeal clearly advocated a restrained approach to court involvement in claims of excessive or discriminatory pricing.

There are also miscellaneous cases, including clusters of cases concerning alleged abuses in the IT recruitment industry,[123] and the interplay of competition law and the rules of various organisations.[124]

3.3 Interlocutory relief

A key factor which may influence a decision to raise a stand-alone action, particularly in an abuse case, is the potential to obtain some form of interim order to ensure the competitiveness of the claimant is maintained at least in the short term. A very limited number of reported cases have involved applications for interlocutory injunctions, and the earlier difficulties in this context, as evidenced most notably by *Garden Cottage Foods*, have been noted and criticised.[125] However, *Network Multimedia Television Ltd* v *Jobserve Ltd*[126] indicated a more relaxed approach, and, since 2005, two of the

---

122 [2007] EWCA Civ 38 (CA).

123 See, for instance, *Jobserve Ltd* v *Network Multimedia Television Ltd* [2001] EWCA Civ 2021 (CA); *Suretrack Rail Services* v *Infraco JNP Ltd* [2002] EWHC 1316 (Ch).

124 See, for instance *Hendry* and *Fotheringham*, below, and another competition law defence case, *Qualifying Insurers Subscribing to the ARP* v *Ross & Co* [2004] EWHC 1181 (Ch).

125 See A D MacCulloch and B J Rodger, "Wielding the Blunt Sword: Interim Relief for Breaches of EC Competition Law before the UK Courts" (1996) 7 ECLR 393.

126 [2001] EWCA Civ 2021. (See *Network Multimedia Television Ltd (T/A Silicon.com)* v *Jobserve Ltd*, *Times*, 25 January 2001 and [2001] UKCLR 814 (Ch).)

three cases involving claims for interlocutory relief on the basis of reliance on competition law provisions were successful. The claimant in *Adidas-Solomon AG* v *Draper*[127] relied on Arts 81 and 82 and sought interlocutory injunctions. Reference was made[128] to earlier dicta in *Intel Corporation* v *Via Technologies*:[129] "(a) claims and defences under Articles 81 and 82 require careful scrutiny so as to prevent cases lacking in merit going to long and expensive trials but (b) often raise questions of mixed law and fact which are not suitable for summary determination." The court noted that a cautious approach was also appropriate in the context of the developing shape of European jurisprudence and was satisfied that there was a real prospect of success under Arts 81 and 82. A similar approach in relation to the application of the UK prohibitions was evidenced in *Software Cellular Network* v *T-Mobile (UK) Ltd*.[130] Crucially, in relation to the adequacy of damages as a remedy, the claimant argued that its commercial survival would be in doubt if it would be required to await trial, even speedy trial, before launching a full service. On the balance of convenience, and taking into account the cross-undertaking in damages, the potential impact on Truphone favoured the grant of interim remedies. The court relied on the dicta in *Sea Containers Ltd* v *Stena Sealink Ports and Stena Sealink Line*[131] to the effect that if an opportunity is denied to provide a new service "there is sufficient urgency to justify interim measures". Otherwise, a final decision may be "rendered 'ineffectual or even illusory'".[132]

3.4 Defences

Competition law derived rights may also be important as defences to a range of types of action. The majority of competition law judgments until 1999 were intellectual property related cases and they were virtually all defences to actions for infringement of various intellectual property rights.[133] Although the position has now clearly changed and claims now predominate, the Chapter I and II prohibi-

---

[127] [2006] EWHC 1318 (Ch).

[128] At para 24.

[129] [2002] EWCA Civ 1905 (CA), at para 32.

[130] [2007] EWHC 1790 (Ch).

[131] [1995] 4 CMLR 84, paras 58–59.

[132] At paras 58–59. However, cf *AAH Pharmaceuticals Ltd* v *Pfizer Ltd* [2007] EWHC 565 (Ch). An application for interim injunctions to restrain Pfizer from terminating supply agreements and refusing to supply the claimants with prescription drugs, in infringement of Arts 81 and 82 and ss 2 and 18 of the 1998 Act was unsuccessful, particularly because of delays in bringing an application.

[133] See B Rodger [2006] ECLR, n 14 above.

tions[134] are still frequently used as shields, still primarily in relation to IPRs,[135] usually unsuccessfully;[136] as demonstrated in *Microsoft* v *Ling*, where the claimant was granted summary judgment in relation to a purported defence based on the illegality of licensing agreements under the Chapters I and II prohibitions and Arts 81 and 82. However, in *Intel Corporation* v *Via Technologies Ltd*,[137] the Court of Appeal allowed an appeal against a summary judgment in relation to competition law defences based on all four sets of EC and domestic prohibitions that a refusal to license by the claimant was abusive. In relation to the abuse-based defences the Court of Appeal noted the tension between IPRs and the rules of competition, and appeared to anticipate the subsequent CFI *Microsoft* ruling years later, by adopting a broad interpretation of the essential facilities case law.[138]

3.5 Success and evaluation

Unfortunately, it appears that in the majority of cases in which UK competition law has been pled in stand-alone actions, alone or in combination with other provisions, that party has been unsuccessful at that stage of the litigation.[139] There have, of course, been some limited successes: in *Fotheringham*,[140] where a defence succeeded at an interim stage of the litigation process, and the successful interlocutory injunction case, *Software Cellular Network* v *T-Mobile (UK) Ltd*. Nonetheless, the unsuccessful Chapter II and Art 82/ Chapter II combination cases reflect the difficulties in succeeding in establishing an abuse. Some cases are simply weakly pled and fail to

---

[134] And Arts 81 and 82, for instance, in *Sportswear Co SpA* v *Stonestyle Ltd* [2005] EWHC 2097 (Ch) and [2005] EWHC Civ 830 (CA); and *HMSO* v *AA*, above. See also *Murphy* v *Media Protection Services Ltd* [2008] EWHC 1666 (Admin) and *Football Association Premier League Ltd* v *QC Leisure* [2008] EWHC 44 (Ch) and [2008] EWHC 1411 (Ch).

[135] See also, for example, *BHB Enterprises plc* v *Victor Chandler (International) Ltd* [2005] EWHC 1074 (Ch), which, although not strictly an IPR case, was an unsuccessful defence (and counterclaim) based on Art 82 and the Chapter II prohibition, based on allegations of excessive pricing in relation to the use of pre-race data.

[136] See, for example, *Hewlett-Packard Development Co LP* v *Expansys UK Ltd* [2005] EWHC 1495, [2007] ECC 9 which involved a joint application of the Chapter II prohibition and Art 82. See also the non-IPR case of *P & S Amusements Ltd* v *Valley House Leisure Ltd* [2006] EWHC 1510 (Ch) involving an unsuccessful defence in a beer tie case based on the Chapters I and II prohibitions.

[137] [2002] EWCA Civ 1905 (CA), reversing [2002] EWHC 1159 (Ch).

[138] In particular "*Magill*" (Joined Cases C–241 & 242/91P) [1995] ECR I–743.

[139] See B Rodger [2006] ECLR and [2009] GCLR, n 14 above.

[140] *Fotheringham & Son* v *The British Limousin Cattle Society Ltd* 2004 SLT 485 (Ex Div).

set out the basic requirements for an abuse, as in *PIK Facilities Ltd* v *Watson's Ayr Park Ltd*,[141] where the defence failed at the first hurdle of establishing the relevant market.[142] Similarly, in *Chester City Council* v *Arriva plc*[143] it was stressed that each element of an abuse case needed to be established and the case fell at both the relevant market and dominance stages.[144] Furthermore, the complex nature of a successful abuse plea was highlighted in *BHB Enterprises Ltd* v *Victor Chandler (International) Ltd*:[145]

> "it seems to me that particular care is to be expected of a party who pleads breach of s 18 of the Act or an Article 82 offence. These are notoriously burdensome allegations. The recent history of cases in which such allegations have been raised illustrate that they can lead to lengthy and expensive trials. Mere assertion in a pleading will not do. Before a party has to respond to an allegation like that, it is incumbent on the party making the allegation to set out clearly and succinctly the major facts upon which it will rely."[146]

The difficulties in this area have been reduced by the greater readiness of courts in recent years to grant interlocutory remedies, but until very recently there has been a dearth of OFT activity in relation to the Chapter II prohibition (or Art 82) which could form the basis of follow-on actions at the CAT or High Court.[147] Furthermore, the lack of reported case law may simply reflect the likelihood that stronger cases based on Art 82 may be more likely to settle either before or after litigation has commenced.[148]

---

141 [2005] CSOH 132.

142 At para 43: "The defenders' averments in answer 5 touching upon the issue of the relevant market display, in my opinion, vagueness, ambiguity and confusion. I conclude that the defenders have not relevantly averred what is the relevant market in this case." Furthermore, it was held that the requirement of indispensability was not satisfied.

143 [2007] EWHC 1373 (Ch).

144 See also *Land Rover Group Ltd* v *UPF (UK) Ltd (in administrative receivership)*, n 97 above, where the claimant unsuccessfully sought an interlocutory order for specific performance, the court doubting the existence of dominance in relation to arguments based on s 18 and Art 82; and *Getmapping plc* v *Ordnance Survey* where there was a lack of a credible case on the potential existence of abusive conduct.

145 [2005] EWHC 1074 (Ch).

146 *Ibid*, at para 43. See also *HMSO* v *AA Ltd* [2001] EC 34, at para 21, where it was held that the defendant's claim would not give rise to a viable plea of alleged abuse under Art 82 "because the adverse consequences of allowing a plea under Article 82 into a case are so severe and may involve enormous cost, not just to the parties, but to court time, it is incumbent upon the court to look carefully at what is and what is not pleaded."

147 See the OFT infringement decision in relation to Cardiff Bus in November 2008 at http://www.oft.gov.uk/advice_and_resources/resource_base/ca98/decisions/cardiffbus, its first infringement finding in relation to the Chapter II prohibition for circa 5 years. See also R Nazzini, Chapter 5 below, and R Whish, Chapter 1 above.

148 See B Rodger, "The Hidden Story ..." [2008] ECLR 96, n 35 above.

4 THE OFT PROPOSALS FOR REFORM

Following a period of consultation, in November 2007 the OFT published recommendations to enhance private means of redress in relation to competition law and improve and extend the provisions introduced by the Enterprise Act.[149] In particular there are proposals to reform the system of representative actions. Currently, consumers must elect to opt in to a representative action brought under s 47B of the Competition Act, and it is recognised that this constrains the vitality of this provision, especially in comparison with US-style class actions. There is currently limited scope for collective redress generally in the UK courts. In England and Wales, there is the possibility of bringing a test case, consolidation and single trial of multiple actions, a GLO (Group Litigation order) and a representative action. However, the Civil Justice Council has recently issued a Report outlining the limitations of each of these options and recommending the introduction of a new collective procedure, allowing particular cases to proceed on an opt-in or opt-out basis.[150] Similarly, the OFT has proposed the introduction of a combination of the opt-in/opt-out procedures for consumer representative actions,[151] with judicial discretion as to whether in the circumstances a general representative action, a representative action on behalf of named individuals or individual actions would be the most appropriate way to proceed. Perhaps more importantly, recognising the limits on public enforcement action, the finite resources of the OFT and the need to prioritise high-impact outcomes, the OFT also recommended further consultation by the Government as to whether representative bodies should be permitted to institute stand-alone actions, and, if so, how best to facilitate this change. Furthermore, given the barriers to justice which may confront small- and medium-sized businesses, they recommended that consideration should also be given to the possible extension of the provisions on representative actions from consumers to businesses.[152] The lacuna in the existing provisions, which the OFT

---

[149] *Private Actions in Competition Law: effective redress for consumers and business*, OFT 916resp, available at http://www.Qit.gov.ult/shared oft/reports/comp policy/oft916te.sp.pdf. See OFT Press Release 162/07, 26 November 2007.

[150] *Improving Access to Justice Through Collective Actions, Developing a More Efficient and Effective Procedure for Collective Actions* (Final Report, Nov 2008, Civil Justice Council). The ongoing Civil Courts Review in Scotland is also considering ways of enhancing collective redress. See the recent BIS White Paper, *A Better Deal for Consumers: Delivering Real Help Now and Change for the Future* (Cm 7669, July 2009), http://www.berr.gov.uk/files/file52072.pdf. and the limited proposals for the appointment of a Consumer Advocate.

[151] See OFT Recommendations at paras 7.01–7.35, particularly at paras 7.28–7.29.

[152] *Ibid*, at paras 6.1–6.9. The consultation should consider whether to allow representative bodies to bring follow-on and/or stand-alone actions on behalf of businesses and the appropriate model for such representative actions.

recommendations seek to deal with, was demonstrated by the High Court ruling in *Emerald Supplies Ltd* v *British Airways plc*.[153] Rather surprisingly, given the relative timidity of the Commission's White Paper, the OFT Recommendations could have been pre-empted by the draft Council Directive circulated during the summer of 2009 but withdrawn subsequently, which proposed the introduction *inter alia* of a group action and a form of opt-out representative action for competition law damages actions across the Community.[154]

5 CONCLUSIONS

Contrary to what one may have anticipated from the Member State which produced the *Crehan* ruling and saga and whose legal systems are closest in terms of legal traditions to the United States, there is still not extensive private enforcement experience before the UK courts, including the CAT, and one would search in vain for a final judgment in a damages action.[155] However, there have been significant developments over the last 10 years. There are dedicated provisions introduced by the Enterprise Act designed to facilitate follow-on actions before the CAT, and the CAT has delivered some interesting and important judgments, clarifying various aspects of the litigation process under the follow-on mechanism. However, given the number of infringement decisions by the relevant competition authorities, notably the OFT and European Commission, over the last 10 years, the follow-on procedure has not been utilised as widely as expected, particularly given certain advantages inherent in and developed under the CAT follow-on procedure: namely the ability to rely on an infringement decision to establish liability; the different limitation periods; the closely managed and expedited process and the potential cost advantages for unsuccessful claimants. The available funding mechanisms and costs rules can clearly act as a major incentive or disincentive to claimants and/or lawyers in relation to competition law claims,[156] and are arguably the most important factor in deter-

---

153 [2009] EWHC 741 (Ch).

154 Proposed Council Directive on rules governing damages actions for infringements of Articles 81 and 82 of the Treaty, Arts 3–6.

155 However, in Germany there is considerable evidence of high levels of litigation activity involving competition law (circa 200 cases per year over the last 10 years) in a database maintained by the Bundeskartellamt.

156 See A Riley and J Peysner, "Damages in EC Antitrust Actions: Who pays the Piper?" (2006) European Law Review 748; J Peysner, "Costs and Funding in Private Third Party Competition Damages Actions" [2006] Competition Law Review 97. See fuller discussion on the incentives in "Making Antitrust damages more effective in the EU: welfare impact and potential scenarios", available at http://ec.europa.eu/competition/antitrust/actions-damages/documents.html#link1.

mining whether to proceed with a claim. In comparison with the basic High Court rule, with limited exceptions and cost-control possibilities, the CAT's discretionary cost powers offer greater flexibility to potential claimants and this may reduce cost pressures for claimants before the CAT.[157] There is evidence that we may be at the start of an era of an increasing frequency of follow-on actions before the CAT. The anticipated publication of OFT decisions in relation to a number of early resolution cases during the last 18 months, involving price-fixing of transatlantic passenger surcharges, dairy products and tobacco, may stimulate follow-on litigation, on an individual or collective basis.[158] Nonetheless, the High Court also has a role to play,[159] particularly in stand-alone actions which appear to be gaining in significance,[160] but also where it may be advantageous to rely on the 6-year limitation period before the High Court or as a litigation tactic to raise follow-on proceedings in the High Court prior to the completion of the appeal process following an infringement finding.

As discussed, there are OFT proposals which seek to build on the experience developed by the courts and CAT to date, but the recommendations have been with the relevant government department, the Department of Business, Innovation and Skills ("BIS"), for over 18 months and it remains uncertain whether any reforms will be introduced,[161] at least prior to any modifications which may be required as a result of implementation of the Commission's White Paper proposals. There is private enforcement practice in the UK, but it is obscured as a result of the prevalence of out-of-court settlements which are not made public. A particularly interesting development is the settlement of cases at the CAT where mediation has been used

---

[157] J Peysner [2006] Competition Law Review 97, n 156 above. See also EU White Paper at para 2.9, indicating that it would be useful for Member States to reflect on their cost rules and to examine the practices existing across the EU. The OFT 2007 Recommendations include the introduction of CFAs in representative actions to allow for increases of greater than 100% on lawyers' fees, codifying courts' discretion to cap cost liabilities, the provision for cost protection where appropriate in addition to establishing a merits-based litigation fund.

[158] Note the settlement in the United States District Court for the Northern District of California in relation to that cartel: see https://www.airpassengerrefund.com/Default.aspx.

[159] As has the Court of Session in Scotland.

[160] Note that s 16 of the Enterprise Act allows for transfer of proceedings in relation to the determination of an infringement issue from the High Court to the CAT but the provision has not, as yet, been activated. See C Brown, "Section 16 Enterprise Act 2002 – time for activation?"

[161] See the recent BIS White Paper, *A Better Deal for Consumers: Delivering Real Help Now and Change for the Future* (Cm 7669, July 2009), http://www.berr.gov.uk/files/file52072.pdf. and the limited proposals for the appointment of a Consumer Advocate.

to resolve the dispute.[162] Settlements are an inescapable reality in all forms of commercial litigation but their ubiquity is particularly problematic in a competition law context where, as the author has argued before, the absence of developed procedural and substantive rules appears to be both a cause and effect of settlement practice; arguably restricting, discouraging and disincentivising appropriate competition law claims.[163] Increased awareness of the scope for consumer (and business) redress, enhanced by the increasing prominence and influence of the US antitrust bar, combined with adoption of the OFT recommendations for reform, may lead to a greater role for private enforcement in the UK in the next 10 years.

---

[162] See, for instance *Burgess Ltd* v *W Austin & Sons (Stevenage) Ltd and Harwood Park Crematorium Ltd* (Case 1088/5/7/07). It should be stressed that this chapter does not consider competition-related disputes which are settled through arbitration. See, for instance, E Stylopoulos, "Powers and Duties of Arbitrators in the Application of Competition Law: an EC approach in the light of recent developments" [2009] ECLR 118.
[163] B Rodger, "The Hidden Story ..." [2008] ECLR 96, n 35 above.

CHAPTER 4

THE CONSISTENCY PRINCIPLE: SECTION 60 OF THE COMPETITION ACT 1998

*Ben Rayment**

This chapter considers the influence of the "consistency principle" on the development of UK competition law in the last 10 years. The consistency principle is contained in s 60 of the Competition Act 1998 ("the 1998 Act") and requires broadly that the 1998 Act be interpreted in harmony with EU competition law.

More specifically, the purpose of s 60(1) is:

> "to ensure that so far as is possible (having regard to any relevant differences between the provisions concerned), questions arising under this Part in relation to competition within the United Kingdom are dealt with in a manner which is consistent with the treatment of corresponding questions arising in Community law in relation to competition within the Community."

It is further provided that:

> "(2) At any time when the court determines a question arising under this Part, it must act (so far as is compatible with the provisions of this Part and whether or not it would otherwise be required to do so) with a view to securing that there is no inconsistency between –
>
> (a) the principles applied, and decision reached, by the court in determining that question; and
>
> (b) the principles laid down by the Treaty and the European Court, and any relevant decision of that Court,[1] as appli-

---

* Barrister, Monckton Chambers, former Legal Secretary to the Competition Appeal Tribunal. All views expressed are those of the author.

[1] Although "important and authoritative", the Court of Appeal has questioned without deciding whether an Advocate General's Opinion is a decision of the European Court for

cable at that time in determining any corresponding question arising in Community law.

(3) The court must, in addition, have regard to any relevant decision or statement of the Commission.

(4) Subsections (2) and (3) also apply to –

(a) the OFT; and
(b) any person acting on behalf of the Director, in connection with any matter arising under this Part.

(5) In subsections (2) and (3), "court" means any court or tribunal.

(6) In subsections (2)(b) and (3), decision includes a decision as to –

(a) the interpretation of any provision of Community law;
(b) the civil liability of an undertaking for harm caused by its infringement of Community law."

When enacted there were those who understandably predicted that s 60 was a recipe for litigation, especially in determining whether the section applied or not, which turned on identifying a "corresponding question" in relation to competition under both EC and UK laws and the question of whether or not there was a "relevant difference" between their provisions so as to justify not following the Community approach in domestic law.[2]

However, save in all but a few cases, s 60 has not given rise to a significant number of disputes in the case law of the courts or the CAT and decisional practice of the OFT and sectoral regulators over the last 10 years.[3] Rather, as explained below, the thesis of this chapter is that the influence of s 60 has generally been minimal in relation to substantive issues of competition law. Section 60 has had a more prominent role in relation to determining matters of procedure – perhaps somewhat unexpectedly – but even here its influence, although important, has to date probably only been indirect.

In what follows, the influence of s 60 is examined, first, in relation to substantive issues of competition law, and, second, in relation to

---

the purposes of s 60(2)(b). *Napp Pharmaceuticals Ltd* v *Director General of Fair Trading* [2002] EWCA Civ 796, per Buxton LJ at para 37.

[2] Eg P Willis, "Procedural Nuggets from the 'Klondike Clause': The Application of s. 60 of the Competition Act 1998 to the Procedures of the OFT" (1999) 20 ECLR 314. See also K Middleton, "Harmonisation with Community law: The Euro Clause" in B Rodger and A MacCulloch, *The UK Competition Act: A New Era for UK Competition Law*, (2000, Hart, London).

[3] See, for further consideration of various aspects of the decisional practice, R Whish, Chapter 1 above; D Bailey, Chapter 2 above; R Nazzini, Chapter 5 below; and G Monti, Chapter 6 below.

questions of procedure. The question of whether s 60 has made UK law overly EC-centric is also touched upon.

1 INFLUENCE ON SUBSTANTIVE ISSUES OF COMPETITION LAW

1.1 A modest impact?

The reasons why the contribution of s 60 to matters of substantive law has been modest are on reflection relatively easy to identify.

First, the Chapter I and Chapter II prohibitions of the 1998 Act were closely modelled on the provisions of Arts 81 and 82 EC. To this extent the consistency principle was already "hard wired" into the 1998 Act. Moreover, with the introduction of the system of decentralised enforcement of EC law in 2003 only 3 years after the coming to force of the 1998 Act, both EC and UK law have flowed more closely through the same enforcement channels.

Thus in many situations there is relatively little controversy as to how s 60 should apply. In the case of two appeals raising the meaning of "agreements" and "concerted practices" under the 1998 Act there was no possible dispute that this issue was to be determined in a manner consistent with the jurisprudence of the European Court.[4] Whether or not that jurisprudence is clear is a separate matter to which law applies to the question in issue under s 60.

Second, while the legislator may have assumed that the task of applying the 1998 Act would be made a lot easier by importing via s 60 the whole *corpus iuris* of EC competition law, the reality has been that not all of the issues that have arisen under the 1998 Act in the first 10 years have had a ready analogue in EC law that could simply be identified and applied in the name of consistency.

For example, the first case brought by the OFT under the 1998 Act comprised in part a rare allegation of abuse by excessive pricing.[5] In the absence of an EC law solution "prepared earlier" with which to ensure consistency, it has instead in such cases been for the UK system to find its own answers. Indeed, such domestic analysis reached without the benefit of much assistance from EC authority has the potential in turn to feed back into the application of EC law. Consistency was not necessarily a one-way street even before the advent of the decentralised enforcement of EC competition law.

---

[4] *JJB Sports plc and Allsports Ltd* v *OFT* [2004] CAT 17 (judgment on liability); *Argos Ltd and Littlewoods Ltd* v *OFT* [2003] CAT 24 (judgment on liability).

[5] *Napp Pharmaceuticals Ltd* v *Director General of Fair Trading* [2002] CAT 5, [2002] Comp AR 259.

In *Aberdeen Journals* the CAT observed that "the cost-based rules set out in *AKZO* and *Tetra Pak II*, while providing guidance, are not an end in themselves and should not be applied mechanistically".[6] The CAT pointed out that the European Court's own jurisprudence in *Compagnie Maritime Belge*[7] demonstrated that the guidance available in *AKZO* and *Tetra Pak II* is open to development depending on the circumstances. This approach helps to show why the requirement of consistency does not act as a straitjacket, constraining the CAT from reaching a particular result warranted in its view by the circumstances of a case. As the CAT has stated in a similar context, "competition law is not an area of law in which there is much scope for absolute concepts or sharp edges".[8]

In another case, despite the numerous decisions in EC law dealing with the question of whether any entity is an "undertaking" for the purposes of Arts 81 and 82 EC, the CAT found no ready answer in that jurisprudence when required to determine whether a Northern Irish healthcare trust was acting as an "undertaking" when purchasing residential and nursing care from a private company.[9] Applying s 60, the CAT approached the issue in the manner in which it thought the European Court would approach it, as regards the principles and reasoning.[10] Interestingly, it might be regarded as at least implicit in the CAT's approach that where there is no relevant EC authority actually on point or in prospect there is no danger of inconsistency arising if it decides the matter. The alternative would be to make a preliminary reference to the ECJ under Art 234.[11]

The discovery by the OFT of widespread bid-rigging and cover pricing within the UK construction industry has required the CAT to

---

[6] *Aberdeen Journals* v *OFT* [2003] CAT 11, at para 380. These comments were made in the context of an argument set out at paras 378–379 to the effect that where a dominant firm is using spare capacity it is entitled to price against a competitor on a marginal basis so long as its marginal revenue exceeds its marginal costs. The CAT did not need to decide the issue on the facts of the case.

[7] *Compagnie Maritime Belge* v *Commission* (Cases T–24–26 & 28/93) [1996] ECR I–1365, at para 146, finding an abuse notwithstanding that the members of a liner conference had not been shown to have incurred losses, only a reduction in profits.

[8] *The Racecourse Association* v *OFT* [2005] CAT 167, at para 167.

[9] *BetterCare* v *Director General of Fair Trading* [2002] CAT 77.

[10] *Ibid*, at para 32. Subsequent developments in EC law, notably *FENIN* v *EC Commission* (Case T–319/99) [2003] ECR II–357, have cast doubt on aspects of the CAT's approach, although *Bettercare* was referred to in the Opinion of the Advocate General, demonstrating the "dialogue" that now arises between UK and EC competition law.

[11] There is no difficulty in obtaining such a ruling on EC law where national law requires the same interpretation to be given as EC law. *A Leur-Bloem* v *Inspecteur der Belastingdienst* (Case C–28/95) [1997] ECR I–4161; *Bernd Giloy* v *Hauptzollamt Frankfurt am Main Ost* (Case C–130) [1997] ECR I–4295. There has to date not been a single preliminary reference in relation to proceedings under the 1998 Act.

consider how such arrangements are to be analysed under the 1998 Act. In doing so there was no issue that it should ensure consistency of treatment with EC law; rather the greater challenge for the CAT was that EC law was relatively undeveloped on this issue.[12]

1.2 Effect on trade

The main substantive issue of competition law that has given rise to controversy under s 60 has been the correct approach to the requirement that an agreement or conduct "may affect trade within the United Kingdom". Moreover, the issue is one that has given rise to a difference of opinion between the CAT and the High Court.

Aberdeen Journals v Office of Fair Trading[13]
Aberdeen Journals appealed to the CAT against a decision of the OFT finding that it had abused a dominant position in the market for the supply of advertising space in local newspapers (paid for and free) in the Aberdeen area from 1 to 29 March 2000, contrary to the Chapter II prohibition of the 1998 Act. The abuse consisted in Aberdeen Journals charging rates for advertising in its free newspaper at less than average variable costs with the intention of driving its sole competitor, the Independent, out of the market. Aberdeen challenged the finding of abuse on a number of grounds,[14] including that its pricing would not affect trade within the UK.

Aberdeen Journals submitted that s 60(2) required the OFT to prove that the abuse had a material effect on trade within the UK.[15] The CAT found on the facts that there was plainly a material effect on trade within the UK. Although the relevant trade at issue was local in nature, the CAT noted that pricing below average variable cost, even for a short period, can have a significant effect on the business of competitors by forcing them to lower their own prices or to accept a loss of business.[16] Moreover, although it was true that the period of the infringement was 29 days, the fact that the conduct had gone on for years prior to the coming into force of the 1998 Act meant that the effect on trade during those 29 days was sufficiently established.

However, the CAT went on to accept the submission of the OFT that there was no need under UK law for it to establish an

---

[12] *Apex Asphalt and Paving Co Ltd* v *OFT* [2005] CAT 4. See, eg, A Riley, Chapter 10 below.

[13] [2003] CAT 11.

[14] See, for a fuller discussion of the case, R Nazzini, Chapter 5 below.

[15] [2003] CAT 11, at paras 453–462.

[16] *Ibid*, para 457.

appreciable effect on trade within the UK in the way that is required under EC law.[17] The CAT reached this conclusion for two essential reasons. First, the effect on trade requirement as a matter of EC law was a jurisdictional boundary between Community and domestic law. That, according to the CAT, was a "relevant difference" between the 1998 Act and the provisions of Community law. Second, the fact that there was no such *de minimis* rule under the Chapter II prohibition was supported by the fact that s 40 of the 1998 Act enables the Secretary of State to prescribe by regulations "conduct of minor significance" in relation to which a person is immune from any penalty that might be imposed for breach of the Chapter II prohibition under s 36(2). The relevant regulations provide that conduct by an undertaking with an applicable turnover of less than £50 million in the previous business year is outside the scope of the Chapter II prohibition.[18] In this case, due to its parent companies, Aberdeen Journals did not benefit from this immunity. The CAT concluded that an undertaking which does not benefit from s 40 could not claim to benefit from a further *de minimis* rule under the Chapter II prohibition. According to the CAT, an absence of an effect on trade will only arise when either there is no "trade" or the effect on trade is wholly outside the UK.[19]

P&S Amusements v *Valley House Leisure*[20]

The lease of a business carrying on a bar and night club under the name of Gaiety's on the Golden Mile in Blackpool contained a beer tie.[21] The landlord sought to enforce the beer tie by means of an injunction and the tenant raised a defence that the provision infringed both Chapter I and Chapter II prohibitions, essentially by obliging him to purchase beer at a higher price than could be obtained elsewhere. Subject to the competition law issues the tenant was bound by the tie.

On an application for summary judgment the landlord attempted to strike out the competition law arguments on the grounds of

---

[17] See *Volk* v *Vervaecke* (Case 5/69) [1969] ECR 295; *Beguelin* v *Commission* (Case 22/71) [1971] ECR 949; *Bagnasco* v *Banco Popolare di Novara* (Case C–215/96) [1999] ECR I–135 (Arts 81 and 82 EC); and *Hugin* v *Commission* (Case 22/78) [1979] ECR 1869 (a case under Art 82 EC).

[18] Competition Act 1998 (Small Agreements and Conduct of Minor Significance) Regulations 2000, SI 2000/262.

[19] The OFT has followed the approach of the Tribunal in its decision making: see *Abuse of a dominant position by Cardiff Bus* (CA98/01/2008), 18 November 2008, paras 3.20–3.21.

[20] *P&S Amusements Ltd* v *Valley House Leisure Ltd* [2006] EWHC 1510 (Ch).

[21] Ie a requirement allowing the Landlord to nominate the supplier from whom the tenant was to obtain his beer.

defective pleading, including the absence of any allegation that the agreement had an effect on trade within the UK. The tenant argued that it was not necessary to demonstrate such an effect and relied on *Aberdeen Journals*.

In the event the court held – perhaps unsurprisingly – that there was no appreciable effect *on competition* by virtue of the effect of the tie on the tenant. However, in his judgment the Chancellor indicated that, given his conclusion on the absence of any appreciable effect on competition, he was not deciding the question in the instant case. Nevertheless, he made plain that he was not persuaded by the analysis in *Aberdeen Journals*. Understandably the Chancellor was concerned: first, that the words imposing the requirement that there be an effect on trade within the UK were rendered otiose by the CAT's approach; and, second, applying the CAT's approach would involve applying the domestic prohibition to *de minimis* or insignificant effects contrary to the established approach of EC competition law. Although not stated in terms, it is clear that he did not consider there was any "relevant difference" between the provisions of UK and EC competition law.

Analysis

In terms of s 60(1) it is clear that the Chancellor, unlike the CAT, did not view the provisions of EC and UK law as containing any relevant difference. Indeed there is no difference between the terms of the provisions in question in both EC and UK law: both require an effect on trade to be established. Strictly speaking, his approach to relevant differences is closer to the words of s 60(1). The CAT's approach effectively involves taking account of wider relevant differences between the provisions concerned beyond their terms to encompass matters such as their purpose.

However, this minor quibble aside, it is clear that the CAT's approach does not involve any inconsistency between EC and UK law, which is the overall objective of s 60. Moreover, there is nothing in s 60 that requires the same approach to be taken to the same provisions where unusually, as here, this results in no inconsistency.

The reason why there is no inconsistency is the fact that there must necessarily be a difference between the concepts of appreciable effect on competition and appreciable effect on trade in EC law as explained by Advocate General Reischl:

> "... it would ... appear unacceptable to treat the criterion of an effect on trade as being virtually the same as an effect on competition. That would be an interpretation contrary to the wording, according to which the element of an effect on trade is of particular importance in

> delineating the sphere of application, which can only mean that the element must have an independent meaning."[22]

However, as *Aberdeen Journals* makes plain, there is no need for such delineation of jurisdiction between EC and UK law in UK law given that the dividing line is already provided in EC law.

The Chancellor's concern that the CAT's approach would result in the law applying to trivial situations is addressed via the requirement that there must be an appreciable effect on competition. Where there is such an effect it would be extraordinary to find at the same time there was no appreciable effect on trade in a part of the UK. The Chancellor's concern remains that this would render otiose the requirement under the 1998 Act to establish an effect on trade. However, the inescapable reality is that those words are otiose by virtue of an overzealous attempt by the draftsman to "hard wire" consistency between the provisions of EC and UK law apparently without fully understanding the separate role that the concept of an effect on trade plays in EC law. However, that concept has no relevance in domestic law and treating it effectively as otiose will have no impact on consistency with EC law; nor will it result in UK law applying to trivial situations as – consistent with both EC and UK law – it will remain a requirement to establish an appreciable effect on competition.[23]

1.3 Infringements committed "intentionally or negligently"

Section 36(3) of the 1998 Act provides that the OFT may only impose a penalty if the infringement has been committed "intentionally or negligently". In *Napp*[24] it was submitted by the appellant that in order to impose a penalty the OFT was required to show that Napp was aware or ought to have known that it had resorted to methods of competition which were abnormal and could not be regarded as a form of competition on the merits. In particular, Napp relied by analogy on the concept of *mens rea* as applied in theft cases under the English criminal law.[25] Moreover, it also submitted that the OFT had failed, as required by the 1998 Act, to address its mind to the question of whether the infringement was committed intentionally rather than negligently or vice versa, particularly where the infringement was novel.

---

[22] *Hugin* v *Commission* (Case 22/78) [1979] ECR 1869.

[23] It is an interesting question outside the scope of the present chapter whether over the first 10 years of the 1998 Act the CAT has tended to conclude there was an appreciable effect on competition in small local markets more readily than the OFT.

[24] *Napp Pharmaceuticals Ltd* v *Director General of Fair Trading* [2002] CAT 5, [2002] CompAR 259.

[25] See *R* v *Ghosh* [1982] 2 QB 1053 (HL).

The CAT rejected those submissions, agreeing with the OFT that whether an infringement was "intentional or negligent" under s 36(3) of the 1998 Act is a threshold question which "corresponds" for the purposes of s 60 to the position under Art 15(2) of Council Regulation 17.[26]

The Tribunal noted that s 36(3), unlike Art 15(2), does not refer to the need to take into account the gravity and duration of the infringement when fixing the penalty. However, those factors are referred to in the OFT's Guidance under s 38 for setting the amount of a penalty.[27] Nonetheless, notwithstanding the "slightly different structure under sections 36 and 38 of the Act, as compared to Article 15(2)", the CAT was satisfied that there was no "relevant difference" between the provisions concerned for the purposes of s 60. Accordingly, the CAT concluded on the basis of EC authority that in determining the threshold question the OFT was only required to decide whether the infringement was committed either intentionally or negligently,[28] but was not required to determine specifically which it was.

The CAT held that an infringement is committed intentionally if the undertaking must have been aware that its conduct was of such nature as to encourage a restriction or distortion of competition.[29] In relation to the term "negligently", the CAT noted that there was little guidance on this concept in EC law, but held that an infringement would be committed "negligently" if the undertaking ought to have known that its conduct would result in a restriction or distortion of competition.[30] For the purposes of the threshold question it was not necessary to decide precisely where the concept of "negligently" shaded into the concept of "intentionally" nor to attempt an exhaustive judicial interpretation.

Where the words "intentionally" and "negligently" may require such further interpretation in future is in relation to the use of those words in connection with the gravity of the infringement under the OFT's penalty guidance as opposed to the so-called threshold question that arises under s 36(3) and Art 15(2).[31] On that issue EC law arguably does not raise a corresponding question as EC law only

---

[26] That provision is now to be found in Art 23(2) of Council Regulation 1/2003/EC.

[27] For the latest version of that guidance, published under s 38 of the 1998 Act, see OFT 423: OFT's Guidance as to the appropriate amount of a penalty (December 2004), at para 2.15.

[28] *SPO* v *Commission* (Case C–137/95P) [1996] ECR I–1611.

[29] *Napp*, n 24 above, at para 456, citing *Musique Diffusion Française* v *Commission* (Case 100/80) [1983] ECR 1825, para 112 and *Parker Pen* v *Commission* (Case T–77/92) [1994] ECR II–549, para 81.

[30] *Napp*, n 24 above, at para 457, citing *United Brands* v *Commission*, at paras 298–301.

[31] Above, n 26.

refers to the gravity or duration of the infringement as aggravating or mitigating factors.[32]

2 INFLUENCE ON PROCEDURAL ISSUES

Section 60 is expressed as applying "in relation to competition". The effect of this qualification in relation to procedural matters raised questions when the 1998 Act came into force.[33] In particular it was not clear whether it extended to procedural issues, arising out of the DGFT's powers of investigation and enforcement under the Act or imported general principles of EC law such as proportionality, non-discrimination and fundamental rights. In debates in Parliament it was indicated that general principles of Community law were to be imported by s 60.[34] What remained unclear were the implications this might have for the OFT's procedures, for example in relation to its treatment of third parties and complainants,[35] a subject on which the 1998 Act was silent. The question was eventually considered by the CAT in a decision in 2004 with surprising results for many.

2.1 Treatment of third parties

Pernod Ricard v *Office of Fair Trading*[36]
The case arose out of a decision by the OFT, following a 2-year investigation, to accept "voluntary" undertakings from Bacardi in order to address its concerns in respect of certain of Bacardi's on-sale distribution arrangements in the UK. Pernod, who had complained about those arrangements, sought to challenge that decision before the CAT on the grounds that it should have been consulted before the decision to close the OFT's file was taken. Pernod relied both on the procedural obligations that are afforded to complainants as a matter of EC law, which it said applied by virtue of s 60, and on general obligations of fairness under English administrative law.

There was a preliminary issue as to whether the CAT had jurisdiction to hear the appeal at all as it only has jurisdiction to determine appeals in this context in respect of a decision "... as to

---

[32] See Art 23(3) of Regulation 1/2003.

[33] See, for instance, K Middleton in Rodger and MacCulloch, n 2 above.

[34] *Hansard*, col 963 (25 November 1997).

[35] Ie persons not a party to a particular investigation under the Act, which may include competitors, suppliers, customers and end-consumers.

[36] [2004] CAT 10. See D Bailey, "The Impact of Pernod v OFT on section 60 and the enforcement of UK competition law" [2004] Comp Law 153.

whether the Chapter I prohibition has been infringed".[37] The CAT took a broad view and found that a decision that the assurances addressed the competition concerns was such a decision, namely that the prohibition had not been infringed.[38] Having determined the issue of jurisdiction the CAT was required to address the procedural issues. The CAT identified the extensive provisions governing the rights of complainants in competition cases under EC law at the time the contested decision was taken in this case – 30 January 2003 – which included both of the rights effectively claimed by Pernod as follows:[39]

- To make a complaint to the EC Commission.[40]
- If the EC Commission proceeded to issue a statement of objections, to receive a non-confidential copy of the statement of objections, and to make written (and usually oral) comments on the statement of objections.[41]
- If the EC Commission came to the view that there were insufficient grounds for acting on the complaint, to be so informed in writing and be given an opportunity to make written comments before the complaint was rejected.[42]
- To be given reasons if the Commission decided not to continue with the examination of a complaint, including the facts and legal considerations relied on, such reasons to be sufficiently precise and detailed to enable the Court of First Instance to review the Commission's use of its discretion to define priorities.[43]
- To have the fate of the complaint settled by a decision of the EC Commission against which an action may be brought.[44]

The CAT then analysed whether s 60 conferred similar rights on complainants under UK law. First, it held that the corresponding question was "what are the principles of administrative fairness which apply in relation to competition",[45] ie in the sphere covered by the competition rules of the EC Treaty. Although this question did not arise directly "in relation to competition", nevertheless it still

---

[37] Section 46.

[38] For further detail on many of the cases in which this issue arose in the first 10 years of the 1998 Act, see B Rayment, "What is an appealable decision under the Competition Act 1998?" [2004] Comp Law 132.

[39] *Pernod*, para 225.

[40] Article 3(2) of Regulation 17/62.

[41] Article 19(2) of Regulation 17; Arts 7 and 8 of Regulation 2842/98.

[42] Article 6 of Regulation 2842/98.

[43] *Ufex* v *Commission* (Case C–119/97P) [1999] ECR I–1371, at paras 90–91.

[44] *Ibid*, at para 86.

[45] [2004] CAT 10, at para. 229.

arose indirectly "in relation to competition" according to the CAT.[46] The importance of complainants meant that procedures for handling such complaints were important, in the CAT's view, for how effectively the 1998 Act is enforced.

As to the question of any "relevant differences" in s 60(1), the CAT pointed out that it was not a case of a positive provision of the Act or of subordinate legislation precluding an approach which is in conformity with Community law. Rather, it was simply that the existing procedural framework did not according to the CAT expressly provide for complainants' rights in the same way as Community law. The CAT noted that the general principles of Community law were intended to be incorporated via s 60. The CAT also noted that "... the system as it has evolved under Community law appears to have worked satisfactorily, and has been an important element in ensuring fairness, transparency and rigour in decision making".[47]

For good measure the CAT also made it plain in its decision that it would have quite separately decided that Pernod should have been consulted on grounds of fairness in domestic administrative law.[48]

Accordingly, the CAT concluded that the OFT had been under a duty to provide the statement of objections to Pernod and to consult it on the decision it proposed to make.[49] However, the Tribunal was less convinced as to the substance of Pernod's complaint as it did not automatically quash the OFT's decision on the grounds of the procedural failings it identified.

Analysis

The CAT's broad interpretation of the meaning of "questions arising ... in relation to competition within the United Kingdom ..." in this case has not received universal approval. Indeed the OFT has said that while it accepts (as it must) the result on the particular facts of that case, it has not accepted the general proposition that s 60 applies to detailed questions of the procedure it must follow in competition cases.

Technically speaking, there are certainly arguments to the effect that the CAT went too far in suggesting the OFT was obliged under s 60 to follow the way in which the EC Commission deals with third parties. In the first place, it is certainly arguable that the issue of what procedure the OFT should follow did not arise in relation to competition. Second, the fact that there was nothing to preclude following

---

46 [2004] CAT 10, para 229.
47 *Ibid*, para 234.
48 *Ibid*, para 253.
49 *Ibid*, para 246.

the EC approach arguably overlooks the fact that the legislator in the UK did not make comparable provision for the treatment of third parties. To that extent there was arguably a relevant difference in the provisions concerned. Ultimately, the requirement under s 60 is to ensure that there is no inconsistency between the principles applied rather than an express requirement to follow a particular procedure. In procedural terms there is usually more than one way of doing things without sacrificing fairness and effective decision-making. Indeed, the CAT itself was careful to link its decision to the specific facts of the case and did not itself rely exclusively on s 60 but also on domestic administrative law principles. Third, although some statements in Parliament were arguably supportive of the line taken by the CAT, there were others that were definitely less so.[50]

However, in the author's view, the key to understanding the decision in *Pernod* is not a close technical analysis of s 60 but a broader perspective on some of the issues of concern about the operation of the 1998 Act in its early years. In particular, the CAT's case law indicates that it was concerned that decisions taken to close investigations, sometimes after a significant period of investment of public resources, were not sufficiently thorough and, as in *Pernod*, were taken with little or no consultation with third parties.[51] This, as it indicated in *Pernod*, raised in its view issues of both administrative fairness and effective decision-making.

2.2 Developments post-*Pernod*

Following *Pernod*, the OFT and other concurrent regulators have, without accepting the correctness of the CAT's analysis of s 60, developed their procedures for dealing with third parties, which prior to *Pernod* were largely non-existent.[52]

These developments recognised that the procedural standards applied in such cases needed to be improved in line with the CAT's concerns. The OFT's Guidance on "Involving Third Parties in Competition Act investigations" now states:

> "The OFT's experience suggests in particular that the adoption of a policy providing such third parties with an opportunity to comment on the OFT's provisional findings in a formal and structured manner

---

[50] "In making the procedural rules, the [OFT] is not obliged to secure that there is no inconsistency with EC procedural law since [it] will not be 'determining a question' under Part I." Per Lord Simon, *Hansard*, HC, vol 696, col 961 (25 November 1997).

[51] These concerns emerge in the numerous cases dealing with the OFT's and other sectoral regulators' case closure decisions under the 1998 Act. See Rayment, n 38 above.

[52] "Involving third parties in Competition Act investigations" (OFT 451, April 2006). Other sectoral regulators such as Ofcom have developed their own procedures.

> is likely to contribute to robust decision making at the administrative stage by ensuring that their views are fully taken into account before a definitive conclusion is reached."[53]

Although the result of *Pernod* has not been to import wholesale the rights enjoyed by third parties before the EC Commission into the OFT's procedures that the CAT's approach to s 60 would have implied, the steps taken after the CAT's judgment have nevertheless led to a welcome rapprochement and greater consistency in terms of approach under UK and EC law in this area. Taken together with other statutory[54] and administrative reforms introduced into the enforcement process by the OFT, *Pernod* has played a small but significant role in overhauling part of the procedural framework within which the 1998 Act has come to be enforced.

As to s 60, although it figures prominently in the CAT's judgment, ultimately its influence has only been indirect in provoking the changes outlined above to the way in which third parties are involved in investigations under the 1998 Act. Indeed, in its Guidance the OFT only makes specific reference to *Pernod* in the context of the CAT's observations on the requirements of procedural fairness in this context deriving from domestic administrative law.[55] Nonetheless, it is well established that procedural fairness depends on the particular administrative context.[56] In that regard EC competition law remains the closest comparator to UK competition law even in relation to the administrative procedures before the OFT and other regulators.

In the circumstances, it is difficult to believe that the CAT's exposition of the considerable gap between EC and UK law in this context did not have a significant influence on the new procedures that have been developed under domestic law. Ultimately, this demonstrates that even where s 60 does not formally apply there may be good and powerful reasons why consistency, or the lack of it, with EC competition law should influence what are regarded as fair and effective procedures in domestic law.

3 A NARROW FOCUS?

A concern expressed when s 60 was enacted was that UK courts should not become "blinkered" by the consistency principle in their approach to interpretation and should take into account the wealth

---

53 OFT 451, para 1.3.

54 Eg the ability of the OFT to accept binding undertakings in respect of competition concerns it has: see Sch 8, para 3A(2) to the 1998 Act.

55 OFT 451, para 1.8.

56 *R* v *Secretary of State for the Home Department, ex p Doody* [1994] 1 AC 531, per Lord Mustill at 560. Cited by the CAT in *Pernod*, at para 235.

of US, Commonwealth and other European competition laws.[57] Moreover, EC competition law itself draws on such laws from time to time.[58] There is no suggestion that the CAT has been blinkered in its application of UK competition law during the first 10 years of the 1998 Act. Indeed, the CAT has said that decisions in other antitrust jurisdictions are of general interest to it.[59] However, the relevance of other competition laws to particular issues under the 1998 Act always needs to be carefully justified by the parties and an apparent "read across" may on further examination not be appropriate.[60] The CAT has observed that the conceptual basis of US law may in particular be different to that underlying the provisions of EC and UK law. This was evidenced in *Aberdeen Journals* in the context of the Chapter II prohibition on abuse of a dominant position.[61]

In *Aberdeen Journals*, the appellant argued that it had not abused a dominant position because it had no realistic possibility of recouping the losses it was incurring by reason of its allegedly predatory strategy. It referred to US authority including *Brooke Group* v *Brown & Williamson Tobacco*.[62] However, the CAT distinguished that case, decided under the Robinson Patman Act, on the basis that the defendant who had engaged in below cost sales only had a 12 per cent market share, there being no requirement of dominance. In those circumstances the prerequisite of recoupment was plainly relevant to whether competition could actually be harmed by the actions of a company with a relatively modest market share. The CAT was not persuaded that this was the case under the Chapter II prohibition and EC law as the requirement of dominance would effectively establish the relevant detrimental effect of the conduct, at least where there is a risk that competitors will be eliminated.[63]

---

[57] A Robertson, "UK and EC Competition Laws: Will They Operate in Complete Harmony?", in N Green and A Robertson (eds), *The Europeanisation of UK Competition Law* (1999, Hart, London), at p 102.

[58] See A G Roemer in *Consten & Grundig* v *Commission* (Cases 56 & 58/64) [1966] ECR 299.

[59] *Aberdeen Journals* v *Office of Fair Trading* [2003] CAT 11, at para 451.

[60] In *Aberdeen Journals* the Tribunal did not consider that the relevance of s 46(1) of the Australian Trade Practices Act 1974 to which it had been referred had been explained (at para 451).

[61] [2003] CAT 11, at paras 436–446.

[62] 509 US 209 (1993).

[63] *Aberdeen Journals*, above, at para 439. The Tribunal referred to Case *Tetrapak II* v *Commission* [1996] ECR I–5983, at para 44 of the judgment and para 78 of the Advocate General's Opinion, in support of its conclusion. Evidence of recoupment may well provide relevant evidence of a predatory strategy: see *Compagnie Maritime Belge*, n 7 above, per AG Fennelly at para 136.

4 CONCLUSION

As discussed in the preceding sections, s 60 has raised some interesting issues during the first 10 years of the 1998 Act. However, for the reasons discussed above, the impact of s 60 on the development of substantive competition law in the UK has been relatively limited. As the CAT itself has observed, there are few absolute concepts in competition law. As such, the relatively open-ended nature of competition law means that the main disputes tend to arise not at the level of interpretative consistency with EC law but in the detailed application of those relatively open-ended rules to the detailed facts of specific cases. The biggest surprise has been the suggestion by the CAT in *Pernod* that s 60 required the OFT to adopt procedures that were consistent with those applied by the EC Commission in relation to third parties and complainants. Although the legal basis for that approach may be questioned there is little doubt that the UK system was underdeveloped in this area or that the *Pernod* case in 2004 was undoubtedly a factor in bringing about much-needed reform. Any litigant claiming in future that the OFT's procedures in this area are not consistent with EU law are likely to be met, somewhat ironically, with the argument that there is now a "relevant difference between the provisions concerned" due to the introduction of the OFT's Guidance following the *Pernod* judgment, which itself relied on s 60.

CHAPTER 5

A WELFARE-BASED COMPETITION POLICY UNDER STRUCTURALIST CONSTRAINTS: ABUSE OF DOMINANCE AND OFT PRACTICE

*Renato Nazzini**

This chapter examines the role of the OFT in shaping UK competition policy on abuse of dominance and its contribution to the wider development of EU competition law. Since 1 March 2000, the Office of Fair Trading ("the OFT")[1] has had the power to apply the Chapter II prohibition[2] of the Competition Act 1998. Furthermore, since 1 May 2004, the OFT has also had the power and, in certain circumstances, the duty to apply Art 102 TFEU. The Chapter II prohibition is modelled on Art 102 and the two provisions are, for all practical purposes, the same. Furthermore, under s 60 of the Competition Act 1998, so far as is possible (having regard to any relevant differences between the provisions concerned), questions arising in relation to competition within the UK are to be dealt with in a manner which is consistent with the treatment of corresponding questions arising in EU law in relation to competition within the European Union. In particular, under s 60(2) of the Act, the OFT must act (so far as is

---

* Reader in law, University of Southampton. This chapter was written while the author was a Visiting Professor at the University of Turin. The author would like to express his thanks to all colleagues and friends at the Dipartimento di Scienze Giuridiche for their generous support. The views expressed are purely personal.

[1] Under s 2(1) of the Enterprise Act 2002, brought into force by art 2 of SI 2003/766, on 1 April 2003 the functions of the Director General of Fair Trading ("the DGFT") were transferred to the Office of Fair Trading ("the OFT"), a body corporate created under s 1 of that Act. This chapter continues to refer to the DGFT as the person who exercised the relevant functions under the Competition Act 1998 up to 1 April 2003.

[2] For an overview of the Chapter II prohibition, see R Whish, *Competition Law* (6th edn, 2009, OUP, Oxford) pp 353–62 and M Furse, *Competition Law of the EC and UK* (6th edn, 2008, OUP, Oxford), pp 321–326.

compatible with the provisions of the Act) with a view to ensuring that there is no inconsistency with the principles laid down by the Treaty on the Functioning of the European Union and the case law of the EU courts and any relevant decision of the EU Courts. Under s 60(3) of the Act, the OFT must, in addition, have regard to any relevant decision or statement of the European Commission.[3]

Article 82 EC remains one of the most controversial areas of EU competition law. At the end of 2008, after a 4-year process in which the OFT has been heavily involved, the European Commission published guidance on the application of exclusionary abuses.[4] However, such guidance, in stark contrast with other sets of guidelines issued by the Commission, is confined to setting out the Commission's enforcement priorities rather than providing guidance on the substance of the Art 101 TFEU prohibition. It is trite that several approaches to the application of Art 102 TFEU co-exist which may be broadly divided into structuralist and welfare-based approaches. A structuralist approach would prohibit conduct which has a negative impact on the market structure or the process of competition *per se*, assuming that such conduct is socially undesirable (including, as the case may be, due to negative welfare effects). A welfare-based approach would prohibit conduct which has a negative impact on an appropriate measure of social welfare. It is not clear what the appropriate measure of social welfare should be but the current trend appears to favour consumer welfare.[5] The European Commission has only recently embraced a

---

[3] On s 60 of the Competition Act 1998, see Whish, *Competition Law*, pp 362–367; Furse, *Competition Law of the EC and UK*, pp 54–56; B J Rodger and A MacCulloch, *Competition Law and Policy in the EC and UK* (4th edn, 2009, Routledge-Cavendish, London/New York) pp 145–146; D Bailey, "The Impact of Pernod v OFT on section 60 and the Enforcement of UK Competition Law" [2004] Comp Law 153. For a broader discussion of the interaction between EC and UK law, see B J Rodger, "Interrelationship with Community Competition Enforcement" in B J Rodger and A MacCulloch (eds), *The UK Competition Act: A New Era for UK Competition Law* (2000, Hart, Oxford), pp 45–74.

[4] Communication from the Commission: Guidance on the Commission's enforcement priorities in applying Article 82 of the EC Treaty to abusive exclusionary conduct by dominant undertakings [2009] OJ C45/7. The OFT had published for consultation a draft guideline on *Assessment of conduct* in April 2004, OFT 414a <http://www.oft.gov.uk> (accessed on 10 June 2009), hereinafter "draft guideline on *Assessment of conduct*". However, the publication of the final version of this guideline was put on hold following the announcement by DG Comp of the establishment of an ECN Working Group on the Review of Art 82 EC. The OFT has published a number of other guidelines on the Chapter II prohibition and Art 82, all available at <http://www.oft.gov.uk> (accessed on 10 June 2009). They are: *Abuse of a dominant position* (OFT 402, December 2004), hereinafter "*Abuse of a dominant position*"; *Assessment of market power* (OFT 415, December 2004), hereinafter "*Assessment of market power*"; and *Market definition* (OFT 403, December 2004), hereinafter "*Market definition*".

[5] For an overview, see R Nazzini, "Welfare Objective and Enforcement Standard in Competition Law" in U Bernitz and A Ezrachi (eds), *Private Labels, Brands and Competition Policy* (2009, OUP, Oxford).

welfare-based approach in its prioritisation guidance. The EU Courts, on the other hand, continue to follow a structuralist approach under which an abuse is established if the conduct of the dominant undertaking is capable of having an effect on the competitive structure of the market.[6] In the UK, the OFT has been a strong proponent of a welfare-based approach both in speeches by senior officials[7] and through its involvement in a number of international fora, including the ICN working group on unilateral conduct[8] and various OECD roundtables.[9]

Given the structuralist approach of the EU case law and the stated welfare-based policy,[10] the first question which arises is to ascertain which approach the OFT has adopted in practice.[11] This would be particularly interesting in the current debate as the effective application of a welfare-based approach would demonstrate that such an approach is administrable whereas a major objection to it has always been that it is too difficult to enforce. Second, a review of how a welfare-based approach is applied in practice could be useful to competition authorities around the world as they shape

---

[6] Eg *British Airways* v *Commission* (Case T–219/99) [2003] II–5917, upheld on appeal in *British Airways* v *Commission* (Case C–95/04P) [2007] ECR I–2331; *Manufacture française des pneumatiques Michelin* v *Commission* (Case T–203/01) [2003] II-4071 (*Michelin II*); *Microsoft* v *Commission* (Case T-201/04) [2007] ECR II-3601, para 664.

[7] "Reform of Article 82", opening keynote speech to the British Institute of International and Comparative Law, London, by Philip Collins, Chairman, Office of Fair Trading, 24 February 2006, <http://www.oft.gov.uk/shared_oft/speeches/spe0206.pdf> (accessed on 10 June 2009); and "Abuse of market power", speech to the 31st conference of the European Association for Research in Industrial Economics, Berlin, by Sir John Vickers, Chairman, Office of Fair Trading, 3 September 2004, <http://www.oft.gov.uk/shared_oft/speeches/spe0304.pdf> (accessed on 10 June 2009).

[8] UK Response to the ICN Unilateral Conduct Working Group Questionnaire, <http://www.internationalcompetitionnetwork.org/media/library/unilateral_conduct/questionnaire/UnitedKingdomQuestionnaireResponse.pdf> (accessed on 10 June 2009).

[9] OECD Policy Roundtable on Guidance to Business on Monopolisation and Abuse of Dominance, 2007, written submission from the United Kingdom, <http://www.oecd.org/dataoecd/50/33/40880976.pdf> (accessed on 10 June 2009), pp 44–45; and OECD Policy Roundtable on Competition on the Merits, 2005, written submission from the United Kingdom, < http://www.oecd.org/dataoecd/7/13/35911017.pdf> (accessed on 10 June 2009), pp 199–210.

[10] This inherent tension has not escaped the attention of commentators: see B Allan, "The Control of Dominant Firms in the UK: The Jurisprudence of the CAT" [2007] Comp Law 265, 269–270.

[11] As a commentator rightly pointed out when the Competition Act came into force, notwithstanding s 60, the nature of the issues relating to abuse of dominance inevitably gives the decision-maker a margin of discretion. It is the way in which the OFT "exercises that discretion which will determine how far the Chapter II prohibition really promotes competition": see B Sufrin, "The Chapter II Prohibition" in Rodger and MacCulloch, *The UK Competition Act*, pp 120, 147.

their competition policy according to their own legal framework and objectives. Third, given the significant constraint that s 60 of the Competition Act 1998 and general principles of EU law impose on UK courts and authorities, the identification of the enforcement standards adopted by the OFT would demonstrate how a welfare-based approach could be developed consistently with EU law. Finally, the analysis of the developments in the law of abuse of dominance in the UK may indicate the potential for improvements and refinements in competition enforcement both in the UK and elsewhere.

In order to answer these questions, this chapter reviews the OFT cases in which the Chapter II prohibition and Art 102 TFEU have been applied or considered and any subsequent judgment on appeal by looking at the analysis of dominance and the abuse test.[12] This chapter is structured as follows: first, it examines the OFT decisional practice and any subsequent appeal judgments in relation to dominance; second, it discusses which enforcement standards have been applied in the assessment of the abuse; third, conclusions are drawn.

1 A WELFARE-BASED APPROACH TO DOMINANCE

1.1 The analytical framework

In OFT practice, dominance[13] is always found with very high market shares, considerably higher than 50 per cent, which are sufficient in law to give rise to a presumption of dominance.[14] The finding of dominance never rests on market shares alone but almost invariably includes an assessment of actual competition, potential competition (with a focus on behavioural barriers to entry), and, where relevant,

---

[12] Given the focus of this chapter on how the principal UK competition authority entrusted with the enforcement of the abuse of dominance prohibition has developed a given policy agenda, the decisions of the courts in civil litigation fall outside its scope. However, it would be wrong to underestimate the role of the courts in civil cases in the development of UK and EC competition law. See, for instance, *Attheraces Ltd* v *The British Horseracing Board Ltd* [2007] ECC 7 on excessive prices and price discrimination. Equally, the decisions of the sectoral regulators and any subsequent judgments on appeal are not discussed as they may raise different policy issues because of the interaction between competition law and regulatory objectives. On these aspects, see G Monti, Chapter 6 below.

[13] This chapter focuses only on single dominance. There have been no infringement decisions based on collective dominance. Collective dominance has been discussed in some cases but never in a fully reasoned and evidenced decision. For an example, see *Assessment of a complaint by Brannigan Publishing ("Brannigan"); Newsquest (Sussex) Limited ("Newsquest"); and Johnston Press Limited ("Johnston Press")*, Annex b, <http://www.catribunal.org.uk/files/Let1073Bran090606.pdf> (accessed on 16 June 2009) (*Brannigan*), upheld on appeal in *Terry Brannigan* v *Office of Fair Trading* [2007] CAT 23.

[14] *AKZO Chemie BV* v *Commission* (Case C–62/86) [1991] I–3359, para 60.

buyer power[15] and regulatory constraints.[16] The following sections discuss the use of dominance as a screen to filter out cases where no substantial competitive harm is likely and identify cases in which such harm is possible; the role of barriers to entry in the assessment of dominance; and the link between dominance and the analysis of the abuse.

1.2 Dominance as a screen

A structuralist approach would tend to find dominance based on structural factors alone such as market shares and concentration ratios. This approach is embodied in the emphasis that EU law places on market shares[17] and the *AKZO* presumption of dominance for undertakings with a market share of 50 per cent or more.[18] A welfare-based approach to dominance would not rely on market shares alone but would systematically assess, in every case, actual competition, potential competition and, if relevant, buyer power and other constraints. This is consistent with the idea that dominance is a screen to identify cases where substantial market power[19] is present and filter out cases in which no substantial economic harm is likely. On the other hand, under a welfare-based

---

15 Decision of the Director General of Fair Trading no CA98/2/2001, *Napp Pharmaceutical Holdings Ltd and Subsidiaries*, 30 March 2001 (*Napp*), paras 119–121, partly upheld on appeal in *Napp Pharmaceutical Holdings Ltd* v *Director General of Fair Trading* [2002] CAT 1, [2002] CompAR 13, [2002] ECC 13 (*Napp* v *DGFT*) but with the CCAT not addressing buyer power in its judgment although this may have been because the appellant did not challenge the DGFT's finding this point in its appeal (permission to appeal was refused by the CCAT in *Napp Pharmaceutical Holdings Ltd* v *Director General of Fair Trading* [2002] CAT 5, [2002] CompAR 259 and a further application for leave was rejected by the Court of Appeal in *Napp Pharmaceutical Holdings Ltd* v *Director General of Fair Trading* [2002] EWCA Civ 796, [2002] 4 All ER 376); Decision of the Director General of Fair Trading no CA98/20/2002, *BSkyB investigation: alleged infringement of the Chapter II prohibition*, 17 December 2002 (Case CP 01916-00) (*BSkyB*), paras 319–320; Decision of Director General of Fair Trading no CA98/3/03, *Exclusionary behaviour by Genzyme Ltd*, 27 March 2003 (Case CP/0488–01) (*Genzyme*), paras 268–275, partly upheld on appeal in *Genzyme Ltd* v *Office of Fair Trading* [2004] CAT 4, [2004] CompAR358 (*Genzyme* v *OFT*), paras 241–258; Decision of the Office of Fair Trading no CA98/01/2008, *Abuse of a dominant position by Cardiff Bus*, 18 November 2008 (Case CE/5281/04) (*Cardiff Bus*), para 5.10.

16 *Napp*, paras 112–35, upheld in *Napp* v *DGFT*, paras 161–9; *Genzyme*, paras 276–281, upheld in *Genzyme* v *OFT*, paras 259–289; *Cardiff Bus*, paras 5.11–5.12.

17 See already *Hoffmann-La Roche* v *Commission* (Case 85/76) [1979] ECR 461, paras 39–41. More generally on the concept of dominance in EU law, see G Monti, "The Concept of Dominance in Article 82" (2006) 2 ECJ 31.

18 *AKZO Chemie BV* v *Commission*, para 60.

19 Although dominance is not synonymous with substantial market power, for the purpose of this chapter the two terms will be used interchangeably unless the context requires otherwise. The OFT takes the view that an undertaking will not be dominant unless it has substantial market power: see *Abuse of a dominant position*, para 4.11.

approach to dominance, a low market share may alone be evidence of lack of dominance. This position, which may appear to be a paradox at first sight, reflects the belief that economic harm is only likely when the dominant undertaking has substantial market power. Substantial market power generally requires a high market share. While there may be exceptions, with low market shares the risk of false positives[20] and over-deterrence[21] outweighs the benefits of intervention.

In most circumstances, low market shares are considered to be conclusive evidence of lack of dominance. In *ICL/SYNSTAR*,[22] the only issue was whether there was a separate market for the maintenance of ICL mainframe computers. Given that customers engaged in whole-life costing and were willing to switch and reputation was an important competitive factor, no separate secondary market existed and ICL was not dominant.[23] In *TM Property Services Ltd*, the finding of absence of dominance was based on the low market shares of the vertically integrated undertakings.[24] However, even when market shares are low, the OFT is not exclusively concerned about false positives but takes into account also the risk of false negatives. In *DSG Retail*,[25] the complaint related to abuse of dominance by a major retailer of personal computers (PCs) which had entered into exclusive agreements with two leading manufacturers. Notwithstanding a non-concentrated market[26] and DSG's market share well below 40 per cent on the appropriately defined market,[27] before making a finding of absence of dominance[28] the

---

[20] In this chapter, a false positive denotes a case of intervention when intervention was not warranted. A false negative denotes a case of non-intervention when intervention was warranted. See "The cost of inappropriate interventions/non interventions under Article 82", (Economic discussion paper, OFT864, September 2006), a report prepared for the Office of Fair Trading by Lear, <http://www.oft.gov.uk/shared_oft/economic_research/oft864.pdf > (accessed on 18 June 2009).

[21] Over-deterrence denotes the effect of a policy or enforcement which discourages socially desirable conduct. Under-deterrence denotes the opposite effect of not deterring socially undesirable conduct.

[22] Decision of the Director General of Fair Trading no CA98/6/2001, *ICL/SYNSTAR*, 20 July 2001 (*ICL/SYNSTAR*).

[23] *ICL/SYNSTAR*, paras 26–33 and 36–37.

[24] Decision of the Office of Fair Trading no CA98/07/2004, *TM Property Services Ltd's complaint against MacDonald Dettwiler (Hub) Ltd and MacDonald Dettwiler (Channel) Ltd (trading as Transaction Online)* 18 August 2004 (Case CE–2941/03) (*TM Property Services Ltd*), paras 104–117.

[25] Decision of the Director General of Fair Trading no CA98/3/2001, *Dixons Stores Group Ltd/Compaq Computer Ltd/Packard Bell NEC Ltd*, 6 April 2001 (*DSG*).

[26] *Ibid*, para 66.

[27] *Ibid*, paras 72 and 97.

[28] *Ibid*, paras 97–98.

OFT examined product differentiation[29] and barriers to entry both upstream and downstream.[30]

The role of dominance as a screen against false positive errors is further demonstrated by the fact that the OFT has so far not relied on the presumption of dominance when a firm's market share is more than 50 per cent.[31] Market share alone is a poor indicator of market power[32] and reliance on the presumption might therefore trigger intervention in cases where economic harm is unlikely. In *Napp*, notwithstanding the dominant undertaking, the supplier of a drug called MST, had held market shares of more than 90 per cent on the relevant market for a number of years,[33] the DGFT thoroughly assessed the significance of barriers to entry,[34] buyer power,[35] and regulatory constraints.[36] The decision noted the presumption of dominance in EC law but did not explicitly rely on it.[37] Interestingly, on appeal, the DGFT did rely on the presumption of dominance, arguing that Napp was dominant by virtue of its market share alone.[38] The Competition Commission Appeal Tribunal ("the CCAT")[39] upheld the finding of dominance based on market shares, regulatory barriers to entry, and Napp's first mover advantage, reinforced by the importance of product reputation for general practitioners in the community segment of the market,[40] and

---

[29] *Dixons Stores Group Ltd/Compaq Computer Ltd/Packard Bell NEC Ltd*, paras 73–87.

[30] *Ibid*, paras 88–96.

[31] For a strong policy statement to the effect that there is no market share threshold to define dominance, see *Brannigan*, para 16.

[32] In *Assessment of market power*, the OFT takes a more cautious position which is expressed as follows: "[A]n undertaking's market share is an important factor in assessing dominance but does not determine on its own whether an undertaking is dominant" (see para 2.11). The presumption of dominance is stated at para 2.12 immediately followed by the statement that the OFT considers that it is unlikely that an undertaking will be individually dominant if its market share is below 40%.

[33] *Napp*, paras 96–100.

[34] *Ibid*, paras 101–118.

[35] *Ibid*, paras 119–121.

[36] *Ibid*, paras 122–137.

[37] *Ibid*, para 96.

[38] *Napp* v *DGFT*, para 154.

[39] By virtue of ss 2 and 3 of the Enterprise Act 2002, with effect from 1 April 2003, the Competition Appeal Tribunal ("the CAT"), established under s 12 of the Enterprise Act 2002, replaced the CCAT as the statutory tribunal with power to hear, *inter alia*, appeals on the merits from certain decisions of the OFT. This chapter continues to refer to the CCAT up until 1 April 2003.

[40] The decision identifies two segments of the market for the supply of sustained release morphine in the UK: (1) the community segment, which refers to the supply of the product to pharmacies in the community where the product is prescribed by general practitioners; and (2) the hospital segment, which refers to the supply of the product to hospitals for patients who are in hospital or hospice where the product is prescribed by hospital doctors or specialists (*Napp*, para 22).

their lack of price sensitivity, and their reluctance to switch. The CCAT considered it unnecessary to rely on the further entry barriers identified in the DGFT's decision, particularly sunk promotional expenditure and strategic barriers.[41]

In *Aberdeen Journals II*, the DGFT held the undertaking in question to be dominant based on its market share of more than 70 per cent of the relevant market by value.[42] However, the decision went on to note that existing competition on the market was weak and that significant barriers to entry existed.[43]

In *BSkyB*, the dominant undertaking had a 100 per cent market share on the relevant sports channel market[44] for 10 years,[45] and a market share consistently above 95 per cent on the market for the supply of premium films for at least 3 years.[46] Although BSkyB's market shares were sufficient to presume dominance – and the DGFT said so in relation to the relevant sports channel market[47] – the decision examined barriers to entry and buyer power.

In *Genzyme*,[48] notwithstanding market shares of 100 per cent over more than 10 years on the market for the supply of Gaucher disease drugs in the UK,[49] and prospective market shares in the short to medium term of over 90 per cent,[50] the DGFT conducted a systematic analysis of barriers to entry to the market,[51] reviewed the possibility of new entry in the future,[52] and assessed whether

---

[41] *Napp* v *DGFT*, paras 153–160.

[42] Decision of the Director General of Fair Trading no CA98/14/2002, *Predation by Aberdeen Journals Ltd (Remitted case)*, 16 September 2002 (Case CE/1217–02) (*Aberdeen Journals II*), para 148, partly upheld on appeal in *Aberdeen Journals Ltd* v *Office of Fair Trading* [2003] CAT 11, [2003] CompAR 67 (*Aberdeen Journals* v *OFT*). The DGFT submitted that the case law of the EU Courts entitled him to rely on market shares alone: *Aberdeen Journals* v *OFT*, para 106. In relation to the same infringement, the DGFT had adopted a previous decision which had been set aside by the CCAT in *Aberdeen Journals Ltd* v *Director General of Fair Trading* [2002] CAT 4, [2002] Comp AR 167. The CCAT had remitted the matter to the DGFT (*ibid*). On these earlier developments, see J Holmes, "Aberdeen Journals Limited v The Director General of Fair Trading" [2002] Comp Law 117; G Niels, "Newspaper War in Aberdeen: Was Predation Involved?" [2002] Comp Law 177; and G Murphy, "Director-General's GBP 1.33 million fine for predatory pricing set aside for now" [2002] ECLR 368.

[43] *Aberdeen Journals II*, paras 148–9. On barriers to entry, see paras 145–147. The CAT upheld this analysis: *Aberdeen Journals* v *OFT*, paras 309–313.

[44] *BSkyB*, n 15 above, para 270.

[45] *Ibid*, para 284.

[46] *Ibid*, para 273.

[47] *Ibid*, para 271.

[48] *Genzyme*, n 15 above, paras 126–158.

[49] *Ibid*, para 227.

[50] *Ibid*, paras 228–229.

[51] *Ibid*, paras 230–255.

[52] *Ibid*, paras 256–267.

buyer power was such as to counterbalance Genzyme's market power.[53] The Competition Appeal Tribunal ("the CAT") endorsed this approach. Although the Tribunal stated that a market share of 90 per cent or above, which had continued throughout the period of infringement and was likely to continue for several years, would be sufficient, depending on the circumstances, to infer the existence of dominance,[54] it went on to consider barriers to entry,[55] the likelihood of future entry,[56] and buyer power,[57] placing considerable emphasis on evidence of actual exercise of market power by Genzyme.[58]

In *Harwood Park Crematorium*,[59] the OFT had defined a wider upstream market for the supply of crematoria services to funeral directors including all crematoria within a 30-km radius of Stevenage and Knebworth,[60] and a narrow downstream market for the supply of funeral directing services to consumers comprising only Stevenage and Knebworth.[61] As a result, Austins, the firm of funeral directors owning Harwood Park crematorium, was held not to be dominant on the upstream market mainly because of its low market share (slightly above 15 per cent).[62] The CAT set aside the OFT's decision, holding that the OFT had erroneously defined the upstream market more widely than the downstream market for funeral directing services.[63] As a consequence, Harwood Park's market share was over 90 per cent, which in itself would be "indicative of dominance"[64] but not, it appears, sufficient proof given the CAT took into account the barriers to entry to the market[65] and Austins' market behaviour.[66]

In *Cardiff Bus*, even if the market shares of 66 per cent on a

---

[53] *BSkyB*, n 15 above, paras 268–275. For a criticism of the assessment of dominance in this case, see, however, D Ridyard, "The Genzyme case and the OFT's margin squeeze muddle" [2004] ECLR 44, 44–45.

[54] *Genzyme* v *OFT*, n 15 above, para 225.

[55] *Ibid*, paras 227–237.

[56] *Ibid*, paras 238–239.

[57] *Ibid*, paras 241–258.

[58] *Ibid*, paras 252–258.

[59] Decision of the Office of Fair Trading no CA98/06/2004, *Refusal to supply JJ Burgess & Sons Limited with access to Harwood Park Crematorium*, 29 June 2004 (Case CP/0055/02) (*Harwood Park Crematorium*).

[60] *Ibid*, para 45.

[61] *Ibid*, para 54.

[62] *Ibid*, paras 57–60.

[63] *ME Burgess, JJ Burgess and SJ Burgess (trading as JJ Burgess & Sons)* v *Office of Fair Trading* [2005] CAT 25, [2005] CompAR 1151 (*Burgess* v *OFT*), paras 166–245.

[64] *Ibid*, para 246.

[65] *Ibid*, para 247.

[66] *Ibid*, paras 247–249. For a further discussion of this aspect of the case, see the section on barriers to entry, below.

network basis[67] and over 70 per cent on a flow-by-flow basis[68] gave rise, in law, to a rebuttable presumption of dominance,[69] the OFT did not rely on this presumption. It went on to consider whether potential competition,[70] countervailing buyer power[71] and the regulatory framework[72] constituted a sufficient competitive constraint on the allegedly dominant undertaking.

1.3 Barriers to entry

The concept of barrier to entry is not legally defined. A structuralist approach would regard any factor that deters or delays entry as a barrier to entry.[73] A welfare-based approach would seek to distinguish between costs of entry generally, which cannot be regarded as a barrier to entry, and asymmetries between entrants and incumbents which are welfare-reducing.[74]

The OFT defines entry barriers as "factors that allow an undertaking profitably to sustain supra-competitive prices in the long term, without being more efficient than its potential rivals".[75] This definition points towards a welfare-based approach to entry barriers. A factor is a barrier to entry only if: (a) entry by equally efficient or more efficient rivals is prevented; and (b) as a consequence, the dominant undertaking can sustain supra-competitive prices[76] in the long term. It is clear that this situation is welfare-reducing both in terms of total welfare (because of the deadweight loss of market power which would be reduced following at least equally efficient entry) and in terms of consumer welfare (because of prices higher than those which would

---

67 *Cardiff Bus*, para 5.83.

68 *Ibid*, para 5.84.

69 *Ibid*, paras 5.59–5.62 and 5.83–5.86.

70 *Ibid*, paras 6.1–6.101.

71 *Ibid*, para 5.10.

72 *Ibid*, paras 5.11–5.12.

73 J S Bain, *Barriers to New Competition* (1956, Harvard University Press, Cambridge) regarded the "condition of entry" as "a structural condition" defined as the advantages of the established sellers which allowed them to keep prices above the competitive level without attracting new entry (p 3).

74 G J Stigler, "Barriers to Entry, Economies of Scale and Firm Size" in G J Stigler, "Barriers to Entry, Economies of Scale, and Firm Size", in *The Organization of Industry* (1968, Irwin, Homewood), pp 67–70; R Bork, *The Antitrust Paradox: A Policy at War with Itself* (1978, Basic Books, New York), pp 310–323; F M Fisher, "Diagnosing Monopoly" (1979) 10 Quarterly Review of Economics and Business 7; C. Von Weizsacker, "A Welfare Analysis of Barriers to Entry" (1980) 11 Bell Journal of Economics 399.

75 *Assessment of Market Power*, para 5.3.

76 Note that the correct test is supra-competitive prices and not supra-competitive profits. A less efficient incumbent shielded by entry barriers may not be earning supra-competitive profits because of X-inefficiencies or because the market power rents are appropriated by other firms (on this latter point, see *BSkyB*, paras 290–292).

be sustainable following at least equally efficient entry). The OFT decisions confirm this approach, which has been endorsed by the CAT.

When the OFT finds that the undertaking in question is dominant, it is only in exceptional cases that the analysis does not include a thorough assessment of actual competition, potential competition and, where relevant, other constraints such as buyer power. This is the case when there is a 100 per cent market share together with an insurmountable regulatory barrier to entry. Regulatory barriers are artificial and, unless they have been specifically set for the purpose and with the effect of maximising social welfare, they can be presumed to lead to inefficiency.[77] In *Companies House*, a non-infringement decision, the OFT held that, because companies in England and Wales had a statutory obligation to provide certain information to Companies House and the latter also received information from the Registrar for Companies in Scotland, it had a statutory monopoly in the supply of bulk and magnetic products containing this information.[78]

In *Napp*, regulatory barriers to entry were found to exist but not to be such as to deter firms from entering the UK market if there were profits to be made. Rather, regulatory barriers had the effect of delaying entry.[79] More importantly, however, the DGFT found that Napp enjoyed a strong and persistent first mover advantage as a result of having introduced the first brand of sustained release morphine which enjoyed patent protection for 12 years.[80] This raised a barrier to entry to the community segment of the market where reputation, lack of price sensitivity, and reluctance to switch were significant.[81] To overcome these obstacles, a new entrant would have to establish a significant presence in the hospital segment and to invest heavily in promotional activities in the community segment.[82] However, Napp's reputation for aggressive pricing behaviour when bidding for hospital contracts constituted a strategic barrier to entry to the latter segment.[83] Barriers to entry, therefore, were not simply factors which made entry more costly or more difficult but factors which enabled Napp to behave strategically by excluding rivals from

---

[77] Even the most strenuous proponent of the Chicago school policy approach to competition law accepted that "artificial" barriers were properly characterised as barriers to entry: Bork, *The Antitrust Paradox*, 311. However, Bork understands artificial barriers to entry as exclusionary practices (*ibid*).

[78] Decision of the Director General of Fair Trading, *Companies House, the Registrar of Companies for England and Wales*, 25 October 2002 (Case CP/1139–01) (*Companies House*), para 17.

[79] *Napp*, paras 102–103.

[80] *Ibid*, para 104.

[81] *Ibid*, paras 104–109.

[82] *Ibid*, para 110–113.

[83] *Ibid*, para 114–118.

the market segment which potential competitors had to enter in order to be successful.

In *Aberdeen Journals II*, the DGFT identified two barriers to entry: the cost of sustaining and expanding presence in the market in order to attract advertisers,[84] and the incumbent's reputation for predation.[85] Arguably, although the point was not developed in the decision, the former was simply the cost of competing in the market. However, it gave the dominant undertaking the ability and incentive to behave strategically by establishing a reputation for predation, thus further reducing expected post-entry profits. This could ultimately deter entry by equally efficient undertakings. The CAT on appeal upheld this analysis.[86]

In *BSkyB*, the focus was also on strategic barriers rather than on economies of scale or sunk costs *per se*. As regards the relevant sports channel market, the DGFT considered that the establishment of an entirely new competition of the standard of the Football Association Premier League (FAPL) was unrealistic,[87] and that BSkyB's exclusive rights on FAPL content were an absolute barrier to entry.[88] Nor did competition for the market negate BSkyB's substantial market power because the auction was not to supply the auctioneer.[89] As a consequence, any anti-competitive exploitation of the FAPL rights would have no impact on the outcome of future auctions.[90] As regards the relevant market for the supply of premium film channels, the DGFT considered that the BSkyB portfolio of studio contracts with staggered renewal dates was a barrier to entry because it meant that a new entrant could not compile a new premium film channel unless it took a number of such contracts from BSkyB[91] as they came up for renewal at different times.[92] This was reinforced by BSkyB's matching rights, which meant that BSkyB had a right of first refusal or preferred status in the negotiation when contracts expired.[93] However, in relation to both relevant markets, the DGFT did not come to a view as to whether BSkyB's vertical integration constituted a barrier to entry by

---

84 *Aberdeen Journals II*, para 145.

85 *Ibid*, paras 146–147.

86 *Aberdeen Journals* v *OFT*, paras 309–313.

87 *BSkyB*, para 283.

88 *Ibid*, para 284. Similarly, in *Du Pont*, also a non-infringement decision, the OFT found that Du Pont had 100% of the relevant market and exclusive worldwide rights relating to the manufacture and the distribution of the product. See Decision of the Office of Fair Trading no CA98/07/2003, *Refusal to supply unprocessed holographic photopolymer film: EI du Pont de Nemours & Company and Op Graphics (Holography) Ltd*, 9 September 2003 (Case CP/1761/02) (*Du Pont*), paras 24–25.

89 *BSkyB*, para 287.

90 *Ibid*, para 288.

91 *Ibid*, paras 293–295.

92 *Ibid*, paras 296–300.

93 *Ibid*, paras 301–303.

giving BSkyB the ability and incentive to exclude a new provider of a premium content channels from BSkyB's retail customer base, which was arguably essential for the commercial viability of any such new entrant.[94] However, it is clear that the DGFT considered that vertical integration could constitute a further strategic entry barrier.

In *Burgess*, as explained above, the CAT held that a market share of 90 per cent was "indicative" of dominance but did not stop there. It considered that there were "insurmountable" barriers to entry to the market because of planning regulations.[95] This absolute regulatory barrier coupled with a 90 per cent market share would have been sufficient to establish dominance. However, the CAT considered that it was necessary to rely on the direct evidence of the undertaking's exercise of market power and, in particular, on the fact that it had increased prices further than other crematoria in the area while also increasing the number of cremations, and had restricted the choice of funeral directors of consumers wishing to use Harwood Park crematorium.[96] Finally, the CAT considered it relevant that the dominant undertaking had been able to raise its downstream rival's costs and had the ability to exclude it from the market.[97] This analysis demonstrates that the CAT adopted a welfare-based approach to entry barriers. The evidence of exercise of market power and ability to exclude highlights the welfare-reducing effect of the regulatory barrier to entry.

In *Cardiff Bus*, the OFT held that the Cardiff Bus network constituted a barrier to entry by giving the incumbent the ability to raise switching costs for customers. This would force a new entrant to replicate the full scale of the incumbent's network, which, however, would entail significant up-front costs, some of which would be sunk. The incumbent could, therefore, deter entry if per capita scale economies were greater than per capita switching costs. Accordingly, full-scale entry was unlikely.[98] Small-scale no-frills entry was feasible but the incumbent's reputation for aggressive entry response constituted a strategic barrier to entry against small-scale no-frills rivals.[99] These findings were confirmed by the history of entry, exit, and expansion in the market.[100] Therefore, it is not simply economies of scale or sunk costs that constitute barriers to entry. What matters is the ability of the dominant undertaking to take advantage of scale

[94] *BSkyB*, paras 304–311.
[95] *Burgess* v *OFT*, para 247.
[96] *Ibid*, paras 247–249.
[97] *Ibid*, paras 248–249.
[98] *Cardiff Bus*, paras 6.3–6.63.
[99] *Ibid*, paras 6.64–6.79.
[100] *Ibid*, paras 6.81–6.95.

economies and sunk costs in order to exclude as efficient rivals with a negative effect on social welfare.

1.4 Dominance as an integral part of the analysis of the abuse

A structuralist approach would tend to detach the assessment of dominance from the analysis of the abuse. Such an approach rests on the belief that certain conduct is harmful in concentrated market structures where one firm is dominant. Therefore, once dominance has been found, all that is left is to decide whether the undertaking engaged in a prohibited form of conduct. A welfare-based approach would integrate the assessment of dominance in the analysis of abuse. Unilateral conduct may be harmful because the undertaking has substantial market power which gives it the ability and incentive to exclude competitors thereby reducing social welfare. It would not make sense to establish dominance and then focus exclusively on abuse without explaining how the abuse of market power results in harm to social welfare.[101] This proposition can be illustrated by focusing on four aspects.

First, the abuse itself may be evidence of dominance if the harm to competition or consumers tends to show that the undertaking under review has substantial market power.[102] In *Burgess* v *OFT*, the CAT held that Austins' ability to raise its rival's costs and to exclude it from the market was evidence of dominance.[103] This approach may be criticised as circular to the extent that it purports to infer dominance from the abuse in a simplistic way. However, this is not what the CAT did in the *Burgess* case. The abusive behaviour was only one piece of evidence which did not dispense with the analysis of actual competition and barriers to entry. Furthermore, if the finding of abuse entails the assessment of potential or actual competitive harm,[104] then inferring dominance from the abuse

[101] It has even been argued that "[t]he economic approach implies that there is no need to establish a preliminary and separate assessment of dominance. Rather, the emphasis is on the establishment of a verifiable and consistent account of significant competition harm, since such an anti-competitive effect is what really matters and is already proof of dominance". See Report by the EAGCP, "An economic approach to Article 82", July 2005, <http://ec.europa.eu/competition/publications/studies/eagcp_july_21_05.pdf> (accessed on 11 June 2009). As explained above, the OFT does not follow this approach but assesses dominance as a necessary preliminary step in the analysis.

[102] *Ibid.*

[103] *Burgess* v *OFT*, paras 248–249.

[104] For the purpose of this chapter, competitive harm denotes the actual or likely effects of the behaviour under review which the OFT has, from time to time, adopted as an element of the abuse test. These tests are discussed below in the section on the enforcement standards and theories of harm.

carries a much lesser risk of false positives insofar as competitive harm is unlikely unless the undertaking in question has substantial market power.

Second, the abuse may be a strategic barrier to entry which protects or reinforces the incumbent's substantial market power. In a cluster of predation cases, namely *Napp*, *Aberdeen Journals II*, and *Cardiff Bus*, the incumbent's predatory conduct was found to be a strategic barrier to entry which directly prevented the entry or expansion of rivals[105] or deterred future entry by establishing a reputation for predation.[106] This approach has been extended beyond predation theory. In *Genzyme*, a margin squeeze case, the DGFT held that Genzyme's tying practice, by reserving to itself the downstream market for homecare services, raised barriers to entry to the upstream market for the supply of the drug. On the assumption that Genzyme would not be prepared to provide homecare services in respect of a competing drug, a patient switching drug would also have to switch homecare service provider. This would further increase the already significant resistance to a new drug and protect Genzyme's market power on the upstream market.[107]

Third, a trend emerges in the cases which attempts to explain the harmful effects of the abuse as a direct consequence of the undertaking's substantial market power. Already in *Napp*, the theory of harm rested on the inextricable link between predatory conduct in the hospital segment and the charging of supra-competitive prices in the community segment.[108] In *Aberdeen Journals* v *OFT*, the CAT held the dominant undertaking was incurring losses on one newspaper in order to protect profits on another.[109] The reasonable assumption, given the previous finding of dominance, was that such profits were supra-competitive. In *Cardiff Bus*, the OFT held that the dominant undertaking was likely to be able to recoup its losses, relying, *inter alia*, on the analysis of dominance and barriers to entry.[110]

---

[105] *Napp*, paras 114–118.

[106] See, for the treatment of the abuse in the context of the assessment of dominance, *Napp*, para 115; *Aberdeen Journals II*, paras 146–147; *Cardiff Bus*, paras 6.64–6.80. The same entry-deterring effect is also part of the analysis of the effects of the abuse on competition: see *Napp* v *DGFT*, paras 275–288; *Aberdeen Journals II*, para 210; *Cardiff Bus*, paras 7.241–7.243.

[107] *Genzyme*, paras 331–350. On appeal, the CAT found that the abuse, if successful, would have had some adverse effect upstream but not as great as suggested by the OFT: *Genzyme* v *OFT*, para 639.

[108] *Napp*, paras 192–196; *Napp* v *DGFT*, paras 261 and 299.

[109] *Aberdeen Journals* v *OFT*, para 445.

[110] *Cardiff Bus*, para 7.254.

Finally, if the harmful effects of the conduct are directly linked to the undertaking's market power, it is possible to assume that the greater the market power, the more serious the anti-competitive effects. This approach was adopted by the CAT in *Napp* v *DGFT*.[111] When rejecting the appellant's objective justification arguments, the CAT considered it relevant that Napp was a virtual monopolist[112] and that there was a link between the degree of dominance and the abuse because "[i]n a situation where the barriers to entry protecting an incumbent monopolist are already high, even a modest raising of further barriers by the pricing actions of that monopolist is potentially a serious matter".[113] In *Genzyme*, the DGFT adopted this principle and held that the effect of blocking or delaying entry of a new competitor was all the more serious in a market where the incumbent had a monopoly position and new entry was the only way in which its market power could be challenged.[114] This approach is sound as long as it does not slip into the application of stricter liability standards to undertakings with very high market shares. As applied so far by the CAT and the OFT, the link between the degree of dominance and the magnitude or seriousness of the anti-competitive effects is a correct application of the welfare-based approach to the Chapter II prohibition and Art 102 TFEU whereby what matters is not the undertaking's market share or form of conduct but the effect of unilateral conduct on social welfare.

2 ENFORCEMENT STANDARDS AND THEORIES OF HARM

2.1 Enforcement standards in structuralist and welfare-based approaches

A structuralist approach tends to adopt stricter enforcement standards, possibly close to *per se* rules. This approach relies on the assumption that where the structure of the market is already weakened, certain forms of conduct are almost inevitably harmful. A welfare-based approach would seek to develop administrable enforcement standards going beyond per se rules and incorporating

---

[111] See Rodger and MacCulloch, *Competition Law and Policy in the EC and UK*, p 149 and S Kon and S Turnbull, "Pricing and the dominant firm: implications of the Competition Commission Appeal Tribunal's judgment in the Napp case" [2003] Comp Law 70, 77–78.

[112] *Napp* v *DGFT*, para 260.

[113] *Ibid*, para 286. See also para 343, where the CAT rejected a "meeting competition" defence based, *inter alia*, on the degree of market power held by Napp.

[114] *Genzyme*, para 345. See also *Brannigan*, para 41, where *Aberdeen Journals* was distinguished on the fact that in that case the dominant undertaking had a "virtual monopoly".

an analysis of the likely effect of a given practice on welfare. The OFT has not applied per se infringement rules but has sought to develop standards based on the likelihood of exclusion of equally efficient competitors[115] or on consumer harm.[116] The CAT has endorsed this approach although, on occasions, this has in fact resulted in the application of a stricter standard than the OFT.[117]

2.2 *Per se* infringement rules

Per se rules in EU law and OFT practice

A structuralist approach often relies on per se rules which prohibit certain forms of conduct. Examples of this approach may be the rules set out in the case law of the EU Courts on predation, rebates, and refusal to supply. The case law on predation establishes a presumption of predation for prices below average variable costs which could be applied mechanistically as simply prohibiting prices below average variable costs subject to objective justification.[118] The case law on rebates can be read as prohibiting retrospective rebates which tend to make it more difficult or impossible for competitors to enter or compete in the market and to restrict the buyer's freedom to choose their suppliers, subject to objective justification based on a

---

[115] For a well-known formulation of the test as giving rise to a presumption of infringement, see R Posner, *Antitrust Law* (2nd edn, 2001, University of Chicago Press, Chicago), p 194. The test has some shortcomings, particularly because of the difficulty in ascertaining whether a competitor is as efficient as the dominant firm in certain cases: H Hovenkamp, "Exclusion and the Sherman Act" (2005) 72 UChiLRev 147, 154–155. It has also been argued that, in principle, an appropriate welfare-based test should focus directly on the welfare effects of the behaviour: R O'Donoghue and J A Padilla, *The Law and Economics of Article 82* (2006, Hart, Oxford), p 190.

[116] On the consumer harm test, see S C Salop, "The Controversy over the Proper Antitrust Standard for Anticompetitive Exclusionary Conduct", 2006 Fordham Corp L Inst 477 (B Hawk (ed), 2007) and S C Salop, "Exclusionary Conduct, Effect on Consumers, and the Flawed Profit-Sacrifice Standard" (2006) 73 Antitrust LJ 311. The criticism of the consumer harm test focuses on its lack of administrability and consequent risk of false positives and over-deterrence: G Werden, "Identifying Single-Firm Exclusionary Conduct: From Vague Concepts to Administrable Rules", 2006 Fordham Corp L Inst 509, 538–539 (B Hawk (ed), 2007); G Werden, "Identifying Exclusionary Conduct under Section 2: The 'No Economic Sense' Test" (2006) 73 Antitrust LJ 413, 431–432; A D Melamed, "Exclusive Dealing Agreements and Other Exclusionary Conduct – Are There Unifying Principles?" (2006) 73 Antitrust LJ 375, 380–381.

[117] Allan, "The Control of Dominant Firms in the UK: The Jurisprudence of the CAT" 272–273.

[118] *AKZO Chemie BV* v *Commission*, paras 71–2. The Court of Justice has repeatedly rejected the argument that recoupment should be part of the test: *Tetra Pak International SA* v *Commission* (Case C–333/94P) [1996] ECR I–5951, para 44; *France Télécom SA* v *Commission* (Case C–202/07P), 2 April 2009, paras 103–114.

strict correlation between economies of scale and the amount of the rebate.[119] At its most extreme, the case law on refusal to supply may be interpreted as laying down a rule which prohibits a dominant undertaking from discontinuing supplies to an established customer which abides by normal commercial practices, subject to objective justification.[120] The OFT, however, has never exclusively relied on evidence of prices below average variable costs or average avoidable costs for a finding of predation; has not applied the case law of the EU Courts on rebates when it had the opportunity to do so; and has sought to refine the test for the refusal to supply to an existing customer by requiring proof of anti-competitive effects.

Predation

As regards predation, the OFT and the CAT have held that prices below average variable costs may be objectively justified. In *Napp* the DGFT accepted in principle that an objective justification was open to Napp even if the prices charged in the hospital segment were below average variable costs. Napp argued that its conduct was objectively justified because each loss-making sale in the hospital segment generated follow-on sales in the community segment and was, therefore, overall profitable.[121] The DGFT rejected this argument as Napp's discounts did not result in overall increased sales as it would be in a pro-competitive loss-leading scenario.[122] They excluded competitors from the hospital segment and, as a result, prevented them from competing effectively in the community segment, thereby allowing Napp to earn supra-competitive profits in this latter market segment.[123] The CCAT doubted whether the presumption of predation when a virtual monopolist such as Napp prices below direct costs could be rebutted but, "as a precaution", ruled on the issue and upheld the DGFT's finding.[124] The judgment of the CCAT has rightly been described as "a rejection of a *per se* cost-based approach to predatory pricing".[125]

---

[119] *Hoffmann-La Roche* v *Commission*; *Michelin* v *Commission* (Case 322/81) [1983] ECR 3461 (*Michelin I*); *British Airways* v *Commission* (Case T–219/99), upheld on appeal in *British Airways* v *Commission* (Case C–95/04P); *Michelin II*; *Irish Sugar* v *Commission* (Case 228/97) [1999] ECR II–2969.

[120] *United Brands* v *Commission* (Case 27/76) [1978] ECR 207, para 182. The test for refusal to supply remains unclear in EU law. See R Nazzini, "The *Microsoft* Case and the Future of Article 82" (2008) 22(2) Antitrust 59, 60.

[121] *Napp*, para 192.

[122] *Ibid*, para 194.

[123] Ibid, paras 192–196.

[124] *Napp* v *DGFT*, paras 231–339.

[125] Kon and Turnbull, "Pricing and the dominant firm: implications of the Competition Commission Appeal Tribunal's judgment in the Napp case", n 111 above, 86.

In *Aberdeen Journals II*, the DGFT found that the dominant undertaking had failed to cover its variable costs in March, May and June 2000[126] and that it intended to expel its only competitor from the market by incurring substantial losses.[127] However, the DGFT accepted that, as a matter of law, prices below average variable costs only gave rise to a presumption of predation and that such a presumption might be rebutted by evidence of objective justification.[128] On the facts, the DGFT found that the conduct was objectively justified in May and June 2000 due to the need to move the production of the newspaper to Leicester as a result of the threat of industrial action in the Aberdeen production facility.[129]

In *First Edinburgh/Lothian*, the OFT went even further. It held that prices below average variable costs on a significant number of bus routes and for periods of many months were a form of legitimate competition on the merits.[130] The OFT took the view that First Edinburgh engaged in aggressive pricing by deliberately incurring losses in order to establish a more comprehensive network in the Greater Edinburgh area and rationalising depot utilisation.[131] At no stage did First Edinburgh intend to force Lothian from the Greater Edinburgh area or believe that it was capable of so doing.[132] On the contrary, the OFT found that Lothian had been profitable throughout and there was no risk of First Edinburgh forcing Lothian out of the market or weakening it as a rival.[133] In conclusion, First Edinburgh's conduct, and Lothian's reaction to it, were characterised as legitimate competition between rival undertakings, which ultimately benefited consumers within the Greater Edinburgh area by resulting, for a time, in lower fares and higher route frequencies, with no danger that this would lead to competition being weakened in the future.[134] It was material to this conclusion that First

---

[126] *Aberdeen Journals II*, para 184.
[127] *Ibid*, paras 181–183.
[128] *Ibid*, para 185.
[129] *Ibid*, para 205. The CAT endorsed this approach on appeal: *Aberdeen* v *OFT*, paras 357–358, although, as in *Napp* v *DGFT*, the Tribunal raised the bar for the dominant undertaking and commented that "[t]he presumption of abuse will rarely, if ever, be rebutted if the pricing policy under scrutiny originates as an aggressive response to market entry by a competitor, or is directed towards eliminating a competitor. An objective justification will normally be particularly difficult to establish if there is evidence of selective price cutting by a dominant undertaking that is targeted specifically towards the customers or potential customers of a competitor".
[130] Decision of the Office of Fair Trading no CA98/05/2004, *First Edinburgh/Lothian*, 29 April 2004 (Case CP/0361–01) (*First Edinburgh/Lothian*).
[131] *Ibid*, para 68.
[132] *Ibid*.
[133] *Ibid*, paras 76–79.
[134] *Ibid*, para 83.

Edinburgh was not dominant in the Greater Edinburgh area but on a neighbouring market.[135] The aggressive pricing policy was a pro-competitive market penetration strategy.

Rebates

As regards rebates, the only OFT decision containing a conclusive finding as to whether the practice constituted an infringement relates to the bundled discounts in *BSkyB*. These are discounts across different products whereas the case law of the EU Courts relates to single product discounts.[136] However, it is striking that, for multi-product retroactive rebates, the OFT applied a test of likely foreclosure of an as efficient single-product competitor. In *BSkyB*, the DGFT examined certain wholesale bundled discounts which, allegedly, distorted downstream competition and foreclosed entry to the wholesale premium channel market.[137] The pay-to-basic discount was a retroactive rebate on all units purchased and depended on the achievement of targets based on the ratio of BSkyB premium channel subscribers and the number of basic cable subscribers. This resulted in a range in which the cost to the distributor of taking additional BSkyB premium subscribers was very low. A new entrant would have to match this price in order to be a viable competitor.[138] The discount could also distort downstream competition by incentivising distributors to increase the number of BSkyB premium channel subscribers rather than basic subscribers. Basic-only strategies, however, were potentially important as a means of market penetration by bundling basic packages with telephony, e-mail, and internet access.[139] The DGFT applied a two-limb test: (a) whether the discount resulted in

[135] *First Edinburgh/Lothian*, paras 42–48.

[136] *Hoffmann-La Roche* v *Commission*; *Michelin I*; *Virgin/British Airways* [2000] OJ L30/1, upheld in *British Airways* v *Commission* (Case T–219/99) and, on appeal, in *British Airways* v *Commission* (Case C–95/04P); and *Irish Sugar* v *Commission*. Because of the way the parties argued their cases, the OFT had to distinguish the case law on rebates not when dealing with the bundled rebates issue but when addressing the mixed bundling issue. Deciding on two applications under s 47 of the Competition Act 1998, as in force at the time, the OFT rejected the contention that the assessment of mixed bundling was governed by the case law of the EU Courts on rebates and that the test should be whether the pricing practice had a tendency to restrict the buyer's freedom to choose its suppliers. The OFT distinguished the case law of the EU Courts because it did not concern mixed bundling and held that it was entitled to analyse the issue from first principles: Decision of the Office of Fair Trading under section 47 relating to decision CA98/20/2002: *Alleged infringement of the Chapter II prohibition by BSkyB* (*BSkyB s 47 decision*), para 176.

[137] *BSkyB*, para 601.

[138] *Ibid*, paras 610–615.

[139] *Ibid*, paras 616–620.

average prices of incremental units below their incremental costs;[140] (b) whether an actual or realistic potential foreclosure effect existed (likelihood of foreclosure).[141] On the facts, certain distributors had not received the discounts in question and all of them had moved away from the critical range during the relevant period, so the discounts were found not to be likely of having a foreclosure effect.[142] As for the distortion of downstream competition, the DGFT found evidence that this had not happened.[143]

At least twice, the OFT has investigated single-product rebates which, unlike the rebates in *BSkyB*, would have fallen squarely within the case law of the EU Courts. In both cases, the OFT decided to close the investigations based on its administrative priorities either because of lack of consumer detriment[144] or because of lack of evidence of substantial foreclosure effects.[145]

Refusal to supply

In relation to refusal to supply, the OFT has sought to narrow the scope of the dominant undertaking's duty to deal. The problem is that, given that some degree of foreclosure of a rival is almost inevitable in refusal to supply cases if the input in question is indispensable or even simply a superior product, is it possible to say that any foreclosure is sufficient to establish an abuse? If so, how does one distinguish the protection of competition from the protection of competitors?

In *Du Pont*, the OFT held that it was not an infringement of the Chapter II prohibition for a monopolist holding exclusive worldwide rights relating to the manufacture and distribution of a product to terminate a supply contract with a downstream firm.[146] In this case, the OFT was clearly concerned about false positives. It took the view that the product in question was not an essential facility – defined as an infrastructure, access to which is necessary to compete and duplication of which would be either impossible or extremely difficult – but the outcome of research and development which resulted in a unique product. To deprive a firm of its freedom to choose its trading partners in such circumstances would be "an excessive degree of interference".[147] More puzzlingly, the decison also held that the

---

[140] *BSkyB*, paras 613–614.
[141] *Ibid*, para 639.
[142] *Ibid*, para 639.
[143] *Ibid*, para 644.
[144] *Walkers Snacks Ltd*, case closure summary, 2 May 2007, <http://www.oft.gov.uk/advice_and_resources/resource_base/ca98/closure/Walkers> (accessed on 10 June 2009).
[145] *British Airways*, case closure summary, 30 April 2007, <http://www.oft.gov.uk/advice_and_resources/resource_base/ca98/closure/British-Airways2> (accessed on 19 June 2009).
[146] *Du Pont*, paras 26–34.
[147] *Ibid*, para 29.

refusal to supply would not eliminate all downstream competition because Du Pont itself was withdrawing from the downstream market. Therefore, the behaviour under review did not appear to have an anti-competitive purpose.

In *Capita Business Services Ltd and Bromcom Computers plc*,[148] Capita gave the OFT voluntary assurances that it would provide "interface information" to a third party to enable it to have access to data on Capita's server. The OFT had reasonable grounds for suspecting that Capita was dominant in the schools information management system sector because of its "stable and high market shares ... the presence of entry barriers such as high switching costs for schools, the generally risk averse and financially constrained nature of schools as purchases and the low market shares of competitors". The refusal to supply interface information to the complainant could have limited "innovation and choice" by excluding competition between Capita's own products and the competitor's products. While it would be wrong to read too much in a case closure summary, it is clear that the theory of harm relied upon was not simply foreclosure but consumer harm.

In *Harwood Park Crematorium*, the OFT considered that a vertically integrated undertaking providing both crematoria services on an upstream market and funeral directing services on a downstream market (Austins) had not abused its dominant position by refusing to continue to grant access to the crematorium to a downstream competitor (Burgess). This finding was based on Austins not being dominant on the upstream market.[149] However, the OFT went on to consider whether, even if the undertaking in question had been dominant on the upstream market, the refusal to supply would have been anti-competitive. The OFT's conclusion was that not only was the behaviour under review not carried out with anti-competitive intent[150] but, more importantly, it would not cause substantial harm to competition. The downstream competitor was not likely to exit the market as a result of the alleged abuse and there was at least another substantial downstream competitor on the relevant market.[151]

The CAT set aside the decision of the OFT.[152] Having found that Austins was dominant on the upstream market,[153] the

[148] *Capita Business Services Ltd and Bromcom Computers plc*, case closure summary, 2 May 2003, http://www.oft.gov.uk/shared_oft/ca98_case_closures/2003.pdf (accessed on 18 November 2009).

[149] *Harwood Park Crematorium*, paras 56–61.

[150] *Ibid*, paras 82–84.

[151] *Ibid*, paras 84–92.

[152] For a comment on the case, see J Skilbeck, "Burgess v Office of Fair Trading" [2005] Comp Law 94.

[153] *Burgess* v *OFT*, paras 246–252.

Tribunal held that Austins had infringed the Chapter II prohibition by refusing to give Burgess access to the Harwood Park Crematorium, thereby strengthening its dominant position on the downstream market for funeral directing services to the detriment of consumers.[154] The OFT argued that competition law should protect competition and not competitors and that there was no evidence of substantial harm to competition downstream. The CAT found that the refusal to supply had the likely effect of eliminating Burgess from the downstream market. The elimination of one of only two competitors on a market where the dominant undertaking had a market share of over 75 per cent and there were barriers to entry would have the likely effect of, at the very least, weakening effective competition.[155] The Tribunal, however, did not stop here but went on to consider that the elimination of Burgess would strengthen Austins' downstream dominant position.[156] Finally, the Tribunal held that significant consumer detriment was shown because there was demand for the services of Burgess and the refusal to supply deprived consumers of a choice they valued.[157]

Although it did not uphold the OFT's test, the CAT did not interpret the EU case law as requiring only the termination of an established supply contract with a customer which abides by normal commercial practices and the absence of objective justification as sufficient elements to find that the practice under review was abusive. The CAT applied a test which required, at the very least, the likely elimination of a competitor resulting in the weakening of competition and the strengthening of the dominant undertaking's market power on a market (in this case, importantly, in a downstream market other than that in which the abuse was committed) and significant consumer detriment. What the CAT did not accept was that a competition authority or a court could set a threshold below which the elimination of a competitor leading to consumer harm would not be an abuse because sufficient competitive constraints still existed on the market.[158] This conclusion is correct in policy terms because to hold otherwise would be to open the door to arbitrariness in decision-making with a potential significant risk of false negatives.

---

[154] For a summary of the legal principles applied by the CAT, see Whish, *Competition Law*, p 701.

[155] *Burgess* v *OFT*, paras 317–319.

[156] *Burgess* v *OFT*, paras 317 and 319.

[157] *Ibid*, paras 320–321. The *Burgess* case has cast doubt on the earlier, somewhat puzzling, *Du Pont* decision, discussed above in this section.

[158] *Burgess* v *OFT*, paras 330–336.

2.3 Likely foreclosure effects

If *per se* infringement rules are not favoured, which tests has the OFT applied in practice? The test most frequently applied by the OFT seems to be the likely foreclosure of an as efficient competitor, a test explicitly adopted in margin squeeze cases by both the Court of First Instance[159] and the English Court of Appeal.[160] This test is, however, by no means limited to margin squeeze.

Starting with predation, the test which the OFT has applied more frequently is whether the dominant undertaking's conduct deviates from normal competition[161] and is likely to exclude an equally efficient rival. To determine whether the dominant undertaking deviated from what constitutes normal competition, the OFT considers two elements: (a) whether the undertaking incurred losses;[162] and (b) whether there is evidence of a plan to eliminate a competitor. Likely foreclosure effects are then determined with regard both to actual competition (the exclusion or marginalisation of the prey) and potential competition (the entry-deterring effect of an established reputation for predation). Given that the profitability analysis is carried out based on the costs and revenues of the dominant undertaking, the likely foreclosure effect relates to a competitor that is at least as efficient as the dominant undertaking.

---

[159] *Deutsche Telekom AG* v *Commission* (Case T–271/03) [2008] II-477, paras 186–193, upheld on appeal in *Deutsche Telekom AG* v *Commission* (Case C–280/08P) [2008] OJ C223/31.

[160] *Albion Water Ltd* v *Water Services Regulation Authority (formerly Director General of Water Services)* [2008] EWCA Civ 536, [2008] BusLR 1655, para 105.

[161] By conduct which deviates from normal competition, the OFT means conduct which would not be profitable absent exclusion: see *BSkyB*, para 591 and *Cardiff Bus*, para 7.10. This concept of "normal competition" has its origin in the "profit sacrifice" and the "no economic sense" tests which have been put forward in the literature as tests for the lawfulness of unilateral conduct in competition law: see Bork, *The Antitrust Paradox*, p 144; Werden, "Identifying Single-Firm Exclusionary Conduct: From Vague Concepts to Administrable Rules" (n 116 above), 509; Werden, "Identifying Exclusionary Conduct under Section 2: The 'No Economic Sense' Test" (n 116 above), 413. For a strong criticism of the profit sacrifice standard, see Salop, "Exclusionary Conduct, Effect on Consumers, and the Flawed Profit-Sacrifice Standard" (n 116 above), 311. As explained in the text, the OFT does not rely on the profit sacrifice or the no economic sense standard as self-standing tests for abuse but as guiding principles to determine whether the conduct under review constitutes normal competition. If it does not, a further test must be applied for an abuse to be established (generally whether the conduct in question is likely either to exclude an equally efficient competitor or to cause consumer harm).

[162] The profitability analysis in predation cases is not a straightforward matter. The CAT was trenchant in its criticism of the OFT in *Claymore Dairies Ltd* v *Office of Fair Trading* [2005] CAT 30, an appeal against a non-infringement decision relating to alleged predation in the milk industry in Scotland.

In *Napp*, the DGFT did not confine himself to an analysis of Napp's prices, which were selectively below average variable costs, but examined the foreclosure effect of the practice. The effect was an actual effect insofar as there was evidence that a competitor (BIL) had exited the market as a consequence of Napp's behaviour.[163] However, the DGFT also considered the likely foreclosure effect of Napp's behaviour on other competitors[164] and potential entrants.[165] On appeal, the CAT found that "the overwhelming inference from the totality of the evidence is that Napp's prices in the community segment, and its market shares in both the hospital and community segments, have been protected, at least in part, by the foreclosure effects of Napp's hospital discount policy".[166] This appears to be a finding of actual effects. On the other hand, the Tribunal did not find it necessary to decide whether BIL had left the market as a result of Napp's conduct but found Napp "to have effectively, albeit indirectly or potentially, foreclosed the community segment of the market as a whole by blocking, to a substantial extent, the only viable point of entry".[167] These apparently conflicting statements of the Tribunal and the use of the adverbs "effectively" and "potentially" in the same sentence can only be explained if what the Tribunal had in mind was that a likely foreclosure effect would be sufficient although probably on the facts actual foreclosure was established.

In *Aberdeen Journals II*, the DGFT found that the dominant undertaking's conduct consisted in pricing below average variable costs and resulted in losses[168] with the intention of expelling the only competitor from the market.[169] The decision went on to find that the conduct in question had a threefold harmful effect: (a) it had a direct effect on the business interests of Aberdeen Journal's only competitor;[170] (b) it raised a barrier to entry to the market;[171] and (c) it could establish a reputation for predation which deterred entry to the other markets where the parent companies of Aberdeen Journals were present.[172] While the effect on the rival and the raising of a strategic entry barrier

---

[163] *Napp*, paras 159, 168, and 173–175.

[164] *Ibid*, para 168, where the DGFT found, on the evidence, that "there is a risk that Napp's discount policy will have the effect of eliminating competition altogether".

[165] *Ibid*, para 168.

[166] *Napp* v *DGFT*, para 287.

[167] *Ibid*, para 283.

[168] *Aberdeen Journals II*, paras 155–180.

[169] *Ibid*, paras 181–183.

[170] *Ibid*, para 210.

[171] *Ibid*, para 210.

[172] *Ibid*, para 211.

to the relevant market were actual effects, the erecting of a reputational entry barrier in other markets was a likely effect.[173]

In *First Edinburgh/Lothian*, First Edinburgh's prices below average variable costs were a form of normal competition. Furthermore, Lothian, the alleged prey, had been profitable throughout and there was no risk of First Edinburgh forcing Lothian out of the market or weakening it as a rival.[174] The conduct under review did not deviate from what constitutes normal competition and was not likely to eliminate a competitor.

In *Cardiff Bus*, the OFT clarified that whether the dominant undertaking resorted to methods other than "normal" competition[175] must be assessed *ex ante* and not *ex post*. In that case, a new entrant, 2 Travel, launched a new, no-frills service on selected bus routes in the Cardiff area. The incumbent bus operator reacted by introducing its own, loss-making, no-frills services during the same periods of the day and on the same routes as 2 Travel's services. The incumbent's no-frills service was withdrawn as soon as the rival exited the market.[176] Cardiff Bus claimed that it had introduced the no-frills services – in reaction to 2 Travel's entry – with the intention of market testing the no-frills concept and that its decision to withdraw the no-frills services was taken on the basis of an unexpected lack of customer demand, as well as driver shortages. Particularly in industries with high fixed costs or when new products or services are launched, profitability depends not as much on the unit price charged but on overall actual demand. Should the cost/revenue element of the predation test – however formulated or defined – be satisfied whenever the dominant undertaking is found to have incurred losses *ex post*, or should the rationality of the practice under review – and its likely exclusionary effect – be assessed *ex ante*, that is, at the time when the business decisions were made?

The OFT held that, in principle, the rationality of the dominant undertaking's behaviour should be judged on the basis of the facts as they would have appeared to the dominant undertaking at the time when the relevant business decision was made.[177] In other

[173] The DGFT made these findings in the context of the analysis of the conduct's effect on trade within the United Kingdom. The legal test relied on the presumption of predation when prices are below average variable costs and on the absence of objective justification. From the overall decision, however, it is possible to say that the theory of harm relied on by the DGFT was that the predation had an actual or likely foreclosure effect. This approach was endorsed by the CAT on appeal in *Aberdeen Journals* v *OFT*.

[174] *First Edinburgh/Lothian*, paras 76–79.

[175] *Cardiff Bus*, para 7.15.

[176] *Ibid*, para 7.4.

[177] *Ibid*, para 7.23.

words, the normal competition test must be applied *ex ante* and not *ex post*. However, on the facts, Cardiff Bus provided no convincing contemporaneous evidence to support its claim that its no-frills services were introduced to test market demand for such services.[178] On the contrary, the OFT identified evidence that rebutted Cardiff Bus's explanation that it was conducting a market test. This included evidence that Cardiff Bus planned to launch its no-frills services not as a true market testing exercise, but in order to divert potential customers away from 2 Travel. For instance, Cardiff Bus avoided advertising and promoting its new no-frills services, which was at odds with a genuine market testing exercise.[179] Furthermore, there was evidence that the losses were incurred with the intention of forcing the rival out of the market, thus protecting Cardiff Bus's existing dominant position.[180] Finally, the very fact that the continuing operation of the services was loss-making was considered to be inconsistent with Cardiff Bus's market test argument.[181]

In the same decision, while stating that for an abuse to be established the case law of the EU Courts only requires that the conduct under review carried the risk of eliminating competition,[182] the OFT went on to examine the likely effects of Cardiff Bus's predatory conduct on actual competition (that is, on the prey)[183] and on potential competition (by establishing a reputation for predation thus raising a barrier to entry to the market).[184]

The approach in predation cases is consistent with the test adopted in margin squeeze cases. In *BSkyB* the DGFT applied an as efficient competitor test to assess whether the dominant undertaking was engaging in abusive margin squeeze. The test was whether the margin between the price BSkyB charged its downstream rivals and BSkyB's own retail prices was sufficient at least to cover BSkyB's

---

[178] *Cardiff Bus*, paras 7.58–7.74.

[179] *Ibid*, paras 7.76–7.85.

[180] *Ibid*, para 7.225. Evidence of exclusionary intent included such circumstantial evidence as the fact that the no-frills services were launched at or around the same time, and on the same routes, as 2 Travel's no-frills bus services (*ibid*, paras 7.103–7.121) and were withdrawn when 2 Travel exited and as a consequence thereof (*ibid*, paras 7.137–7.149). To put it another way, targeting and selectivity were held to be relevant evidence of exclusionary intent. Further evidence included the substantial preparations made by Cardiff Bus to respond aggressively to 2 Travel's entry (*ibid*, paras 7.88–7.102), and ongoing assessment by Cardiff Bus of the threat posed by 2 Travel (*ibid*, paras 7.131–7.136).

[181] *Ibid*, para 7.87. The OFT thus applied an *ex ante* approach but subjected the dominant undertaking's claims to careful scrutiny. This line of reasoning demonstrates the acute awareness on the part of the OFT of the need to balance the risk of false positives and false negatives in its enforcement policy.

[182] *Ibid*, para 7.229.

[183] *Ibid*, paras 7.231–7.240.

[184] *Ibid*, paras 7.241–7.243.

own costs of transformation.[185] It mattered not whether BSkyB's rivals were more efficient, which would, as BSkyB argued, allow the latter to charge them a higher price,[186] or less efficient, which would mean that their inability to compete effectively was not, or not only, the result of BSkyB's alleged abuse. If BSkyB's prices would allow an equally efficient competition to earn a normal profit, then downstream competition is not distorted.[187] The methodology applied was to allocate costs to the distribution arm of BSkyB (DisCo) and to compare historical revenues with historical costs in periods of 6 months taking into account the appropriate return on turnover. On the facts, the DGFT found that there was no margin squeeze because, over an overall period of 22 months, the results showed only limited temporary losses.[188] This methodology is consistent with a test of likely foreclosure of an as efficient competitor.

In *Companies House*, the OFT found no infringement of the Chapter II prohibition by the application of a margin squeeze because the prices charged by the dominant undertaking to downstream rivals would have allowed a competitor as efficient as the downstream arm of the dominant firm to earn a reasonable rate of return. Although not explicitly adopting an as efficient competitor test,[189] such a test is implicit in the methodology applied.[190] This methodology is consistent with a standard requiring likely foreclosure of an as efficient competitor.

In *Genzyme*, the dominant undertaking supplied a drug for the treatment of a rare disease called Gaucher disease. Prior to 5 May 2001, HealthCare at Home (HH) had been Genzyme's distributor. Under the agreement, HH bought the drug at full list price and resold it to hospitals at a discounted price (the concessionary price) and to the community at the full list price, which included the price of home delivery and home care service. Genzyme paid HH different unit fees for units sold to the hospitals and to the community and a management fee.[191] On 5 May 2001, Genzyme terminated the distributorship agreement and launched its own home delivery and home care service. As before, it charged the NHS a price which included the price of the drug and the price for home delivery and home care services in the community (the NHS price). Genzyme was

---

185 *BSkyB*, para 370.

186 *Ibid*, paras 360–362.

187 *Ibid*, paras 352–370.

188 *Ibid*, paras 541–547.

189 *Companies House*, para 29, setting out as a benchmark "an efficient firm" and not a firm as efficient as the dominant undertaking. See also *TM Property Services Ltd*, para 130.

190 *Companies House*, para 33.

191 *Genzyme*, paras 110–114.

only prepared to supply the drug to HH at the NHS price plus VAT thus denying HH any margin. It also refused to allow hospitals to sell on the drug, bought at the cheaper concessionary hospital price, to HH.[192] The DGFT characterised this abuse as a margin squeeze[193] and stated the test as including the exclusion of "reasonably efficient competitors".[194] However, on the facts, the issue whether the downstream competitor was as efficient or reasonably efficient did not arise as a zero margin would clearly exclude all competitors, at least as long as only price competition is taken into account. The OFT found that the effect of the behaviour was to eliminate all competition in the downstream market and to raise a barrier to entry to the upstream market.[195] Genzyme engaged in this conduct with the intention of monopolising the downstream market.[196]

The CAT upheld the finding of margin squeeze.[197] It held that the bundling of the price of the drug and the price of home delivery and homecare services facilitated the margin squeeze although it was not a standalone abuse.[198] As regards the effect on competition, the CAT held that the effect of foreclosing the downstream market was sufficient to establish the margin squeeze abuse.[199] As to whether proof of likely or actual foreclosure effects was required, on the facts it was clear that the only downstream rival was sustaining losses pending the proceedings and was likely to exit the market should the margin squeeze not cease. It appears, therefore, that the likely elimination of the (only) competitor was held to be sufficient.[200]

In *Claymore Dairies Ltd* v *OFT*, the CAT suggested that the likely exclusion of an equally efficient competitor was relevant to the assessment of *de facto* exclusive contracts.[201] Finally, as explained above, in *BSkyB*, the only occasion on which the OFT had to consider rebates, the DGFT applied a test of likely foreclosure of an as efficient competitor to the assessment of bundled discounts.[202]

---

[192] *Genzyme*, paras 115–120.

[193] *Ibid*, paras 364–381.

[194] *Ibid*, para 364.

[195] *Ibid*, para 382. On the theory of harm of foreclosure of the upstream market, see the discussion of Genzyme's alleged bundling abuse above.

[196] *Ibid*, para 378.

[197] *Genzyme* v *OFT*, paras 549–555.

[198] *Ibid*, para 561.

[199] *Ibid*, para 625.

[200] *Ibid*, para 562, where the CAT said that "the effect of the margin squeeze is potentially to eliminate Healthcare at Home and other providers from the supply of Homecare Services to Gaucher patients".

[201] *Claymore Dairies* v *OFT*, para 295.

[202] *BSkyB*, para 639.

2.4 The problem of actual foreclosure effects

Are likely foreclosure effects sufficient to find an abuse or must actual effects be established,[203] at least when the infringement has terminated or has been continuing for a long enough period for actual effects to occur? In *Consignia plc and Postal Preference Service Ltd*,[204] the granting by Consignia to a consumer lifestyle survey company of an exclusive licence of the Royal Mail trademark was held to be capable of infringing the Chapter II prohibition if it foreclosed rivals on the UK consumer lifestyle survey market.[205] However, the decision found that there had been no infringement because there was no evidence of actual foreclosure.[206] It appears that the investigative approach adopted in the case was to obtain evidence of the current impact of the exclusivity and the views of the downstream customers. The analysis of the evidence led to the conclusion that there was no competition problem on the market, but it is not possible to infer from this case that actual foreclosure effects were held to be necessary in law for an abuse to be established.

In *ANL*,[207] a commitments decision, the competition concerns related to actual foreclosure arising out of exclusive agreements preventing a new entrant to the market from taking advantage of a key distribution channel.[208] The agreements had already been in place for more than 5 years[209] and the complainant alleged that it intended

---

203 The case law of the EU Courts appears to support the proposition that likely effects are generally sufficient: *Compagnie Maritime Belge Transports SA* v *Commission* (Joined Cases T–24, T–26 & 28/93) [1996] ECR II–1201, para 149, upheld on appeal in *Compagnie Maritime Belge Transports SA* v *Commission* (Joined Cases C–395 & 396/96P) [2000] ECR I-1365 (however, note that the point in question did not arise in the appeal); *British Airways* v *Commission* (Case T–219/99), paras 293, 297 and 298 and *British Airways* v *Commission* (Case C–95/04P), paras 96–102 (however, at para 101 the Court of Justice declared inadmissible the ground of appeal relating to the relevance of evidence of lack of actual effects); *Microsoft Corp* v *Commission* (Case T–201/04) [2007] ECR II–3601, paras 560–562 (where a test falling short of actual effects was justified from an enforcement perspective given the need to intervene before harmful effects occur).

204 Decision of the Director General of Fair Trading no CA98/4/2001, 15 June 2001, *Consignia plc and Postal Preference Service Ltd* (Case CP/0155–01) (*Consignia*). An interim injunction application was rejected by Lawrence Collins J in *Claritas (UK) Ltd* v *The Post Office* [2001] UKCLR 2.

205 This possible theory of harm is set out in *Consignia*, paras 18–22.

206 *Ibid*, paras 28–43. This aspect of the case has been criticised for setting too high a threshold for an abuse to be established: B Rodger, "Early steps to a mature competition law system: case law developments in the first 18 months of the Competition Act 1998" [2002] ECLR 52, 61.

207 Decision of the Office of Fair Trading no CA98/02/2006, *London-wide newspaper distribution*, 1 March 2006 (Case CE/2479/03) (*ANL*).

208 *Ibid*, para 24.

209 *Ibid*, para 26.

to enter the market but could not do so.[210] While actual foreclosure effects were sufficient to constitute a competition concern, this case is not a precedent for the proposition that actual effects are required for an abuse to be established.

In *Genzyme*, the dominant undertaking included in the price of its drug Cerezyme the price of homecare services. Up until 5 May 2001, Genzyme supplied HH with Cerezyme, thus allowing HH to provide home delivery and homecare services to the community. However, Genzyme's price for the drug included the price of home delivery and homecare services, for which HH was remunerated separately under its contract with Genzyme. Therefore, the NHS could not have used any other provider of home delivery and homecare services because the bundled price meant that it would have been charged twice for the price of the drug.[211] Before the CAT, this abuse was not upheld because: (a) there was no evidence that the NHS sought an alternative provider to HH or that any other homecare services provider sought to obtain Cerezyme from Genzyme on discounted terms or otherwise; (b) the NHS knew of, and acquiesced in, Genzyme's practice of including homecare services in the NHS list price of Cerezyme; (c) it was not shown that Genzyme acted contrary to any aspect of the NHS system in including homecare services in the NHS list price for Cerezyme; and (d) it was not obvious how Genzyme would have been remunerated for the supply of homecare services had it "unbundled" the list price of Cerezyme, other than by virtue of a separate contract with the NHS but the NHS never sought or suggested any such separate contract.[212] Therefore, the Tribunal ruled that "the effect on competition of Genzyme's 'bundling practice' in the period March 2000 to May 2001, although theoretically established, was not proved to have had a sufficient adverse effect on competition, in the particular circumstances of this case, to be characterised as an abuse for the purposes of the application of the Chapter II prohibition".[213] While the CAT clearly ruled that there were no actual foreclosure effects, it is unclear whether *Genzyme* v *OFT* establishes that, when the abuse has ended, actual foreclosure must be shown. A possible reading of the judgment is that not any practice which is theoretically capable of having foreclosure effects is an abuse. In *Genzyme*, not only did the practice not have actual effects but, on the same facts, it appears that no foreclosure effect was likely given that the NHS did not wish to use alternative

---

[210] *ANL*, para 1.
[211] *Genzyme*, para 308.
[212] *Genzyme* v *OFT*, paras 527–548.
[213] *Ibid*, para 548.

providers and, in any event, there were no alternative providers wishing to enter the market.

The only case so far in which the DGFT appears to have required both conduct deviating from normal competition and actual foreclosure is *BSkyB*. In that case, the DGFT considered an allegedly abusive mixed bundling.[214] The different combinations of channels offered by BSkyB at different prices were such that the incremental price of the sports premium channels or the films premium channels depended on which other channels were being bought by the distributor. For instance, in 2001, the price for Sky Premier was £12.55 and the price for Single sports was £12.05 but the price of Sky Premier and Single sports bought as a package (a bundle) was £14.56. The implied incremental price of a single sports channel was £2.01 and the implied incremental price of Sky Premier was £2.51.[215] The complainants alleged that this pricing structure foreclosed competition. To put it simply, the argument was that a new entrant would not be able to offer the full range of BSkyB's channels. Customers would, therefore, buy BSkyB's packages and, potentially, a new entrant's premium channel. As a consequence, a new entrant's premium channel would have to be priced at or below the implied incremental price of BSkyB's premium channel in order to be competitive. Given that such a price would not allow the new entrant to be viable, entry was foreclosed.[216] The DGFT started from the idea of "normal competition", derived from the *Hoffmann-La Roche* case law.[217] Consistently with the predation analysis, the key principle was said to be whether, absent any entry deterrence, the mixed bundling represented a clear deviation from a profit maximising strategy. A Chapter II infringement would be established if, absent objective justification, the implied incremental price of a channel was below the incremental avoidable cost of supplying that channel to an additional subscriber "together with evidence of foreclosure".[218] When setting out the test, the decision did not specify whether likely or actual foreclosure was required. On the facts, the incremental price of the bundle was below the incremental avoidable cost of supplying the channel in question only in one instance but, in that instance, there was no sufficient evidence that BSkyB's mixed bundling "has, in fact, foreclosed entry".[219] A relevant factor which

[214] For an economist's commentary on this aspect of the case, see A Majumdar, "Mixed Bundling, Economic Analyis and BSkyB" [2003] Comp Law 135.

[215] *BSkyB*, paras 550–553.

[216] *Ibid*, paras 556–561.

[217] *Hoffmann-La Roche* v *Commission*, para 91.

[218] *BSkyB*, para 592.

[219] *Ibid*, paras 594–600.

may have led to the application of the higher threshold of actual foreclosure was that the provision of BSkyB premium channels was characterised by very high fixed and common costs, but very low marginal costs, and BSkyB was selling into a market with varied but unknown consumer preferences.[220] Therefore, mixed bundling was in principle an efficient way of recovering fixed costs and consistent with normal competitive behaviour.[221] Another possible reading of this case is that lack of actual foreclosure effects *ex post* demonstrates that foreclosure was not likely *ex ante* although it was theoretically possible.

2.5 Consumer harm

In some cases, the OFT and the CAT have gone further than the test of likely or actual foreclosure. They have identified the negative effect of the practice under review on price and output, which could be properly defined as a consumer harm test.[222]

Recoupment

In *Napp*, Napp's exclusionary conduct in the hospital segment of the market allowed it to charge excessive prices in the community segment.[223] The CCAT categorised Napp's ability to charge excessive prices in the community sector as a form of "recoupment".[224] The link between the exclusionary behaviour in the hospital segment and the simultaneous recoupment in the community segment was, however, not part of the legal test. In the CCAT, the DGFT argued

---

[220] *BSkyB*, para 568; *BSkyB s 47 decision*, para 179.

[221] *Ibid*, paras 568–576 and 589–592; *BSkyB s 47 decision*, paras 179–184, 192–201 and 206–209.

[222] For the purpose of this chapter, consumer harm denotes any harmful effects on the customers of the dominant undertaking, including lower output, higher prices, lower quality, less innovation, or less choice. On the broad definition of "consumer detriment" in the current practice, see P Marsden and P Whelan, "'Consumer Detriment' and its Application in EC and UK Competition Law" [2006] ECLR 569.

[223] *Napp*, paras 142–143. In fact, at the time of the decision, a commentator rightly noted that "it may seem somewhat unusual for a decision that appears in essence to be about discriminatory pricing to refer so centrally to excessive and predatory pricing" (M Furse, "Caught napping: DGFT and Napp Pharmaceutical Holdings Ltd" [2001] ECLR 477, 479). As the same commentator acknowledged, this approach was consistent with the guideline on *Assessment of Individual Agreements and Conduct* then in force (*ibid*, also for the quotation from the guideline in question). This approach would also be consistent with the draft guideline on *Assessment of conduct*, paras 3.4–3.5. In other words, by a conscious policy choice, the OFT regards price discrimination as abusive on a case-by-case basis focusing on whether it is exclusionary or exploitative (or it has both effects, as in *Napp*). This approach may not be easy to reconcile with certain precedents of the EU Courts: M Furse, "Monopoly price discrimination, Article 82 and the Competition Act" [2001] ECLR, 149, 154–155.

[224] *Napp v DGFT*, paras 261 and 299.

that the excessive pricing abuse was not self-standing, but depended upon Napp's exclusionary conduct in the hospital segment which enabled Napp to charge excessive prices in the community segment.[225] However, the CCAT did not construe this argument as meaning that excessive pricing could only be abusive if it was made possible by the dominant undertaking's exclusionary behaviour, holding that such a contention would have been wrong in law.[226] Therefore the Tribunal did not comment further on the legal or policy significance on the link between the exclusionary and the exploitative abuse but went on to hold that the abuse of excessive pricing was established on the facts.[227]

Simultaneous recoupment must be distinguished from loss-leading, which is a strategy of incurring losses on some products in order to obtain higher revenues from the sale of complementary products. Loss-leading is not a deviation from normal competition. In *TM Property Services Ltd*, the OFT held that loss-leading objectively justified prices below average variable costs in circumstances in which the practice was open to the other competitors and total revenues exceeded total costs. It was material that the OFT found no intention to eliminate a competitor.[228] In *Napp* v *DGFT*, the CCAT considered whether Napp's behaviour was objectively justified because the revenue generated by each loss-making sale in the hospital segment was the revenue of the sale in question plus the revenue of additional sales in the more lucrative community segment ("net revenue test").[229] Upholding the DGFT decision, the CCAT rejected this argument because of three conceptual weaknesses: (a) the net revenue test did not distinguish between legitimate competition and abuse of dominance – abusive conduct may be profitable when forgone profits are recouped in another sector or at a later time;[230] (b) the hospital and community segments were not part of a system price as it was not possible to evaluate system costs;[231] (c) the test did not take account of the overall competitive significance and effect of Napp's behaviour on competition.[232] In reality, Napp's discounting practice in the hospital

[225] *Napp* v *DGFT*, paras 364–365.
[226] *Ibid*, para 434.
[227] *Ibid*, para 429.
[228] *TM Property Services Ltd*, para 128. However, note that, because of the finding of absence of dominance in this case, the OFT did not reach a concluded view on the abuse (para 129).
[229] *Napp* v *DGFT*, para 229.
[230] *Ibid*, paras 259–262.
[231] *Ibid*, paras 263–264. A system price is the price of complementary products supplied by the same undertaking (eg razors and razor blades) whereby the price of one product will be set taking account of the demand for the other.
[232] *Ibid*, paras 265–266.

segment raised a further barrier to entry to the market with the effect of protecting its market power.[233] It was not open to competitors to recoup any losses incurred in the hospital segment by charging higher prices in the community segment as the linkages between the two segments available to Napp were not equally available to other market players due to a number of factors including asymmetry of market shares, profit flows, promotional activity requirements, switching costs, and price levels in the community segment.[234] The fact that Napp intentionally adopted its pricing policy in order to foreclose the market reinforced the finding of abuse although eliminatory intention was not required as a matter of law.[235]

In *Aberdeen Journals* v *OFT*, the CAT upheld the DGFT's analysis, which relied on likely foreclosure effects. The CAT stated that the law did not require proof of the possibility of recoupment whenever there is a risk that competitors will be eliminated.[236] However, the Tribunal added that predatory pricing may be a rational policy for a dominant undertaking when it is pursued in one sector in order to protect profits and market share in another sector and that this is a form of recoupment.[237] On the facts, the dominant undertaking was incurring losses on one newspaper in order to protect profits on another. The DGFT would not be expected to provide "any further evidence of 'recoupment' in order to prove an abuse of a dominant position".[238] Why would the Tribunal make these comments if recoupment is not part of the legal test? A possible answer may be that, as in *Napp* v *DGFT*, the Tribunal was setting forth a theory of harm, a plausible explanation as to why, on the facts, the conduct under review had a negative effect on price and output.

The *Aberdeen Journals* v *OFT* understanding of recoupment, which is wider than increased post-predation prices and includes the protection of existing market power, was applied in *LME (Interim Measures)*. In that case, the London Metal Exchange argued that, as a not-for-profit organisation, it had no incentive to raise the price of its services post-predation. The OFT held that the predation could still protect an entrenched dominant position thus leading to inefficiency.[239]

---

233 *Napp* v *DGFT*, paras 267–288.

234 *Ibid*, paras 291 and 229.

235 *Ibid*, paras 307–333.

236 *Aberdeen Journals* v *OFT*, para 443.

237 *Ibid*, para 445.

238 *Ibid*.

239 Direction given pursuant to Section 35 of the Competition Act 1998, *London Metal Exchange*, 27 February 2006: *LME(Interim Measures)*, para 39. The direction was then withdrawn and investigation was later closed due to the small value of the market and the lack of customer concern: see (CE/4478–04) *Complaint against the London Metal*

In *Cardiff Bus*, the OFT for the first time addressed the issue of second-phase recoupment. However, it adopted the approach of the CAT in *Aberdeen Journals* v *OFT* by making clear that the case law did not require proof of recoupment.[240] It then set out the circumstances that rendered "plausible the possibility of recoupment"[241] as a way of putting forward a theory of harm which was, nonetheless, not part of the legal test. Consistently with the CAT judgment in the *Aberdeen Journals* case and with the OFT decision in *LME (Interim Measures)*, recoupment is defined widely to include a price increase above the levels prevailing before the predation, or as the avoidance or postponement of a price decrease that would have occurred as a result of competitive pressure from the rival that was the target of the predatory conduct, or, finally, as the establishment of a reputation for predation that deters future entry.[242] On the facts, the OFT relied on a the analysis of entry barriers[243] and post-exit price levels, including a 40 per cent price increase, to conclude that "Cardiff Bus may therefore have benefited by being able to continue to behave to a greater extent independently of any effective competitive constraint on its behaviour".[244]

Finally, although not a form of recoupment in the strict sense, it will be recalled that the CAT in *Burgess* held that the refusal to supply would result in an increase of Austins' downstream market power.[245]

Consumer choice

Some cases make reference to the impact of the dominant undertaking's behaviour on consumer choice although not necessarily as part of the legal test. In *Burgess*, the CAT held that the refusal to supply deprived consumers of a choice they valued.[246] Significantly, the CAT considered whether there was demand for the services of Burgess[247] and, probably, considered consumer

---

Exchange (LME) by Spectron plc, case closure decision, April 2007, <http://www.oft.gov.uk/advice_and_resources/resource_base/ca98/closure/LME> (accessed on 17 June 2009).

240 *Cardiff Bus*, paras 7.229 and 7.247–7.251.

241 *Ibid*, para 7.252.

242 *Ibid*, para 7.253.

243 *Ibid*, para 7.254.

244 *Ibid*, para 7.257.

245 *Burgess* v *OFT*, para 317.

246 Allan, "The Control of Dominant Firms in the UK: The Jurisprudence of the CAT" (n 117 above), 275 rightly points out that *Burgess* v *OFT* is not an example of the Chapter II prohibition being applied to protect a competitor. Rather, the CAT was concerned with the protection of the competitive process and consumer choice.

247 *Burgess* v *OFT*, paras 320–321.

detriment as an element of the legal test.[248] In the same vein, in *Genzyme*, the DGFT held that the bundling abuse deprived the NHS of the choice of home delivery and homecare provider.[249] The CAT did not disagree in theory but found that the NHS never sought an alternative provider,[250] nor did any alternative provider try to enter the market in the relevant period.[251] In *Cardiff Bus*, the OFT held that the conduct under review reduced consumer choice by pre-empting the emergence of a new service (no-frills bus services).[252] However, the OFT made clear that it did not regard the reduction of consumer choice as part of the legal test.[253]

2.6 Non self-correcting excessively high or excessively low prices

Excessively high prices

In *Napp*, the DGFT held that the prices charged by Napp in the community market segment were excessive. The excessive pricing test in the decision was that a price is excessive and abusive if: (a) the price is above that which would exist in a competitive market; and (b) it is clear that high profits will not stimulate successful new entry within a reasonable period.[254] The second limb of the test did not receive as much attention in the decision as the first. However, it is the more important.[255] The following elements pointed to the unlikelihood that high profits would stimulate new entry within a reasonable period: (a) unlike prices in the hospital segment where Napp's drug MST had been subject to competition, the price of MST in the community segment had not fallen since the expiry of Napp's patent in 1992. Instead, Napp had maintained excessively high margins on the sale of MST in the community segment of the market without effective competition from successful new entry;[256] (b) the high prices in the community segment were made possible, at least in part, by Napp's

---

[248] *Burgess* v *OFT*, paras 311(1) and (2), 320, 323, 330. But see para 327, where the CAT seems to suggest that the possibility of elimination of all competition in a neighbouring market would be sufficient to establish an abuse as a matter of law. On the facts, however, not all competition would have been eliminated as at least one other significant competitor would have stayed on the market even if Burgess had exited.

[249] *Genzyme*, para 308.

[250] See, for the summary of the Tribunal's conclusions, *Genzyme* v *OFT*, para 547.

[251] *Genzyme* v *OFT*, para 547.

[252] *Cardiff Bus*, para 7.246.

[253] *Ibid*, para 7.229.

[254] *Napp*, para 203.

[255] The same test was applied, but with a different formulation, in *TM Property Services Ltd*, para 138. In that case the OFT found that there was probably no abuse although it did not reach a final view on the issue (see paras 139–146).

[256] *Napp*, para 232.

exclusionary conduct in the hospital segment;[257] (c) taking account of the fact that MST enjoyed patent protection from 1980 to 1992, Napp had considerable time and opportunity to recoup its initial investment and compensate it for the risk it had taken; and (d) Napp's advertising costs were relatively low.[258] The CCAT held that the excessive pricing test in the decision was a permissible approach. By saying so, it endorsed both elements of the test, including the circumstance that high profits will not stimulate successful new entry within a reasonable period.[259]

Excessively low prices

In *BetterCare II*,[260] the OFT considered that excessively low prices by a dominant buyer may constitute an abuse only in exceptional circumstances.[261] The rationale for the test mirrors the excessive pricing test adopted in *Napp*. In the absence of barriers to exit by suppliers from the relevant market, a purchaser which paid excessively low prices would be unable to obtain supply beyond the short term even if it was a monopsonist. Excessively low purchase prices will normally be self-correcting and would not, absent price discrimination, usually justify action under Chapter II of the Competition Act 1998 or under Art 102 TFEU. What might amount to exceptional circumstances was not clarified. However, it is suggested that the presence of barriers to exit is crucial as it provides the monopsonist with the ability and the incentive to exploit its market power. The reference to price discrimination is also left unclear, but it is likely to denote exclusionary price discrimination.[262]

---

257 *Napp*, para 232.

258 *Ibid*, para 233.

259 *Napp* v *DGFT*, para 391.

260 Decision of the Office of Fair Trading no CA98/09/2003, *BetterCare Group Ltd/North & West Belfast Health & Social Services Trust* (Remitted case), 18 December 2003 (Case no CE/1836–02) (*BetterCare II*). The previous decision (Notice of decision of Director General of Fair Trading, CA/98/11/2002, *The North & West Belfast Health and Social Services Trust*, 30 April 2002 (CP/0829–01)) and the judgments of the CAT (*BetterCare Group Ltd* v *Director General of Fair Trading* [2002] CAT 6 and *BetterCare Group Ltd* v *Director General of Fair Trading* [2002] CAT 7) did not deal with either dominance or abuse. For a commentary on the 2002 judgment, see J Holmes, "Bettercare Group Ltd v The Director General of Fair Trading" [2002] Comp Law 109 and K Currie and C Bright, "Is Bettercare a bitter pill" [2003] ECLR 41.

261 *BetterCare II*, para 56. On the abuse of excessively low prices, see also Decision of the Director General of Fair Trading no CA98/19/2002, *The Association of British Travel Agents and British Airways plc*, 11 December 2002 (Case CE/1471–02) (*The Association of British Travel Agents and British Airways plc*). On this latter case, see G Murphy, "BA's reduction of booking payments to travel agents not abusive behaviour, says OFT" [2003] ECLR 411.

262 *BetterCare II*, para 59, where it is stated that price discrimination can be abusive where there is evidence that prices were excessive or where it is used to exclude competitors. In other words, mere price discrimination without more is not an abuse.

3 CONCLUSIONS

This chapter examined the policy and practice of the OFT in the enforcement of the Chapter II prohibition and Art 102 TFEU. The focus on the OFT and any judgments on appeals against OFT decisions allowed for a discussion of how a stated welfare-based policy could be implemented in a legal environment which, through s 60 of the Competition Act 1998 and general EU law principles, retains major elements of a structuralist approach. The introduction to this chapter set out some broader policy questions. The answers to them flow naturally from the above analysis but an attempt will be made here to summarise them briefly.

First, which approach has the OFT applied in practice? The OFT has, quite robustly and consistently, applied welfare-based tests both to the assessment of dominance and to the examination of the abuse. As regards dominance, in no case has the OFT relied exclusively on market shares for a finding of dominance even when the undertaking in question was close to having a 100 per cent share of supply; a welfare-based concept of barriers to entry has been adopted whereby the focus is not simply on ease of entry but on the welfare effects of entry-related factors; and, finally, dominance has been an integral part of the assessment of the abuse. As regards abuse, the OFT has rejected the concept of per se infringement rules. Instead, it has focused on foreclosure analysis, and particularly on the likely foreclosure of an equally efficient competitor. In some cases, the analysis was taken further and the OFT assessed the likely consumer harm resulting from the conduct under review although often as part of the articulation of a theory of harm beyond the scope of the legal test.

Second, is the welfare-based approach adopted by the OFT administrable? The answer appears to be in the affirmative. The CAT has endorsed the OFT approach through its thorough, on the merits appeal process. No infringement decision in this area has been ultimately set aside in full, yet, in *Burgess*, the CAT substituted its own infringement decision having set aside the OFT non-infringement decision. Even on this occasion, however, it would be wrong to argue that the CAT applied a structuralist approach. On the contrary, *Burgess* in one of the few cases reviewed in this chapter where consumer detriment appears to have been part of the legal test.

Third, what lessons can be learned for competition policy around the world as a number of new competition regimes look for the right enforcement standards suited to their economies? This review of the OFT practice demonstrates that it is possible to adopt a welfare-based approach which results both in robust enforcement decisions and takes into account the risk of false positives. Perhaps the most important lesson for new competition regimes is the key role of a thorough assessment of dominance. The review of the OFT cases and the CAT jurisprudence shows that such an assessment can be carried out in a structured and predictable way in order to filter out cases where harm is unlikely and provide a sharp focus for assessment of the abuse.

Fourth, is a welfare-based approach consistent with the case law of the EU Courts, which, through different routes and with different qualifications, is binding on the UK authorities both when they apply Art 102 TFEU and when they apply the Chapter II prohibition? Again, the answer is in the affirmative but, this time, with a significant qualification. The analysis of the OFT practice and the CAT jurisprudence shows that a test of likely foreclosure of equally efficient competitors is fully compatible with EU competition law. Indeed, as demonstrated by the legal analysis in *Burgess*, the law can even be interpreted, in certain cases, as requiring proof of consumer detriment. However, in certain circumstances, EU law leaves little room for manoeuvre. Notable examples are the case law on rebates and the case law on recoupment in predation cases. As regards rebates, the OFT has either distinguished the case law or closed cases on administrative priority grounds because of a lack of substantial foreclosure effects or consumer detriment. The latter approach is not entirely satisfactory, not least because it cannot apply in civil litigation. The UK experience confirms that this is an area where the case law of the EU Courts is very difficult to reconcile with a welfare-based approach. As regards recoupment, the OFT has adopted two different approaches. In *Napp*, it proved simultaneous recoupment by establishing that exclusionary behaviour in one market segment allowed the dominant undertaking to charge excessive prices in another market segment. In *Cardiff Bus*, it set out a plausible recoupment theory but made it clear that it was not part of the legal test.

Fifth, what does this chapter conclude about the challenges that UK competition law is facing in this area? Three observations can be made. First of all, there has been for some time a paucity of infringement decisions. It is beyond the scope of this chapter to explore why this is the case but one significant conclusion of the present research is that the problem does not lie in the administrability of the substantive standards. The search for an answer must be directed elsewhere and, probably, in the realm of procedure and institutional arrangements. Second, the analysis highlighted one technical issue of great importance which needs to be resolved in an "effects-based world": the question of the significance of actual foreclosure effects. The better view appears to be that the OFT practice and the

CAT jurisprudence only require *ex ante* likely foreclosure effects. The lack of actual foreclosure effects *ex post* plays a significant role but only as relevant evidence going to whether foreclosure effects were likely *ex ante*. However, this view has not yet been clearly confirmed by the CAT or the courts. Finally, this chapter identified an emerging trend to include in the decision or judgment a theory of harm, generally focused on the effect of the practice under review on consumers, which is, however, explicitly not part of the legal test. It is unclear what the effect of this trend is going to be. There is a risk that such theories of harm may harden over time and, through the thorough and intensive litigation process in the UK, will colour the outcome of individual cases and even "contaminate" the governing legal principles. Some may favour this development as it would bring UK enforcement practice and jurisprudence closer to a full-scale case-by-case economic analysis which focuses directly on the welfare effects of the practice under review. However, a note of caution should be sounded in this regard. So far, the OFT and the CAT have developed administrable standards based on foreclosure and, to a more limited extent, on consumer detriment consistently with the case law of the EU Courts. Moving away from this only just laboriously gained, and yet still not firmly held, terrain could be dangerous when one abandons the sphere of legal rules for *ad hoc* standards that do not fulfil the criteria of *ex ante* certainty and *ex post* administrability. If there is one valuable lesson to be learnt from the cases reviewed here, it is that legal rules can be applied consistently with economic principles without jeopardising certainty and administrability. The future efforts should not be to move away from those rules but in the direction of developing and refining them.

CHAPTER 6

UTILITIES REGULATORS AND THE COMPETITION ACT 1998

*Giorgio Monti**

In addition to the Office of Fair Trading (OFT), six Authorities, whose main role is the regulation of a particular economic sector, have "concurrent powers" to enforce the provisions of the Competition Act 1998 (hereinafter "CA 1998") and Arts 101 and 102 TFEU (ex Arts 81 and 82 EC).[1] These are: the Office of Communications (Ofcom);[2] the Water Services Regulation Authority (Ofwat);[3] the Office of Rail Regulation (ORR);[4] the Gas and Electricity Markets Authority (GEMA) for England and Wales;[5] the Northern Ireland Authority

---

* Reader in Law, London School of Economics. With thanks to Zoe Fiander for excellent research assistance, and to her and Barry Rodger for helpful comments on an earlier draft.

[1] See s 54 of and Sch 10 to the Competition Act 1998 (establishing concurrency for UK competition law). Regulation 3 of the Competition Act 1998 and Other Enactments (Amendment) Regulations 2004, SI 2004/1261 (designating the OFT and regulatory authorities as national competition authorities for the purposes of Art 35 of Regulation 1/2003 on the implementation of the rules on competition laid down in Articles 81 and 82 of the Treaty [2003] OJ L1/1).

[2] Communications Act 2003, s 371. (Unless otherwise indicated, all further references to the publications of Ofcom (or Oftel as it was) are available from www.ofcom.gov.uk.)

[3] Water Industry Act 1991, s 31(3). Originally the industry was regulated by the Director General of Water Services. He and his staff were called the Office of Water Services (abbreviated Ofwat). Since 2006 a regulatory body has been set up (Water Act 2003, Pt 2) to replace the Director General, but the new agency is still known as Ofwat. (Unless otherwise indicated, all further references to the publications of Ofwat are available at: http://www.ofwat.gov.uk/.)

[4] Railways Act 1993, s 67(3). (Unless otherwise indicated, all further references to the publications of ORR are available at: http://www.rail-reg.gov.uk/.)

[5] Gas Act 1986, s 36A(3), Electricity Act 1989, s 43. (Unless otherwise indicated, all further references to the publications of Ofgem are available at http://www.ofgem.gov.uk.)

for Utility Regulation (NIAUR);[6] and the Civil Aviation Authority (CAA).[7] Postcomm (the Authority regulating the postal sector) does not have concurrent powers, but has used its regulatory powers to monitor the dominant player (Royal Mail) and it is believed that if it did have concurrent powers, these would not affect its approach much.[8] Concurrency means that these authorities may exercise, in the markets they are empowered to regulate, the same powers as the OFT, which include: considering complaints, imposing interim measures, seeking information from undertakings, imposing financial penalties, and accepting commitments from undertakings. The justification for empowering the Authorities to apply competition law is threefold: first, when utilities markets were opened to competition, it became apparent that the Authorities needed to apply competition law powers to ensure markets remained competitive (indeed some tried to deploy their regulatory powers to monitor competition);[9] second, it was considered that Authorities, by dint of their close scrutiny of the relevant markets, would be best placed to apply competition law and to evaluate complaints about restrictive practices; third, concurrency allows an Authority to decide which enforcement power (competition law or regulation) is most appropriate in a given case. That said, there was criticism that having multiple competition enforcers created significant practical risks: duplication of work, inconsistency, and opacity.[10] To avoid these, considerable effort has been devoted to ensuring effective co-ordination among the seven competition Authorities.

The chapter begins by explaining the provisions that govern the allocation of cases among the Authorities, the relationship between CA 1998 powers and sector regulation, and the relationship between regulators and the courts. Then it considers two government reviews that studied the application of competition law by the Authorities. The remainder of this chapter examines the decisions of three Authorities that have used their competition powers (Ofcom, GEMA, Ofwat). The first two have been selected because they are the Authorities that have used CA 1998 the most, while Ofwat provides an interesting case study on the relationship between Authorities and the Competition Appeal Tribunal, and between sector regulation

[6] Electricity (Northern Ireland) Order 1992 (SI 1992/231) (N I 1), reg 46; Gas (Northern Ireland) Order 1996 (SI 1996/275) (NI 2), reg 23.

[7] Transport Act 2000, s 86.

[8] Memorandum of Understanding between Postcomm and the OFT (June 2003).

[9] Eg Oftel inserting a condition on BT's licence that was modelled on Arts 81 and 82 EC. Upheld in *R* v *Director General for Telecommunications, ex p British Telecom plc* [1996] EWHC Admin 391.

[10] For a review of the debates, see T Prosser, "Competition, Regulation and Public Service" in B J Rodger and A MacCulloch, *The UK Competition Act* (2000, Hart, Oxford).

and competition law. The survey focuses on two issues: first, what competition concerns have arisen and whether there are distinctive issues that arise in these sectors (whether because of the economic conditions of newly liberalised, network industries or because of the authority's approach in a given sector); second, the relationship between competition law and other regulatory powers and objectives. The major preoccupation of the authorities has been the investigation of abuses of dominance, and readers are referred to the chapter by Renato Nazzini for further discussion of the application of the Chapter II prohibition of CA 1998.[11]

1 CO-ORDINATION

1.1 Co-ordinating enforcement among the agencies

The principle that underpins the Concurrency Regulations is that one Authority should be involved in each case, to avoid double jeopardy.[12] Therefore, if an Authority wishes to take action it must first inform the other six, and upon notification all must agree which of them is to take the case forward, no action being allowed before this is done. Only the Authority with jurisdiction will apply CA 1998, although it is possible to transfer the case to another Authority at a later date. The criteria applied when deciding on the allocation of a case is who is "better or best placed" to deal with it, with four considerations that help make this determination: the Authority's knowledge of the economic sector; whether the case affects more than one economic sector; any previous contacts between the parties and the Authority; and an Authority's recent experience with the undertakings or with similar issues.[13] Any investigation to which criminal penalties might apply (eg into a cartel) will be taken by the OFT.[14] The Department of Trade and Industry and HM Treasury report, *Concurrent Competition Powers in Sectoral Regulation*, noted that the process of allocating cases appeared to work well, indicating that the OFT would pass cases to the relevant regulator when it concerned that regulator's economic sector. However, no difficult case has yet arisen to test the effectiveness of the system of case allocation.[15] It is worth bearing in mind that the six sector-specific Authorities are also national competition authorities for the

[11] See Chapter 5 above.

[12] Competition Act 1998 (Concurrency) Regulations 2004, SI 2004/1077, reg 6.

[13] OFT, *Concurrent application to regulated industries* (OFT 405, 2004), para 3.13.

[14] *Concurrent competition powers in sectoral regulation* (URN 06/1244, May 2006), para 2.3, fn 17 (available at: http://www.berr.gov.uk/files/file29454.pdf). (Hereinafter "DTI/Treasury Report".)

[15] *Ibid*, para 3.2.

purposes of EC competition law. Therefore, if a practice is one to which Arts 101 or 102 TFEU apply, then a second case allocation may take place to determine which EU competition authority is well placed to pursue the case.[16]

Co-ordination is also achieved through the Concurrency Working Party established in 1997 and designed to facilitate a consistent approach by the authorities in applying the CA 1998. It meets six times a year and is a forum to discuss how the co-operation arrangements function and matters of common interest, to share information, and to co-ordinate the application of competition law.[17] With regard to the latter, the OFT, in conjunction with each Authority, has published guidelines explaining how the provisions of the CA 1998 and Arts 101 and 102 TFEU are to be applied in each sector.[18] These are discussed further below, for now we merely highlight their importance in ensuring that there is a co-ordinated approach to the interpretation of competition law among the Authorities, which ensures a uniform application of the law for the most part, while taking into account the specific features of each sector.

1.2 Co-ordinating competition law and regulatory powers

A second issue that requires consideration is how an Authority chooses between applying competition law and its regulatory powers to address a given practice when both might apply. Three questions arise: first, how the authority should go about deciding whether to apply CA 1998 or its sector-specific powers; second, if it chooses to apply CA 1998, whether it is able to use these powers to pursue regulatory goals; third, if there has been an intervention by the regulator, whether this prevents a subsequent application of CA 1998.

The first two questions can be treated together. Consider a situation where there is a condition in a licence that is akin to a prohibition under competition law. For example, operators of gas distribution networks have a monopoly over the territory where they operate and a duty not to discriminate under the Gas Act 1986,[19] but also a duty not to discriminate arising from competition law. If the practice in question does not affect trade between Member States

---

[16] Commission Notice on Co-operation within the Network of Competition Authorities [2004] OJ C101/43.

[17] Further information is available in OFT 405, n 13 above.

[18] The OFT has sole power to issue soft law guidance, but it must consult the relevant regulatory authorities when the guidance applies to them: CA 1998, ss 38(7) and 51(4).

[19] See Gas Act 1986, s 9, Condition 4 of the Gas Transporters Licence Standard Conditions.

(so that EC law does not apply) then the Authority's duty is to apply competition law where it is more appropriate to proceed under CA 1998 than under sector-specific powers.[20] However, little guidance is offered to explain how this determination is to be made. If the practice in question affects trade between Member States, the matter is affected by the requirements of Art 3 of Regulation 1/2003: if the Authority decides that it is more appropriate to use competition law it must apply EC competition law as well as national law and must avoid the application of stricter national law. Regarding the second question: when proceeding under CA 1998, the Authority should not have regard to the broader policy goals it has as regulator of the sector, but it may do so if the policy goal is one to which the OFT could have regard in exercising its powers under CA 1998, and all statutes give effect to this with provisions that are similarly worded.[21] This is designed to ensure that competition law is not used in a regulatory manner. Similarly, if the proceedings involve EC competition law the Authority must ensure its approach is consistent with that set out by the competition *acquis*.[22] Thus, non-competition considerations may be taken into account by the authorities only insofar as they may also be taken into account by the OFT, the Commission, or as determined by the relevant appellate courts.

According to the Court of Appeal, the rule forbidding the consideration of wider regulatory tasks in applying competition law "serves to underline the separation between the competition law powers and the wider regulatory powers of the Authority".[23] However, a complication arises because of Art 3(3) of Regulation 1/2003. This allows the application of national law which is stricter than EC competition law provided that the "provisions of national law … predominantly pursue an objective different from that pursued by Articles 81 and 82 of the Treaty". The OFT suggests that on a case-by-case basis, the Authority will have to consider whether, in applying its regulatory powers, it may be considered to be applying competition law (for example, when enforcing a non-discrimination obligation that falls foul of a licence condition but which may also be characterised as an abuse of dominance).[24] If so, then the Authority is forbidden from making reference to its broader policy objectives even when applying its regulatory powers. On the other hand, if the Authority

---

[20] OFT 405 (n 13 above), para 4.3.

[21] Communications Act 2003, s 371(11) and (12); s 4B; Gas Act 1986, s 2(6A) and (6B); Railways Act 1993, s 4(7A)(7B); Water Industry Act 1991; OFT 405 n 13 above, para 4.1.

[22] Regulation 1/2003, Art 3(1), with some exceptions provided in Art 3(2) and (3).

[23] *Dŵr Cymru Cyfyngedig v Albion Water Ltd and Water Services Regulation Authority (formerly Director General of Water Services)* [2008] EWCA Civ 536, para 22.

[24] OFT 405 n 13 above, para 4.4.

is exercising its regulatory powers to pursue an objective that is different from competition law, then it is free to apply its powers without having regard to EU competition law.[25] The upshot is that even when the Authority chooses not to use its powers under CA 1998 or Arts 101 and 102 TFEU, but relies on its sector-specific powers, it may be deemed to be pursuing a competition law-related objective anyway, and so be limited in what steps it may take. This might apply to the non-discrimination obligation imposed on gas transporters, as s 9(1A) of the Gas Act imposes a duty on the gas transporter to "facilitate competition in the supply of gas". Enforcement of this duty by the regulator might be seen as enforcement of a rule that pursues the same objective as Arts 101 and 102 TFEU. However, this case-by-case approach has been criticised because Art 3(3) requires that one should look at the objective of the national legislation, and not its exercise in an individual case.[26] On this basis, every time the Authority chooses to enforce its sector-specific powers, its actions are *de iure* not enforcement using competition law, but are taken having regard to the wider duties imposed on the regulator by statute.[27] That said, as will be illustrated below, there is no neat division between the Authorities' competition law enforcement functions and their other regulatory duties since often these other duties must be pursued by promoting competition. From a broader policy perspective this suggests that the role played by regulatory authorities may require reconsideration in order to articulate more clearly the division between competition law and sector-specific regulation.[28]

As regards the third question, CA 1998 provides that the Chapters I and II prohibitions are excluded when the conduct in question is in compliance with a legal requirement.[29] For example, Vodafone's agreements with its distributors fixing the retail price for pre-pay mobile phone vouchers would have constituted an infringement of the Chapter I prohibition but it was found that this practice was required by Vodafone's licence, and therefore no action could be taken under CA 1998.[30] However, there is no immunity if a regulator merely authorises a practice which may be anticompetitive, although the Competition Appeals Tribunal ("the CAT") has taken the view that the fine may be reduced if the regulator was aware of a possible

---

[25] OFT 405 n 13 above, para 4.8.

[26] E O'Neill and E Saunders, *UK Competition Procedure* (2007 OUP, Oxford) paras 3.29–3.31. Similarly, *ORR Competition Act Guideline: Application to Services Relating to Railways* (August 2005), paras 3.7–3.11.

[27] Gas Act 1986, s 4AA.

[28] T Prosser, "Theorising Utility Regulation" (1999) 62 MLR 196.

[29] CA 1998, Sch 3, para 5(1).

[30] Oftel, "Complaint Submitted under the Competition Act 1998 by the Federation of Wholesale Distributors 5 April 2002".

infringement and appears to have encouraged the practice. We discuss this point further in section 4 below with reference to the *National Grid* case.

1.3 The role of the courts

Decisions by the Authorities may be appealed to the CAT, whose task is to determine the appeal on the merits, and whose powers go beyond confirming or quashing the decision, but also extend to making any decision that the authority could have made.[31] The CAT has interpreted the reference to an appeal "on the merits" to mean that it has "full jurisdiction to find facts, make its own appraisals of economic issues, apply the law to those facts and appraisals, and determine the amount of any penalty".[32] These extensive powers are not exercised on every appeal but they show that the Tribunal is a considerable player not only in developing the law but in scrutinising the decisions of the Authorities in detail. However, the Court of Appeal has placed certain limits on the Tribunal's powers.

In supervising the performance of the authorities, the CAT has demanded that Authorities provide greater detail in their decisions to reject complaints.[33] Running slightly counter to this, it has been suggested that the Tribunal is eager to see Authorities resolve cases quickly, especially when the complainant is a small operator.[34] In one instance, having decided that the authority's rejection of a complaint was wrong, it required the authority (Ofcom) to reach a conclusion (either a finding of no infringement, or a decision to issue a statement of objections) within 5 months.[35] However, the Court of Appeal considered that the Tribunal had gone too far: while it was entitled to "express its own view as to how urgently the case should be dealt with", it is not "able to give directions to the regulator in relation to the conduct of the further investigation".[36] This is helpful for Authorities as they are entitled to prioritise work as they see fit, taking into account the resources at their disposal (although a failure to re-investigate may be susceptible to judicial review).

---

[31] See CA 1998, Sch 8, para 3(1) and (3).

[32] *Freeserve* v *Director General of Telecommunications* [2003] CAT 5, para 107.

[33] Eg *ibid*, paras 131 (requiring more detailed analysis of market definition) and 212 (criticising the lack of detail on the reasons for dismissing the predatory pricing complaint).

[34] R Whish "Appeals to the Competition Appeal Tribunal under the Competition Act 1998 and the Enterprise Act 2002" in P Vaas (ed), *Regulatory Review 2006/2007* (2007 University of Bath).

[35] *Floe Telecom Ltd (in liquidation)* v *Office of Communications*, Order of the Tribunal, 1 December 2004.

[36] *Office of Communications* v *Floe Telecom Ltd* [2006] EWCA Civ 768, para 35.

In aiding the development of the law, the CAT in one case, in addition to dismissing an appeal against an Ofcom finding that there was no infringement of competition law, went on to set aside other parts of Ofcom's decision even when this was not necessary to determine the appeal. Thus Ofcom was worried that its success in front of the Tribunal would turn out to be a Pyrrhic victory as the parts of the decision that were set aside risked undermining Ofcom's policy in the relevant markets. Therefore it appealed against those parts of the CAT's judgment setting aside its decision even if that did not affect the outcome of the present dispute. The Court of Appeal hesitated in hearing an appeal of this nature because it should give priority to appeals of real significance to the parties, but in the end agreed with Ofcom's concerns and issued a general warning to Tribunals to desist from ruling on points that are unnecessary for deciding the appeal: "[d]eciding no more than is necessary may be described as an unimaginative, unadventurous, inactive, conservative or restrictive approach to the judicial function, but the lessons of practical experience are that unnecessary opinions and findings of courts are fraught with danger."[37] The main danger is that the opinions may be wrong because the Tribunal did not have full representation on the issues, and may be damaging when relied upon by others.[38]

2 GOVERNMENT REPORTS

Two reports have investigated concurrency and the relationship between competition law and sector-specific regulation: the DTI/Treasury Report, *Concurrent competition powers in sectoral regulation*, in 2006; and the House of Lords Select Committee on Regulators' report, *UK Economic Regulators* in 2007.[39] Three points emerge from these reports: the working of case allocation provisions; the use of CA 1998 by the Authorities; and the interaction between sector-specific regulation and CA 1998.

As noted in the section above, the DTI/Treasury considered that the processes for allocating cases had worked well; however, it also encouraged further co-ordination measures, which the OFT and the

---

[37] *Office of Communications T-Mobile (UK) Ltd* v *Floe Telecom Ltd* [2009] EWCA Civ 47, para 20.

[38] On the merits, the Court of Appeal agreed with Ofcom that the Tribunal's interpretation of the relevant legal issues was incorrect and ordered that the portion of the CAT's order setting aside a part of Ofcom's decision should in turn be set aside.

[39] See n 14 above; House of Lords, Select Committee on Regulators, 1st Report of Session 2006–07, *UK Economic Regulators* (HL Paper 189–I) http://www.publications.parliament.uk/pa/ld200607/ldselect/ldrgltrs/189/18902.htm.

Authorities have now implemented. The Select Committee echoed this sentiment, indicating that there appeared to be a good working relationship between the Authorities and the OFT, while noting some instances where the regulated undertakings reported poor co-ordination among the OFT, Competition Commission, and the Authorities.[40]

Regarding the use of CA 1998, the Select Committee was concerned that a sector regulator might not be "assiduous enough in investigating competition issues".[41] Two entrants in the water industry market (Albion Water and Aquavitae) and a consumer group (Energywatch) were not satisfied with the authorities' responses to their complaints.[42] The Committee was not specific as to why the Authorities might under-enforce CA 1998, although both it and the DTI/Treasury reported the views of some commentators that this might be a deliberate policy to avoid conflict with the industries they regulate,[43] and it recommended that complainants should be given the option of requesting the OFT to take the lead in investigating complaints. This is not a helpful suggestion because it risks harming the working relationship between the OFT and the Authorities: the OFT taking a case is evidence that it does not trust the authority. What is needed instead is a better understanding of why CA 1998 might be underutilised by some Authorities, a question we pursue below.

Regarding the relationship between competition law and regulatory powers, both reports subscribe to the well-established view that regulatory powers are necessary to create the conditions for competition, but that economic regulation should recede in time, leaving the need to apply only competition law.[44] This is at odds with what is happening: the number of staff employed by Authorities had increased by 9.14 per cent between the financial years 2004/05 and 2006/07;[45] and regulatory intervention is not abating. Nor is this view sustainable in light of the remaining natural monopoly segments of all utility networks, nor with the broader duties that have been imposed on regulators.[46] Furthermore, the statutes themselves do not foresee the end of sector-specific regulation: while the Authority's primary objective

---

[40] *UK Economic Regulators*, *ibid*, paras 6.17–6.26.

[41] *Ibid*, para 6.34, echoing the views of an earlier report: Better Regulation Task Force, *Economic Regulators* (July 2001).

[42] *UK Economic Regulators*, paras 6.34 and 6.35

[43] DTI/Treasury Report n 14 above, para 4.8.

[44] *Ibid*, para 1.4.

[45] *Ibid*, para 7.38.

[46] For a critique, see P Larouche, "A Closer Look at Some Assumptions Underlying EC Regulation of Electronic Communications" (2002) 3 Journal of Network Industries 129.

in the regulated sectors is "to protect the interests of consumers ... wherever appropriate by promoting effective competition",[47] this wording acknowledges that it may not always be appropriate to protect consumers by competition. Nor does it assume that promoting competition will necessarily require the relaxation of regulatory controls, for instance, imposing on a dominant firm the duty to share facilities with competitors may protect consumers by enhancing competition, but, if the dominant firm has a natural monopoly, continued regulatory intervention will be required to ensure the market remains competitive.[48]

That said, the DTI/Treasury Report provides a reasoned argument in favour of greater reliance on competition law powers by suggesting that regulators are risk averse when they prefer to apply sector-specific regulation in that they feel more confident in applying these rules because companies prefer rule-based regulation. However, the DTI/Treasury suggest that if significant efforts were made to apply competition law (which may include decisions being lost on appeal to the CAT), this could create a valuable set of precedent that would guide Authorities and deter undertakings more effectively than the continued application of sector-specific rules. This suggests that a period of costly transition away from rule-based regulation to principle-based regulation is necessary before greater use can be made of CA 1998. Further, according to the DTI/Treasury, the costs outweigh the benefits: (1) rule-based regulation can have unanticipated anti-competitive effects; (2) rules may stifle the development of competitive pressures that would improve market outcomes; (3) compliance with general principles can be more flexible and stimulates innovation; (4) competition law sets a higher hurdle for intervention and prevents over-regulation; (5) CA 1998 affords greater third-party scrutiny of regulatory decisions; (6) competition law principles deter all anti-competitive conduct while rule-based regulations prevent only specific forms of conduct.[49] However, this might be too idealistic a scenario: first, regulators have to pursue other public policy objectives than competition; second, EU directives (for example, in electronic communications) may require the imposition of regulatory remedies in certain circumstances (for example, when an undertaking holds significant market power); third, even in the most competitive of the regulated sectors (electronic communications) there is continued use of regulatory tools; fourth, regulators might find they have better tools to tackle market failures through

[47] Communications Act 2003, eg s 3(1)(b); Gas Act 1986, s 4AA(1); Water Industry Act 1991, s 2(2B).

[48] Contra DTI/Treasury Report n 14 above, paras 2.24–2.27.

[49] *Ibid*, para 4.11.

the use of regulatory powers.[50] Thus, a more realistic objective is to examine how to achieve the best mix between regulation and competition law.

Finally, it is worth noting the Select Committee's views about the success of deregulation: some sectors (electronic communications and energy) are more competitive than others (water, where "competition had barely made an appearance at all"),[51] with a mixed picture in airports and rail.[52] This roughly tallies with the use of CA 1998: Ofcom and Ofgem have been significantly more active in considering the application of CA 1998, while the other regulators have lagged behind. It demonstrates that creating the conditions for competition also creates incentives for incumbents to defend their established position and the need for competition law enforcement.

3 OFCOM

3.1 The application of competition law by the regulator

Of the utility regulators, Ofcom (and its predecessor Oftel)[53] has been the most active in applying CA 1998 (between 2004 and early 2007 it opened 200 inquiries, 60 of which could have been considered using competition law, and opened 10 CA 1998 investigations),[54] although it has yet to find an infringement. As may be expected, the bulk of its investigations have concerned exclusionary abuses, and the main target of complaints and investigations has been BT. On the whole, the approach taken by Ofcom in interpreting the concepts of dominance and abuse is in line with that of the OFT.

Procedurally, Ofcom is able to draw on previous work it has undertaken in the sector to help with defining markets and assessing dominance, which allows it to address these questions more efficiently than would a generalised competition authority, thus justifying giving sector regulators competition powers. That said, the CAT has imposed a requirement that, in cases where a non-infringement decision is reached, the authority has to indicate "at least briefly" what the relevant markets are and whether or not any assumption

---

50 On this point, see Ofgem's response to the DTI/Treasury Report (12 December 2006) (available at www.oft.gov.uk).

51 See n 39 above, para 7.6. Further analysis relating to the lack of competition in the water sector leads to the conclusion that Ofwat should apply the regulatory powers to improve competition (paras 7.16–7.23).

52 *Ibid*, paras 7.3–7.3.

53 The functions of Oftel were transferred to Ofcom by the Communications Act 2003.

54 Ofcom response to DTI/Treasury Report, *Concurrent competition powers in sectoral regulation* (12 January 2007) (available at www.oft.gov.uk).

of dominance has been made.[55] There is a risk that this lengthens proceedings in instances where there are no antcompetitive effects so that even outlining possible relevant markets seems superfluous.[56] It also runs against the CAT's concerns about the length of time competition authorities take in resolving disputes, discussed above.

Ofcom has addressed a number of methodological questions arising from its investigations into price squeeze and predatory pricing claims. In predatory pricing cases, Ofcom's view is that recovering losses post-predation is a relevant consideration, but this runs counter to the ECJ's position;[57] it has also taken the view that an average variable cost floor is not suitable because of the high levels of capital costs involved in network industries and so it has used long run incremental cost (LRIC) as the floor below which pricing will be deemed predatory, which is in line with the Commission's practice.[58] In price squeeze investigations, Ofcom uses an "equally efficient operator" test, considering "whether the dominant undertaking would be profitable in the downstream market if it had to pay the same input prices as its competitors".[59] In one decision, it considered whether a "reasonably efficient entrant" test should be applied but took the view that this might be a "more relevant test if there were an objective to promote competition under sectoral powers".[60] This is consistent with the regulators' duties not to use competition law in a regulatory manner.

Finally, a long-running dispute has led to discussion on whether an anticipated illegal use of a facility can justify a dominant undertaking's refusal to supply. The issue arose in 2003 when VIP complained about a termination of a "GSM gateway service" by T-Mobile, and Floe made a similar complaint with respect to Vodafone. In brief, both T-Mobile and Vodafone are dominant in the market for wholesale voice call termination on their network; their termination charges for calls that originate from a fixed handset are regulated, but remain high enough to spur the search for alter-

---

[55] *Freeserve*, n 33 above, para 131.

[56] Eg Oftel, *BT 118500 directory enquiries number* (31 December 2003); Ofcom, *Vodafone/O2/Orange/T-Mobile* (26 May 2004).

[57] OFT/Oftel, *Application in the telecommunications sector* (OFT 417), para 7.14 (note that these guidelines were published before 2003, so they may not represent current thinking). The ECJ has recently confirmed that recoupment is not an element that must be proven to establish predatory pricing: *France Télécom* v *Commission* (Case C–202/07 P), judgment of 2 April 2009.

[58] See OFT 417, *ibid*, para 7.15; eg Ofcom, *BT 0845 and 0870 retail price change* (19 August 2004); Ofcom, *BT Wholesale Calls* (16 June 2005).

[59] OFT 417, *ibid*, para 7.26, and Oftel, *BT UK-SPN calls service* (22 May 2003); Ofcom, *Vodafone/O2/Orange/T-Mobile* (26 May 2004).

[60] Oftel, *BTOpenworld* (20 November 2003), paras 3.22–3.26.

native, cheaper ways of calling mobile phones. The GSM gateway is a means of avoiding the termination charge whereby a call that originates from a fixed handset is made to appear like a call originating from the same network as that of the person receiving the call. When the calling party and the called party are on the same mobile network, termination charges are lower than in a fixed-to-mobile call. T-Mobile and Vodafone originally afforded VIP and Floe with access to their GSM gateways but this was later withdrawn. The Director General of Telecommunications ("the Director") found that the use that VIP and Floe made of the gateway was unlawful and concluded that "a dominant undertaking would be objectively justified in refusing to supply a customer where the products or services to be provided were to be used in an unlawful manner".[61] The CAT found that the analysis of the legality of the use of the public GSM gateway by the Director was flawed. Therefore the issue of the defence did not require examination but the Tribunal addressed it, giving the following indications: "where the relevant authorities have pronounced that an activity is illegal, competition law cannot and does not require the dominant undertaking to participate in the furtherance of an illegal act."[62] However, "where there may be doubt as to the legality of an activity or where the relevant authority has announced that it is not for the time being taking enforcement action ... We do not consider that the dominant undertaking can necessarily rely ... on its own interpretation of the illegality of the activity objectively to justify conduct that would otherwise be an abuse of a dominant position."[63] This very restrictive approach is arguably in line with that of the CFI in *Hilti*,[64] but when Ofcom re-investigated the issue, and again came to the conclusion that the use of the public GSM gateway is unlawful, it provided a more generous approach for justifying the refusal to supply. Its principal finding was that T-Mobile and Vodafone "would potentially have been committing a criminal offence" by continuing to supply VIP and Floe. This triggered the application of para 5(2) of Sch 3 to CA 1998 so that the refusal to supply was carried out "in order to comply with a legal requirement", which in this case was the duty to desist from criminal conduct. The policy behind this conclusion was

---

[61] Ofcom, *Vodafone re-investigation* (29 June 2005), para 38. Ofcom *T-Mobile re-investigation* (29 June 2005), para 35.

[62] *Floe Telecom Ltd* v *Ofcom* [2004] CAT 18, para 333.

[63] *Ibid.*

[64] *Hilti* v *Commission* (Case T–30/89) [1991] ECR II-1439, where the CFI held that the dominant undertaking could not refuse to supply goods when it feared there was a safety risk in their use by the undertaking requesting them. There were laws prohibiting the sale of dangerous products and enforcement bodies with powers to enforce these rules.

that "[i]t would defeat the purpose of the competition rules if they were to act to promote competition in a particular economic activity which is itself unlawful".[65] If this approach was not accepted, Ofcom ruled, relying on *United Brands*, that "a dominant undertaking is objectively justified in refusing to supply a customer if it does so as a means of protecting its legitimate commercial interests and [its actions] are reasonable and proportionate".[66] In examining the legitimate commercial interests of T-Mobile and Vodafone, Ofcom said that had these firms supplied VIP and Floe respectively, they themselves "would have faced a genuine risk of committing a criminal offence"[67] and so were justified in wishing to avoid prosecution and the resulting commercial damage. The termination was proportionate and there was no need for the undertakings to refer the matter to the regulator because, even without enforcement action, the activity in question remained unlawful and therefore it was legitimate to cease those illegal commercial transactions.[68] Ofcom's broader defence is to be welcomed given the uncertainties that regulated industries would face with the CAT's approach.

There has been little examination of whether dominant undertakings are exploiting their dominant position. Two decisions touched on this issue and offer useful insights. One was a complaint against BT regarding the wholesale access to DSL broadband products where purchasers complained that some contract terms were unreasonable and the levels of service poor.[69] Regarding the quality of service, it was noted that inefficiency could amount to an abuse but that there was insufficient evidence of an effect on competition or consumers. That said, it noted that BT had undertaken to improve this service by introducing Service Level Agreements and Service Level Guarantees, but it found that BT had been "cautious" and "unambitious" in this regard, and accordingly the Authority would monitor how BT reassessed its contractual relations.[70] A similar preference for self-regulation can be seen in that an investi-

---

[65] *T-Mobile re-investigation*, n 61 above, para 194.

[66] *Ibid*, para 243, citing *United Brands* v *Commission* (Case 27/76) [1978] ECR 207.

[67] *Ibid*, para 245.

[68] *Ibid*, para 256.

[69] This complaint could be characterised both as an exploitative abuse (BT taking advantage of its dominance to harm firms downstream) or exclusionary (BT harming downstream rivals, since BT was also competing with the complainants on the retail market).

[70] Oftel, *Complaint Submitted under the Competition Act 1998 by the XDSL Wholesale Products Industry Group* (January 2002), paras 23–26. In 2004, however, the market for wholesale broadband access was subjected to more detailed regulation under the Communications Act 2003 to ensure the development of competition (Ofcom, *Review of the wholesale local access market* (16 December 2004)).

gation into the prices charged for making calls to hospital patients was closed after Ofcom decided that a better way forward would be to encourage co-operation between the Department of Health and the service providers with a view to developing a new pricing structure.[71] The solutions in these two cases are of interest because they show that, beyond competition and regulation, a potentially fruitful enforcement strategy to ensure compliance with competition law is to encourage self-regulation. This is especially the case given the difficulties that competition authorities face when regulating excessive pricing or detailed contractual arrangements in high technology markets.

3.2 The interface between competition law and sector regulation

In relation to broadcasting markets, s 317(2) of the Communications Act 2003 stipulates that "[b]efore exercising any of their Broadcasting Act powers for a competition purpose, Ofcom must consider whether a more appropriate way of proceeding in relation to some or all of the matters in question would be under the Competition Act 1998". If Ofcom decides to use CA 1998 then it may not use the Broadcasting Act powers in relation to the same issue. Ofcom stated that it will follow the same approach in markets for electronic communications networks and services.[72] The discretion it has cannot be fettered in advance and a case-by-case determination of which powers are more appropriate must be carried out.[73] However, in its decisions there is little substantive discussion to explain why CA 1998 is more appropriate.[74] Accordingly, the only guidance on why Ofcom prefers CA 1998 is found in its public statements, and these identify a general policy of minimising the application of regulatory powers, and identify a number of advantages that obtain when applying the Act. For instance, a now superseded document suggested that CA 1998 was more advantageous when tackling anti-competitive conduct

---

[71] *Ofcom's Investigations Programme: Report on activity between 1 October 2005 and 31 March 2006*, p 20; *Ofcom own-initiative investigation into the price of making telephone calls to hospital patients* (18 January 2006).

[72] Ofcom, *Draft Enforcement Guidelines* (2006), para 10.09. Absent a final version, they "reflect how Ofcom now conducts its investigations, including our approach to prioritisation": *Ofcom's Investigations Programme: Report on activity between 1 April and 30 September 2008*.

[73] This is in contrast with the view Oftel took in its *Competition Act Strategy* (2002) where it indicated that when considering behaviour that could contravene both CA 1998 and the sectoral regime, it would carry out an investigation under CA 1998 from the start.

[74] Eg Oftel, *Disconnection of Floe Telecom Ltd's services by Vodafone Ltd* (3 November 2003), para 17; Ofcom, *T-Mobile: disconnection of VIP Communications Limiteds services* (31 December 2003), para 15.

because it afforded greater powers of investigation, effective powers to issue interim measures, the power to apply financial penalties, and it would "make it easier for operators to develop compliance systems and cultures by replicating successful examples from other sectors".[75] In contrast, regulatory powers were best used residually when the authority had to fulfil its sector-specific duties.

While Ofcom is comfortable in applying CA 1998, there remains scope for applying regulatory powers. The major reason for this is that some forms of conduct are hard to pin down as abuses of dominance and the authority finds that sector-specific rules are applied with more ease. Two examples illustrate this. One is broadband migration: Ofcom has introduced a new regulation requiring all broadband providers to follow a set of rules to ensure customers can switch easily from one provider to another. Switching costs had the effect of limiting competition, and reducing incentives for providers to ensure they provided customers with the best service. It would be tricky to handle this issue using competition law because each provider (whether dominant or a new entrant) would have an incentive to try and keep its subscribers, so the only way to tackle this would be to bring a case alleging all providers had abused a collective dominant position. However, the law on this point is uncertain.[76] Furthermore, the regulatory approach allowed Ofcom to impose a more effective remedy to guarantee customers could switch, perhaps reflecting the wider duty to protect vulnerable customers.[77] The second example is the consultation on termination rates for calls to mobile phones. This entails the regulation of prices to a market where each mobile phone operator is dominant (because if A wants to call B on B's mobile phone he cannot avoid having the call routed through B's phone network) but Ofcom is reluctant to deregulate and merely enforce CA 1998 if charges are too high, for the following reasons: (1) competition law does not provide for "ready-made solutions" to problems found in telecoms markets; (2) competition law provides less certainty for regulated players than do price controls; (3) competition law enforcement is not likely to cause an increase in competition in a market where there is no effective competition yet; (4) finally, deregulation would entail operators negotiating with each other and disagreements would have to be resolved by Ofcom.[78]

These two examples illustrate the general point made by one commentator: "Ofcom may make claims to be a competition

---

[75] Oftel, *Competition Act Strategy* (2002).

[76] G Monti, "The Scope of Collective Dominance Under Article 82 EC" (2001) 38 CMLRev 131.

[77] Ofcom, *Enforcement Report* (12 May 2009), pp 16–18.

[78] Ofcom, *Wholesale mobile voice call termination: Preliminary consultation on future regulation* (20 May 2009), paras 6.89–6.94.

authority, with special expertise in telecommunications. In reality it is much more than that; it is a regulatory agency with powers to manage the market going way beyond those of a normal competition body."[79]

4 GEMA

4.1 The application of competition law by the regulator

Allegations of exclusionary abuse have formed the bulk of GEMA's work, which is in line with its enforcement strategy.[80] Between 2000 and 2004 it received 44 complaints, but most were not followed up, mainly due to lack of evidence.[81] In five cases that were investigated more fully, it found no infringement of the Chapter II prohibition, but in the one decision where it found an infringement (*National Grid*), it imposed a significant fine of £41.6 million, which was (at the time of writing) the second highest fine by a competition authority in the UK.[82] To date, a combination of its decisions and the OFT's guideline, *Application in the Energy Sector*,[83] indicate that there are some distinguishing features to the application of competition law in this sector, which we review first before turning to look more closely at the *National Grid* case and what lessons it holds for the application of competition law in regulated industries.

The guideline notes a number of instances where specific features of energy markets warrant distinct approaches. For example, when issues of market definition are under scrutiny, certain market features may require a modified approach: wholesale price movements may be greater than 5–10 per cent (which is the usual benchmark for the hypothetical monopolist test) therefore an alternative approach may be required; and since electricity (and to some extent gas) cannot be stored easily there is the possibility of market power being present for brief periods, unlike other markets. In terms of dominance, a situation of inelastic supply and demand conditions (for example, in wholesale markets) might indicate that a relatively small player may have sufficient market power to be found dominant below the normal thresholds.[84] These difficulties are exemplified by GEMA

---

[79] E Pitt, "Competition Law in Telecommunications" in I Walden and J Angel (eds), *Telecommunications Law and Regulation* (2nd edn, 2005, OUP, Oxford).

[80] OFT, *Application in the Energy Sector* (OFT 428, 2005), para 3.3, noting the need for particular vigilance towards incumbents.

[81] "Complaints considered by Ofgem under the Competition Act 1998". Unfortunately Ofgem has not made available any comparable data for later years.

[82] GEMA, *National Grid Competition Act Decision* (21 February 2008).

[83] OFT 428, n 80 above.

[84] *Ibid*, para 3.21. In these settings risks of exploitative abuse arise: para 3.25.

closing its CA 1998 investigation into Scottish Power and Scottish Southern Energy in the wholesale electricity market. The suspected abuse concerned a 4-week period during which the two firms held a dominant position because of transmission constraints between England and Scotland and when prices charged by these two firms were much greater than those charged by comparable generators. The Authority determined that the likelihood of finding an infringement of CA 1998 was low and that a regulatory approach would be preferable to address this manifestation of market power.[85] A follow-on report on market power in the electricity wholesale sector indicated specific concerns about the appropriateness of CA 1998 as a tool to address possible abuses, in particular the complexity in applying the dominance test when market power is intermittent and limitations in addressing and remedying exploitative abuses.[86]

The *National Grid* decision concerned an abuse in the market for the provision and maintenance of domestic gas meters that took place as soon as this market was opened to competition in 2004. All customers who are supplied with gas must receive it through a meter.[87] National Grid is the dominant meter operator and its business model was to retain ownership of the meters it made available to gas suppliers and an annual rental charge was used to recover the cost of supplying the meter. To facilitate competition the regulator decided to encourage gas suppliers to look for new meter operators by allowing them to replace National Grid meters at short notice without a penalty charge. Substantial entry would eliminate the rental income stream that National Grid anticipated, since the meters have little value once removed. As a result National Grid renegotiated the contracts with gas suppliers (beginning with its largest customer, British Gas) and two models were drawn up: (1) for meters installed before 2004 (legacy meters), the gas supplier would gradually reduce the number of meters it bought from National Grid and pay a charge if the number of meters rented fell below that which was agreed; (2) for meters installed after that date, there would also be a charge if meters were replaced prematurely. The regulator found that these contracts excluded competitors contrary to the Chapter II prohibition and Art 82 EC.

In relation to dominance, National Grid had high market shares in the market for gas meters (no distinction was drawn between legacy and new meters): 98 per cent in 2002 and 89 per cent in 2007. However, the CAT expressed caution as to whether one might

---

[85] "Ofgem closes Competition Act 1998 case against Scottish Power and Scottish Southern Energy", Information Note R/4 (19 January 2009).

[86] "Ofgem, *Market Power Concerns in the Electricity Wholesale Sector* (March 2009).

[87] Gas Act 1986, Sch 2B, para 2.

conclude there is dominance from such high market shares (as the case law of the ECJ suggests) because, after the lifting of a statutory monopoly, even vigorous entry may not cause a substantial dent in the incumbent's market share, but "such market entry may well mean that the incumbent has little effective market power and is destined to lose market share rapidly in future".[88] Therefore, in this kind of circumstance market shares raise no presumption of dominance. Nonetheless, the CAT confirmed dominance by finding high entry barriers and weak buyer power. One factor that dented buyer power was that both parties believed that the Authority would be opposed to large-scale switching of meters from National Grid to new entrants and this weakened the suppliers' hand while strengthening National Grid's bargaining position.[89] In considering whether the contracts were abusive, the question asked was akin to that in other industries: whether the contracts went "too far in protecting National Grid from the consequences of competition and whether the agreement's foreclosing effect is too severe to be justified by National Grid's desire to protect the revenue stream generated by its meters".[90] The CAT agreed that the contracts were capable of and did foreclose entry to the detriment of consumers, but disagreed with the Authority that the contracts stifled the roll out of so-called "smart meters" (which transmit information about each customer's use directly to the supplier without requiring a personal visit as do contemporary meters), attributing this to other reasons, not least the role of government in managing what would be a major project.[91]

Perhaps the key issue for the application of competition law in regulated industries is found in the CAT's decision to reduce the fine from £41.6 million to £30 million because it found that the Authority had been closely involved in discussions about the new contracts, and, although it did not provide formal approval, the CAT understood National Grid's "surprise and dismay" at the decision and the fine.[92] Two lessons can be drawn from this: first it appears that utilities regulators have an obligation, when opening new markets and when closely involved with the incumbent in discussing the latter's plans, to offer some assistance. The Tribunal noted:

> "We are surprised that the Authority did not consider that it was part of its role either as an industry regulator or as a competition law enforcement agency to steer the industry participants away from

---

[88] *National Grid* v *Gas and Electricity Market Authority* [2009] CAT 14, para 51.
[89] *Ibid*, para 70.
[90] *Ibid*, para 93.
[91] See now Department of Energy and Climate Change, *A consultation for Smart metering for Electricity and Gas* (May 2009).
[92] *National Grid*, n 88 above, para 209.

making private arrangements which risked jeopardising the competitive process to a serious degree".[93]

However, the second lesson is that, even if the regulator fails to do this, it does not provide the dominant firm with a complete defence, only a reduction in the fine. However, these two findings appear to be in conflict with each other: surely if the regulator becomes involved and gives the impression of approving a scheme it later defines as abusive, the undertaking merits stronger protection.[94]

4.2 The interface between competition law and sector-specific regulation

In common with other authorities, GEMA should consider applying CA 1998 first before using its powers under the energy legislation.[95] In a letter responding to the DTI/Treasury Report, it gave an insight into the six major factors that influence its choice between applying CA 1998 or regulatory powers: (1) the complainant's wishes; (2) the speed of intervention; (3) the efficiency with which a given enforcement route would address the issues; (4) the resource implications; (5) the deterrent effect; (6) the availability of damages. The Authority considered that while the choice would be made on a case-by-case basis, making these criteria public would "promote consistency and a structured approach".[96] These general criteria conflict with the government's desire to phase out regulation but instead suggest that on a case-by-case basis the authority determines the most effective enforcement strategy.

It seems that, in addressing harm to final consumers, GEMA has preferred to rely on its regulatory powers. At the time of writing, it is consulting on a series of proposals that are designed to further enhance the benefits that consumers may reap from competitive markets. Its strategy is to amend the suppliers' obligations in two ways: first, by placing further controls on retailers to improve the information available to consumers and to make it easy for a consumer to switch from one energy provider to another.[97] These measures are designed to address two concerns: that a significant portion of consumers have yet to switch supplier, and that most people who switch do not find the cheapest supplier – indeed a

---

[93] *National Grid*, para 208.

[94] See the arguments developed in G Monti "Managing the Intersection of Utilities Regulation and EC Competition Law" (2008) 4(2) Competition Law Review 123.

[95] See n 80 above.

[96] Ofgem response to DTI/Treasury Report, 12 December 2006 (available from www.oft.gov.uk).

[97] Ofgem, *Energy Supply Probe – proposed retail market remedies* (15 May 2009).

significant number pay more after switching.[98] The second part of the strategy is to impose two licence conditions on suppliers to avoid discrimination: "a requirement for any difference in the terms and conditions offered in respect of different payment methods to be cost reflective; and a prohibition (limited to three years) of undue discrimination in any terms and conditions offered to customers."[99] The latter is of interest from a competition law perspective, because the concern it addresses is that the six energy suppliers tend to offer cheaper contracts in areas where they are new entrants and keep higher prices in those areas where they formerly held monopolies. Thus, price discrimination might be addressed under CA 1998 but, given that the Authority has identified an industry-wide practice, it seemed more practical to address it by way of regulation. A further advantage of regulation is that the Authority has consulted widely on these proposals, whereas action under CA 1998 does not afford the same possibilities for participation. Nonetheless, one might question the wisdom of the proposal by reference to a well-known judgment of the ECJ, *United Brands*,[100] which prohibited price discrimination by the dominant undertaking selling bananas in various EU countries. As one critic noted at the time, the upshot was that, while before bananas were sold at lower prices in poorer countries and higher prices in wealthier ones, the judgment would lead to higher prices.[101] Likewise in this case, banning price discrimination reduces the incentives to sell energy at low prices. Indeed, the Authority's study revealed that the impact of this measure on competition was "ambiguous".[102] However, the study concluded that the impact on vulnerable consumers would be positive, and the Authority concluded by placing more weight on the protection of this group in recommending these measures. This is in line with the wider statutory duties that are imposed on it, and facilitates the achievement of objectives that cannot be obtained with competition law enforcement. Accordingly, those that have criticised this policy option on grounds that it is anti-competitive have failed to consider the broader regulatory objectives that the Authority is obliged to consider.[103]

---

[98] House of Commons Business and Enterprise Committee, Energy prices, fuel poverty and Ofgem, Eleventh Report of Session 2007–08 (HC 293–I), pp 53–54.

[99] Ofgem, *Addressing undue discrimination – final proposals* (15 April 2009), para 1.7.

[100] See n 66 above.

[101] W Bishop "Price Discrimination under Article 86: Political Economy in the European Court" (1981) 44 MLR 282.

[102] See n 99, above para 5.67.

[103] "Ofgem regulator resigns over 'anti-competitive' pricing proposals", *The Times,* 13 June 2009; R Milne, "Ofgem's attempt to end 'unfair pricing' could severely impede the competitive market", *Utility Weekly*, 12 June 2009.

5 OFWAT

5.1 The application of competition law by the regulator

Ofwat is in charge of regulating a number of regional monopolies. Plans to increase contestability are under consideration but at present the agency plays a significant role in regulating the economic performance of 21 monopolies in England and Wales.[104]

Once competition is stimulated, however, the dominant incumbent will have incentives to thwart new entry. To date there have been two unsuccessful complaints (one by a water company accusing another of predatory pricing, one by a waste collector complaining that a water company was diverting such business to its waste collection subsidiary)[105] and one finding of abuse: a price squeeze practised by Dŵr Cymru to damage Albion. Albion had secured a contract to supply one firm (Shotton) with water. Albion bought the water from Dŵr Cymru who in turn obtained it from United Utilities. The dispute began when Albion sought to change its purchasing strategy: buying the water directly from United Utilities and paying Dŵr Cymru for transporting the water through its network, a "common carriage" agreement. Albion complained that the price that Dŵr Cymru was offering to charge for this was so high that it made it unprofitable for Albion to resell the water to Shotton. The regulator ruled that there was no price squeeze but on appeal the CAT exercised its powers to carry out further investigations and ruled that there had been a price squeeze. The CAT was particularly concerned that Dŵr Cymru's actions threatened the existence of the only new entrant in the market at that time, and was critical of the regulator's apparent reluctance to recognise the value of the new entrant's services to consumers and for competition.[106] The Court of Appeal confirmed both the finding of a price squeeze and the CAT's power to make a decision of abuse where it has the evidence that allows it to reach such a finding.[107] However, it remains to be seen how far this case sets a precedent for future disputes between new entrants and incumbents. We consider this in the following section.

---

[104] M Cave, *Independent Review of Competition and Innovation in Water Markets: Final Report* (April 2009).

[105] Ofwat, *Thames Water Utilities Ltd/Bath House and Albion Yard* (30 March 2003); *Southern Water Services Ltd: provision of new infrastructure in East Kent* (2 August 2004).

[106] See, eg *Albion Water Ltd* v *Water Services Regulation Authority* [2006] CAT 23, paras 893–895.

[107] For discussion of the CAT's analysis of price squeeze, see F Parker, "When is a Pipe not Just a Pipe?" [2005/2006] 4 Utilities Law Review 151

5.2 The interface between competition law and sector-specific regulation

Since December 2005 the Water Industry Act 1991 ("WIA 1991"), as amended, provides for an access regime which gives new entrants a right to access an incumbent's infrastructure to deliver water services. If terms and conditions between the new supplier and the incumbent cannot be agreed, Ofwat is empowered to make a determination of what these terms and conditions should be.[108] The question to be explored is how far this affects the application of CA 1998. A convenient place to begin is the first price determination made by Ofwat under WIA 1991 in the dispute between Anglian Water Services and Aquavitae. Aquavitae complained about the access price offered by Anglian Water both under WIA 1991 and CA 1998. Ofwat took the view that it was more appropriate to apply WIA 1991 for the following reasons: WIA 1991 provided a bespoke approach to the dispute, it would allow for a speedier resolution (given that no questions of dominance and abuse would have to be assessed), Ofwat could decide a definitive access price, it would not be an efficient use of resources to proceed under CA 1998 as well, and the regime in WIA 1991 was specifically designed to tackle the dispute at hand.[109] However, in making its determination under the statute, Ofwat complained that the formula for calculating the access price was unsatisfactory because it did not allow the regulator to give access to competitors so that they were able to undercut the incumbent, and urged reform.[110] Given this conclusion, should Ofwat not have considered applying CA 1998 and examined whether the access price offered by Anglian could have been characterised as an abuse of dominance? Then, unbound by the perceived defects in WIA 1991, Ofwat would have been able to tailor an effective remedy that introduced competition. According to the CAT in *Albion Water*, this route remained open because the WIA 1991 did not disapply the Chapter II prohibition.[111] However, the Court of Appeal took the view that it was unlikely that CA 1998 would bite, because it is not applicable when the conduct in question is in compliance with a legal requirement, making reference to para 5(2) of Sch to 3 CA 1998.[112] Accordingly, once Ofwat determines the

---

[108] Water Industry Act 1991, s 66.

[109] Ofwat, *Final determination by the Water Services Regulation Authority determining terms for wholesale access prices offered by Anglian Water Servces Ltd to Aquavitae (UK) to four customers* (28 March 2008), para 4.6.

[110] Ofwat, "Case highlights the need for change in water competition rules", Press Release PN08/08, 28 March 2008.

[111] *Albion Water*, n 106 above, para 978.

[112] *Dŵr Cymru*, n 23 above, para 23.

price, the dominant undertaking has no duty to offer a better price. If the CAT is right, it seems that there would be two routes to applying CA 1998: one would be private litigation; the other would be to try and force Ofwat to apply CA 1998, but this would seem to require Aquavitae to challenge Ofwat's decision not to proceed under CA 1998, and this might be difficult to achieve given that Ofwat has discretion and has given reasons which seem plausible. If the Court of Appeal is right and the undertaking is immune from CA 1998, one commentator has suggested an interesting alternative means by which to challenge Ofwat's finding, based on Art 106(1) TFEU (ex Art 86(1) EC). This provides that in relation to holders of special or exclusive rights, a Member State may not enact or maintain in force any measure contrary to EU competition law. An undertaking such as Anglian has a special right to supply water, and, if the application of WIA 1991 leads to it retaining its dominance, it may be that Ofwat is in breach of Art 106(1) TFEU read jointly with Art 102 TFEU. To avoid this result, Ofwat may be required to interpret WIA 1991 in a manner that is compliant with competition law, lest it be found in breach of EC law and potentially subject to damages claims by injured parties.[113] These legal difficulties suggest more attention must be paid to devising a clearer relationship between CA 1998 and utilities regulation.

Given the absence of competition, consumers' economic interests must be safeguarded by regulation: pricing, for instance, is regulated at regular intervals, and other aspects of each firm's performance are regulated by the Guaranteed Standards Scheme Regulations ("GSS Regulations"),[114] which include requirements that firms respond promptly to complaints and queries from customers, give notice about interruptions of supply, maintain a minimum amount of water pressure, and make payments to customers when in breach of any service standard. Failure to achieve these standards could also constitute exploitative abuses, prohibited by CA 1998, s 18. The overlap between the application of regulatory powers and CA 1998 is managed by s 22A(13) of WIA 1991 (as amended by s 48 of the Water Act 2003):

> "An enforcement authority shall not impose a penalty under this section where it is satisfied that the most appropriate way of proceeding is under the Competition Act 1998."

Prima facie it is not clear what might make CA 1998 more appropriate when the allegation is a breach of a service standard as the

---

[113] F Parker, "Applying the Cost Principle: Ofwat's First Wholesale Access Price Determination" [2006/2007] 16 Utilities Law Review 214, 216.

[114] The current version is: Water Supply and Sewerage Services (Customer Service Standards) Regulations 2008, SI 2008/594, with effect from 1 April 2008.

level of monetary fine is likely to be identical (no penalty may exceed 10 per cent of the company's turnover under both statutes):[115] when calculating the fine imposed on Severn Trent Water, Ofwat relied in part on the fining policy of the OFT and even the EC Commission in competition cases. In this decision, as in others, there is but a perfunctory statement explaining why the penalty was not imposed under CA 1998: that the infringement is a breach of the GSS Regulations, therefore CA 1998 is inappropriate.[116] This is unsatisfactory because the reason s 22 penalties are under consideration is precisely because there has been a failure of regulatory standards, and in this context WIA 1991 demands that consideration should be given to applying CA 1998 in lieu. There is a pragmatic reason why Ofwat prefers to fine a company under WIA 1991: the basis of the infringement in Thames Water was in fact over 11,000 separate infringements (including missed appointments, interruptions of water supply, and failures to deal with sewers). In an action under CA 1998, Ofwat would have to explain why each of these failures constituted abuse, and, while it is well established that sloth is an abuse of dominance, the precise parameters of exploitative abuse are not well determined. But expediency is not the same as appropriateness. It may be that action under CA 1998 would be most appropriate when Ofwat takes the view that consumers should have a right to seek damages for pecuniary and non-pecuniary losses suffered. On the other hand, consumers' interests may be better served by applying sector-specific rules, as in some cases (eg Thames Water) the firm undertook to make missed payments.[117] Earlier, voluntary payment of a lower sum is preferable to later, court ordered payment of a higher sum. So the possibility of compensation afforded by CA 1998 does not make a compelling case why action should be taken under that statute. The best reason to explain why applying WIA 1991 is more appropriate than CA 1998 is that Ofwat is testing a firm's compliance with industry standards, and its decision offers guidance to all regulated firms on how to comply with these standards, while a determination that failures amount to an abuse of dominance is not as helpful an interpretation of the relevant regulatory obligations. Thus, ensuring adequate behaviour by all regulated firms is best served by enforcement of sector-specific rules. Accordingly, as with the broad guidelines suggested by Ofgem, it appears appropriate that an Authority should weigh up the relative merits of applying competition law and regulation in an explicit

---

[115] WIA 1991, s 22A(11) (as amended).

[116] "Notice of Ofwat's imposition of a penalty on Thames Water Utilities Limited" (16 April 2008), Annex 1, p 54.

[117] *Ibid*, para 51.

manner to provide clear guidance on what action it considers to be best suited for different types of case.

6 CONCLUSIONS

This survey of the application of CA 1998 by regulators reveals a paradox: while considerable effort has been made to ensure that concurrency does not lead to inconsistency and duplication, there has been relatively little application of CA 1998 by the Authorities. There is no evidence that this is the result of regulatory capture, as revealed by frequent interventions by the Authorities using sector-specific powers. Perhaps the DTI/Treasury's suggestion that the preference for regulation is caused by path dependence, with Authorities unwilling to experiment with CA 1998 when they feel comfortable using regulatory powers, is accurate. On the other hand, it may be argued that the kinds of cases that Authorities should be considering under CA 1998 (exclusionary abuses by incumbents) are very difficult ones and even general competition authorities are slow to bring these cases, for both practical reasons (the significant amount of evidence and expert economic analysis required, the likelihood of a successful appeal by the defendant, and, as noted above in the review of Ofcom and GEMA's practice, specific market conditions require a slightly different approach to applying competition law concepts, making enforcement more demanding), and also because the line between lawful and unlawful exclusion is so blurred that there is a fear they will over-enforce competition law and thus harm competition in the long run. Furthermore, as evidenced in Ofwat's approach, it seems reasonable to favour the application of sector-specific rules when these appear to be tailor-made to tackle the dispute.

When CA 1998 has been applied, the resolution of the dispute has often hinged on the relevant regulatory framework: in *Floe*, the regulatory scheme rendering the use of public GSM gateways unlawful was the basis on which Ofcom considered there would be a defence to any abuse; in *National Grid,* the fine was reduced when it was found that the regulator had been aware of the defendant's plans; and in *Albion Water*, subsequent regulation in the sector meant that future price squeeze cases would likely be controlled by means other than CA 1998. Furthermore, in many instances when CA 1998 has not been applied and sector-specific regulation has been used instead, it might have been possible to intervene with competition law: in regulating the price of gas, in monitoring the performance of water supply companies, and in regulating mobile termination rates and migration to other internet service providers. All these matters can fall within the scope of the Chapter II prohibition but in each case there was good reason not to apply CA 1998: the pursuit of non-competition objectives in the gas sector and the practical benefits of using regulatory powers in the water and telecoms sector. Taken cumulatively, these examples suggest that more is required to explain the relationship between competition law and regulation so that an appropriate enforcement mix is achieved. This task must start by denying the government's view that regulation must give way to competition law, and this can be achieved by establishing a legitimate space for sector-specific regulation and for competition law.

Harlow and Rawlings suggest five models of regulatory legitimacy, which some take to operate cumulatively.[118] The first source of legitimacy is the presence of a legislative mandate: while competition law has a single mandate, sector regulation embodies a wider range of potentially conflicting goals, and the risk is that "the more discretion there is the less a statutory mandate can be used to justify actions and policies".[119] On the other hand, it has been argued that it is precisely the nature of public law to require decisions based on multiple factors, and the task of public lawyers to develop approaches that help the decision-makers do so in ways that are not arbitrary.[120] Second, expertise legitimates action: here both OFT and sector regulators score highly. Third, the efficiency and effectiveness of the regulator can be used to legitimise its activity, although this is a difficult, if not impossible, attribute to measure. For instance, the mere fact that the authorities do not enforce competition law significantly is not necessarily a measure of their ineffectiveness, but may be because firms comply or because there are better regulatory tools to address market failures. Fourth is oversight, and here competition law scores more highly because the process of judicial oversight is much more intensive thanks to the CAT's role, while judicial review of regulatory decisions is less thorough. A final model of legitimacy is the presence of fair administrative procedures. Here both score highly: competition law enforcement can be triggered by complaints, however the final decision is that of the authority, while regulators consult widely also at the stage of imposing remedies. In sum, while taken cumulatively it may be argued that competition law enforcement benefits from greater legitimacy, there are sufficient indicators that render regulatory intervention equally legitimate.

---

118 C Harlow and R. Rawlings, *Law and Administration* (2nd edn, 1997, Butterworths, London), pp 309–315.

119 *Ibid*, p 310.

120 T Prosser, "Privatization, Public Ownership and Public Services" (1994) 1 Juridical Review 3.

Having established the legitimacy of both forms of intervention, three conclusions follow: first that a regulator should be free to select between using competition law and regulation, but that a coherent policy mix must be designed. Here the framework suggested by Ofgem, discussed in section 4.2 above, marks a helpful starting point, and it is also echoed by the Office of Rail Regulation, whose overriding principle in determining whether to use CA 1998 or regulation is "to use the most effective, efficient and expeditious solution".[121] While it may be overly ambitious to design a detailed scheme to explain when CA 1998 will be used and when regulation will apply, the Concurrency Working Party seems an ideal forum for the discussion and publication of a framework to explore criteria to determine the relative merits of competition law and regulation. The difficulties noted in section 5.2 regarding what rules to apply to fix access prices to new entrants in the water sector shows that this is not an easy task, but that it is a necessary one. Second, that an Authority using its regulatory powers is free to reach decisions that are based on non-competition considerations set out in the statutes even at the expense of creating more competitive markets. This is not affected by EU law: while EU law imposes an obligation on a Member State to disapply national law when this authorises or facilitates an infringement of EU competition law,[122] the Court has also recognised that restrictions of competition may be justified if in the public interest.[123] The regulator's legitimacy cannot be challenged merely because it avoids a pro-competitive solution, but only when it fails to offer good reasons based on public policy to restrict competition. Third, undertakings subject to sector-specific regulation need more certainty as to the application of CA 1998 when there has been regulatory intervention. It seems that regulated undertakings merit protection from the application of CA 1998 not only when national law requires them to act in anti-competitive ways (as CA 1998 provides) but also when regulation makes the undertaking's conduct reasonable. This can be supported from Ofcom's analysis in *Floe*, which suggested an objective justification arose when the dominant firm's refusal to deal stemmed from its perception of a risk that dealing with the rival would be a criminal offence. One might consider whether the same result should obtain when the

---

[121] *ORR Competition Act Guideline: Application to Services Relating to Railways* (August 2005), para 3.23.

[122] *Consorzio Industrie Fiammiferi* v *Autorità Garante della Concorrenza e del Mercato* (Case C–198/01) [2003] ECR I-8055.

[123] *Wouters* v *Algemene Raad van de Nederlandse Orde van Advocaten* (Case C–309/99) [2002] ECR I-1577.

undertaking places reasonable reliance on the regulator, as did the defendants in the *National Grid* decision: merely reducing the fine may not be sufficient to reflect the undertaking's reliance placed on the Authority, even in the absence of a formal decision.

CHAPTER 7

BETWEEN SCYLLA AND CHARYBDIS: MARKET INVESTIGATIONS AND THE CONSUMER INTEREST

*Christian Ahlborn and Daniel Piccinin**

While 10 years have passed since the (first) UK competition law reform, market investigations, in their current incarnation, were only introduced in March 2003. Nevertheless, over 6 years and nine Competition Commission investigations later, this chapter takes a look at this unique policy instrument which straddles competition policy, consumer policy and control of anti-competitive state conduct.

Section 1 sets out the history and background of the system of market investigations and describes its key elements. Section 2 provides an overview of the market investigations which have been carried out since the entering into force of the Enterprise Act 2002 ("the Enterprise Act"). Section 3 describes the hybrid nature of market investigations while sections 4–6 set out particular issues arising from the various policy aspects of market investigations. Section 7 concludes.

1 KEY FEATURES OF UK MARKET INVESTIGATIONS

1.1 History and background

The UK market investigation regime is unique among competition policy enforcement regimes in the combination of the scope of issues that it addresses and the powers that are given to the competition authorities who operate it.[1] However, although it is unique, its

---

* The authors are competition lawyers with Linklaters. They are very grateful to Oyebola Ajayi and Zarina Bart for their research assistance, and to Bill Allan, Laura Carstensen and Vicky McMaw for their thoughtful comments. All views expressed in the chapter, however, are solely those of the authors.

[1] G Niels, H Jenkins, J Casanova, "the UK market investigations regime: taking stock after 5 years" (2008) 7 Competition Law Journal 346.

introduction was more evolutionary than revolutionary as a development of the old Mergers and Monopolies Commission ("MMC") investigations under the Fair Trading Act 1973 ("the FTA 1973"), which gave the MMC power to investigate and remedy "monopoly situations".

Prior to 1998, the monopoly provisions of the FTA 1973 were the main substantive provisions of competition law outside the area of merger control. They covered two distinct forms of monopoly situations: single firm monopoly situations (where a single firm had a market share of at least 25 per cent) and complex monopoly situations (where a set of independent firms, with an aggregate market share of at least 25 per cent, so conducted their affairs as to prevent, restrict or distort competition).[2] However, the Competition Act 1998 ("the Competition Act") introduced the Chapter I and Chapter II prohibitions, UK equivalents to the Arts 81 and 82 EC prohibitions of anti-competitive agreements and abuse of dominance respectively, thus entrusting the Office of Fair Trading with the primary enforcement powers to deal with antitrust issues, leaving the monopoly investigation regime to focus on complex monopoly situations (as single firm conduct could largely be dealt with under Chapter II of the Competition Act). The importance of the OFT and the antitrust prohibitions grew again on 1 May 2004 with the coming into force of the Modernisation Regulation,[3] which gave the OFT shared responsibility for enforcing Arts 81 and 82 (in addition to the UK equivalents) and, as described below, limited to some extent the UK competition authorities' ability to apply competition law inconsistent with EC law.

1.2 Scope of monopoly investigation and substantive provisions

The OFT describes the scope of market investigations as follows:

> "Market investigations are concerned with something different from particular anti-competitive agreements or abuses of dominance. Their purpose is to determine whether the process of competition is working effectively in markets as a whole."[4]

This scope is reflected in the breadth of the statutory power for the OFT to refer markets for investigation by the Competition

---

[2] FTA 1973, s 6.

[3] EC Regulation 1/2003 of the European Parliament and of the Council of 16 December 2002 on the implementation of the rules on competition laid down in Articles 81 and 82 of the Treaty [2003] OJ L1/1.

[4] OFT, *Market investigation references: OFT Guidelines* (hereinafter *OFT Guidelines*) (March 2006), para 2.2.

Commission. Section 131(1) of the Enterprise Act 2002 empowers the OFT to refer a market for investigation if it identifies:

> "any feature, or combination of features, of a market in the UK for goods or services [which] prevents or distorts competition in connection with the supply or acquisition of any goods or services".

Section 131(2) defines "features" to include "either the structure of the market or the conduct of one or more persons who is active in the market concerned or of their customers". The OFT defines "competition" to be the "process of rivalry between firms seeking to win customers' business" and considers that the concept of a "prevention or distortion" of competition should also be interpreted widely.[5]

1.3 Institutions and procedure

Market investigations follow a two-stage process: a reference of a market investigation is made by the OFT (often following a market study as explained below), certain sectoral regulators or (in limited circumstances) the Secretary of State to the Competition Commission, which carries out the investigation. Judicial review is carried out by the Competition Appeal Tribunal ("the CAT") with appeals from the CAT to the Court of Appeal.

In practice, the OFT is the relevant phase I authority in the overwhelming majority of cases. The OFT performs its statutory function of keeping markets under review, including launching market studies on its own initiative, in response to complaints or at the request of parts of the government. Section 11 of the Enterprise Act 2002 established a regime whereby designated consumer bodies (such as Which? or Citizens' Advice) may make "super complaints" to the OFT, whereupon the OFT has 90 days to respond publicly to the complaint, indicating what action it intends to take (such as launching a market study or referring the market for investigation by the Competition Commission) in relation to the complaint and its reasons for doing so.

Where the OFT concludes that a market requires further review either in response to a super complaint or otherwise, it will carry out a preliminary analysis and then generally launch a short study (six months) or long study (12 months). On 8 April 2009, the OFT announced that it would in future aim to consult on a reference to the Competition Commission within 6 months if a reference is being considered so as to reduce the amount of duplication with the

---

[5] *OFT Guidelines*, paras 4.1 and 4.2.

Competition Commission's work.[6] The OFT may also refer a market investigation on the basis of an investigation under its Competition Act powers.[7]

Where the requirements for a market investigation reference in s 131 are met, the OFT has discretion rather than a duty to refer the market to the Competition Commission (unlike in the case of merger control).[8] The OFT's guidance sets out four criteria that it uses to assess whether or not to refer a market for investigation:[9]

(1) whether it would be more appropriate to deal with the competition issues with the OFT's antitrust enforcement powers;
(2) whether "undertakings in lieu" that can address the competitive problems identified by the OFT can be agreed (although the OFT notes that this would be uncommon);
(3) the scale of the competition problems identified; and
(4) the availability of remedies and the value of a Competition Commission report.

Although the OFT's reference must at least identify the goods or services to which the investigation relates, it need not limit the scope of the Competition Commission's investigation any further than this. Thus, the Competition Commission is not limited to the features of the market identified by the OFT as potentially having an adverse effect on competition. However, the OFT may limit the scope of the reference to certain suppliers, customers or regions and, to the extent that the reference is so limited, the Competition Commission is bound by those limits unless the OFT subsequently varies them.[10]

Once a market has been referred to the Competition Commission for investigation, the Competition Commission has 2 years in which to reach its conclusion and publish its final report – including any remedy package that it decides upon.[11] This 2-year period does not include the remedies consultation or implementation period, however, during which the legal instruments (undertakings or orders) giving effect to the remedy package are consulted upon and implemented. However, on 8 April 2009 the Competition Commission announced that in future it would aim to publish its final report with 18 months instead of the statutory maximum of 2 years.[12]

---

[6] "OFT and CC working together to improve competition regime", OFT Press Release 41/09.
[7] *OFT Guidelines* para, 3.4.
[8] See N Parr, Chapter 8 below.
[9] *OFT Guidelines*, para 2.1.
[10] Enterprise Act 2002 (EA 2002), s 133.
[11] EA 2002, s 137.
[12] Competition Commission, "CC Publishes Corporate Plan", CC Press Release 17/09.

Section 179 of the Enterprise Act provides that applicants may seek review in the CAT of decisions of the OFT, Secretary of State, or Competition Commission in relation to market investigations. It is therefore possible to challenge either the OFT's decision as to whether or not to refer a market for investigation or the Competition Commission's findings or remedies if the market is referred. However, s 179(4) provides that the CAT shall apply the same standard of review as a court in a judicial review application, meaning that the CAT does not conduct a "full merits review" of the relevant decision.[13]

1.4 Enforcement powers and remedies

Section 138 of the Enterprise Act 2002 imposes a duty on the Competition Commission to take action (where reasonable and practicable) to remedy any adverse effect on competition and any consumer detriment that may be expected to follow from the adverse effect on competition. To this end, ss 159 and 161 empower the Competition Commission to accept undertakings from market participants or to impose any orders listed in Sch 8 to the Enterprise Act. Sch 8 entrusts the Competition Commission with an extremely wide range of remedial powers to address any adverse effects on competition identified in a market investigation. The Competition Commission's Guidance categorises these remedies as follows:[14]

"(a) remedies designed to make a significant and direct change to the structure of a market by a requirement, for example, to divest a business or assets to a newcomer to the market or to an existing, perhaps smaller, competitor;
(b) remedies designed to change the structure of a market less directly by reducing entry barriers or switching costs, for example, by requiring the licensing of know-how or intellectual property rights or by extending the compatibility of products through industry-wide technical standards;
(c) as a particular category of (b), recommendations for changes to regulations found to have adverse effects on competition or detrimental effects on customers, for example, by limiting entry to a market;
(d) remedies directing firms (whether sellers or buyers) to discontinue certain behaviour (for example, giving advance notice of price changes) or to adopt certain behaviour (for example, more prominently displaying prices and other terms and conditions of sale);

---

[13] See D Bailey, Chapter 2 above.
[14] Competition Commission Guidelines, para 4.18.

(e) remedies designed to restrain the way in which firms would otherwise behave, for example, the imposition of a price cap;
(f) monitoring remedies, for example, a requirement to provide the OFT with information on prices or profits."

In determining which, if any, remedies to impose or recommend, the Competition Commission first identifies remedies "that would be effective in dealing with the adverse effects on competition of the market features rather than seeking to deal with any detrimental effects on customers".[15] Section 134(7) of the Enterprise Act also provides that the Competition Commission may have regard to any impact of its remedies on "relevant customer benefits" that may be connected with the feature of the market identified as responsible for the adverse effect on competition. However, the Competition Commission considers that it would not normally be the case that such a feature brings benefits to customers, as the adverse effect of competition would normally be expected to harm consumers.[16]

1.5 Policy goal

Although the Enterprise Act 2002 technically requires the Competition Commission to remedy "adverse effects on competition" irrespective of whether the adverse effect has caused any consumer detriment (unless the adverse effect is beneficial for consumers), the OFT and Competition Commission both interpret "adverse effects on competition" from a consumer welfare perspective. Thus, they are not necessarily focused on simple measures such as the number of firms in the market or the degree of concentration, but rather by the extent to which firms are incentivised to compete to "win customers' business" and therefore generate good outcomes for consumers (through price, quality, service, innovation, etc).[17]

2 MARKET INVESTIGATIONS: OVERVIEW OVER THE LAST 6 YEARS

2.1 Stage 1: reference stage

The OFT has carried out a total of 33 market studies since 2002 and has a further three currently in progress. These have covered a wide range of markets, with most but not all addressing issues in markets for which the customers are individual consumers (some

---

[15] Competition Commission Guidelines, para 4.2.
[16] *Ibid*, para 4.2.3.
[17] See eg, paras 1.16–1.18 of the Competition Commission's Guidance and para 4.1 of the OFT's *Guidelines*.

exceptions being the market studies into public sector procurement and the distribution of medicine). However, only four market studies have resulted in market investigation references to the Competition Commission:

(1) *Classified Directory Advertising Services*;
(2) *Payment Protection Insurance (PPI)*;
(3) *BAA Airports*; and
(4) *Store Card Services*.

In addition to the four market investigation references arising from OFT market studies, the OFT has also referred the following three markets to the Competition Commission in response to "super complaints":

(1) *Groceries* (super complaint by the Association of Convenience Stores ("ACS") and successful CAT challenge to the OFT's initial decision not to refer);
(2) *Home Credit* (super complaint by NCC); and
(3) *Northern Irish Personal Banking* (super complaint by General Consumer of Northern Ireland and Which?).

Finally, the OFT also referred the *Market for the Supply of LPG* without either a market study or a super complaint. Instead, on this occasion the OFT simply conducted a "preliminary investigation", met the requirement for consultation by writing to LPG suppliers and then referred the market to the Competition Commission. The only other market to have been referred to the Competition Commission is the *Market for the Leasing of Rolling Stock*. This market was referred by the Office of the Rail Regulator following a market study at the request of the Department for Transport.

Ofcom, the regulator for the communications and media sector, and Ofgem, the regulator for the energy sector, have also conducted market studies with a view to possible references to the Competition Commission, but to date have not made any references. However, undertakings in lieu of a reference have been given, notably to Ofcom in 2005 when BT agreed to functional separation of its network from its other operations to avoid a reference to the Competition Commission.[18]

Although the Secretary of State has not to date made any references to the Competition Commission pursuant to his powers under s 132 of the Enterprise Act, the House of Commons Business and Enterprise Committee published a report on 21 April 2009

[18] Ofcom, *Final Statements on the Strategic Review of Telecommunications, and Undertakings in Lieu of a Reference Under the Enterprise Act 2002*, (September 2005).

recommending that the Secretary of State exercise these powers in respect of the pub market.[19]

2.2 Stage 2: Competition Commission stage

As indicated above, the Competition Commission has conducted nine market investigations (including those still underway). The Competition Commission identified an "adverse effect on competition" in each of these investigations and accordingly imposed remedies in all of them.

2.3 Appeals: the CAT

Issues relating to market investigations have come before the CAT on four occasions, one of which is currently in progress. First, in 2005, the Association of Convenience Stores ("ACS") sought judicial review of the OFT's decision not to refer the groceries market for investigation by the Competition Commission. The ACS argued, *inter alia*, that the OFT had mistaken the level of certainty as to the existence of adverse effects on competition required for a reference decision. Before the CAT could determine the matter, however, the OFT indicated that it wished to withdraw its decision not to refer the market because it considered its decision was not fully reasoned. The CAT therefore quashed the OFT's decision and directed it to consider the issue again, whereupon the OFT decided to refer the market to the Competition Commission.[20]

The second application to the CAT in relation to a market investigation also related to the groceries investigation. One of the remedies imposed by the Competition Commission in that case was a recommendation that planning laws be altered to include a "competition test" in relation to new stores or extensions by incumbents with high market shares in local markets. Tesco appealed against this decision on the basis that the Competition Commission had not conducted a thorough cost–benefit analysis, and the CAT agreed.[21] The Competition Commission has now conducted that analysis and concluded that the competition test should still be included in the remedy package, albeit subject to a new *de minimis* threshold.[22]

The third application to the CAT in relation to a market investigation was brought by Barclays following the Competition

---

[19] House of Commons Business and Enterprise Committee, *Pub Companies*, Seventh Report of Session 2008–09.

[20] *Association of Convenience Stores* v *OFT* [2005] CAT 36.

[21] *Tesco plc* v *Competition Commission* [2009] CAT 6.

[22] Competition Commission, *Groceries Market Investigation: Remittal of the Competition Test by the Competition Appeal Tribunal* (2 October 2009).

Commission's decision in the *PPI* investigation. Barclays' challenge was aimed primarily at the Competition Commission's remedy of a ban on the marketing of PPI at the point of sale on similar grounds to the Tesco appeal. Again, the CAT agreed that the Competition Commission had failed to give sufficient consideration to the potential harm that the remedy could cause and so has remitted the issue to the Competition Commission for further consideration.[23]

Finally, BAA has brought an application in relation to the *BAA Airports* investigation, challenging the decision to require BAA to sell two of its three London airports.[24] However, BAA's case is narrower than those brought by Tesco and Barclays, as BAA is not challenging the decision on the ground that the Competition Commission's analysis was flawed, but on grounds of bias (one member of the panel had links to a group potentially interested in Gatwick airport) and that requiring the sale in the economic downturn would impose disproportionate economic costs on BAA.

3 THE NATURE OF MARKET INVESTIGATIONS: A HYBRID POLICY

3.1 Nature and scope

"Classic" competition policy – at least as practised in most jurisdictions outside the UK – is generally based on the entrustment of an administrative body (either through its own enforcement powers or as a prosecutor in the courts) with the preservation of the competitive status quo, rather than seeking to improve competition or consumer outcomes beyond what the market would deliver in the absence of any "foul play" by competitors. As it has developed in light of modern economic thought, this "classic" competition policy generally involves the prohibition of certain forms of conduct as anti-competitive based on the following core elements of analysis:

(1) *Significant market power*: competition policy has generally come to accept that the existence of significant market power is a prerequisite for firms to cause significant harm to competition (with the exception of hard-core collusion).
(2) *An anti-competitive act*: the second element is an anti-competitive act by a firm with market power (whether on the supply or demand side). The anti-competitive act could be a merger, an agreement or unilateral behaviour such as predatory pricing or a refusal to deal.

---

23 *Barclays Bank plc* v *Competition Commission* [2009] CAT 27.

24 *BAA Ltd* v *Competition Commission* (CAT Case 1110/6/8/09).

(3) *Consumer harm*: modern competition policy generally also requires demonstration of consumer harm (although in some cases, such as cartels, this may be assumed), for example in the form of higher prices, reduced quality or reduced choice.[25]
(4) Finally, there has to be *causality* between the anti-competitive act and the consumer harm.

Market investigations, however, have a more ambitious objective and a correspondingly wider scope than "classic" competition policy. The Competition Commission is not required to treat any aspect of market structure or behaviour as "given", but rather has an extremely wide brief to identify any aspect of the market to which changes could be made that would significantly improve competition. As a result of of the breadth of the Competition Commission's mandate, it is not limited by any of the four key elements of "classic" competition policy outlined above. Given that adverse effects on competition may arise even without significant market power (for instance, if firms are competitively constrained but consumers are ineffective at exploiting these competitive constraints because they are largely "inert"), there is no requirement for the Competition Commission to identify market power (although in practice market power is often relevant to the Competition Commission's analysis). Moreover, because the adverse effect on competition may arise from some aspect of market structure or consumer behaviour, there is no requirement that any anti-competitive act be identified (let alone causally linked to consumer harm). It is sufficient for the Competition Commission to show that "the process of competition" is not working effectively (in the sense of producing good outcomes for consumers) and indeed the fact that consumers themselves are responsible for the negative outcomes identified is no barrier to the Competition Commission's duty to intervene on their behalf.

Due to their wider scope, market investigations are a hybrid of four different policy areas:

(1) "classic" competition policy (as defined above);
(2) extended competition policy (ie addressing market power but without any anticompetitive act);
(3) consumer policy (including issues of transparency, search and switching costs – both real and imagined);
(4) control of anti-competitive state conduct.

We will address each of these four areas in turn.

---

[25] It is often sufficient to demonstrate harm to the immediate customers of the firms engaging in the anti-competitive conduct rather than necessarily to end-users as well.

3.2 Classic competition policy aspects of market investigations

The terms of the Competition Commission's mandate in the market investigation powers set out in the Enterprise Act 2002 are clearly cast widely enough to cover conduct that would constitute violations of the classic antitrust offences: in other words, an anti-competitive agreement or unilateral act would also amount to a "feature or combination of features which prevents, restricts or distorts competition".[26]

A legal difficulty that arises from this overlap is that the Competition Commission is not empowered to apply Arts 101 and 102 TFEU, and yet, when investigating conduct that engages either prohibition, the Modernisation Regulation requires that national competition authorities apply those provisions as appropriate. Moreover, with respect to agreements within Art 101 TFEU, national competition authorities cannot apply a more restrictive approach than that taken by European law (the same is not true for Art 82). The difficulty is that, in the UK, only the OFT (and the sectoral regulators) have jurisdiction to apply the EU prohibitions. Accordingly, if the Competition Commission were to consider any agreements within the terms of Art 101 TFEU or any conduct within Art 102 TFEU, it would need to bring these to the attention of the OFT to investigate, and at least with respect to the agreements, the Competition Commission could not impose any remedies additional to those imposed by the OFT.

The OFT's guidance on market investigations indicates that it attempts to avoid this overlap of market investigations with antitrust enforcement by applying its Competition Act powers whenever there is a potential infringement of the antitrust offences. It will only consider a reference to the Competition Commission in one of two circumstances:[27]

(1) when it has reasonable grounds to suspect that there are market features, which prevent, restrict or distort competition, but not to establish a breach of the Competition Act prohibitions;
(2) when an action under the Competition Act has been or is likely to be ineffective for dealing with the adverse effect on competition identified (for example, because of the more limited remedies available).

For this reason, the OFT has stated that:

> "Market investigation references are therefore likely to focus on competition problems arising from uncoordinated parallel conduct by several firms or industry-wide features of a market in cases where

[26] EA 2002, s 134(1).
[27] *OFT Guidelines*, para 2.2.

the OFT does not have reasonable grounds to suspect the existence of anti-competitive agreements or dominance."[28]

This means that the large number of market investigations should fall outside the scope of classic competition policy. As we will see, this is indeed the case.

Nevertheless, a number of potential areas of overlap remain, primarily with Art 102 TFEU:

(1) control of single firm dominance, particularly where the anti-competitive conduct of a single firm is associated with structural features of the market or customer conduct or where a structural remedy may be appropriate;
(2) control of collective dominance: where parallel behaviour in an oligopolistic market is concerned, there may be an overlap with Art 102 TFEU but the European case law gives relatively limited guidance as to the scope of the prohibition;
(3) in certain circumstances, network effects of vertical agreements.

Only one of the nine market investigations addresses issues that could arguably be described as classic competition policy, namely *Classified Directory Advertising Services*. Given that this investigation was concerned with whether undertakings that had been given following an earlier investigation under the FTA 1973 required amendment or further undertakings in light of market developments (including further instances of potentially anti-competitive conduct), it should not be considered strong evidence of willingness on the part of either the OFT or the Competition Commission to deal with classic competition policy issues in market investigations.

3.3 Extended competition policy aspects of market investigations

As noted above, the scope of competition policy applied in market investigations goes far beyond classic competition policy of prohibiting anti-competitive acts. We refer to those cases in which the Competition Commission intervenes to address market power directly, or aspects of market structure that give rise to market power (for example, high degree of concentration, barriers to entry, network effects, etc) as "extended competition policy" cases.

The clearest example of this kind of application is the *BAA Airports* investigation,[29] in which BAA had a virtual monopoly in airport ownership in London and southern Scotland. Although it had

---

[28] *OFT Guidelines*, para 2.4.

[29] Competition Commission, *BAA airports market investigation – A report on the supply of airport services by BAA in the UK* (19 March 2009).

not engaged in any conduct that could be described as anti-competitive, the Competition Commission has required the divestment of two airports in London and one in Scotland on the basis of a finding that the common ownership of these airports was leading to adverse outcomes for consumers because the lack of competition reduced investment incentives.

3.4 Consumer policy aspects of market investigations

Section 131(2) of the Enterprise Act 2002 extends the concept of a "feature of a market" to include the behaviour of any person in the market, so the Competition Commission's market investigation powers extend beyond what would ordinarily be called "competition policy" to address problems that stem from aspects of consumer behaviour.[30] Thus, even in a market with a large number of suppliers who in normal circumstances would compete aggressively, if consumers are (either because of real or perceived search or switching costs or through some imperfection in their decision process) not active searchers or switchers such that firms lack the incentive to compete and therefore offer low quality service or high prices, this may be a feature of the market that the Competition Commission seeks to remedy.[31] Often consumers' inertia is found to be the combined result of real and imagined obstacles to search and switching. As the OFT's guidance states:

> "Competition requires customer choice. In order to make informed choices customers need to spend at least some time and effort finding out what alternative products are available to them. Where such search costs are perceived to be high searching is likely to be curtailed. Customer sensitivity about a product may also limit the amount of search that will be contemplated. Depending on other features of the market, reduced searching may blunt sellers' incentives to compete."[32]

In the *Liquefied Petroleum Gas* investigation ("LPG investigation")[33] the Competition Commission identified elements of market structure (that LPG tanks were owned by the supplier, with the result that switching required removal of the tank by the existing supplier and installation of a new tank by the new supplier, with consumers

---

[30] OFT, *Interactions between competition and consumer policy – Economic discussion paper*, para 2.12. As acknowledged in Armstrong, some aspects of these consumer policy issues could arguably be considered to overlap with competition policy, such as the case where real switching costs confer market power on suppliers.

[31] This is roughly the fact pattern for the PPI investigation, the Extended Warranties investigation and the OFT's PCA market study.

[32] *OFT Guidelines* para 7.2.

[33] Competition Commission, *Market investigation into supply of bulk liquefied petroleum gas for domestic use* (29 June 2006).

paying both their existing supplier and their new supplier to switch) that increased real switching costs, but it also said that customers were not well informed as to the existence of alternative suppliers. Similarly, in the *Personal current accounts* (PCA) market study[34] the OFT has identified both real and perceived switching costs.

In contrast to the OFT's consumer protection powers (for instance, under Part 8 of the Enterprise Act 2002, the Consumer Protection from Unfair Trading Regulations 2008[35] or the Unfair Terms in Consumer Contracts Regulations 1999[36] ("UTCCR 1999"), which require some element of unfair conduct on the part of the supplier, in a market investigation context the Competition Commission is not required to show that the consumer harm associated with the consumer behaviour that causes the adverse effects are in any way linked to conduct (whether fair or otherwise) of firms. Nevertheless, it is often the case that where consumers are inert or wrongly perceive search or switching costs to be high, there will be some aspect of firms' behaviour that aggravates or exploits the problem. For example, in the *Northern Ireland Personal Banking* market investigation, the Competition Commission suggested that consumers' inability to drive effective competition was partly because the banks had designed charges that were not only complex, but unduly so, in the sense that they were "more complex than might reasonably be necessitated solely by the wide variety of uses or services offered".[37] Consumers could not cope with the complexity and therefore could not identify the best offer available.

As with the overlap between competition policy in market investigations and antitrust enforcement, there can also potentially be an overlap between the OFT's consumer protection powers and its market investigation reference powers. The OFT's approach to this overlap is to prefer market studies and investigations where there is a market-wide issue or combination of issues that could benefit from the flexibility of analysis and remedial options of market investigations.[38] Where appropriate, the OFT may also use a combination of powers, as it has done in relation to personal current accounts, where it has brought proceedings in the courts to challenge the fairness of unauthorised overdraft charges under the UTCCRs in parallel with a market study into the market as a whole.

---

34 OFT, *Personal current accounts in the UK – OFT Market study* (July 2008), para 5.1.

35 SI 2008/1277.

36 SI 1999/2083

37 Competition Commission, *Northern Irish Personal Banking, Personal current accounts banking services in Northern Ireland market investigation*, para 4.122.

38 H Priest and G Winton, "The OFT market studies" The Beesley Lectures – Lectures on Regulation Series XVIII) (2008).

Examples of markets that have been investigated by the Competition Commission that have raised consumer issues are the *Store Card Credit Services*, *Home Credit*, *Northern Ireland Personal Banking* and *PPI* markets.

3.5 Control of anti-competitive government behaviour

The Competition Commission also considers markets in which government intervention has an adverse effect on competition, often in interaction with other aspects of the market such as consumer behaviour or concentration. In these investigations the Competition Commission identifies the government intervention, shows that it restricts competition, and then demonstrates that the restriction of competition results in consumer harm, thus potentially justifying a recommendation to change the government intervention. Examples include the *Groceries* investigation,[39] in which the Competition Commission considered that certain aspects of the local planning regime acted as barriers to entry, and the *Rolling Stock* investigation,[40] in which the Competition Commission found that the structure and timing of the government's procurement process limited the ability of rolling stock leasing companies to compete with each other.

The Competition Commission's willingness to intervene in a wide range of regulatory matters on consumers' behalf provides an interesting contrast with European competition law where Art 106(1) TFEU focuses on "public undertakings and undertakings to which Member States grant special or exclusive rights" and stipulates that in relation to these undertakings:

> "Member States shall neither enact or maintain in force any measure contrary to the rules contained in the Treaties, in particular to those rules provided for in Article 18 and Articles 101 to 109."

Both regimes allow other considerations to override competition concerns: Art 106(2) TFEU preserves Member States' rights to engage undertakings to perform "services of general economic interest" and effectively disapplies competition law insofar as it would interfere with the Member States' ability to do so, while s 134(8) of the Enterprise Act 2002 allows the Competition Commission to consider whether any restriction of competition caused by government intervention is offset by other benefits of that intervention for customers. All in all, there is a much greater scope for intervention by the Competition Commission and a more intrusive analysis under the

---

[39] Competition Commission, *Market investigation into the supply of groceries in the UK* (30 April 2008), para 7.65.

[40] Competition Commission, *Rolling Stock Leasing market investigation* (7 April 2009).

UK market investigation provisions than is the case for the European Commission under EC law.

This can be explained by two facts: first, any conclusions of the Competition Commission in respect of government actions are mere recommendations which the Government is free to accept or reject while the European Commission has the power to proceed against a Member State to enforce the Art 106(1) prohibition.[41] In addition, there is the fact that European law is supra-national in character and must to some extent be sensitive to the preferences of Member State Governments, as well as the fact that the Competition Commission cannot compel government to change regulations but rather can only recommend such changes.

3.6 Development of Competition Commission policy over time

As Peter Freeman, the Chairman of the Competition Commission, has said, there are dangers in seeking an agenda in the decisional practice of the Competition Commission because it does not have control over the number or type of cases that it reviews over time.[42] Thus, although Derek Ridyard's observation that the Competition Commission appears to have a "preoccupation" with consumer policy issues of transparency, information, search and switching costs reflects the fact that these issues have been central to just over half of market investigations conducted so far (with the *Classified Directory Advertising*, *BAA Airports*, *Rolling Stock* and *Groceries* investigations providing the exceptions),[43] this is, if anything, a reflection on the OFT's priorities rather than the Competition Commission's priorities.[44] Moreover, it appears that this focus on consumer issues may be abating, with three of the four market investigations opened since 2006 not raising any of these issues (the *PPI* investigation being the exception), compared to four of the five investigations commenced prior to 2006 raising at least some issues of consumer policy.

---

[41] The Commission may proceed against a Member State either under Art 106(3) or Art 258 TFEU, depending on the nature of the state measure in question.

[42] P Freeman, "'The Competition Commission's Northern Ireland banking market investigation: some unanswered questions on the role of market investigations' – a reply" (2008) ECLR 497.

[43] D Ridyard, "The Competition Commission's Northern Ireland banking market investigation: some unanswered questions on the role of market investigations" (2008) 29(3) ECLR 173. In Ridyard's defence, of these only the *Classified Advertising* investigation had been concluded at the time that he made his observation.

[44] Even the OFT does not have complete control over its agenda as it is obliged to respond to super complaints and political interference may also require an OFT response in some circumstances.

A clearer view of the development of the Competition Commission's market investigation practice can be gleaned from the change in the type of remedies imposed over time, although of course to some extent this will be a function of the change in type of issues raised in the investigations. The Competition Commission's decisions in the early years of the market investigation regime largely resulted in recommendations and orders concerned with increasing the provision of information to customers, making the process of switching easier and facilitating consumer choice. With the exception of the *Classified Directory Advertising* investigation, the most coercive remedy imposed prior to 2008 was to require store card providers to offer payment protection alongside a package of payment protection and the card. Although the *Classified Advertising* investigation resulted in quite draconian remedies such as price regulation and restrictions on Yell's ability to expand into related market segments, that case should be understood as somewhat exceptional in light of both the subject-matter and the historical context of the investigation (ie Yell was already a price regulated entity following a previous FTA investigation and this investigation addressed the issue that Yell was effectively circumventing the regulations by expanding through a second-tier product that had not yet been regulated).[45]

In contrast to these early decisions, 2008 and 2009 saw the Competition Commission issue final reports in three market investigations imposing more drastic remedies that have been appealed in the CAT: the *Groceries* investigation, the *PPI* investigation and the *BAA Airport* investigation. In respect of the groceries market, the Competition Commission recommended the introduction of a "competition test" that would prevent firms with high market shares in a local market from expanding.[46] Clearly this remedy has the potential to make things worse for consumers rather than better if new entrants are slow to or indeed never enter these markets but the incumbent would have been willing to expand quickly. The CAT quashed the remedy and sent it back to the Competition Commission. After a further investigation the Competition Commission concluded that the benefits outweighed the costs, although the Competition Commission did acknowledge that a *de minimis* threshold would improve the remedy.

In the *PPI* investigation the Competition Commission has prohibited banks from providing PPI at the point of sale of the

---

[45] Competition Commission, *Market investigation into classified directory advertising services* (21 December 2006), para 58.

[46] Competition Commission, *Market investigation into the supply of groceries in the UK* (30 April 2008), para 11.35.

associated credit.[47] Again, even if this does result in increased search and competition, it clearly imposes a cost on consumers (by removing the most convenient distribution channel) and may (if consumers' inertia is robust to the new policy) result in fewer consumers obtaining insurance – the opposite of the intended effect of the remedy. Again, the CAT considered that the Competition Commission had failed to take sufficient account of this issue. Curiously, however, the CAT did not consider the direct effect of the more convenient distribution channel (ie that consumers save time by purchasing PPI at the point of sale rather than shopping around elsewhere) to be a relevant customer benefit for the purposes of s 134(8) of the Enterprise Act. According to the CAT, the Competition Commission's error was limited to failing to consider the indirect effect of the reduction in PPI sales that may follow from this lack of convenience.[48]

In *BAA Airports* there is less concern as to the immediate effect of the remedy (divestment of airports) on competition (although capacity constraints may limit some of the benefits). However, imposing forced divestments on a company that purchased the monopoly assets in good faith (which were put on the market in that form by the Government) and has done nothing more than behave as a regulated monopolist seems like a harsh decision and may ultimately have implications for the government's ability to obtain a good sale price for privatisations of companies with market power in the future (for instance, Royal Mail). The Competition Commission does not appear to have considered this issue in its assessment of the proportionality of the divestment remedy; however, it did note that when Ferrovial acquired BAA the OFT had already commenced a market study that raised the issue of BAA's common ownership of UK airports and so Ferrovial ought to have taken this into account in its purchase price.[49] Of course, the same cannot be said for the private shareholders who participated in the privatisation of BAA in 1987. In any event, the issue does not appear to have been raised by BAA on appeal either. If this unintended consequence is beyond the scope of the issues that the Competition Commission is empowered or required to consider, then that is all the more concerning for the assessment of the potential for the market investigation regime to give rise to harmful effects.

Although it is too early to draw definitive conclusions as to the direction of the Competition Commission, the more recent decisions may reflect a growing confidence that it is possible to achieve large gains

[47] Competition Commission, *Market investigation into payment protection insurance* (29 January 2009), paras 10.34–10.35.

[48] *Barclays Bank plc* v *Competition Commission* [2009] CAT 27, para 135.

[49] Competition Commission, *BAA airports market investigation – A report on the supply of airport services by BAA in the UK* (19 March 2009), para 10.97.

for consumers through strong intervention in markets, including those that actually limit consumer choice or convenience or firms' ability to expand to meet demand. Indeed, it is instructive to note that both in the *PPI* and *Groceries* investigations, the Competition Commission's remedies differed from the approach that it had taken to similar issues in earlier cases. Thus, the Competition Commission's prohibition of selling PPI at the point of sale was in part motivated by the Competition Commission's disappointment that its own weaker, information and choice based remedies imposed in relation to essentially the same issue in the *Extended Warranties* investigation,[50] under the old FTA regime, had removed only a fraction of the total consumer welfare loss caused by the point of sale advantage. The idea of crafting remedies to target the achievement of "first best" results for consumers reflects a highly ambitious and confident approach to consumer and competition policy.

The Competition Commission had also recommended a less mechanistic version of the competition test in its earlier groceries investigation under the FTA 1973 (the Competition Commission recommended that major supermarkets seek approval from the OFT for new stores and extensions, but did not recommend that approval be given solely on the basis of a mechanistic market share and fascia count test).[51] That recommendation was never implemented and the Competition Commission did not refer to its earlier proposal in its assessment of the merits of the current proposed competition test.

4 ISSUES REGARDING COMPETITION POLICY ASPECTS OF MARKET INVESTIGATIONS

4.1 Complexity and error costs in competition cases

Policy makers and scholars have become increasingly aware of the importance of error costs in the evaluation of competition policy. The greater the likelihood of erroneous decisions (in terms of permitting harmful behaviours or prohibiting welfare enhancing behaviour) and the greater the costs of those errors, the more questionable is such a policy. The various elements of the analytical framework for classic competition policy ((i) the assessment of market power; (ii) the identification of an anti-competitive act; (iii) the identification of a counterfactual; and (iv) the assessment of consumer harm resulting from the anti-competitive act) are intended to limit the

---

[50] Competition Commission, *Extended warranties on domestic electrical goods – A report on the supply of extended warranties on domestic electrical goods within the UK* (30 September 2003).

[51] Competition Commission, *Market investigation into the supply of groceries in the UK* (30 April 2008).

error costs and balance type I and type II errors of competition policy enforcement.

The likelihood of enforcement errors is dependent on a number of factors:

(1) *The scope and complexity of the anti-competitive act*: the assessment of an individual act (whether a specific type of behaviour by a dominant firm or a specific agreement between two undertakings) is generally less prone to error than the assessment of the behaviour of a number of firms in the context of joint dominance or the assessment of a network of agreements.
(2) *The relationship between anti-competitive acts and consumer harm*: the clearer and better understood the relationship between a potentially anti-competitive act and the consumer harm, the smaller the likelihood of error. Competition authorities generally get the assessment of horizontal agreements right (to the extent that they are assessed at all) and the impact of horizontal mergers is also well understood. By contrast, where particular acts, such as bundling and/or tying, are often pro-competitive but in certain specific circumstances may also have anti-competitive effects, the authorities are more prone to error.
(3) *The simplicity of the counterfactual*: it is easier to assess the implications of a potential anti-competitive act if the counterfactual is simply the absence of the act in question, ie to assess the impact of a particular agreement against the absence of an agreement or the impact of a rebate against the absence of that rebate. By contrast, the scope of error increases significantly in situations where competition authorities implicitly have to choose the "correct" outcome among a range of possibilities (for example in cases of excessive pricing or other forms of exploitative abuses, where the authorities *de facto* have to define the "right" price).

These considerations have important implications for the competition policy aspects (both classic and extended competition policy) of market investigations:

(1) Where the market investigation policy overlaps with classic competition policy is in relation to complex dominance cases, for example abuse by collectively dominant firms. One reason why "what qualifies as an abuse of collective dominance is underdeveloped in the case law"[52] is that collective dominance cases are difficult to assess and even more difficult to remedy. These cases do not become less difficult merely by pursuing them under a different policy instrument.

---

[52] Paragraph 2.5 of the *OFT Guidelines* on market investigation references.

(2) As far as extended competition policy aspects in market investigations are concerned, the above considerations in respect of error costs suggest that such a policy is highly prone to error: the scope of the investigation generally goes beyond individual acts and may comprise entire markets; the relationship between the "features" in question and consumer harm is far less well understood than even relatively complex anti-competitive acts; and there is no simple counterfactual in market investigations.

Both of these implications will be discussed in more detail in the following two sub-sections.

4.2 Implications for market investigations within the scope of "classic" competition policy

The fact that there are only a very small number of Art 82 or Chapter II cases dealing with abuses of joint dominance or exploitative abuses is not primarily due to a lack of power under those prohibitions. The concept of abuse of joint dominance has been recognised and the definition of abuse has similarly become flexible. Indeed, *Höfner* and *P&I Clubs* suggest that exploitative clauses could be expanded to scenarios where the dominant firm is underperforming.[53]

To the extent that market investigations aim to cover ground which is also covered by Arts 101 and 102 TFEU or Chapters I and II, in particular networks of vertical agreements and abuse of joint dominance, the Competition Commission is likely to run into similar problems as "classic" competition policy, namely complexity of analysis, high likelihood of error and difficulty in identifying an appropriate remedy.

At most, one of the nine market investigations could be described as falling within the scope of classic competition policy. This may reflect the fact that the OFT aims to address those issues under the domestic and EU prohibitions – it may, however, also reflect the fact that some of these issues are just too difficult to tackle.

4.3 Implications for extended competition policy

The main benefit of market investigations is the flexibility that they provide the Competition Commission in improving competitive outcomes for consumers. Thus, in principle, the idea of imposing remedies to address consumer harm that flows directly from market power, irrespective of the existence of anything recognisable as an

---

[53] *Höfner & Elsner* v *Macrotron GmbH* (Case C–41/90) [1991] ECR I–1979, *P&I Clubs*, (Case IV/30.373) Commission Decision 1999/329/EC [1999] OJ L125/12.

"abuse" of that power, seems a natural application of the market investigation system.

However, dispensing with the requirement to establish an anti-competitive act that is responsible for the consumer harm almost inevitably leads to more drastic intervention than in "classic" competition policy enforcement, less rigorous analysis of the prospective effects of the remedy, and hence an increased likelihood of imposing harmful remedies. This is because the requirement to demonstrate anti-competitive conduct provides a (relatively) clear (albeit far from perfectly so in the abuse of dominance context) counterfactual for the assessment of the consumer harm (ie prohibition of the anti-competitive act) and therefore a clear link between the assessment of consumer harm and the net benefits of a remedy.

If the investigation addresses only the existence of market power causing consumer harm, the range of potential remedies open to the Competition Commission to address that market power is highly open-ended (including, for example, price regulation, the encouragement of entry and divestments). The selection of the optimal remedy is likely to be a very difficult task. Some remedies may promise more potential upside gains, but also more downside risks, whereas others may be more modest but at least be sure to do no harm. Moreover, since remedies to address market structure are by their nature generally more intrusive, permanent and far-reaching than the prohibition of a particular form of anti-competitive conduct, the prospect of unintended consequences is far more significant in these cases.

The example of *BAA Airports* illustrates these issues. The Competition Commission observed that BAA was not competitively constrained and that consumer outcomes were in some respects poor. It inferred that consumers were harmed by the lack of competition and therefore has ordered BAA to divest some of its airports to introduce effective competition. Although the competition analysis in this case was relatively straightforward, it is by no means clear that the result will ultimately be positive for society. By demonstrating its willingness to impose divestment obligations on firms that have not engaged in any anti-competitive conduct, the Competition Commission has effectively signalled that investing in monopoly assets (either through purchasing existing assets or investing to build or improve them) creates an exposure to the risk of what is effectively expropriation.[54] The repercussions of this intervention, both in UK airport markets and in other UK markets could potentially be serious. Moreover, these repercussions

[54] Although BAA will of course receive payment for the airports it sells, the new purchasers will clearly not pay the value of the airports as monopolies (which was the basis on which BAA was acquired) and will also be negotiating the purchase in the knowledge that BAA is required to sell.

are not necessary to achieve the aim of increased competition. First, at least in the case of privatisations, the entire issue could in many cases be avoided if the Government consulted with the competition authorities prior to conducting the privatisation on a monopoly basis. Second, even if *ex post* rectification of an anti-competitive privatisation is required, there is no reason why this could not be done with adequate compensation for investors. If it is true that social welfare is improved by requiring divestments, then it should be feasible for the Government to compensate investors for the full value of the divestment businesses (on a monopoly basis), rather than limiting their compensation to what they can reap from a forced sale without the benefit of their monopoly. At the very least, the decision as to whether to require a forced divestment without adequate compensation should be made by the Government rather than an independent authority.

4.4 Absence of deterrent effect

Classic competition policy has two effects. First, as a direct result it alters the behaviour of the firms which have been subject to the investigations. Firms will amend or cease to operate agreements which are held to contravene competition law and dominant firms will stop behaviour which has been found to be abusive.

In addition, competition policy also affects firms which are not subject to an investigation through a general deterrent effect. This deterrent effect is dependent on: (a) the extent to which unlawful conduct is identifiable *ex ante*; (b) the impact of the sanctions (for example, size of a fine); and (c) the likelihood of detection.

In the context of classic antitrust enforcement, this deterrent effect is often considered to be more important than the direct effect.[55] This is because – especially in the case of cartels – the conduct is relatively easy for firms to identify as unlawful *ex ante*, the sanctions are high and with the OFT's leniency policy the likelihood of detection is also high. The deterrent effect is weaker for abuse of dominance because of the complexity of the law and likelihood of detection (or enforcement activity), but nevertheless the possibility of enforcement action is likely to be a factor driving some clearly dominant firms' business activities (for better or worse). The effect of market investigations is almost exclusively limited to the firms and markets which are subject to an investigation. This direct impact is generally wider than in classic competition cases as investigations do not focus merely on a narrow anti-competitive act.

---

[55] See, eg, Deloitte, *The deterrent effect of competition enforcement by the OFT* (November 2007), para 2.7.

At the same time, market investigations have no or almost no wider deterrent effect beyond the remit of their investigation. First and foremost, this is because there are no acts comparable to those prohibited by Arts 101 and 102 TFEU or Chapters I and II which are *ex ante* prohibited and therefore capable of being deterred. Moreover, the assessment of the types of features (including conduct by firms) that form the subject of the market investigations is too complex to be clearly identified in advance. This is not to say that market investigations could not have an impact on how firms behave in the future (it may well be the case, for example, that firms may be more wary to purchase a monopoly from the UK Government in future); however, that impact may be hard to predict and indeed may be unintended.

Finally, there is only a handful of market investigations every year and no private enforcement mechanism, meaning that the likelihood of any given adverse effect on competition forming the subject of a market investigation is very low. This means that any benefit from a market investigation has to flow directly from the positive impact of the investigation in the market in question and that that impact has to be sufficiently large to outweigh the non-trivial costs of the market investigation process in terms of management time, costs for advisers, etc. The Competition Commission's approach to evaluating the consumer benefit of its market investigations is to calculate the annual consumer detriment of the adverse effect on competition that it identifies and remedies. It does not, however, make any attempt to measure the effectiveness of its remedies in removing this detriment.[56] One study that attempted to do this estimated that the Competition Commission's remedy package only reduced consumer detriment by 5 per cent.[57]

4.5 The risk of crowding out: incongruent powers and legal standards

One would normally expect that greater powers of intervention of an authority are linked to a higher threshold for intervention. However, while the Competition Commission has no power to fine (unlike the OFT in antitrust enforcement cases), its powers to intervene in the market are otherwise greater under the market investigation provisions than under Arts 81 and 82 and Chapters I and II. Thus, whereas the OFT can only intervene to stop the anti-competitive act under its antitrust enforcement powers, as outlined above, the Competition Commission has almost unlimited power to

---

[56] See, eg, Competitive Commission, "Estimated costs to consumers of mergers and market outcomes against which the CC took action between April 2007 and March 2008"(July 2008).

[57] LECG, *Evaluating the impact of the Supply of Extended Warranties on Domestic Electrical Goods Order 2005, prepared for the OFT* (October 2005).

reshape the market to remedy any "adverse effect on competition" that it identifies.

At the same time (as demonstrated above), the threshold for intervention under the market investigation regime is lower (not higher) than under Arts 101 and 102 TFEU. There is no need to demonstrate significant market power or to identify an anti-competitive act.

There is therefore a temptation for the authorities to circumvent the stricter standards under Art 102 TFEU and to use the greater powers under the market investigation. This temptation can be seen in the OFT's *Guidelines*, which state that the OFT may refer a market to the Competition Commission on the basis of a suspected violation of Art 102 TFEU if it considers that enforcement action under that provision would be insufficient to remedy the adverse effect on competition.[58]

5 ISSUES REGARDING CONSUMER POLICY IN MARKET INVESTIGATIONS

From the early days of the market investigation regime, the OFT and Competition Commission have recognised the power of the regime to pursue consumer policy on a scale well beyond what is possible under the various consumer protection powers conferred on the OFT and other regulators. Whereas consumer protection legislation generally only allows the OFT to prevent particular instances or categories of unfair behaviour on the part of firms, market investigations potentially allow for the wholesale restructuring of the market to facilitate (or even mandate) active consumer participation and encourage effective competition.

Although, as Derek Ridyard acknowledged, it is difficult to argue against the provision of information to consumers, the Competition Commission has recently indicated its willingness to go far beyond this in the reshaping of markets in pursuit of consumer policy objectives, raising new issues that do not generally arise in the consumer protection context.[59] For instance, in the *PPI* investigation the Competition Commission chose to address a "point of sale advantage" by banning the sale of PPI at the point of sale of the associated credit product as well as banning single premium products. As Armstrong points out, this is a highly interventionist consumer policy result, and has the effect of disadvantaging some consumers (ie those who would prefer to purchase at the point of sale) even if it also has the effect of benefiting others. Although Armstrong notes that in theory remedies of this kind

---

[58] *OFT Guidelines*, para 2.3.

[59] D Ridyard, "The Competition Commission's Northern Ireland banking market investigation: some unanswered questions on the role of market investigations" (2008) 29 (3) European Competition Law Review 173.

can improve aggregate consumer welfare, "the informational requirements to assess the likely benefits of the intervention are formidable in even the simplest situations", which is why "such policies should only be contemplated if no information or education remedy would work instead".[60] Even in those cases, Armstrong calls for "rigorous cost–benefit analysis (which is usually sorely lacking in consumer policy)" before imposing the remedy. This is precisely the basis on which the CAT decided to quash the Competition Commission's remedy.

Moreover, even to the extent that on a cost–benefit analysis remedies of this kind are beneficial, the issue is more complex than simply assessing aggregate consumer welfare. As the Competition Commission itself noted, decoupling PPI from credit would likely adversely affect the price of credit and therefore make those consumers who prefer not to take PPI worse off.[61] Arguably, a competition authority is not well placed to make distributional assessments of this kind and indeed the Enterprise Act 2002 provides no guidance as to what principles the Competition Commission should adopt (for example is maximising aggregate consumer welfare the objective, or should the authority adopt a "first harm no consumers" approach?).

5.1 Interaction of competition policy and consumer policy in market investigations

The OFT likes to highlight the synergies generated from its role as a combined competition and consumer policy enforcement agency. It identifies market studies and market investigations as the key tools that enable it to exploit these synergies by addressing competition and consumer issues together, as well as potentially addressing issues raised by one with remedies imposed in relation to the other. As a prime example of this approach the OFT cites its campaign for more competition in relation to personal current accounts, where the OFT has issued proceedings under the UTCCR 1999 against unauthorised overdraft charges as well as conducting a market study to address wider issues.[62] The OFT's agenda may have far-reaching implications for current accounts, potentially heralding the end of "free when in credit" banking in the UK.

However, competition and consumer policy do not always work in tandem. For instance, as the OFT acknowledges, efforts to improve competition by encouraging entry may complicate markets

---

[60] M Armstrong, *Interactions between competition and consumer policy – Economic discussion paper* para 6.5.

[61] Competition Commission, Market investigation into payment protection insurance (29 January 2009), paras 10,442–10,464.

[62] H Priest and G Winton, "The OFT's market studies" (*The Beesley Lectures*).

for consumers, thus creating or exacerbating informational obstacles to search.[63] At the same time, efforts to improve transparency for consumers may simultaneously improve transparency of strategic conduct for firms, with the result that tacit co-ordination becomes more feasible.

A focus on consumer choice may also result in reduced opportunities for synergies from vertical integration or incentives for innovation, as illustrated by the recent campaign against eBay's attempt to require its customers to use eBay's proprietary PayPal payment service. In the absence of market power, vertical restraints of these kinds would ordinarily be considered socially desirable in competition analysis, but consumer policy may prefer the interests of some segments of the consumer population who would prefer to combine eBay's platform with other payment technologies. Allowing these issues to be dealt with by the same authorities in the same investigations may indeed be the most efficient means to avoid unintended consequences and secure "virtuous circles" of remedy effects, but it is not at this stage clear that the OFT or Competition Commission have in place a systematic approach to weighing up these potentially competing concerns.

6 OTHER POLICY OBJECTIVES AFFECTED BY MARKET INVESTIGATIONS

As explained above, once a market has been referred to the Competition Commission, it is required (where reasonable and practicable) to use its powers to remedy any adverse effects on competition that it identifies. Thus, its sole policy objective is to improve competition for the benefit of consumers. However, because its mandate and powers are so wide, in many cases the remedies imposed by the Competition Commission may have implications for other policy objectives that go far beyond competition or consumer policy issues. For instance, Peter Freeman, Chairman of the Competition Commission, noted that in the *Groceries* investigation the Competition Commission received submissions urging the consideration of issues as wide-ranging as:

> "social cohesion and environmental distinctiveness; the effect of the potential loss of small corner shops on the local community, especially in rural areas; the effect of availability of relatively cheap alcoholic drinks in supermarkets on 'binge drinking' and street safety; the interests of UK farming and security of UK food supply; and the consequences for suppliers in the developing world (and the

---

[63] OFT, *Interactions between competition and consumer policy – Economic discussion paper*, para 4.5.

environmental impact) of seeking to provide seasonal fresh fruits to UK consumers throughout the year".[64]

Although it would clearly be impracticable (if even desirable) for a body such as the Competition Commission to consider such a range of issues when conducting a market investigation, the fact that the Competition Commission is required to take what may in some cases be quite drastic action with wide-ranging implications by reference only to a very narrow policy goal is highly concerning. The kind of market design function that the Competition Commission seeks to carry out in market investigations – for instance, by breaking up BAA's airport monopoly to encourage capacity expansion – is generally a function reserved for Parliament rather than an independent administrative authority, precisely because only Parliament is well placed to weigh up the potentially competing policy concerns.

7 CONCLUSIONS

The market investigation regime has turned out to be a flexible competition (and consumer) policy instrument. So far the Competition Commission has resisted the temptation to substitute Art 82 EC (and Chapter II) with market investigations and to benefit from the lower intervention thresholds and stronger enforcement powers. During the early years of market investigations, the Competition Commission exercised significant self restraint: investigations had a relatively narrow focus (largely around transparency and consumer protection) and involved relatively non-intrusive remedies (for example, obligation to provide more information to customers).

These early cases clearly helped to bridge the gap between competition policy and consumer policy and to introduce competition policy concepts into consumer policy. Although it was by no means clear that the OFT and Competition Commission had developed a systematic approach to dealing with the tensions between competition and consumer policy that accompany the oft-cited synergies, it is probably fair to say that these investigations were at least not harmful. The question was more whether the intervention by the Competition Commission in these early cases resulted in consumer benefits which were sufficiently large to outweigh the significant costs of a 2-year investigation. In the *PPI* investigation, the Competition Commission itself raised some doubts about the effectiveness of its intervention in the *Extended Warranties* investigation under the previous FTA regime.

---

[64] P Freeman, "Is competition everything?" (2008) 7(3) Competition Law Journal 214, at 215.

More recently, the approach of the Competition Commission in market investigations seems to have become more aggressive, both in terms of scope of intervention and the nature of the remedy employed:

(1) in the *Groceries* investigation the Competition Commission recommended the introduction of a "competition test" in the planning regime that would limit expansion possibilities for incumbents with large local market shares;
(2) in the *PPI* investigation the Competition Commission imposed a ban on selling PPI at the point of sale of the associated credit and on single premium PPI products;
(3) in the *BAA Airports* investigation the Competition Commission ordered the divestment of three of BAA's airports.

It is no surprise that, in contrast to the earlier cases, aspects of each of the latter three investigations have been challenged before the CAT.

The wider-ranging and more aggressive approach to market investigations has highlighted the drawbacks which come with its flexibility, namely the absence of a rigorous analytical framework of "classic" competition policy and, almost inevitably, a greater likelihood of policy errors.

It remains to be seen whether in future the Competition Commission will be able to navigate between the Scylla of non-intrusive but potentially ineffective intervention of early years and the Charybdis of a more robust but also potentially more error-prone policy of recent years.

CHAPTER 8

THE COMPETITION COMMISSION, MERGER CONTROL AND THE SLC TEST

*Nigel Parr**

A couple of years after the UK competition law regime had been extensively overhauled by the Competition Act 1998 ("CA 1998"), the Government turned its attention to the system of merger control (the focus of this chapter) and market investigations (or monopoly inquiries, as they were known under the Fair Trading Act 1973 ("FTA 1973")). Part 3 of the Enterprise Act 2002 ("EA 2002") introduced extensive reforms to UK merger control, although two of the key distinguishing characteristics[1] of the regime were preserved, namely the system of voluntary notification and the dual enforcement regime by two separate institutions, the Office of Fair Trading ("the OFT") and the Competition Commission ("the CC").

When the proposals which became the EA 2002 were first announced, the issues which appeared in the headlines were:

(a) the removal of ministerial involvement from UK merger control in all but exceptional cases; and
(b) the introduction of a formal competition-based test against which to assess mergers, as opposed to the existing more broadly based "public interest" test.

These key changes were not expected by practitioners to lead to a fundamental shift in assessment in light of the OFT's focus on

---

* Partner of Ashurst LLP. The author would like to thank Alexi Dimitriou and Catherine Hammon for their assistance in the preparation of this chapter.

[1] Unlike the CA 1998 which mirrors the EC competition law regime, there is minimal read-across between the UK and EC merger control regimes and there is no equivalent to s 60 of the CA 1998 in the EA 2002.

competition issues and ministerial practice of following the OFT's advice in making references to the CC. Practitioners were more interested in the impact of:

(a) the significant changes to the CC's role and procedures as a result of becoming a decision-making body rather than an advisory body, including in particular issues surrounding the standard of proof;
(b) procedural developments and changes, in particular the discussion of potential remedies in light of the publication of the CC's provisional findings, plus the emergence of a much greater degree of concern regarding the treatment of completed mergers; and
(c) the grant of judicial review jurisdiction to the Competition Appeal Tribunal ("the CAT"), particularly in light of the detailed and forensic approach it had taken in hearing appeals under the CA 1998.

Finally, this chapter will consider two of the most significant areas of current debate in relation to further reform of UK merger control, ie the voluntary nature of the regime and the bi-institutional structure. These two key characteristics have come under increasing scrutiny and the accepted wisdom that both are desirable has started to be challenged.

1 REMOVAL OF MINISTERIAL INVOLVEMENT AND RESIDUAL PUBLIC INTEREST PROVISIONS

1.1 Depoliticisation of UK merger control

The removal of ministerial involvement from the decision-making process was a key change introduced by the EA 2002 and was trumpeted as depoliticising the UK merger control regime. The CC and OFT were promoted from being advisory bodies, recommending a course of action to the Secretary of State who took all decisions, to being decision-makers in their own right. In the vast majority of cases,[2] the CC now has the power to take a final decision on whether a merger should be permitted or prohibited, and the final decision on what remedies (if any) should be required as a condition of clearance.

Ostensibly, this was a significant reform. However, in practice, it had been the formal policy of ministers since October 2000[3] to

---

[2] That is, except where the Secretary of State has made a reference on public interest or special public interest grounds.

[3] Department of Trade and Industry, "Byers Announces Major Overhaul of Mergers System", Press Release, 26 October 2000.

follow the recommendations of the CC (and the OFT) in all but exceptional circumstances. Since the 1980s, ministers had adopted a policy of referring cases to the CC primarily on competition grounds. In practice, therefore, it had long been the situation that the cases in which the Secretary of State took a different decision from that recommended by the competition bodies were a small minority. From a practical perspective, therefore, the EA 2002 reforms did not involve the Government relinquishing a significant decision-making role, and in any event it reserved to itself the power to intervene in exceptional cases where politically necessary.

1.2 Development of the public interest regime

Of arguably greater significance has been the development of the public interest regime, which was initially expected to be limited to national security issues. At the committee stage of the passage of the legislation through Parliament, Melanie Johnson, the responsible minister, stated:

> "We have no plans to specify new public interest considerations. Merger reform has been the subject of extensive consultation and we have considered thoroughly whether anything beyond national security should be in the Bill. We do not expect to specify further issues in relation to the current scope of the merger control regime. It would be unwise, however, to ensure that unforeseen circumstances could not be dealt with if there were a compelling case in the public interest. We must ensure that we can meet unforeseen circumstances ..."[4]

However, before the EA 2002 entered into force, a second area of public interest was added – to ensure the accurate presentation of the news, free expression of opinion and plurality of the media.[5] Arguably this was not a controversial addition, as it took place in the context of abandoning the special newspaper merger provisions contained in the FTA 1973 and a broader reform of communications regulation in the UK.[6]

A much more controversial addition to the public interest provisions took place in late 2008, at the height of the financial crisis, when a third public interest consideration – maintaining the stability

---

[4] *Hansard*, HC Standing Committee B Debate on the Enterprise Bill, 9th Sitting, col 343 (30 April 2002).

[5] Section 58(2A), (2B) and (2C) of the EA 2002, which specify the media public interest considerations, were inserted by s 375(1) of the Communications Act 2003.

[6] These reforms were introduced by the Communications Act 2003, which overhauled the regulatory regime governing the media sector.

of the UK financial system – was added.[7] This amendment was made to allow the Government to wave through the acquisition of HBOS, a major UK retail bank on the brink of collapse, by another UK retail bank, Lloyds TSB, notwithstanding clear competition concerns which would normally have warranted a reference to the CC.[8] It would be difficult to argue that this case does not represent a repoliticisation of UK merger control, albeit one that arguably represents an isolated instance rather than the start of a trend.

This case brought into sharp relief the extent to which ministers have retained significant political power in relation to mergers:

- first, the financial services sector had been, and continues to be, under close scrutiny by the EC and UK competition authorities, and the waving through of a financial services sector merger was inconsistent with that existing pattern of enforcement. In that context, the Government's intervention can be viewed as being driven by purely political concerns in the face of an exceptional financial crisis;
- second, although the concept of the public interest is apparently limited by the considerations specified in the EA 2002, under s 42(3) the Government is able to intervene in a merger on the basis of a public interest consideration which is not specified, but which should in the opinion of the Secretary of State be specified. In the *Lloyds/HBOS* case the new ground for intervention was added by statutory instrument during the course of the OFT's first-stage review of the merger. Ultimately, therefore, the scope of the public interest in merger control is not formally limited but is a matter for the Government's discretion on a case-by-case basis, much as it was under the FTA 1973; and
- finally, under Art 21 of the EC Merger Regulation[9] (which permits Member States to take steps to protect their legitimate national interests in relation to a merger which is being scrutinised by the EC Commission), a national government is able to take steps to protect essential national interests such as national security and media plurality, in addition to any steps which the Commission might take in light of competition concerns. There is no scope, however, for a Member State to "trump" or overturn the competition analysis, for example, by allowing national interest considerations to take precedence over competition concerns. By contrast,

[7] Section 58(2D) of the EA 2002 was inserted by art 2 of the Enterprise Act 2002 (Specification of Additional Section 58 Considerations) Order 2008, SI 2008/2645.

[8] The OFT's advice to the Secretary of State was that the merger raised material competition concerns: see OFT, Anticipated acquisition by Lloyds TSB plc of HBOS plc, Report to the Secretary of State for Business Enterprise and Regulatory Reform (24 October 2008).

[9] EC Regulation 139/2004 of the Council on the control of concentrations between undertakings (the EC Merger Regulation) [2004] OJ L24/1.

s 45(6) of the EA 2002 allows a minister to rule that public interest considerations trump any competition concerns, such that an anti-competitive merger can be cleared unconditionally in light of overriding public interest considerations. In the *Lloyds/HBOS* case, it was considered that a swift merger of the two banks to avoid the collapse of a major UK retail bank was essential to maintain confidence in the UK banking system regardless of the competition concerns which could arise from the merger.[10]

Notwithstanding the normally exceptional nature of the public interest regime, the Government's treatment of the Lloyds/HBOS merger amply demonstrates that it remains able to deal with "unforeseen circumstances ... if there were a compelling case in the public interest"[11] and to force through politically necessary mergers notwithstanding the EA 2002 reforms, as well as to prohibit mergers on public interest grounds.

The majority of public interest cases to date have been national security cases, typically involving defence sector businesses contracting with the Ministry of Defence and raising issues concerning the protection of classified information and technology, security clearance of individuals and/or the retention of particular skills and capabilities within the UK. To date, no references to the CC have been made on national security grounds – the public interest concerns in such cases are typically addressed with undertakings.

The media plurality public interest provisions have only been invoked once to date, but in relation to a controversial case which was referred to the CC. Following an announcement that Virgin Media (the only UK cable network operator) was considering a bid for ITV (the leading UK terrestrial television operator), BSkyB (the leading satellite television operator) purchased a 17.9 per cent stake in ITV as a blocking tactic against the Virgin Media bid. The Secretary of State chose to invoke the public interest provisions, and referred the merger to the CC not only because of the competition concerns identified by the OFT, but also because of his concerns that "as a result of the merger situation, there may not be a sufficient plurality of persons with control of the media enterprises serving the

---

[10] A challenge to the legality of the Secretary of State's decision to clear the merger before the CAT was unsuccessful: see *Merger Action Group* v *Secretary of State for Business, Enterprise and Regulatory Reform* [2008] CAT 36. This case generated comments that normal competition policy might have been suspended during the current recession – a point which the UK (and EC) competition authorities consistently rebuff. See, eg, the keynote address by Peter Freeman to the Law Society Competition Section Annual Conference, "The world turn'd upside down" (21 May 2009).

[11] As explained by Melanie Johnson in the Commons Standing Committee stage, cited in n 4 above.

UK cross-media audience for national news and the UK TV audience for national news".[12]

Following the CC's inquiry and report on the competition and public interest issues, the Secretary of State accepted (as the EA 2002 required him to do) the CC's conclusions that the acquisition of a 17.9 per cent stake constituted a merger and that the merger had resulted in a substantial lessening of competition. He also concluded that the merger would not be against the public interest. These conclusions were challenged before the CAT by both BSkyB (as regards the conclusion that the merger was anti-competitive) and Virgin Media (as regards the conclusion that the merger was not against the public interest).

Other aspects of this case are discussed in more detail below, but it is worth noting in the context of the current section that the EA regime has introduced a bright line distinction between competition issues and other public interest issues. Under the FTA 1973, mergers were assessed by reference to a general public interest test which included (and was in practice dominated by) an assessment of the impact of the merger on competition. Under the EA 2002, the distinction between competition issues and wider (but defined) public interest issues is explicit and governs the division of jurisdiction between the competition authorities and the Secretary of State, since the Secretary of State is bound to follow the advice and recommendations of the OFT and/or CC as regards the competition assessment.

2 PUBLIC INTEREST TEST TO COMPETITION TEST

2.1 The new SLC test – a sea change in the analysis of mergers?

As discussed above, one of the key changes under the EA 2002 which caught the headlines was the shift from assessing mergers by reference to a general "public interest test" to a test focused expressly on competition analysis, namely whether the merger may be expected to result (or, if completed, has resulted) in a substantial lessening of competition (known as the "SLC test").

Although this was, on the face of it, a major policy shift, in practice the impact was much less pronounced. From the mid 1980s, the government of the day, whether Conservative or Labour, had taken merger control decisions primarily on competition grounds

[12] See the Secretary of State's decision: Alistair Darling, *The reference by Alistair Darling, the Secretary of State for Trade and Industry, of the British Sky Broadcasting Group's acquisition of a 17.9% shareholding in ITV plc to the Competition Commission under Section 45(2) of the Enterprise Act 2002* (24 May 2007).

notwithstanding the potentially broader "public interest test" under the FTA 1973. The OFT and CC had long focused their competition analyses on well-established economic principles and, in practice, the FTA public interest test was interpreted by the OFT and practitioners alike as a substantial lessening of competition test.[13]

The change of legal test was not therefore expected to alter the basis or methodology of the OFT's or CC's assessment[14] and the first few months of the new regime proceeded on that basis. However, in the first application to the CAT for review of a merger control decision under s 120 of the EA 2002, both the meaning of the test for reference and the division of responsibility between the OFT and the CC were thrown into doubt.

2.2 *IBA Health*: early scrutiny of the respective roles of the OFT and CC

In response to a challenge by IBA Health, a competitor, to the OFT's decision to clear the proposed merger of iSOFT and Torex, the CAT handed down a ruling which appeared to lower the threshold at which the OFT's legal duty to refer a potentially anti-competitive merger to the CC was engaged.[15] In particular, the CAT ruled that in order to clear a merger without a reference, the OFT had to satisfy itself of two points:

(1) that there was no significant prospect of a substantial lessening of competition; and
(2) that there was no significant prospect of an alternative view being taken in the context of a fuller investigation by the CC.

Considerable concerns were expressed in relation to the second limb of this test. The general view of practitioners was that the judgment risked emasculating the OFT, a body widely respected for the skill and sophistication of its merger analysis, by reducing it to a first-stage filter whose role was simply to distinguish between those cases that very clearly raised no issues and those cases which, even if the

[13] See the speech of John Vickers, "Competition economics and policy – A speech on the occasion of the launch of the new social sciences building at Oxford University" (3 October 2002), at 7–8 (available on the OFT's website).

[14] Indeed the lack of any expected substantive difference between an FTA public interest assessment and an EA SLC analysis was emphasised by the transitional provisions for the replacement of the FTA regime with the regime introduced by the EA 2002. These provided for the OFT simply to switch the legal basis of any ongoing merger case on its books on 20 June 2003 from the FTA 1973 to the EA 2002, potentially midway through its analysis (although different arrangements were set out for Merger Notice cases). See EA 2002, Sch 24, paras 13 and 15–19.

[15] *IBA Health Ltd* v *Office of Fair Trading* [2003] CAT 27.

OFT did not perceive them to merit a reference, could be the subject of a credible counter view. In this connection, it was widely thought that the CAT's approach could lead to a chilling of merger activity in the UK compared with other merger regimes in Europe and the USA.

The CAT's ruling was appealed to the Court of Appeal. The Court of Appeal's judgment, which did not overturn the outcome reached by the CAT but crucially overruled the CAT's reasoning on the substantive assessment test for reference, is generally regarded as having put the regime back onto a workable footing but also raised important questions about evidence, reasoning and the depth of the OFT's investigation.[16] As now expressed by the OFT, the duty to refer is engaged where "the OFT has a reasonable belief, objectively justified by relevant facts, that there is a realistic prospect that the merger will lessen competition substantially".[17]

The question remained, however, whether after *IBA Health* the OFT was more likely to make a reference to the CC in circumstances where previously it would have weighed potentially conflicting evidence and decided on balance to clear a merger. It was suggested that in borderline cases a reference was now more likely to be made, particularly where there was conflicting evidence.[18] The increase in risk arose primarily because of the emphasis in *IBA Health* on the adequacy of the OFT's reasoning. As a consequence, for a period immediately following *IBA Health*, marginal cases were probably more likely to be referred than under the FTA regime. In the period immediately following *IBA Health*, in 2004 and 2005, references to the OFT increased to their highest level since the introduction of the EA 2002, as is shown in Figure 1.

Indeed, as is shown in Figure 2, there is some evidence that the number of unconditional clearances by the CC increased in 2004 and 2005, indicating that some of the additional references from the OFT to the CC may not have been necessary.

---

[16] *OFT* v *IBA Health Ltd* [2004] EWCA Civ 142.

[17] See the OFT's draft guidance for consultation: OFT, *Mergers – jurisdictional and procedural guidance* (OFT 526con, March 2008) at para 2.6; see also OFT, *Guidance note revising "Mergers – substantive assessment guidance"* (OFT 516a, October 2004).

[18] The OFT's Annual Plan for 2004–05 anticipated that 20–25 cases would be referred or cleared subject to undertakings in lieu out of an estimated 30–50 more complex cases (see OFT, *The Office of Fair Trading Annual Plan 2004–2005* (HC 460, March 2004), at 20); in its Annual Plan for 2003–04, by contrast, it anticipated only 10–20 references from the same number of complex cases (and, in fact, 12 were made) (see OFT, *The Office of Fair Trading Annual Plan 2003–2004* (HC 899, June 2003), at 23). The 2004/2005 Annual Plan expressly commented that the estimates were based on "experience, and the Court of Appeal's clarification of the substantive merger test". However, by 2006 the OFT had become more robust to whether to refer a merger to the CC, and merger references dropped materially for the next few years.

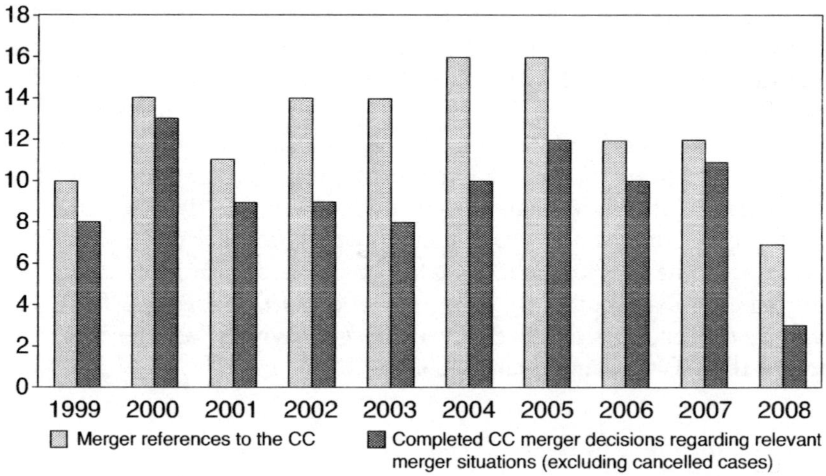

Figure 1 OFT merger references to the CC under the and CC completed merger decisions (1999–2008)

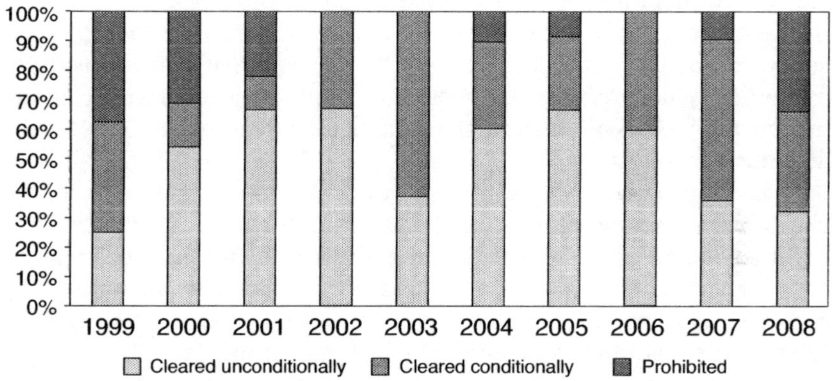

Figure 2 Completed CC merger decisions regarding relevant merger situations by type (excluding cancelled cases) (1999–2008)

However, by 2006 both the number of merger references and the proportion of unconditional clearances by the CC had reduced, reflecting the OFT's increased evidence gathering in its merger review processes by that date,[19] allowing it to support its decisions

[19] The increased evidential burden before the OFT is a consequence not only of the CAT's comments on the adequacy of reasoning in the OFT's decisions in *IBA Health*, but of subsequent CAT criticism of the OFT's failure to verify and cross-check factual statements relied upon in its decision: see *Unichem Ltd* v *Office of Fair Trading* [2005] CAT 8.

by reference to compelling evidence that potentially anti-competitive mergers did not in fact trigger its duty to refer.

In conclusion, and with the perspective of a few years, *IBA Health* can be seen as having shaken up the assumptions that it was "business as usual" under the new EA regime. There is no doubt that the decisions of the OFT are now more fully reasoned and, it is suggested, the first-stage review undertaken by the OFT is now amongst the longest and most onerous of any merger control regime. As regards the work of the CC, however, there is no evidence that more mergers are currently being referred than under the FTA 1973, or that the proportion of referred mergers which fail the SLC test before the CC has significantly changed.

2.3 The meaning of the SLC test

Although the concept of "substantial lessening of competition" is not defined in the EA 2002, the OFT's and CC's competition analysis is rooted firmly in the principles of industrial economics and has strong parallels with merger assessment by competition authorities around the world, including the US and European authorities.

More specifically, the OFT and CC view competition as a process of rivalry between firms in terms of price, quality and innovation. A merger which substantially lessens competition over time, giving rise to an SLC, will reduce the beneficial effects of rivalry to the detriment of consumers.

It is appropriate to identify a number of key points as to the breadth and scope of this interpretation. First, the SLC test was adopted as a result of concerns that a test based solely on the creation or enhancement of a dominant position might not be sufficiently broad to capture all possible anti-competitive effects of mergers.[20] Second, a substantial lessening of competition might still arise even if only some (as opposed to all) customers may be expected to suffer as a result of a merger. This may be the case if some (but not all) customers are able to safeguard their interests because they possess significant countervailing buyer power or are more able to switch to alternatives. Third, the competition concerns are not limited to price increases, but extend to all dimensions of competition including impacts on innovation and product quality. Finally, the emphasis is on harm to customers (and ultimately consumers), not competitors, or any other interest group. This point is reinforced by the fact that

---

[20] See further John Vickers (previous Chairman of the OFT), "Merger Policy in Europe: Retrospect and Prospect" (2004) 25 ECLR 455. Vickers' view was that there was a "gap" in a dominance test in relation to mergers which do not create or enhance a single dominant firm or have co-ordinated effects, but otherwise have non-co-ordinated effects.

the UK authorities may clear a merger or allow it to proceed with less stringent remedies in circumstances where, notwithstanding a realised or expected substantial lessening of competition, they expect the merger to result in specific customer benefits. The consultation draft of the new joint CC and OFT Merger Assessment Guidelines states that an SLC is unlikely to be found without an expectation of adverse effects for consumers.[21]

The task of the OFT and the CC is to assess the facts of individual cases against a potentially very broad standard of economic assessment. In this regard, in contrast to the position under the FTA 1973, there is now considerable guidance available as to how mergers may lead to competitive harm, from regulators' own guidelines, sponsored research papers, the OFT's decisions under the EA 2002 and reports of the CC. Nevertheless, the CC has emphasised that it will not follow its guidelines slavishly, but will assess the specifics of individual cases according to their circumstances and may depart from its guidelines if appropriate.[22] That said, it would nevertheless be prudent for any authority departing from its guidelines to explain why it has done so – indeed, the CAT has implied on a number of occasions that it would expect any significant departure from the approach set out in published guidelines to be explained and justified for the case in question.[23]

Notwithstanding the legal and institutional changes introduced by the EA 2002, it is strongly arguable that the substantive assessment of mergers in the UK has not changed under the new legislation. However, there is no doubt that the level of sophistication of the CC's analysis is ever increasing,[24] not, it is suggested, as a consequence of the change in the test for merger assessment but more as a reflection of:

- the changes in the CC's role, and its role as a decision-maker;
- the changes to the CC's procedure, and in particular the introduction of greater transparency of its analysis and workings; and
- the grant of jurisdiction to the CAT, a specialist competition body, to review the CC's decisions, and the need for the CC to support its decisions by reference to cogent evidence and analysis.

---

[21] OFT/CC, *Merger Assessment Guidelines – A joint publication of the Competition Commission and the Office of Fair Trading – Consultation Document* (hereinafter "the Draft Merger Assessment Guidelines") (April 2009), at paras 4.4–4.5.

[22] CC, *Merger References: Competition Commission Guidelines* (CC2, April 2007), at para 1.4. See also OFT/CC, Draft Merger Assessment Guidelines (April 2009), at para 1.5.

[23] See *Unichem* v *OFT* [2005] CAT 8, eg, at para 199.

[24] This observation is supported by the first external review of the quality of merger decisions taken under the EA 2002 (Deloitte LLP, *Review of merger decisions under the Enterprise Act 2002* (18 March 2009)), discussed in section 4 below.

These factors and their impact on the UK merger control regime are considered in the following sections.

3 CHANGES TO THE CC'S ROLE: BECOMING A DECISION-MAKER

3.1 What is the standard of proof?

Section 36(1) of the EA 2002 provides:

> "[...] the [Competition] Commission shall, on a reference under section 33, decide the following questions –
> (a) whether arrangements are in progress or in contemplation which, if carried into effect, will result in the creation of a relevant merger situation; and
> (b) if so, whether the creation of that situation *may be expected to result* in a substantial lessening of competition within any market or markets in the United Kingdom for goods or services." (emphasis added)

The EA 2002 therefore imposes a duty on the CC to decide whether a relevant merger situation will be created and, if so, whether that situation "may be expected" to result in a substantial lessening of competition. It would appear to follow that the burden of proof rests upon the CC to demonstrate why a substantial lessening of competition may be expected.

In its guidelines,[25] the CC has stated that, for it to reach an adverse decision, either the merger must have resulted in a substantial lessening of competition or the CC must expect such a result. The CC will usually have such an expectation, the guidelines state, where it considers that it is more likely than not that a substantial lessening of competition will result.

The Court of Appeal considered the issue of the standard of proof in its *IBA Health* judgment, and concluded that it is the normal civil standard of the balance of probabilities. In this connection, as regards the meaning of "may be expected to result", the Court of Appeal held that:

> "the words 'may be expected to result' in paragraph (b) of both s.33(1) and 36(1) involve a degree of likelihood amounting to an expectation. In paragraph 182 of its judgment CAT expressed the view that these words connoted more than a possibility and adopted what they described as a crude way of expressing the idea of an expectation as a more than 50% chance. No doubt this is right when

---

[25] CC, *Merger References: Competition Commission Guidelines* (CC2, April 2007), at para 1.19. See also OFT/CC, Draft Merger Assessment Guidelines (April 2009), at para 2.10.

applied to the single question which the Commission is required to answer under s.36(1)(b)."[26]

In comparing the standard of proof for the OFT and the CC, the Court of Appeal further commented that:

> "The difference between s 33 [the reference test for the OFT] and s36 lies in the nature of the conclusion to be arrived at. The question for the OFT is whether it '*believes* that SLC is or may be the case'; the [CC] is required to '*decide*' whether there will be SLC. Thus for the OFT, unlike the [CC], belief in the possibility of SLC is enough to trigger the next stage."[27]

The question of how the CC should apply the standard of proof in relation to the SLC test was in issue before the CAT in the jointly heard challenges by Sky and Virgin Media to the conclusions of the CC and the Secretary of State in relation to the *Sky/ITV* merger.[28] The overarching concern in this case was that Sky might be able to use the material influence flowing from its 17.9 per cent stake in its competitor, ITV, to influence ITV's future investment and/or finance-raising decisions in such a way as to create a substantial lessening of competition on the "all television" market (ie terrestrial, satellite and cable television). BSkyB argued that there were three elements to the SLC test:

(1) the CC must decide whether a particular event or course of events has occurred or may be expected to occur;
(2) having made that finding, the CC must decide whether that event or course of events has resulted in a lessening of competition, or may be expected to result in a lessening of competition, within any market or markets in the United Kingdom for goods or services; and
(3) the CC must decide whether any such lessening of competition is substantial.

According to Sky, *each* of these elements had to be established separately on the balance of probabilities in respect of each future investment relied upon, and by reference to all relevant evidence, which must be identified, with an explanation as to why that particular investment is more likely than not to occur.

The CAT disagreed. It noted that:

> "As far as SLC is concerned ... we agree with the [CC] that the appropriate question for the [CC] to ask itself is whether Sky may

---

[26] *IBA Health Ltd* v *Office of Fair Trading* [2003] CAT 27, per Mance VC at para 46.
[27] *Ibid.*
[28] *British Sky Broadcasting Group plc* v *(1) The Competition Commission (2) The Secretary of State* and *Virgin Media, Inc* v *(1) The Competition Commission (2) The Secretary of State* (heard together) [2008] CAT 25. At the time of writing, the CAT's decision was the subject of an appeal to the Court of Appeal.

> be expected (i.e. on the balance of probabilities) to have the opportunity to exercise its material influence so as to give rise to an SLC in a relevant market. This is not the same as asking whether it is more likely than not that a specific investment opportunity will materialise."[29]

In rejecting Sky's formulation of how the statutory tests should be applied, the CAT held that even where there may be a range of ways in which competition in a market might be lessened substantially, the CC is not required to establish that each potential transaction identified by it is more likely than not to occur. It was sufficient that the CC had identified what it considered to be plausible examples of the kind of investment opportunities which might well present themselves within a 2- or 3-year period and over which the CC expected Sky to able to exercise material influence. In the CAT's view, "Sky's suggested approach would not only be more than is required in law, but it would also be wholly unrealistic, and would probably emasculate the merger regime".[30]

In light of the CAT's judgment, the standard of proof for the CC is therefore a broad question of whether, on the balance of probabilities, the merger may be expected to result in a substantial lessening of competition on a particular market. The standard of proof applies in an overarching way to the whole assessment, and is not required to be attained for each individual element which contributes to the overall SLC conclusion. An appeal against the CAT's judgment was heard on 29–30 October 2009, and judgment was awaited at the time of writing.

In the context of an *ex ante* merger assessment, however, even this broad characterisation of the relevant standard of proof raises further questions. First, in a forward-looking analysis, is it possible to say with any certainty at all what will or will not occur? Second, given that judicial review of the CC's decisions is undertaken by a specialist competition tribunal, it is reasonable for the CC to be subject in practice to a more intensive review of its decisions than might be the case if it were subject to judicial review by the non-specialist administrative court. In other words, is the intensity of review which is now applied to the decisions of the CC (and the Secretary of State in public interest cases) higher because of the specialist expertise of the CAT? These two issues are considered further below.

---

[29] See the CAT's judgment, at para 75.

[30] *Ibid.*

3.2 Is the "standard of proof" concept appropriate in forward-looking merger analysis?

Merger control analysis, particularly in relation to mergers which have not completed,[31] can be seen as involving two discrete steps:

(1) identifying competitive conditions in the relevant market as they currently exist or have existed in the past (usually the relatively recent past in a merger control context) – which *is* something that can be considered to a standard of proof such as the balance of probabilities; and
(2) making a judgment about what "will" or "may" or "may be expected to" happen to market conditions in the future in the context of a specific legal test about the effect of a merger on competition, by reference to the facts established on the basis of a standard of proof.

It is in respect of this latter, and most crucial, step that the notion of a standard of proof sits awkwardly. Is it possible to make a judgment about the future (in effect, a risk analysis or evaluation of the likelihood of something happening), with all the variables that entails in terms of factors that can influence the outcome, to a particular standard of proof?

This difficulty has been recognised in other contexts by the courts. For example, Lord Hoffmann in *Rehman* (which concerned national security) stated:

> "... I agree with the Court of Appeal that the whole concept of a standard of proof is not particularly helpful in a case such as the present. ... the question in the present case is not whether a given event happened but the extent of future risk."[32]

The issue was also articulated by the Court of Appeal in *Karanakaran*:

> "The civil standard of proof, which treats anything which probably happened as having definitely happened, is part of a pragmatic legal fiction. It has no logical bearing on the assessment of the likelihood of future events or (by parity of reasoning) the quality of past ones."[33]

---

[31] Even if a merger has been completed, the 4-month time limit in s 24 of the EA 2002 for referring a case to the CC means that the merged businesses will rarely have been operational for a significant period and the likely impact of the merger on the relevant market will still be substantially a forward-looking analysis.

[32] *Secretary of State for the Home Department* v *Rehman* [2002] 1 All ER 122, at para 56.

[33] *Karanakaran* v *Secretary of State for the Home Department* [2000] 3 All ER 449, per Sedley LJ. See also *Re B (Children) (Care proceedings: standard of proof)* [2009] 1 AC 11, which discusses the relationship between the seriousness of the allegations and the standard of proof (and concludes that "there is no logical or necessary connection between seriousness and probability" (at para 72)).

As has been commented on above, the issue of the standard of proof was considered in detail in the CAT's review of the *Sky/ITV* case. Sky had argued that the CC should be required to show that each element of its analysis met the balance of probabilities threshold. The CAT, however, agreed with the CC (supported by Virgin Media on this point) that the CC is required to evaluate the evidence as a whole and come to a conclusion "in the round" on the basis of the balance of probabilities.[34] In agreeing that the notion of a standard of proof in relation to the prediction of future events is not particularly helpful, the CAT referred to *Rehman* and *Karanakaran* quoted above and observed that:

> "Sky's insistence on the [CC] establishing particular future events or courses of events on the balance of probabilities is unrealistic and, to paraphrase the words of Lord Mustill, seeks to introduce a spurious degree of precision into the statutory tests (*see R v Monopolies and Mergers Commission Ex p. South Yorkshire Transport Ltd* [1993] 1 W.L.R. 23, at 29)".[35]

Sky has raised the proper standard of proof before the CAT in merger cases under s 120 as one of its grounds for appeal.

3.3 Is the intensity of review applied to the decisions of the CC higher because of the specialist expertise of the CAT?

The question was raised in the challenges before the CAT to the CC and Secretary of State's decisions in *Sky/ITV* as to the appropriate standard of review for the CAT to apply under s 120 of the EA 2002, and, in particular, whether the CAT should apply a greater degree of intensity of review than the general courts in light of its specialist expertise?

Section 120 itself states:

> "In determining such an appeal, the [CAT] shall apply the same principles as would be applied by a court on an application for judicial review."

Sky argued that, although the same principles of law should be applied, this did not mean that the CAT should apply them in the same way as the administrative court:

---

[34] See *British Sky Broadcasting Group plc* v *(1) The Competition Commission (2) The Secretary of State* and *Virgin Media, Inc* v *(1) The Competition Commission (2) The Secretary of State* (heard together), CAT, Transcript of "Hearing – Day Two" (4 June 2008) at 31 (available on the CAT's website).

[35] *British Sky Broadcasting Group plc* v *(1) The Competition Commission (2) The Secretary of State* and *Virgin Media, Inc* v *(1) The Competition Commission (2) The Secretary of State* (heard together) [2008] CAT 25, at para 78.

> "Parliament has by design chosen to allocate the power of review to the Tribunal, a specialist body, as opposed to a generalist court, and must be taken to have anticipated the particular consequences for the intensity of review that would follow from that choice."[36]

In considering this issue, the CAT referred to the judgment of the Court of Appeal in *IBA Health*, which had emphasised that in exercising its judicial review jurisdiction, "the essential question" for the CAT "was no different from that which would have faced a court dealing with the same subject-matter".[37] The CAT agreed that it is a specialist forum and that as such it "will enjoy a degree of familiarity with the statutory regime, the relevant case-law and some of the legal and economic concepts which arise" and might be able to use its knowledge to reach speedier conclusions and indeed might be "a more demanding and/or less deferential tribunal" than a generalist court might be.[38] However, the CAT went on to state:

> "... in our view none of this means that the Tribunal is applying judicial review principles in a different way or is exercising a higher intensity of review than would be the case if the matter were before the Administrative Court. Further, by no means all of the findings which may be the subject of a section 120 challenge are such as would necessarily call for expertise in competition law and practice."[39]

The Tribunal went on to emphasise that s 120 clearly did not require an intensity of review to such a degree as to blur the distinction between an appeal on the merits (such as the CAT has jurisdiction to undertake by virtue of ss 46 and 47 of the CA 1998) and judicial review:

> "... the Tribunal must avoid blurring the distinction which Parliament clearly drew between a section 120 review and an appeal on the merits. ... It is one thing to allege irrationality or perversity; it is another to seek to persuade the Tribunal to reassess the weight of the evidence and, in effect, to substitute its views for those of the [CC]. The latter is not permissible in a review under section 120."[40]

The intensity of review by the CAT has also been raised by Sky as one of its grounds for appeal.

In practice, experience suggests that, notwithstanding that the CAT applies the ordinary principles of judicial review, there is no doubt that its specialist knowledge of the competition law field makes it a very vigilant, effective and insightful forum for review.

---

36 [2008] CAT 25 at para 48.

37 *IBA Health Ltd* v *Office of Fair Trading* [2003] CAT 27, at para 100.

38 At para 61.

39 See para 62.

40 See para 63.

This issue is considered further in section 5 below, which discusses the judicial review jurisdiction of the CAT in more detail.

4 CHANGES AND DEVELOPMENTS IN THE CC'S PROCEDURES

In line with its new role as decision-maker, the CC's procedures were overhauled and a number of changes were introduced by the EA 2002. Of particular interest is the publication of detailed provisional findings by the CC before publishing its definitive conclusions which means that, unlike the "hypothetical remedies' discussions under the FTA 1973, dialogue about possible remedies under the EA 2002 takes place in the context of clearly defined competition concerns. Another significant development in the CC's procedure under the EA regime – although not a direct consequence of the EA reforms – is its much greater use under the EA 2002 of its (pre-existing) power to accept undertakings or issue an order to prevent any further integration of completed mergers following a reference. These issues will be considered in turn below.

4.1 Review of potential remedies

Revised procedures for agreeing remedies

The procedures for identifying, negotiating and finalising remedies imposed following a CC reference have been completely overhauled. Under the FTA 1973, it was the duty of the CC, if it found that the merger operated, or might be expected to operate, against the public interest, to make recommendations to the Secretary of State as to how (if at all) the identified detriments might be remedied.[41] It was then for the Secretary of State to decide whether to accept the CC's findings and, in that event, whether to adopt its proposed remedies or to substitute remedies of his own,[42] or indeed to clear the merger unconditionally. The negotiation with the parties of the required remedies was then undertaken by the OFT on the Secretary of State's behalf.

The two main objections to this process were as follows:

(1) The parties were required to have a detailed discussion with the CC about potential remedies at a point in the proceedings at which they did not know if the merger was going to be found to be anti-competitive. The remedies discussion with the CC was conducted by raising the question of "hypothetical remedies", as a means of assessing what remedies might be feasible; how such remedies might be implemented; and their

[41] FTA 1973, s 72(2).

[42] FTA 1973, s 73(2) and (3).

effect on the merged entity. Clearly, this was an inherently artificial approach given that any remedies might have a fundamental effect on the parties' future business and strategy at a time when the CC had not, openly at least, concluded that the merger was detrimental to the public interest. The procedure at times caused the CC to make recommendations that were unworkable; it was also inefficient, since the parties were clearly reluctant to engage in any detailed discussions of the efficacy and practicality of individual remedies whilst maintaining that no remedy at all was necessary.

(2) In its role of negotiating remedies following a CC reference, the OFT was often placed in the difficult position of having to interpret the CC's recommendations and consider objections to them without having been party to the arguments made before the CC or to the CC's reasoning and deliberations.

Both of these difficulties have been addressed by the EA 2002. By granting to the CC the final decision whether to clear, prohibit or approve a merger subject to undertakings or an order, the EA 2002 has provided for a practical discussion on remedies. Moreover, since the CC now publishes its provisional findings,[43] the parties (and also third parties) are afforded the opportunity for a meaningful dialogue with the CC about remedies. Negotiation of the detailed wording of remedies is now also undertaken by the CC itself. The CC has powers under s 82 to accept final undertakings from the parties, or to issue orders under s 83 where such undertakings are not fulfilled, or to issue a final order instead of accepting undertakings, under s 84. It also has powers under s 94 to bring an action before the courts to enforce an order which it has made under ss 83 or 84.

The CC's Rules of Procedure further require the CC to publish a notice of proposed remedies (to the extent that they are not included in the provisional findings), enabling not only the parties to the merger but also third parties to be fully aware of the remedies which are being considered.[44] Publication of this notice is the starting point for the consideration of remedies.

---

[43] Publication of the CC's provisional findings is not akin to the EC law step of publishing a statement of objections in second-stage merger inquiries. Because of the transparency of procedure surrounding the CC's developing thinking, neither the parties nor third parties will be seeing the CC's competition concerns for the first time. It is consequently very unusual for the CC's provisional findings to be overturned. Examples of where the CC's provisional findings on SLC were overturned in the final decision include *Greif Inc/Blagden Packaging Group* (17 August 2007) and *British Salt Ltd/New Cheshire Salt Works Ltd* (8 November 2005).

[44] See CC, *Commission Rules of Procedure* (CC1, 2006), r 11.

The types of remedies accepted by the CC

As under the FTA 1973, the CC is able to impose remedies which are structural (typically requiring divestment of a business to remove the competitive overlap which would give rise to an SLC) or behavioural (ie which do not eliminate the competition concern but seek to control and neutralise it by controlling the parties' commercial behaviour).

Although the CC is open to adopting whichever remedies best address the competition concerns, the preference of the CC has historically been, and continues to be, for structural remedies, for a number of reasons:

- Sections 35(4) and 36(3) of the EA 2002 require the CC to take into account "the need to achieve as comprehensive a solution as is reasonable and practicable to the substantial lessening of competition and any adverse effects resulting from it". As the Explanatory Notes to the EA 2002 comment:

> "The reference to a 'comprehensive solution' will require the [CC] to consider remedies that address the substantial lessening of competition itself (e.g. the features arising from the merger that give rise to the creation of market power) because it is generally more effective to tackle the cause of any problems at their source rather than by tackling the symptoms or adverse effects."[45]

  Structural remedies, which typically eliminate the competition concern at source, meet this requirement more clearly than behavioural remedies, which instead leave the risk of anti-competitive behaviour in place but seek to manage it;
- From a cost perspective, the CC's guidelines indicate that structural remedies are likely to be preferable to behavioural remedies as they address the effect of the merger directly and will require comparatively little, if any, monitoring or enforcement.[46]

The CC's preference for structural remedies is supported by the data in Figure 3, which shows that since 1999 structural remedies have been generally favoured over behavioural remedies.

---

[45] See the Explanatory Notes to the EA 2002, at para 134.

[46] CC, *Merger References: Competition Commission Guidelines* (CC2, April 2007), at para 4.15. See also the OFT's *Substantive Assessment Guidance* (OFT 516, May 2003), at para 8.6.

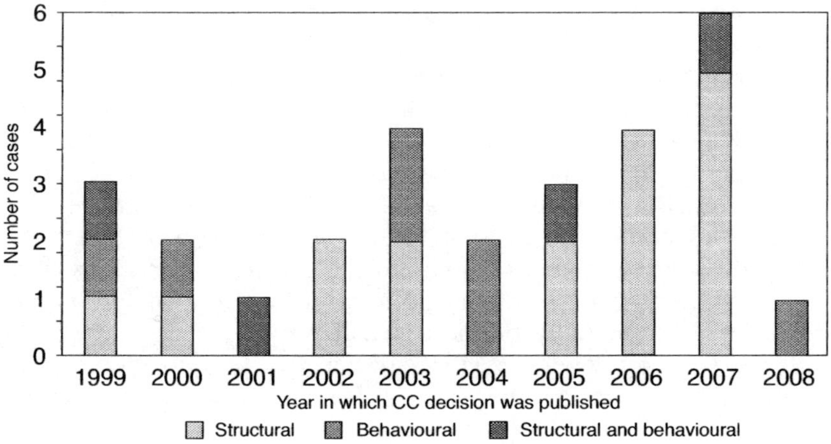

Figure 3 CC remedies by type (1999–2008)

Clarification of the scope of the CC's remedies powers

Two cases before the CAT have considered the issue of the scope of the CC's powers in identifying and imposing remedies on the parties.

In *Somerfield*,[47] the supermarket chain challenged the CC's decision to require it to divest 12 of 115 stores acquired from competing supermarket chain Morrisons. Somerfield claimed, *inter alia*, that the CC had acted unreasonably and without adequate foundation in specifying which of the stores in the relevant local markets Somerfield must divest and imposing restrictions on the identity of the purchaser.

In particular, Somerfield challenged whether, in relation to any particular local market where the CC had identified an SLC, the CC was entitled specifically to require Somerfield to divest the *acquired* store rather than Somerfield's *existing* store in the relevant local market.[48] Somerfield claimed that the CC had unreasonably and without adequate foundation required divestment of these acquired stores, claiming that the SLC identified by the CC would equally have been remedied by the sale of the existing Somerfield store in each area. The CAT, however, noted that, having identified an SLC, the CC had discretion to decide what action it should take for the purpose of removing, mitigating or preventing it.[49] It had to have

---

[47] *Somerfield plc* v *Competition Commission* [2006] CAT 4.

[48] In its application Somerfield had also initially claimed, *inter alia*, that the CC had erred in its finding that the acquisitions would result in an SLC in 12 local grocery markets; however, it dropped this part of its appeal at a case management conference on 19 October 2005.

[49] EA 2002, s 35(3).

regard to the need to achieve as comprehensive a solution as is reasonable and practicable[50] and the requirement that the CC take such action as it considered to be reasonable and practicable.[51] On this basis, the CC had a clear margin of appreciation to decide what reasonable action was appropriate for remedying, mitigating or preventing the SLC created by the acquisition of the disputed stores.

Moreover, the CAT held that, in identifying an appropriate remedy, the CC was entitled to consider that Somerfield should divest the disputed acquired stores, rather than the divestment of its existing stores, unless it was persuaded that the divestiture of alternative stores would be equally or more satisfactory. This was consistent with the CC's guidelines.[52] More specifically, the CC had selected the divestment stores by reference to their attractiveness to potential purchasers, their ability to offer a comparable degree of competition with Somerfield and by reference to a store's profitability, sales area and location.[53] Somerfield claimed that this approach would deprive Somerfield of the better stores in a given area. However, the CAT held that, where the SLC would be equally remedied by the sale of existing or acquired stores/assets, when deciding between which of those assets should be divested all that is required of the CC is to determine whether there is a real risk that the sale of an existing asset would be more problematic, or would take longer, from the point of view of finding a purchaser that was an effective competitor and that the onus was on Somerfield to establish that this was not the case.[54] Moreover, the CAT stated that, given the considerable experience of the CC in business and commercial matters, the commercial features of an asset, such as its profitability, are not outside the CC's margin of appreciation.[55]

The key point arising out of the Somerfield judgment is that the CAT has confirmed that, in considering remedies, the CC is entitled to take restoration of the status quo ante as its starting point. Essentially, this means that it is not for the parties to decide the CC's starting point when considering remedies, unless there is evidence as to why a different starting point is required – but even then the burden of proof is on the parties.

The scope of the CC's powers in setting remedies was also

---

[50] EA 2002, s 35(4).

[51] *Ibid*, s 41(2).

[52] This was consistent with the CC's guidelines, *Merger References: Competition Commission Guidelines* (CC2, April 2007), at para 4.23.

[53] CC, Final Report on *Somerfield plc/Wm Morrison Supermarkets plc* (12 September 2005), at para 11.12.

[54] *Somerfield plc* v *Competition Commission* [2006] CAT 4, at para 116.

[55] *Ibid*, at para 123.

considered in the CAT's judgment in relation to the CC's and Secretary of State's decisions in relation to the *Sky/ITV* reference (discussed above).[56] The CC had recommended to the Secretary of State that Sky should be required to reduce its 17.9 shareholding in ITV down to 7.5 per cent, which Sky argued, before the CAT was excessive.[57] Virgin Media had also challenged this decision, arguing for divestiture of Sky's entire shareholding. The CC had rejected Sky's alternative behavioural remedy proposal to place its voting rights into a voting trust or to undertake not to exercise the votes. The key issue was the level of shareholding which could be expected to give Sky the power to influence general meetings, which was in turn dependent on shareholder turnout at such meetings. In its judgment, the CAT held that the CC was entitled to adopt a cautious, conservative approach to future turnout.[58] This conclusion also suggests that the CC is entitled to take a cautious approach in determining the level of remedy required to alleviate an expected SLC. This approach supplements the wording of s 35(4) of the EA 2002, which states that in determining remedies the CC must take into account "the need to achieve as comprehensive a solution as is reasonable and practicable to the substantial lessening of competition and any adverse effects resulting from it" – it can legitimately err on the side of caution.

In practice, the extent to which the CC can be cautious in determining remedies must be weighed-up against the proportionality of any proposed remedy. Although the EA 2002 does not specifically state that remedies imposed by the CC must be proportionate, the CC itself expressly states in its guidelines that:

> "The Commission will aim to ensure that no remedy is disproportionate in relation to the [substantial lessening of competition] or other adverse effect. If the Commission is choosing between two remedies which it considers would be equally effective, it will choose the remedy that imposes the least cost or that is least restrictive."[59]

In relation to proportionality, the CAT further commented in *Sky/ITV* that, although parties to a merger are entitled to suggest alternative remedies to those proposed by the CC, should the CC reject

---

[56] *British Sky Broadcasting Group plc* v *(1) The Competition Commission (2) The Secretary of State* and *Virgin Media, Inc* v *(1) The Competition Commission (2) The Secretary of State* (heard together) [2008] CAT 25.

[57] On the basis of expected effective voting turnout, Sky argued that a divestiture to below 15% (or a reduction of voting rights to that level) would have been adequate to provide an effective remedy for the SLC found by the CC.

[58] See the CAT's judgment at para 294.

[59] CC, *Merger References: Competition Commission Guidelines* (CC2, April 2007), at para 4.9.

such alternative remedies as not being sufficiently effective having assessed them in light of the facts of the case and the evidence available, the CC is under no obligation to examine the relative proportionality of those alternative remedies as compared to the remedies the CC itself prefers.[60]

Effectiveness of the CC's remedies

A further innovation under the EA 2002 has been the extent to which the CC is prepared to review its own work and to assess the quality and robustness of its own decisions. It has expressly taken steps to measure the effectiveness of its exercise of its new remedies powers.

The first review of the quality of the CC's (and OFT's) remedies decisions taken under the EA 2002[61] was conducted by Deloitte LLP and published in March 2009.[62] This report's aim was to review a sample of merger decisions[63] with the benefit of hindsight and in light of subsequent market developments and to evaluate, on an *ex post* basis, the quality of the forward looking, *ex ante* analysis undertaken at the time by the OFT and CC. As regards the detail of some cases, the study suggests that subsequent events raised questions over whether certain factors relevant to the SLC test were correctly evaluated or given the appropriate weight. For example, it suggests that there may be a tendency for the CC to overstate barriers to entry and expansion and that there may be inconsistency as to whether the CC includes self-supply[64] in its analysis of the relevant market. The review also suggests that greater explanation of the "intervention threshold" applied by the OFT and CC in a particular local market would be helpful. Overall, however, the report concludes that in the

---

[60] *British Sky Broadcasting Group plc* v *(1) The Competition Commission (2) The Secretary of State* and *Virgin Media, Inc* v *(1) The Competition Commission (2) The Secretary of State* (heard together) [2008] CAT 25, at para 308.

[61] There had been two previous *ex post* reviews of the quality of the CC's decision-making but neither dealt with EA inquiries and neither dealt with mergers which had been cleared subject to remedies: see PriceWaterhouseCooper LLP, *Ex post evaluation of mergers* (March 2005) and CC, *Evaluation of the Competition Commission's past cases – Final report* (January 2008).

[62] Deloitte LLP, *Review of merger decisions under the Enterprise Act 2002* (18 March 2009).

[63] The review examined eight cases, selected on the basis of set criteria: three resolved at the OFT stage (*Impress/Alcan* (Case ME/1977/05, 2005), *Boots/Unichem* (Case ME/2134/05, 2006) and *William Hill/Stanley* (Case ME/1716–05, 2005)) and five referred to the CC (*DS Smith/Linpac* (October 2004), *Knauf/Superglass* (November 2004), *Heinz/HP Foods* (March 2006), *Cott/Macaw* (March 2006) and *EWS/Marcroft* (April 2006)).

[64] Ie in-house production which is not available for purchase by third parties but which might be considered as a source of potential competition on the merchant market selling to third parties.

majority of cases subsequent market developments did not raise any substantial doubts about the soundness of the OFT's and CC's decisions.

4.2 Preventing the integration of completed mergers

The CC has always had the power, under s 74(1) of the FTA 1973 and now under s 81(2) of the EA 2002, to order the parties to a completed merger to take no further steps to integrate the merging businesses pending its inquiry. The powers of the CC to make "hold separate" orders under s 81 are specifically envisaged as being "to prevent pre-emptive action" which might prejudice the outcome of the CC's inquiry. In practice the risk is that if the merger is prohibited, restoration of the status quo ante might have become impossible because the two merged businesses have been fully integrated.

This issue came under the spotlight in the *Stericycle*[65] case. In February 2006, Stericycle International LLC ("Stericycle") had purchased a competitor, Sterile Technologies Group Ltd ("STG"). At the time, Stericycle and STG were the two largest clinical waste management service providers in the UK. Merger clearance from the OFT was not sought but the OFT investigated the acquisition of its own initiative and identified it as a qualifying merger under the EA 2002. "Hold separate" undertakings were agreed between the OFT and the parties, to freeze any further integration.

The OFT identified a risk of an SLC and referred the merger to the CC in June 2006, at which point the hold separate undertakings agreed with the OFT were adopted by the CC under s 80(3) of the EA 2002. However, the CC was concerned that if further integration of the parties were to continue, any divestment remedies to restore competitive conditions to the pre-merger situation would be very difficult to implement effectively. Having failed to agree satisfactory undertakings, the CC therefore strengthened the hold separate obligations on the parties by issuing an order ("the Order") under s 81 of the EA 2002 in July 2006, preventing Stericycle and STG from taking any pre-emptive action pending the outcome of the CC's inquiry. The CC also published a direction under the terms of the Order to appoint a Monitoring Trustee to ensure compliance and determine the degree to which the parties had, in fact, integrated. Under para 2(j) of the Order, Stericycle and STG were required to liaise with the CC to ensure that they were still operating separate teams for the conduct of certain defined functions (commercial and

[65] CC, Report on *Stericycle International LLC/Sterile Technologies Group Ltd* (December 2006).

marketing, finance and accounting, environment, and health and safety).

Stericycle appealed to the CAT under s 120 of the EA 2002 for review of the CC's decision to make the Order, challenging the separate teams provision on the basis that it was beyond the scope of the CC's powers under s 81(2) of the EA 2002 and/or that it was disproportionate or unreasonable. The CAT, however, confirmed[66] that the CC has a wide discretion to take reasonable action where it considers that there is a risk of pre-emptive action. Moreover, the CAT commented that the use of the word "might" in the definition of pre-emptive action in s 80(10) of the EA 2002 (which defines the concept of "pre-emptive action") implies a relatively low threshold of expectation.[67] The power under s 81 therefore enables the CC to intervene where it considers that there is at least *some risk* of action being taken by the parties which might prejudice the reference or impede the taking of any action by the CC under the EA 2002.

The CAT also clarified the scope of the powers of the CC in making an order, and the burden of proof in challenging a s 81 order. It is for the applicants to show that the CC's decision is unreasonable and it is not sufficient simply to show that the CC could have taken an alternative decision. In addition, the CC is not under any obligation to explain in detail why it did not adopt possible alternative approaches; it need only provide sufficient reasons for adopting its chosen decision.[68] On the basis of this decision, it would appear that the higher the level of integration that takes place prior to clearance, the more intrusive the measures that can be taken by the CC in order to ensure separation of the businesses during the period of its inquiry.

This case has had a wider long-term impact in that it has contributed to a call from the Chairman of the CC to move to a compulsory pre-closing notification regime in the UK. This radical proposal is discussed further below in the concluding section of this chapter.

5 RECOURSE TO THE CAT FOR JUDICIAL REVIEW OF MERGER DECISIONS

This final section will consider the impact of moving judicial review jurisdiction over CC (and Secretary of State) merger decisions from the High Court to the CAT. As well as considering the reasons for the move, the effectiveness of the CAT in exercising judicial control over

---

[66] *Stericycle International LLC* v *Competition Commission* [2006] CAT 21.

[67] See the *Stericycle* CAT judgment, at para 129.

[68] See *ibid*, at para 149.

the CC will also be considered. The key question of the intensity of review as applied by the CAT, a specialist body, has been considered above in section 3.

5.1 The transfer of judicial review jurisdiction from the High Court to the CAT

Under the FTA 1973, parties and third parties seeking to challenge decisions of the OFT, MMC/CC or Secretary of State had to do so by way of an application for judicial review to the High Court. The very low rate of success of judicial review applications under the FTA regime (only one merger challenge was successful throughout the lifetime of the FTA) meant that, tactically, parties often concluded that the chances of success were too low to justify the expense of a judicial review application and accordingly left (in their eyes) unsatisfactory decisions unchallenged. Case law on the conduct of CC inquiries was therefore fairly scarce and the question was sometimes raised as to whether there was any genuinely effective judicial scrutiny of merger control decisions in the UK. Section 120 of the EA 2002 sought to address any perceived inadequacies in the merger control judicial review regime by moving jurisdiction for judicial review of decisions taken by the OFT, the CC, or the Secretary of State to the CAT.[69]

There were also concerns under the FTA 1973 in relation to the timing of judicial review proceedings in circumstances where the commercial logic behind a particular merger might have changed significantly by the time the court processes had run their course. The relatively lower caseload of the CAT was seen as giving it the capacity to handle merger judicial reviews very swiftly where required. This belief has proved to be correct in practice both by the CAT's decision to impose a 4-week deadline for applications under s 120,[70] and by its very fast handling in just 12 calendar days from application to judgment in both the *IBA Health* case in 2003 and the *Merger Action Group's* challenge to the Lloyds/HBOS public interest clearance in 2008.[71]

---

[69] When originally created under the CA 1998, the CAT was part of the CC, with jurisdiction limited to hearing appeals concerning OFT decisions under the CA 1998. When the EA 2002 granted the CAT judicial review jurisdiction over CC decisions, it became an independent institution, as from 1 April 2003.

[70] See the Competition Appeal Tribunal Rules 2003, SI 2003/1372, r 26.

[71] See *IBA Health Ltd* v *Office of Fair Trading* [2003] CAT 27 and *Merger Action Group* v *Secretary of State for Business, Enterprise and Regulatory Reform* [2008] CAT 36.

5.2 A vigilant and effective JR jurisdiction

As at the date of writing, four applications challenging merger decisions by the CC have been heard by the CAT under s 120 of the EA 2002:[72]

- an appeal by Somerfield plc with regard to the CC's final decision regarding Somerfield's acquisition of 115 stores from Wm Morrison;[73]
- an appeal by Stericycle regarding the imposition of interim relief by the CC with regards to Stericycle's acquisition of Sterile Technologies Group Ltd;[74] and
- joined appeals by Sky and ITV against the decision of the Secretary of State and CC regarding Sky's acquisition of 17.9 per cent of ITV.[75]

Each of these cases has been discussed in the preceding sections of this chapter.

It is clear that the CAT has already had a significant influence on key aspects of the CC's procedure, and judicial scrutiny of merger decisions in the UK can certainly be characterised as active, effective, influential and very swift where required. As the CAT itself anticipated in its review of the *Sky/ITV* case, it is a "more demanding and/or less deferential tribunal" than a generalist court might be and this is particularly notable where it is dealing with expert economics-based evidence. The CAT panel usually includes a CAT member with economics expertise so that the CAT is able to form its own independent view and critique of complex economics submissions.

The vigilance and effectiveness of the CAT's judicial review function has also been demonstrated. Earlier comments in CAT judgments about the quality of OFT decisions had suggested a potentially higher degree of deference to the CC than to the OFT (which since 2000 had been on the receiving end of a fair amount of (constructive) criticism from the CAT in relation to its analysis and procedures under the CA 1998). This impression was first created in the *IBA Health* judgment which (as discussed above), until its reasoning was overturned by the Court of Appeal, threatened to

---

[72] In addition, an application was made by Stericycle regarding the CC's final report, *Stericycle International LLC/Sterile Technologies Group Ltd* (December 2006), but this was ultimately withdrawn.

[73] *Somerfield plc* v *Competition Commission* [2006] CAT 4.

[74] *Stericycle International LLC; Stericycle International Ltd; Sterile Technologies Group Ltd* v *Competition Commission* [2006] CAT 21.

[75] *British Sky Broadcasting Group plc* v *(1) The Competition Commission (2) The Secretary of State* and *Virgin Media, Inc* v *(1) The Competition Commission (2) The Secretary of State (*heard together) [2008] CAT 25.

emasculate the well-respected OFT merger function and give all the real decision-making power to the CC.[76]

However, the CAT has proved that it will call the CC to account where it considers it appropriate. The CAT has a parallel judicial review jurisdiction to s 120 under s 179 of the EA 2002 to review decisions of the CC (and others) in the context of a market investigation under Part 4 of the EA 2002. Tesco challenged the CC's findings in relation to the 2008 *Groceries* market investigation, seeking review not of the substantive findings but in relation to the remedies which the CC identified as being required to address its concerns, and, specifically, in relation to the proposed introduction of a "competition test" into the planning regime for the approval of new supermarkets.[77] Tesco alleged that the CC failed to take into account certain relevant considerations when considering the impact of the competition test and in relation to the proportionality of such a remedy.

The CAT recognised the margin of appreciation which should be given to the CC:

> "the [CC] must be afforded an appropriate margin of appreciation, such that [the CAT] will not interfere in [the CC's] assessments or judgments without good reason",[78]

and cited[79] the comments of Auld J (as he was then) in *R* v *MMC, ex p National House Building Council*[80] in relation to the approach to be taken in reviewing a report of the (then) MMC:

> "the Court … must take care not to subject the [CC's] Report to fine textual or legal analysis as if it were a statute or other legal document. I respectfully adopt the words of Hodgson J about this in *R* v *MMC ex parte Visa International Service* [1991] ECC 291 … '… the Report must not be read as if it were a statute or a judgment … It should be read in a generous not restrictive way and the Court should be slow to disable the [CC] from recommending action considered to be in the public interest or to prevent the [Secretary of State] from acting thereon unless perceived errors of law are both material and substantial' ".[81]

But, having made these comments, the CAT did not hesitate to criticise the CC for what it perceived to be inadequate reasoning in the report:

---

[76] See *IBA Health Ltd* v *Office of Fair Trading* [2003] CAT 27.

[77] *Tesco plc* v *Competition Commission* [2009] CAT 9.

[78] *Ibid*, at para 81.

[79] *Ibid*, at para 79.

[80] [1993] ECC 388 (upheld on appeal: [1995] ECC 89).

[81] [1993] ECC 388, at 398.

> "Bearing well in mind the cautionary words of Auld J (paragraph [79] above), it is nevertheless our view that Tesco is correct in submitting that there is a significant gap in the Commission's analysis in relation to the 'costs' of the competition test. The Report does not fully and properly assess and take account of the risk that the application of the test might have adverse effects for consumers as a result of their being denied the benefit of developments which would enhance their welfare, including by leaving demand 'unmet'."[82]

The CAT went on to find that the CC's proportionality analysis was also "flawed" and that the "omission was not of a trivial nature so as to be incapable of affecting the [CC's] decision ..."[83]

In its *Sky/ITV* judgment (in which the CAT overturned the CC's interpretation of the plurality test set out in s 58 and 58A of the EA 2002) and in the *Tesco* judgment, the CAT has shown that it will not hesitate to overturn elements of the CC's reasoning and analysis where it considers that they are inadequate. Whilst an appropriate degree of deference is given to the CC in its margin of appreciation, this is not to say that the CC is given the benefit of the doubt in cases involving complex competition analysis. On 16 October 2009, following an application under s 120 by Barclays for review of the CC's decision in connection with its market investigation into the provision of payment protection insurance, the CAT held that the CC had failed properly to consider the proportionality of its "point of sale prohibition" remedy, and remitted the matter to the CC for further consideration.[84] In light of these decisions, the strong assumption must be that the CC will continue to be subject to strong and effective judicial scrutiny.

6 CONCLUSIONS AND ISSUES WHICH HAVE EMERGED OUT OF EXPERIENCE OF APPLYING THE EA 2002

Experience since 20 June 2003 when the changes introduced by the EA 2002 entered into force has been broadly positive. Two issues have, however, emerged which challenge two of the key characteristics of UK merger control which have endured since the Monopolies and Mergers Act 1965, namely:

(1) Is it still appropriate to have a voluntary regime with the risk that anti-competitive completed mergers may have to be unwound?

---

[82] [1993] ECC 388, at para 111.

[83] *Ibid*, at para 165.

[84] See *Barclays Bank plc* v *Competition Commission* [2009] CAT 27 in relation to the CC's Report on *Payment Protection Insurance* (January 2009). See also *BAA Ltd* v *Competition Commission* (judgment awaited) in relation to the CC's Report on *BAA Airports* (March 2009).

(2) Is a "Rolls Royce", two-institution system necessary given the prevalence of more streamlined single institution merger control systems in most jurisdictions, and the fact that the largest mergers involving UK companies are likely to be notified to the EC Commission under the EC Merger Regulation?

6.1 Is a voluntary regime still appropriate?

As discussed above, the *Stericycle* case brought to the fore the problems that can arise when a completed merger is found to be anti-competitive. Soon after this experience, the Chairman of the CC started to discuss in public the difficulties raised by the voluntary system. In January 2008, he aired the issues in detail without reaching a conclusion as to whether a mandatory regime would be preferable,[85] but his position had strengthened by May 2008, when he commented:

> "the [CC's] experience of the system since 2002 strongly suggests that another look needs to be taken at moving to compulsory pre-notification so that we are not constantly having to 'unscramble the eggs'."[86]

A number of issues[87] would need to be tackled if such a change were introduced:

- the EA 2002 jurisdictional tests would need to be changed to remove any ambiguities as to whether a particular merger qualified for investigation;[88]
- the OFT would have to deal with a hugely increased proportion of "no issue" filings, which would not be a productive reallocation of the OFT's limited resources;
- the OFT's procedures are currently amongst the most detailed and thorough (and therefore expensive) of any first-stage merger control process in the world: politically, a move to a compulsory regime would involve a significant imposition of red tape on business; and
- finally, there is no doubt that businesses welcome the voluntary nature of the UK regime. A delay for merger clearance is often

---

[85] Speech of Peter Freeman, "Competition Policy – A Process of Constant Renewal" (Lecture as part of the CCS Distinguished Speaker Series, Singapore, 15 January 2008).

[86] Speech of Peter Freeman, "Key challenges at the Competition Commission" (Lecture at King's College London, 28 May 2008).

[87] Some of these issues have been directly acknowledged, as has been pointed out by the Chief Executive of the OFT. See, for example, the interview with John Fingleton in *Global Competition Review* magazine: R Knox, "An Interview with John Fingleton" (2009) 2 GCR 12, at 17–18, and P Scott, "An Interview with Peter Freeman" (2009) 2 GCR 12, at 19–21.

[88] Currently, the share of supply test can be interpreted in various ways such that it is not a "bright line" jurisdictional test.

seen as disruptive and expensive, particularly where there are no substantive competition concerns.[89]

Whilst a compulsory regime would undoubtedly help to resolve the CC's perceived problems in dealing effectively with completed mergers, it is suggested that the powers of the OFT and CC to impose hold separate obligations on the parties could be used to greater effect – and indeed experience suggests that the OFT does now ask for hold separate undertakings more often and at an earlier stage in its proceedings than before the *Stericycle* case. Moreover, the OFT has increased its resources for monitoring merger activity so that the possibility of an anti-competitive merger slipping "below the radar" is minimised. The removal of the share of supply jurisdictional test would also be a significant issue, given its importance in capturing potentially anti-competitive horizontal mergers. Overall, it is suggested that the introduction of a compulsory merger regime would be a disproportionate response to a problem for which the solutions are already incorporated into the EA 2002.

It is understood that legislative proposals on reforms to competition law were shelved as part of the legislative re-prioritisation which followed the financial crisis in autumn 2008 and that one of the proposals for consultation was the introduction of a compulsory merger control system. It remains to be seen whether that debate has been closed for the foreseeable future. Competition-related legislation will probably be required in all Member States in the next couple of years in order to implement expected legislation from Brussels requiring changes to national litigation procedure to facilitate the private enforcement of competition law. It may be that proposals for wider reforms to UK merger control are reactivated at that time.

6.2 Is a "Rolls Royce" bi-institutional system still appropriate?

There is no doubt that the quality and sophistication of the UK merger control regime is first class. In the KPMG Peer Review of Competition Policy 2004, the UK merger authorities came third behind only the US and Germany (and ahead of the European Commission) and interviewees commented that the UK merger regime was "the strongest part of its competition regime" due to the length of time the regime had been in place[90] and due also to

[89] Of course mergers with an international element will often be subject to merger control processes (and delays) in other jurisdictions. However, UK merger control processes are, in the author's experience, amongst the longest in duration so businesses see real commercial value in being able to avoid a UK notification.

[90] Notwithstanding the replacement of the FTA 1973 by the EA 2002, the continuity between the legislative regimes was recognised.

"the staff, which are rated as being the most capable within the UK authorities".[91] In the subsequent KPMG review in 2007, the UK merger regime was ranked second behind only the US.[92]

The CC itself sees virtues in the two-institution approach.[93] But, as has been noted, the UK regime's thoroughness and attention to detail also means that it is amongst the longest in duration and is therefore expensive. In some cases in the author's experience, parties will abandon a merger simply because the synergies expected to be realised by the merger do not warrant the expense of the full CC process.

One area where the bi-institutional structure inevitably creates overlaps is at the point of handover of the case from the OFT to the CC. Experience suggests that the degree of liaison between the OFT and the CC when a reference is made has improved under the EA regime (which places an obligation on the OFT to give the CC such information and assistance as it may need[94]). Although the number of general fact gathering questions posed by the CC has reduced and its questionnaires are now more focused, it remains the case that the CC will often ask for information which is already on the OFT's file.

It has been debated whether streamlined procedures could be introduced to reduce the cost of the CC's proceedings. For example, could the parties simply accept the OFT's findings on certain points – such as market definition or even the OFT's SLC finding – and fast track to the next stage of procedure with the CC? Although such short cuts may be desirable, the statutory framework and decision-making structures which the CC is required to follow make it very difficult to fast track its procedures. Moreover, with an effective and vigilant judicial review forum, the risk of a disgruntled third party challenging any procedural short cuts taken by the CC cannot be ignored.

In the author's experience, a full CC reference is not generally more expensive in terms of adviser's fees than a second-stage merger review by the EC Commission and it is not the case that the latter invariably involves much larger or more significant mergers. Moreover, clients value the high quality of the CC processes with first-class staff, good communication and reasonable transparency. The fact that the businesses under scrutiny have direct access to the

---

[91] KPMG (commissioned by the DTI), *Peer Review of Competition Policy* (May 2004), at para 1.3.1.

[92] KPMG (commissioned by the DTI), *Peer Review of Competition Policy* (June 2007), at para 1.3.1.

[93] Speech of Peter Freeman, "Key challenges at the Competition Commission" (Lecture at King's College London, 28 May 2008).

[94] See EA 2002, s 105(3).

actual decision-makers in the CC process (the members of the CC appointed to the "Group" reviewing the merger) is highly valued and contrasts sharply with the EC Commission where it is very difficult to secure a meeting with the Commissioner responsible for merger control issues. Finally, it is appropriate to observe that if the bi-institutional structure were to be abolished, the case in favour of a full merits appeal before the CAT in merger cases would become compelling.

In conclusion, although the changes to UK merger control introduced by the EA 2002 have been in force for a little over 6 years, it is clear that they have had a significant effect on the decision-making processes of both the OFT and the CC. Moreover, the degree of judicial scrutiny of their decisions has been materially enhanced. As a consequence, it is suggested that the quality of decision-making has also been enhanced, albeit at increased cost to the merging parties. Whether further changes in the form of compulsory pre-notification and/or the move to a single regulator are appropriate is open to debate; in the author's view the case for further changes has not been made.[95]

[95] See *Unichem* v *OFT* [2005] CAT 8, at para 199.

CHAPTER 9

ECONOMIC ANALYSIS IN UK COMPETITION LAW AFTER CA 1998

*Morten Hviid**

In most jurisdictions, including the UK, we have witnessed both a trend towards a more economics based approach to competition law questions and a move towards more quantitative analysis in competition decisions.[1] Given how fundamental economics might appear to be to competition law and its enforcement, it may come as a surprise that such a move can be discerned.[2] Not only has there been a trend, but it has been particularly steep at the EU and EU member state

* ESRC Centre for Competition Policy and Norwich Law School, University of East Anglia. The author would like to thank Pinar Akman, Michael Harker, Barry Rodger, Andreas Stephan, Catherine Waddams and colleagues at the ESRC Centre for Competition Policy at the University of East Anglia for very helpful comments and discussions. The financial support of the UK Economic and Social Research Council (ESCR is also gratefully acknowledged. The usual disclaimer applies.

[1] The chapter will draw heavily on two collections of original essays: P Buccirossi (ed), *Handbook of Antitrust Economics* (2008, MIT Press, and B Lyons (ed), *Cases in European Competition Policy: The Economic Analyis* (2009, Cambridge University Press, Cambridge). These two collections provide an extensive summary of where economics is now and how it has been used within the EU and, in some specific cases, within the UK.

[2] The trend is equally evident for the US, where Lawrence White demonstrates how the use of economics in antitrust enforcement did not really take off until after the 1960s. See L J White, "The Growing Influence of Economics and Economists on Antitrust: An Extended Discussion" (NYU Law and Economics Research Paper No 08–07; Reg-Markets Center Working Paper No 08–05) (2008). This is echoed in some of the chapters in P Buccirossi (ed), *Handbook of Antitrust Economics*, n 1 above.

level, including the UK.[3] An excellent overview by Damien Neven[4] on competition economics in Europe illustrates the growth in the involvement of economics in competition policy within the EU by looking, *inter alia*, at the growth in economic consultancy related to this as well as the growth of professional economists in the agencies since the 1990s. The importance of economics in UK competition law enforcement is also illustrated, in the early years following the introduction of the Competition Act 1998, by the position of academic economists as Director General of Fair Trading and subsequently Chairman of the OFT (following the Enterprise Act 2002)[5] and Chairman of the Competition Commission (formerly the Mergers and Monopolies Commission) respectively. Finally, competition law is an area where communication between economists and lawyers has improved markedly, though there is still much to be done on that front.[6]

The economics relevant to competition law and policy is usually referred to as industrial economics or industrial organisation, typically abbreviated to "IO". In its mission statement, one of the leading journals in this area, *Journal of Industrial Economics*, offers the following definition:

> "[I]ndustrial organisation is the disciplined application of economic principles to explain and predict real-world behaviour of firms, markets and industries."[7]

Thus IO economists may look to see how different market structures shape outcomes; how different behaviours shape market structure; how different outcomes shape structure through dynamics. In these contributions, competition law may either be included as an active ingredient, an exogenous provider of some of the rules constraining the firms, or be the actual subject for analysis. In the latter case, the aim may be to provide an *ex-post* assessment of enforcement, or to offer recommendations about

---

[3] As an illustration of this, consider the background to two books on the use of economics in competition law. J E Kwoka Jr and L J White, *The Antitrust Revolution: Economics Policy, and Competition* (OUP, Oxford) was first published in 1989 and is now in its 5th edition (2008) and has offered ever-changing essays about the use of economics in antitrust cases, predominantly in the US. By contrast, for the EU, the first book offering a similar menu of "the use of economics in competition cases" has just been published: see Lyons (ed), *Cases in European Competition Policy: The Economic Analyis*, n 1 above.

[4] D Neven, "Competition economics and antitrust in Europe" (2006) Economic Policy 741.

[5] See R Whish, "Chapter 1 above.

[6] See, for example the discussion by John Vickers in Neven, "Competition economics and antitrust in Europe", n 4 above, at 781–786.

[7] http://www.essex.ac.uk/jindec/mission.htm.

the design or reform of substantive or procedural law. Finally, it should be kept in mind that IO is independent of jurisdictions in the sense that IO economists share a common framework such that a UK-based IO economist would have the same basic training and understanding and use the same fundamental approach as any other IO economist.[8]

Broadly speaking, IO research can be divided into theoretical and empirical research. Theoretical work has predominantly contributed to two areas: the design of guidelines and the identification of theories of harm. Empirical work has contributed in two different areas: testing the validity of theoretical contributions and offering direct input into cases. Thus, quite apart from any influence economics might have had on the formulation of the substantive law, economics is, broadly speaking, involved in three areas: the design of procedural law; the writing of guidelines; and the actual analysis of cases including *ex-post* case evaluation.

In looking at the 10 years since the introduction of the Competition Act, it is important to look beyond 2000 to pick up more general trends in IO knowledge and understanding. This is an area in which there have been tremendous developments in the last 30 years, particularly but not exclusively in direct policy relevant understanding. IO in the late 1970s was not in particularly good shape. Empirical work was mostly based on relatively weak data and simple estimation methods while theoretical work did not yet have the tools to come to grips with the strategic behaviour of sophisticated firms.[9] Theory was the first area to develop further, by building on significant developments in game theory, which enabled researchers to obtain a more nuanced understanding of the possible outcomes arising from competitive interactions in concentrated markets. The first wave of theory developed on the back on these and other developments in game theory is summarised in the 1989 textbook by Jean Tirole.[10] A large part of this book

---

[8] Growing up (academically) as an IO economist the author knew about Austrian and Marxist economics but was not really aware of the so-called Chicago, Harvard or post-Chicago schools. Knowing about these particular pigeon holes required contact with the writings of US antitrust lawyers and this particular division of IO never seemed particularly helpful. Awareness of the ordoliberal school came much later as a result of interaction with European lawyers. Ordoliberalism is very different from IO and, outside Germany, is unlikely to feature in an economics programme either at undergraduate or graduate level.

[9] One could tentatively associate this with the pre-Chicago state of antitrust analysis in the US and with the Structure-Conduct-Performance paradigm.

[10] J Tirole, *The Theory of Industrial Economics* (1989, MIT Press).

was based on working papers,[11] ensuring that the book was so up to date with developments at the time of publication that, despite the advances since then, it is probably still the premiere text for a graduate IO course. Subsequent developments have been particularly in the area of vertical restraints, where researchers have not just uncovered the strategic effects of various restraints, but also investigated when these could be expected to be used.

While at least some areas of theory were encountering decreasing returns to effort in the late 1980s, there was a huge renaissance in empirical work on IO issues. This was partly sparked by a rapid development and improvement in econometrics methods in other fields of economics, especially labour economics, by much improved statistical packages and most importantly by the availability of better data, not just in terms of the quality of the data but also in its detail.

Thus, even compared with 10 years ago, IO today is in a much better position to offer support to competition law design and enforcement. At least some of the drivers behind the improvement in IO can be associated with the greater involvement of IO economists in competition enforcement,[12] which has introduced economists to new questions and concerns.

Generally, a substantial part of the insights achieved over the period leading up to the Competition Act 1998 have gradually filtered through to policy makers during that period. One difficulty in writing a chapter such as this is that there is a big difference between developments in economics on the one hand (the innovations) and the appreciation of these by the competition law community on the other (the diffusion). To obtain an unscientific but quick impression of the diffusion, the author had a look at the standard textbooks on UK or EU competition law, excluding readers and case books,[13] and

[11] Economics has long had a tradition of research published in working papers in advance of publication in academic journals, with journals, not books, being the preferred means of dissemination. The importance of publishing work as working papers is evident when one considers the lag between submission and publication in economics journals and how this has evolved over the period. For the top journals in 1999 the average time hovered around 2 years and this was for only the relatively small fraction of submitted papers which were eventually published in those journals. For documentation and discussion of this, see G Ellison, "The Slowdown in the Economic Publishing Process" (2002) 110 Journal of Political Economy 947. Even with more electronic-based journals, his conclusions are still likely to be valid.

[12] For illustrations that this has occurred on both sides of the Atlantic, see n 2 above, and Neven, n 4 above.

[13] Notably A Jones and B Sufrin, *EC Competition Law* (2nd edn, 2004, OUP, Oxford). Arguably, this collection contains more economics than most of the textbooks in the table in the text, including two of the standard diagrams.

relatively casually counted the number of pages covering more or less formal economics.[14] The outcome is summarised in the table below which makes a simple point clearly: there is (still) not much of it.[15]

Author and title	*Pages of economics*
Richard Whish, *Competition Law*	73 of 985 pages = 7.4%
Giorgio Monti, *EC Competition Law*	36 of 505 pages = 7.1%
Mark Furse, *Competition Law of the EC and UK*	37 of 471 pages = 7.9%
Barry Rodger and Angus MacCulloch, *Competition Law and Policy in the EC and UK*	14 of 407 pages = 3.4%
Piet Jan Slot and Angus Johnston, *An Introduction to Competition Law*	17 of 350 pages = 4.9%
Joanna Goyder and Albertina Albors-Llorens, *Goyder's EC Competition Law*	16 of 655 pages = 2.4%
Valentine Korah, An Introductory Guide to EC Competition Law and Practice	17 of 474 =3.6%

More seriously, of the books in the table above, only Furse (and to some extent Monti) engages fully with the competition law economics[16] and in my view none of the books would give the reader any level of competence in economics at all. Thus, to get even an intuitive grasp of the economics underlying the law and policy, the reader would have to invest in a specialist book such as Bishop and Walker[17] or Motta,[18] both of which, and in particular the latter, represent a significant step up from the law texts in terms of economic sophistication.

Only Motta's book would equip the reader with the background to tackle the existing economics literature directly. The gap between the UK (and EU) and the US in terms of reading and engaging with

---

14 The author apologises to any author who considers the count found too much or too little economics in their books. In counting pages the author tended to be very generous and broad minded in interpretation rather than simply focusing on the subsection of the introduction with the word "economics" in the title.

15 That is not to say that there is too little or too much – that is up to the reader to decide. Moreover, the fraction may be an over or underestimate. It may be that economics is such an integrated part of competition law that it is seamlessly integrated into the texts to the extent that the casual observer does not even realise it.

16 They are also the only two texts containing one (but only one) of the standard economics graphs.

17 S Bishop and M Walker,, *The Economics of EC Competition Law* (2nd edn, 2002, Sweet & Maxwell, London).

18 M Motta, *Competition Policy*, (2004, Cambridge University Press, Cambridge).

economics, and specifically IO, is very evident. One might wonder about the rationale for this disconnect between law and economics in this area.[19] The message one often hears is that economics is too mathematical, but this comment needs to be understood against the backdrop of how economics in general and IO in particular have developed over the past decades and how it continues to develop.[20] In the development (or innovation) phase, where it is important to be precise in order to understand all the subtleties of the modelling, the analysis and the presentation is typically mathematical and abstract. It is often less so in the diffusion phase when the research community has achieved a better grasp of the models and their implications are more deeply appreciated. Looking at very recent research on new issues may then offer a biased view of how much mathematics economists generally use.

The section below provides an overview of the theoretical and empirical approach of IO economists, highlighting the contribution of game theory and econometrics to our understanding of the competitive process. Section 2 considers some of the contributions made by economics to the areas of vertical restraints, predation, leniency programmes and mergers, particularly but not exclusively, during the last 10 years, and concluding comments are contained in section 3.

1 METHODS IN COMPETITION ECONOMICS

IO economists' output can roughly be subdivided into theoretical and empirical studies; although this distinction is becoming increasingly blurred over time with more recent academic literature combining theoretical models with empirical testing. Theoretical scholars typically use game theory as the method to predict outcomes in particular strategic settings. Empirical research in IO is almost exclusively quantitative, using econometrics as its main method and basing its estimations around increasingly better data and theoretical predictions about relationships between the observables.

1.1 The role of game theory in understanding strategic interaction

When it comes to theoretical research over the last 30 years, the main

[19] See the discussion by John Vickers included in Neven, n 4, above at 785.

[20] It is important for the competition law user of IO to appreciate that economics evolves as do economies. Some of the evolution is driven by policy questions arising out of current or past real problems, be they the writing of guidelines or actual decisions. Both theoretical and empirical studies become dated, and users need to ensure that what they rely on is still considered to be valid.

tool used by IO economists has been, and remains, game theory. Game theory aims to predict outcomes from strategic situations where a small number of actors take decisions in the understanding that outcomes and hence their decisions are interrelated. As an example, the success of an advertising campaign depends critically on what rivals are doing during and after the campaign. Given that competition concerns only arise when there is a small number of strategically interrelated firms in a market or a series of connected markets, game theory would appear to be the most natural starting point when developing competition law methodology.

While the start date of game theory can and has been debated, the foundations were in place by the early 1950s. After many false starts in IO, game theory finally began to deliver on early promises in the 1980s due to two developments. One was the notion of subgame perfection, requiring that strategies should be credible in the sense that, if called upon to carry them out, the firm would do so. For example, this spelled the demise of some of the more fanciful theories of predation and led to the insistence of recoupment as a test for the rationality of the action as predatory. More generally it led to a considerable number of so-called two-stage game models where the researcher considered the joint effect on outcomes by both long-term strategic (for example, investment) decisions and short-term strategic (for example, price) decisions. From this we have a better understanding, not simply about entry and entry deterrence, but more generally about what might determine what we could call the "natural" market structure.[21] The importance of this should be evident when considering interventions which fail to respect any possible "natural" market structure. If there really is only room for three firms, then we can continue to block mergers or break up dominant entities into four or five firms, but ultimately this would be doomed as firms would go bankrupt after an unsuccessful attempt to defy gravity.

The second area was in developing consistent methods for dealing with (the lack of) information.[22] In reality, no firm has complete information about every element of its decisional universe, but it also typically knows something which others do not. Taking costs as an example, firms rarely have perfect knowledge about their costs and in particular are unlikely to have perfect knowledge about all

[21] See work by John Sutton summarised in J Sutton, "Market Structure: Theory and Evidence", in M Armstrong and R H Porter eds, *Handbook of Industrial Economics volume III* (2007, North-Holland).

[22] Both of these contributions were recognised by the Nobel committee in awarding the prize to Reinhard Selten (subgame perfection) and John C Harsanyi (Bayesian games) in 1994 together with John F Nash Jr (Nash equilibrium).

future costs, but they are likely to know more about their own costs than those of their rivals. Being able to handle cases involving uncertainty and asymmetric information led to a number of advances in our understanding.[23] For example, this reinstated one method of predation often cited in UK cases, that of reputation building.[24] Without uncertainty and asymmetric information, building a reputation would have no strategic relevance.

Theoretical economics models are invariably mathematical, formal and based on a set of assumptions which may or may not lead the reader to conclude that not just the baby but also the bath was thrown out with the bathwater. The key benefit, though, is that the assumptions are typically stated explicitly and discussed fully.[25] Economists famously disagree, sometimes even with themselves, but the source of this is usually found in differing views about the underlying assumptions and the extent to which they are empirically plausible. As the understanding of a particular area improves, there is a tendency for the level of mathematical sophistication to be reduced dramatically.[26] Economists need the maths to be precise in what they are stating; and, particularly when an argument or approach is new, clarity is important. As they become more familiar with the model, they often become able to explain their results in terms of relatively simple diagrams. Of course, this may not help in communication with lawyers if the latter are as hostile to diagrams as they are to equations, but hopefully increasing interaction and communication with economists will break down these barriers.

Theoretical models using game theory continue to refine and improve our understanding today. An area which appears particularly fruitful is the inclusion of insights from behavioural economics by allowing the firms or their customers to depart from full rationality in various ways.[27]

---

[23] Many of these advances are associated with the post-Chicago school.

[24] In that we would appear to be ahead of the US: see the conclusion in White, "The Growing Influence of Economics and Economists on Antitrust: An Extended Discussion" n 2 above.

[25] Except that where the assumptions and hence the justifications are well established and standard in the literature, they should be and will be in good scholarly work.

[26] One of the attractions of Jean Tirole's textbook is that in each chapter the basic part uses very limited mathematical apparatus, the sign of a top-class economic scholar.

[27] For a survey of this literature, see G Ellison, "Bounded Rationality in Industrial Organisation" in R Blundell, W K Newey and T Persson (eds), *Advances in Economics and Econometrics: Theory and Applications*, Ninth World Congress (2005, Cambridge University Press, Cambridge).

1.2 The increased use of econometrics

There appears to be some degree of confusion about what econometrics is and how it relates to economics among lawyers. The following quote offers a basic definition of econometrics and its relation to economic theory:

> "Broadly speaking, econometrics aims to give empirical content to economic relations for testing economic theories, forecasting, decision making, and for ex post decision/policy evaluation. ... By emphasizing the quantitative aspects of economic relationships, econometrics calls for a "unification" of measurement and theory in economics. Theory without measurement can have only limited relevance for the analysis of actual economic problems; while measurement without theory, being devoid of a framework necessary for the interpretation of the statistical observations, is unlikely to result in a satisfactory explanation of the way economic forces interact with each other. Neither "theory" nor "measurement" on its own is sufficient to further our understanding of economic phenomena."[28]

The use of econometrics in competition analysis in the UK has increased significantly throughout the decade since the introduction of the Competition Act 1998. Econometrics is used not only in market definitions of merger analysis but in a string of other applications as well.

Early econometric studies, seeking to explain the variation in one continuous variable (such as a price-cost margin) through a relationship with a number of explanatory variables (such as measures of how concentrated the market was), were limited to assuming a simple linear relationship. Subsequent developments in econometrics, econometrics software, data and computer power have enhanced the value of econometric studies. This is not the place to offer a review of these developments[29] but two examples give a flavour of what can now be achieved. Researchers can now explain the variation in variables which take a small number of discrete values, such as "entry" or "no entry".[30] Second, the development of data sets with observations relating to the same set of firms over a period of time, so-called "panel data", together with the techniques

---

[28] See J Geweke, J L Horowitz and H Pesaran, "Econometrics" in S N Durlauf and L E Blume (eds), *The New Palgrave Dictionary of Economics* (2nd edn, 2008) at p 1.

[29] For an excellent review, see P C Reiss and F A Wolak, "Structural Econometric Modeling: Rationales and Examples from Industrial Organization" in J Heckman and E Leamer (eds), *Handbook of Econometrics*, vol 6A (2007, North-Holland), Chap 64.

[30] Another example, used in merger simulations, is where consumers choose between a small number of different products. Such demand is estimated using a so-called "logit model". See, eg C Gollier and M Ivaldi, "A merger in the insurance industry" in Lyons (ed), *Cases in European Competition Policy: The Economic Analysis*, n 1 above, Chap 12.

to exploit the structure of this data fully,[31] has enabled more precise and reliable empirical regularities to be uncovered.

Some of the empirical methods developed to test theories and to gain a better understanding of how industry actually works have a role to play in the analysis of competition cases. Thus new and more advanced empirical methods may be able to improve market definition, measure the extent of the harmful effect of mergers, or the size of the over-charge in cartel cases. In many of these cases the full utilisation of empirical (econometric) methods developed in economics is yet to be achieved, partly due to time constraints, but also because there is not as yet a clear procedural structure to the use of empirical evidence by either side of the argument.[32] While authorities may not have the resources to carry out their own empirical investigation, the parties may have both the resources and the time,[33] and this forces the authorities to spend time evaluating this evidence. This necessitates both that they acquire the necessary expertise to do so and design procedural rules to ensure that they are presented with all the information they need to make an evaluation.

1.3 Economics evidence

One possibly fundamental difference between the US on the one hand and the EU and its Member States on the other is the form of enforcement. In the US the agencies have to go to the courts for a decision, meaning that the lawyers representing the agencies in court have to be comfortable with the economic analysis or else they have to rely on economics experts making witness statements. For the latter, the US has very strict rules about what can be the subject of an expert statement and also about who can be an expert. In the UK, enforcement decisions are taken by the relevant competition authority, primarily the OFT, on the basis of either internal analysis by economists or documents produced by external consultants, including the reports and evidence provided by the parties involved. The CAT and appeal courts do not get involved unless there is an appeal and appeal courts appear generally reluctant to challenge

---

31 For example, there are some features of a market which are likely to vary across firms but not over time, while there are other features which will vary over time but not across firms. This can be used in the estimation process.

32 For an example of the current debate in the US, see D Scheffman and M Coleman, "FTC Perspectives on the Use of Econometric Analysis in Antitrust Cases in J Harkrider (ed), *The Use of Econometrics in Antitrust* (American Bar Association Section on Antitrust), available at http://www.ftc.gov/be/ftcperspectivesoneconometrics.pdf.

33 While the authority has only a limited amount of time to assess a merger, the merging parties may have time to marshal any useful empirical evidence before they even notify the merger to the authorities.

economic "facts".[34] One would conjecture that this might have an effect on how economics is viewed in the two jurisdictions.[35] Understanding how one can "judge" economic expertise in competition law is a relatively new research area in the UK,[36] but looks to be an area with considerable potential.

2 SELECTED AREAS WITH INCREASED ECONOMICS IMPACT

The four areas discussed below – vertical restraints, predation, cartels and mergers – were chosen to illustrate the different ways in which economics has had an impact on UK competition law.

2.1 Vertical restraints[37]

From a policy design perspective, the advances in our understanding of the economics of vertical restraints has had and will continue to have profound effects on how authorities enforce both Chapters I and II. Vertical restraints include non-linear pricing, quantity discounts and rebates, resale price maintenance (RPM), quantity forcing and exclusivity clauses. This is an area which has the potential to drive any user to distraction because not only are there no general results in terms of which restraints are good or bad, the specific results are very sensitive to model assumptions. The immediate implication is that all vertical restraints, including RPM,[38] should be dealt with on

---

[34] See D Bailey, Chapter 2 above in relation to the functions and role of the CAT.

[35] See L M Froeb, P A Pautler, and L-H Röller, "The Economics of Organizing Economists", Vanderbilt Law and Economics Research Paper No. 08-18 (2008) for a related discussion by economists of ways to organise economists within competition authorities. See also D J Gerber, "Competition Law and the Institutional Embeddedness of Economics" in J Drexl (ed), *Economic Theory and Competition Law* (2009, Edward Elgar Publishing) for a perspective from outside economics.

[36] For a recent contribution, see I Lianos, "'Judging' economists: economic expertise in competition law and litigation. A European View", in *New Challenges in European Competition Law* (2009, Kluwer International, The Hague). See also D J Gerber, n 35 above.

[37] There is a number of excellent recent reviews of the economics literature: see P Rey and T Vergé, "Economics of Vertical Restraints" in P Buccirossi (ed), *Handbook of Antitrust Economics*, n 1 above; P Rey and J Tirole, "A Primer on Foreclosure" in Armstrong and Porter (eds), *Handbook of Industrial Economics volume III* (2007, North Holland). For a modern textbook treatment, see M Motta, n 18 above, Chap 6.

[38] It is a matter of some frustration to economists that the message about RPM has not until recently been translated into decision. With the US Supreme Court decision in *Leegin Creative Leather Prods* v *PSKS*, 551 US 877, 127 S Ct 2705 #92007) there may be some light at the end of the tunnel. However, if the US Congress and Senate pass section 148 of the "Discount Pricing Consumer Protection Act", which will restore the *per se* ban on RPM, this light will be an oncoming express train. The Act was introduced on 6 January 2009 but has not been voted on at the time of writing.

a case-by-case basis, ie a rule-of-reason approach. This in itself, as pointed out in Motta,[39] is unhelpful since restraints are ubiquitous and hence authorities and courts would potentially be swamped by cases. Economics has gone some way towards offering guidance on what sort of cases should be subjected to competition scrutiny. In particular, the distinction between within (intra-) and between (inter-) brand competition has proven fruitful.

Within (intra-) brand competition

Where an upstream firm uses vertical restraints to regulate the competition between its brands among two different downstream buyers, in the majority of cases the restraints are there to deal with a co-ordination problem and hence are efficiency enhancing. The typical example is a monopolist selling through two retailers where the restraint may be used to provide incentives for selling efforts, to deal with externalities between the retailers such as free-riding on promotional efforts or to remove double-marginalisation.[40] In the few scenarios where restraints are anti-competitive, these effects will be greatly reduced through competition. The implication is that for intra-brand competition, vertical restraints should only be investigated where market power is very substantial. This fits well with OFT's guidelines on vertical agreements[41] setting out market share thresholds for safe harbours.

Between [inter-] brand competition

The picture emerging from restraints which influence the competition between different brands is one of potentially much more harm, because these restraints can raise rivals" costs, either directly through a margin squeeze or indirectly through foreclosure necessitating closure, or, where available, the procurement of more expensive or less appropriate inputs.

While the economics literature has demonstrated that such foreclosure effects can happen, ie cases where a more efficient firm is foreclosed through vertical restraints raising this firm's costs, it has also demonstrated that it is by no means clear that an incentive to do so exists. Where a firm has the ability to use a specific vertical restraint to foreclose a rival but has no incentive to do so, the authority needs to look elsewhere for possible motivations for the

39 M Motta n 18 above, at p 306.

40 With imperfect competition at more than one level in the vertical supply chain, each such level will mark-up their costs leading to an aggregate mark-up in excess of what a fully integrated monopolist would have done.

41 Office of Fair Trading, *Vertical Agreements* (OFT 419, 2004). See also the European Commission's Notice on Agreements of Minor Importance [2001] OJ C368/13.

restraint. It is a hot debate within economics, as well as between policy makers, when foreclosure is likely or unlikely to arise in equilibrium. The Chicago school argument is that such effects are unlikely. The newer post-Chicago school models demonstrate that there are cases where anti-competitive foreclosure can arise. The latter effect often emerges when strategic behaviour is combined with asymmetric information.

The area of foreclosure is one where there has been significant progress in economics. In their survey of foreclosure, Patrick Rey and Jean Tirole write:

> "For all its prominence in competition law, the notion of foreclosure until recently had poor intellectual foundations. Indeed, the intellectual impetus in the late seventies (reflected in the American antitrust practice of the eighties) cast serious doubt about its validity." [42]

The doubters were from the so-called "Chicago School" and their work has in turn inspired (or should that be provoked) a lot of subsequent research. Rey and Tirole note:

> "The Chicago School view has had the beneficial effect of forcing industrial economists to reconsider the foreclosure argument and to put it on firmer ground. The reconciliation of the foreclosure doctrine and the Chicago School critique is based on the observation that an upstream monopolist in general cannot fully exert its monopoly power without engaging in exclusionary practices."[43]

While economic theory has made considerable progress in understanding how and when foreclosure may arise, this is still an area in which there is a lot of work left to be done. The key role of economics has been to provide theories of harm arising from the various restraints. The OFT's guidelines on vertical agreements[44] rely on the European Commission's Notice Guidelines on Vertical Restraints[45] where in particular the analysis of specific restraints[46] (137–229) shows the influence of economics. Surprisingly neither set of guidelines mention double marginalisation.

Non-linear pricing

One difference between theoretical models of vertical restraints, which spills over into the consequent policy recommendations as well as the possible theories of harm, is whether or not prices

---

[42] Rey and Tirole, "A Primer on Foreclosure", n 37 above, at p 2115.

[43] *Ibid*, at p 2115.

[44] Office of Fair Trading, *Vertical Agreements* (OFT 419, 2004). See also the European Commission's Notice on Agreements of Minor Importance [2001] OJ C368/13.

[45] [2000] OJ C291/01.

[46] *Ibid*, at paras 137–229.

between firms at different levels in a vertical chain are linear or non-linear. A linear price is a simple price per unit purchased. While in modelling terms, the typical non-linear price is a two-part tariff with a fixed fee combined with a per-unit price, non-linearities can arise in many other ways, including rebates, volume discounts, slotting allowances and promotional support. The key element is that, with a non-linear price, the average unit price depends on the number of units purchased.

A vertical chain with different firms at different levels face a possible trade-off between what the firms can secure collectively and what each can secure of this collective value. Thus, where there are two successive monopolists in the vertical chain, each has an incentive to mark up their marginal costs, leading to a price to final consumers in excess of the price a fully integrated monopolist firm would charge. This is known as the double marginalisation problem. Assume that the upstream firm cannot dictate the price the downstream firm charges its customers. The upstream monopolist using a linear price cannot counter the incentive of the downstream firm to mark up this input price, which is part of its costs. The only way to avoid the double marginalisation is then for the upstream firm to refrain from marking up its own marginal costs, but such marginal cost pricing would leave it with no supernormal profits, unless it can make this up in another way, for example through a fixed fee. This is why a non-linear price provides the upstream firm with an extra instrument. Basically, non-linearity is a way for the downstream firm to be provided with the right price signals to set the final consumer price which maximises overall vertical profits while leaving the upstream with a means of sharing in this profit.

If one accepts non-linear pricing as the norm rather than the exception, then many more of the restraints become innocuous.[47] Take a case where there is a single integrated incumbent and a more efficient potential downstream entrant who must purchase an essential input from the incumbent. With a non-linear price the incumbent would be able to extract all the pure profits made by the entrant if the entrant was to be supplied. Hence if the entrant is really more efficient so that it could generate a bigger surplus than the incumbent's own downstream operations, then the incumbent would have no incentive to foreclose the entrant even if it could.

[47] It is important here to be clear that there may still be competition concerns, but these do not relate to the vertical restraint. Thus in the simple example offered in the text, the non-linear price increases efficiency by lowering price, but there is still a monopoly distortion. More generally, when the Chicago School is right that there is only one monopoly profit which can be claimed, one should remember that this monopoly profit still implies a distortion.

Essentially the incumbent could use a fixed fee to extract the extra surplus generated by the more efficient entrant.

Summing up vertical restraints

In a recent survey, Patrick Rey and Tiebaud Vergé summarise the current position as follows:

> "The first lesson that can be drawn from the preceding analysis is that no simple conclusions can be derived on whether any particular type of vertical restraint is pro- or anticompetitive. ... What really matters is not the restraint but the context in which it is used and the goal that it is supposed to achieve."[48]

Economic research on vertical restraints has in turn been inspired by competition law decisions and provided an improved guidance on when these restraints are likely to be harmful to welfare in general and consumers in particular. As an area of research it provides a helpful illustration of how knowledge in IO progresses and demonstrates that, while there is much we know now that we did not know 10 years ago, there is still a long way to go before a settled theory will emerge. While some may find it underwhelming that the main conclusion to draw at this point is that we now know that we know less than we thought we did, this has still had an important impact on policy, not just by making clear that a case-by-case approach is the only appropriate approach but also by giving the authorities as well as firms' advisers a better idea about where the likely problems are, so that firms can be provided with safe harbours and the authorities are not overwhelmed by cases.

Given the ambiguity of the economic effects produced by the various vertical restraints, it is worth checking whether the empirical literature offers some guidance on when the good or bad effects are more or less likely to occur, thereby hopefully giving the authorities further confidence in their resource allocations to cases. Lafontaine and Slade douse the initial hope on this front:

> "Unfortunately, like theory, the empirical evidence is somewhat fragmented. However, it is our belief that with further work, empirical analysis will be able to provide much needed guidance for theorists, policy makers, and the courts."[49]

While commenting on the surprisingly low number of empirical studies (they identify 23), they also find a surprising regularity

---

[48] P Rey and T Vergé, "Economics of Vertical Restraints" in Buccirossi (ed), *Handbook of Antitrust Economics*, n 1 above, Chap 9, at pp 384–385.

[49] F Lafontaine and M Slade, "Exclusive Contracts and Vertical Restraints: Empirical Evidence and Public Policy" in Buccirossi, (ed), *Handbook of Antitrust Economics*, n 1 above, at p 399.

that vertical restraints imposed by outsiders, such as governments, generally harm consumers while voluntarily adopted vertical restraints tend to benefit consumers. While this is suggestive of restraints being less of a competition policy problem, one should keep in mind the low number of cases generally focused on a small number of industries, such as petrol and beer, where the necessary data is available.

2.2 Reputation building through predation

In the UK there has been a number of OFT cases finding predation where the "[T]ypical complaints of predation involve local bus or local newspaper markets".[50] The most recent OFT finding of predation occurred November 2008 and involved Cardiff Bus.[51] The Office of Fair Trading guidelines on Chapter II[52] illustrate the somewhat inconsistent use of economic insights. Thus para 4.25 states:

> "However, the European Court has held that, whenever there is a risk that competitors will be eliminated, there is no need to prove the possibility of recoupment. This is because the weakened state of competition on the market on which the undertaking holds a dominant position will, in principle, ensure that losses are recouped."

This import from the EU goes against the simplest of the insights from economics and is at least to some extent mitigated by the OFT making clear in the guidelines that at least in some cases it will consider the necessity for recoupment. The reason for insisting on recoupment is simple. Predation mostly, though not exclusively, involves below cost pricing.[53] Since this generally benefits consumers and since any explanation for the low price other than the disciplining of a rival generally involves consumer benefits, an authority naturally should be cautious about condemning low prices. A period of below-cost pricing clearly involves a loss for the predator and hence has to be seen as an investment. If such an investment could not be recouped *even* if the predation was successful, then predation

---

50 "Key challenges in public enforcement", a speech to the British Institute of International and Comparative Law by Margaret Bloom, 17 May 2002. Available at http://www.oft.gov.uk/shared_oft/speeches/spe0402.pdf.

51 Decision of the Office of Fair Trading no CA98/01/2008, *Abuse of a dominant position by Cardiff Bus*, 18 November 2008 (Case CE/5281/04).

52 Office of Fair Trading, OFT 402.

53 One can think of any of the "raising-rivals-cost" strategies as an attempt to predate. Thus rather than pricing low, thereby forcing a rival to price below its average variable costs or quit, one could leave prices where they are and instead raise the rival's average variable costs above the "market" price.

could not have been the aim of a reasonable, let alone rational firm. On the other hand, if the *only* circumstance in which such an investment could be recouped is if the predation was successful, then the authority has strong indirect evidence for intent to predate.

Having rejected a very simple, yet persuasive, economics argument, the guidelines in the very next paragraph embrace a much more subtle and sophisticated economics argument:

> "Predatory pricing may be pursued in one sector (or market) in order to protect profits or share of sales in another, perhaps through establishing a reputation likely to deter other would-be entrants. This too can be seen as a form of recoupment." [54]

Economists have demonstrated how firms can generate reputation for particular, seemingly irrational acts because of asymmetric information. Consider a case where a potential predator is active in several markets and where, in each market, predation would not lead to recoupment. Observed below-cost pricing in one market would then appear to be a mistake or as if the predator is "trying it on" to see if it can fool a rival to exit that market. However, no firm can ever be entirely sure of the motivation of a rival. What if there was a small chance that the predator was irrationally aggressive? If the predator was only active in one market then, as long as the chance that the predator was irrational is small enough, that would not change the assessment of the victim that this attempt to predate should be ignored since the predator is most likely to give up the strategy if resisted.[55] However, with the predator active in several markets, then even a rational firm has an incentive to act as if it was an irrational firm and predate. The reason is that firms in other markets will look to history to assess the nature of the alleged predator. If they have observed predatory acts in the past they should logically assume it more likely that this firm is irrationally aggressive, in which case predation against such a firm might be successful. Thus a rational predator would be willing to invest in costly predation in a few markets because it could recoup the investment in developing a reputation for aggressive pricing not from the markets in which it has been predating but from the markets in which it will cash in on its (incorrect) reputation. Note that this theory, which has been taken on board by the OFT, is far more sophisticated than the "rejected" simple recoupment theory. Indeed for the US, Lawrence White points out that this theory has not yet been embraced.[56]

---

[54] Indeed, this reputation effect is argued in *Aberdeen Journals (No 2)* [2003] CAT 21 at para 445.

[55] Recall that the predator is sustaining a loss so long as it pursues the predatory strategy.

[56] See White, "The Growing Influence of Economics and Economists on Antitrust: An Extended Discussion", n 2 above, p 22.

2.3 Cartels[57]

> "Similarly we have seen a greater focus on cartels: large fines and whistle-blowing, encouraged by leniency regimes drawing their inspiration from game theory." Speech by Philip Collins, 24 February 2006.[58]

The effect of economics or, more precisely, game theory, is keenly felt in the design of the enforcement regime surrounding the cartel prohibition.[59] This is particularly the case when it comes to the design of the leniency programme.

Developing instruments which encourage whistleblowing is not a new idea, having been used successfully in other areas of law enforcement such as tax evasion. The idea is to design a system which benefits those who turn informants while harming those who choose not to do so. The contribution of economics and, in particular, game theory has been in the detailed design of such a system aimed at cartel detection. While the basic idea is straightforward, how well it works depends on the details. Since there is always the risk that an illegal conspiracy would come to light, the possibility of offering the first firm or individual to come forward a discount on the expected penalty will in theory have the ability to destabilise the conspiracy. Any member of the conspiracy must continually be weighing up the benefits of reneging on the agreement or continuing it for longer. The benefit of reneging is increased by the possibility of exiting it at a reduced cost by applying for leniency. Moreover, the future benefits of continuing are much reduced by the risk of someone else providing the authority with the necessary information in return for a reduction in their punishment.

Some key details in the design of a leniency programme relate to: (i) who is covered by leniency; (ii) how many can get leniency; and (iii) how leniency interacts with other instruments.

It is in theory unresolved whether leniency should be based on individuals or firms or both. In the UK, where criminalisation of hard-core cartel behaviour was introduced by the Enterprise Act 2002, leniency had to be from both civil and criminal punishment and leniency can be granted to both individuals and firms.

---

[57] For reviews of the recent literature on cartels and on leniency programmes, see J E Harrington Jr, "Detecting Cartels" and G Spagnolo, "Leniency and whistle blowing in antitrust", both in Buccirossi, *Handbook of Antitrust Economics*, n 1 above, at Chaps 6 and 7 respectively.

[58] "Reform of Article 82", Opening keynote speech to British Institute of International and Comparative Law, London by Philip Collins, Chairman Office of Fair Trading, 24 February 2006. Text available at http://www.oft.gov.uk/shared_oft/speeches/spe0206.pdf.

[59] Office of Fair Trading, *Leniency and no-action, OFTs guidance note on the handling of applications* (OFT 803, December 2008).

On brief reflection, it appears that the winner-takes-all design seen in the US[60] has more power to destabilise cartels than the something-for-everyone approach in the UK and EU.[61] A race to the courthouse where winner-takes-all obviously provides a stronger incentive than a race with many prizes. However, this has to be combined with what it takes to be granted leniency.[62] For example, how much information has to be made available for a firm or a person to get leniency? If not enough information is provided in return for leniency it may not be possible for the authority, even using all its other powers, to demonstrate that the other firms were actually involved. Thus the additional information which can be extracted through offering leniency for all who have something useful to contribute may lead to a more efficient leniency programme. In the EU, one of the consequences of a leniency programme which spreads the joy around is frequent and costly appeals often centred on the level of leniency discount granted. Cartel decisions in the UK also appear to be the subject of frequent appeals.[63] It would then be a matter of weighing up the benefits of more information against the costs of more appeals to assess the merit of switching to a winner-takes-all design.

Finally, leniency has to be seen together with all the other tools, especially the nature and size of the punishment, powers of investigation and private enforcement. For example, if the punishment is weak, no one would care about getting leniency. Criminalisation in this respect is a real bonus for the effectiveness of a leniency programme. More subtly, if firms can use potential bankruptcy as an argument to obtain discounts from fines,[64] leniency programmes could be at least partly neutered. This is not simply an abstract idea, demonstrated by the existence of a number of "crisis cartels", without which, arguably, a number of firms would go bankrupt. A consequence of using the full force of the fining system might then be to drive the majority of firms out of business, thereby changing the market structure into one which might be perfectly capable of sustaining the cartel price tacitly. Where a leniency application

---

[60] In the US, the first to come forward gets full immunity. Thereafter, the only way for firms and individuals to obtain a reduction in the sanction is through plea bargaining.

[61] In the UK and EU, the first to come forward may get full immunity, subject to conditions. Even when this prize is gone, firms who come forward in good time will be eligible for some level of leniency discount.

[62] Leniency is used as a catch-all term in the text, something also done in the OFT's own guidelines: see *OFT's guidance as to the appropriate amount of a penalty* (OFT 423, 2004), part 3.

[63] See, eg, table 9.1 in R Whish, *Competition Law* (6th edn, 2009, OUP, Oxford) at pp 367–380.

[64] See A Stephan, "The Bankruptcy Wildcard in Cartel Cases" (2006) Journal of Business Law, 531.

merely alerts the authority to a possible infringement without in itself providing the necessary information for an adverse finding, unless the authority itself has the tools to obtain this evidence, the benefits of the leniency programme may be much reduced. Finally, leniency can generally[65] only be granted for public punishment. Subsequent private follow-on actions may add to the unavoidable punishment and, moreover, might single out the leniency applicant as a cash rich firm to sue for damages. Whether or not firms are joint and severally liable and whether or not there is scope for contribution among those liable for the damages may be crucial factors here.

As regards the design of leniency programmes, an economics approach, often using game theory, has advanced our understanding.[66] The leniency programmes in different jurisdictions still look like works in progress. Providing an assessment of the UK leniency programme, which is outside the scope of this chapter,[67] thus requires some fairly subtle assessments of counterbalancing effects.

2.4 Mergers

While merger control was not revised by the Competition Act 1998, the Enterprise Act 2002 introduced significant changes to the substantial test, moving from a public interest test to a substantial lessening of competition (SLC) test. Further, the Competition Commission became determinative, leading to much more transparent reporting. The importance of economics, and indeed the economic analysis which goes into the merger decisions of the CC, are evident from the post Enterprise Act reports.

It is still worth looking at some of the developments in the economic analysis of mergers from the last decade or so because the pattern here is different. Economics has always been used to a greater extent in merger analysis and this remains so but to a larger extent. However, it is on the whole more a case of an increased use of well-known economic methods and principles rather than newly developed tools and insights. In a few areas there have been some advances and these will be considered briefly.

Merger simulations

Without efficiency savings, a merger will lead to higher prices, but

---

[65] The US is slightly different because of the possibility of treble damages in an antitrust action. The Antitrust Criminal Penalty Enhancement and Reform Act 2004 limits the award of damages to single damages in relation to any firm granted immunity under the leniency programme.

[66] See, eg, the survey by Spagnolo, n 57 above, and the literature cited therein.

[67] See A Riley, Chapter 10 below.

with an SLC standard the question of magnitude remains important, ie is this lessening of competition substantial? With efficiency effects, mergers may potentially lead to lower prices. Assessing the magnitude of the change in prices depends partly on own and cross price elasticities, on the nature of the cost changes and on the way in which firms compete. With better data has come better estimates of the basic ingredients needed to use a simple economics model to forecast the effect on prices from a proposed merger.

These so-called "merger simulation models" assume a particular mode of competition between firms and then use the estimated demand and cost parameters to compute the effect of a subset of the brands or products in the market being controlled by one rather than two firms.[68] The comparison is between equilibria and hence allows for changes in prices and quantities as a result of the less intense competition one would expect when the number of firms is reduced. Where the data is readily available and the industry sufficiently simple, such a simulation can obviate the need to define the market since it can provide the impact on prices directly.

As has been pointed out by Margaret Slade[69] in a paper using data from UK cases on the brewing industry, merger analysis is carried out under a time pressure and hence there is a trade-off between simplicity and accuracy. Slade provides a thorough and very critical analysis of the use of merger simulation in merger analysis, highlighting not only their benefits but also their shortcomings. From her discussion, one gets the impression that this is an area where there is scope for future work but also that this is an instrument which must be handled with care to avoid misleading results.

Co-ordinated effects

Co-ordinated effects in mergers received considerable attention in the EU with the 2002 CFI decision in *Airtours* v *Commission*.[70] Echoes of the *Airtours* test can be found in the Competition Commission guidelines[71] and were, for example, applied by the CC in the Smith Linpack merger.[72] Nonetheless, it is interesting to note that neither

---

[68] See M E Slade, "Merger simulations of unilateral effects" in Lyons (ed), *Cases in European Competition Policy: The Economic Analysis*, n 1 above, for a discussion.

[69] *Ibid.*

[70] [2002] ECR II-2585, [2002] 5 CMLR 317(Case T–342/99). For a recent discussion of the economics of the case, see also E Garces-Tolon, D Neven and P Seabright, "The ups and downs of the doctrine of collective dominance" in Lyons (ed), *Cases in European Competition Policy: The Economic Analysis*, n 1 above.

[71] *Merger References: Competition Commission Guidelines* (CC2, April 2007), paras 3.37–3.43.

[72] Competition Commission report on *D S Smith plc/LINPAC Containers Ltd* (14 September 2004).

the 2003 guidelines nor the April 2009 joint OFT and CC consultation document on Merger Assessment Guidelines mentions the *Airtours* test.

The notion of co-ordinated effects, incorporated in the test set out both in *Airtours* and in the CC guidelines, is very much based on insights from game theory and, in particular, how repetition can help firms collude either explicitly or tacitly. Thus, game theory tells us that where a small number of relatively similar firms with good information about each other's behaviour compete repeatedly, they may be able to co-ordinate their behaviour tacitly. Their similarity will help each firm to reach the same conclusion about what level of price to set, while the repeated nature of interaction combined with good information of past behaviour will ensure that any deviation from this price would be met with a more competitive response, making the deviation unattractive. The CC test looks at three conditions: awareness of competitor behaviour; incentives to conform to the prevailing behaviour; and weak competitive constraints. The first two conditions are exactly what makes co-ordinated behaviour possible. The third ensures that the higher prices are not undermined by entrants or firms not party to the co-ordinated behaviour.

Vertical mergers[73]

Economic insights about vertical mergers are closely related to the insights from vertical restraints since a vertical merger may be perceived as the ultimate vertical restraint as a merger enables the firm to achieve through internal transactions what would otherwise have to be achieved through contractual and other provisions. An immediate implication of this is that if the authorities would allow a vertical merger without any remedies, then they should also be willing to allow any vertical restraints between the same two firms.

Many of the concerns with vertical mergers mirror the concerns with vertical restraints. Thus the consensus appears to be that vertical mergers are often efficiency enhancing rather than anti-competitive, although there are individual instances where they can be anti-competitive, especially where they lead to high degrees of concentration and where subsequent entry is difficult.

3 CONCLUSION

The influence of economics on competition law during the first 10 years of the Competition Act 1998 has been varied. In some cases

---

[73] For a full summary of the economics of vertical mergers, see M H Riordan, "Competitive Effects of Vertical Mergers" in Buccirossi (ed), *Handbook of Antitrust Economics*, n 1 above.

it has been obvious and direct, such as in merger analysis where the substantive test is clearly economics based. In some areas, the influence has come via current research, sparked by past decisions, on the way we think about the infringements. As discussed above, vertical restraints provide an example of this, as does predation. In others, the impact has been more indirect, relating to the way in which the investigative or procedural tools have been shaped, such as in cartel enforcement.

Economics, and particularly IO, is a relatively young field of research[74] and by no means the finished article. Greater integration of law and economics in the area of competition law and antitrust will spark more research by raising more questions and identifying further areas where there are gaps in our understanding. Moreover, better data will enable IO economists to test the theories empirically and to raise further questions to be tackled theoretically or empirically. It is expected that the next 10 years will bring improvements on all fronts. The extent to which this will have an impact on policy and decisions will depend on the communication between economists and lawyers and between academics and practitioners. Here, the author would agree with Sir John Vickers:

> "The proportion of European competition lawyers with a sound understanding of economics is growing but nowhere near that in the US, and the same can be said for the relative ratios of competition economists with a sound understanding of the law. Unless this continues to change rapidly, the transmission mechanism from economics to competition law in Europe will be limited. Lawyers and judges are not generally resistant to good arguments that are put well, so the opportunities for economics are certainly there."[75]

[74] Lawrence White traces the beginnings of IO to the 1930s. See White, "The Growing Influence of Economics and Economists on Antitrust: An Extended Discussion", n 2 above.

[75] See D Neven, "Competition economics and antitrust in Europe", 2006 Economic Policy 741, at pp 785–786.

CHAPTER 10

OUTGROWING THE EUROPEAN ADMINISTRATIVE MODEL? TEN YEARS OF BRITISH ANTI-CARTEL ENFORCEMENT

*Alan Riley**

Ever since the United Kingdom joined the European Economic Community (as it then was) in January 1973, an express prohibition against price-fixing applied via Art 85(1) of the EEC Treaty (subsequently Art 81(1) of the EC Treaty, now Art 101(1) of the TFEU) to agreements which affected trade between Member States on British territory. However, it was only with the coming into force on 1 March 2000 of the Competition Act 1998 that the United Kingdom finally obtained its own domestic regime which expressly prohibited price-fixing, applying to agreements whether or not they affected trade between Member States.[1]

With the Competition Act, the whole panoply of the European adminstrative system for dealing with competition investigations and the accompanying contentious procedure were imported into the British competition system. In addition, the approach to fining policy was largely drawn from the European model. To a degree this was also the case with leniency, but here the British approach

---

* Professor, City Law School, City University, London, and Associate Research Fellow, Centre for European Policy Studies, Brussels.

[1] Prior to the enactment of the Competition Act 1998 there was, of course, the domestic competition statute known as the Restrictive Trade Practices Act 1976. However, this was particularly ineffective at tackling cartels due to: the technical limits of the scope of the Act; the lack of investigative powers; and the numerous steps needed before any individual or undertaking could be sanctioned, all of which rendered the 1976 Act toothless. For a discussion of the 1976 Act, see B Rodger and A MacCulloch, *Competition Law Policy in the EC and the UK* (4th edn, 2008, Cavendish, London), pp 200–202.

was also to adopt some of the lessons from the successful American Corporate Leniency Programme.[2]

The Office of Fair Trading (OFT) could at first sight be criticised on the basis that after 10 years of operation of the system it has in fact dealt with a relatively small number of cartel cases. The OFT has not seen the flood of leniency applications that appeared in the United States or before the European Commission. However, this criticism would be fundamentally misplaced. Given the existence of the EU Leniency Notice,[3] it is likely that most leniency applicants in cases which affect trade between Member States will go to the Commission and not to the OFT.

For domestic cases, the OFT is in an entirely different place from the European Commission's DG Competition or the Antitrust Division of the US Department of Justice. When both of these latter institutions adopted a leniency programme, they did so with the knowledge that large numbers of undertakings had extensive legal liabilities stretching back over several years. Leniency provided an immediate encouragement to come in, confess and remove that legal liability. The OFT was in an entirely different situation. Given that the domestic prohibition applied only from 1 March 2000, there was no tail of legal liability stretching back several years to encourage undertakings to apply for leniency. In addition, despite the fact that price-fixing for agreements affecting trade between Member States was prohibited from 1 January 1973, it is clear from anecdotal evidence[4] and from some of the early cases that many business executives did not grasp that price-fixing was a serious offence under any competition regime.[5] As a consequence, it has been an uphill struggle for the OFT to bring industry round to the understanding that price-fixing is extremely serious, that there are very few real excuses, penalties will be very heavy and that leniency is the only real option to escape those penalties.

From this unpromising start, the OFT has undertaken considerable and effective advocacy work, whereby together with the handful of

---

[2] The Corporate Leniency Programme can be found on the Division's website at http://www.usdoj.gov/atr/public/guidelines/0091.htm

[3] *Commission Notice on Immunity from Fines and Reduction of Fines in Cartel Cases* [2006] OJ C298/17.

[4] In one discussion of several which the author had in preparation for this chapter, a lawyer explained his amazement at one client of a major UK company who expressed the view that price-fixing amounted to no more than a "weights and measures" offence.

[5] See, in particular, the lack of understanding of tenderers caught in collusive bidding that cover bidding is unlawful, and counts as a serious antitrust offence resulting in the imposition of heavy financial penalties: for example, *Apex Asphalt & Paving Co Ltd* v *OFT* [2005] CAT 4; *Richard W Price* v *OFT* [2005] CAT 5; and *Sepia Logistics* v *OFT* [2007] CAT 13.

cartel cases that have come its way, it has sought to establish in the minds of business executives that price-fixing is a serious offence which if discovered will result in heavy penalties. The OFT has also built up a substantial amount of knowhow and experience through the cases it has dealt with, providing it with a base for the future development of the anti-cartel regime.

Clearly, the enactment of s 188 of the Enterprise Act 2002 making price-fixing a criminal offence highlighted the personal danger for business executives in engaging in price-fixing. However, this chapter argues that there are serious questions concerning the viability of Section 188, not least the damaging judgment of the House of Lords in *Norris*[6] which raises serious doubts as to whether s 188 can in fact be effectively deployed by prosecutors; the broader problem with a dishonesty test; and the practical difficulties faced by regulators in a criminal price-fixing trial where the standard of proof is beyond reasonable doubt. It is argued that, unless there is a radical reversal of the *Norris* ruling, together with amendments to s 188 to remove the dishonesty test, it is doubtful that the criminal antitrust regime will be of much value to the prosecution of cartels in the United Kingdom.

This chapter argues instead that serious consideration should be given to a modernisation of the civil regime: to build upon what has already been achieved by the OFT; to modernise the leniency programme and encourage more whistleblowers to come forward; to increase the financial incentives for individual whistleblowers to provide information to the OFT; to strengthen the fines guidelines; to make greater use of individual civil penalties; to cut delays and encourage more rapid settlement and abolish the European administrative model, with cases instead being argued directly before the Competition Appeal Tribunal. This approach, it is argued, would clear the ground for the OFT to take on a greater cartel-busting role in the second decade of its battle against price-fixing.

Section 1 of this chapter provides an overview of the existing UK civil regime, section 2 considers potential reforms in respect of the OFT's leniency guidance, section 3 examines the prospects for reform of the fines guidance, while section 4 looks at the scope for reforming the OFT's procedures, section 5 considers the difficulties faced by the criminal antitrust regime and section 6 in conclusion makes the case for a modernisation of the civil anti-cartel regime.

---

[6] *Norris* v *Government of the United States of America* [2008] UKHL 16.

1 THE BRITISH CIVIL ANTI-CARTEL REGIME

The civil anti-cartel regime is very much modelled on the system already in place within the European Community. It relies on a public regulator to investigate, prosecute and find an undertaking guilty of an infringement at first instance, with a right of appeal to an independent tribunal. The principal difference is that in the British system, the right of appeal includes a full rehearing before the CAT and not merely a judicial review under Art 263 TFEU (ex Art 230 EC) of the Commission's decision before the European Union General Court ("EUGC"), formerly the Court of First Instance ("CFI").

Therefore, as with the Commission, the OFT usually commences an investigation on the basis of its own market intelligence, a complaint or, more usually, upon application for leniency from an undertaking. On the basis of such information, the OFT can obtain search warrants from a High Court judge under s 27 of the CA 1998. Execution of search warrants will not only result in the acquisition of further evidence, but will usually generate more leniency applications (if no applications have yet been forthcoming), which again will result in more evidence falling into the hands of the OFT.

Following assessment of the evidence, where the OFT concludes that there is sufficiently strong *prima facie* evidence to initiate its contentious procedure, it will issue a statement of objections against the defendant undertakings setting out the facts, its reasoned provisional conclusions and the action it intends to take. Defendant undertakings are entitled to inspect the Office's file, make written submissions and attend an oral hearing.

Subsequently, if the OFT concludes it has sufficiently strong evidence it will issue an infringement decision and impose a fine. The fine is subject to the application of the OFT's penalty guidelines and, as in the Community system, is limited to 10 per cent of worldwide turnover. Subsequently, a non-confidential version of the decision will appear on the OFTs website. The defendant undertakings may then challenge the decision on appeal before the Competition Appeal Tribunal, and thence to the Court of Appeal, and ultimately before the Supreme Court.[7]

---

[7] No price-fixing case has yet been subsequently appealed from the Court of Appeal to the House of Lords. In *Argos Ltd* and *Littlewoods Ltd* v *OFT*, and *JJB Sports Ltd* v *OFT* [2006] EWCA Civ 1318 (hereinafter *Football Shirts and Toys Appeal*), an attempt was made to seek leave from the CA to the House of Lords but the CA refused permission to seek leave. There is also the question *post-Bronner* whether the CAT or any of the superior courts would consider making Art 234 references to the European Court of Justice on a novel point of Community competition law. At first sight this is unlikely as most price-fixing cases do not directly raise a novel issue. However, it is not so unlikely to expect at some point an issue such as unequal treatment or succession liability, which directly impacts on price-fixing cases to raise an unargued, novel and important point of competition law which may require an Art 234 reference.

So far the OFT has made 16 infringement decisions relating to price-fixing, market sharing or bid-rigging cartels. In a cartel case there will be several undertakings. The fact, therefore, that there have been only 10 appeals to the CAT and one subsequent appeal to the Court of Appeal[8], indicates that the overwhelming majority of undertakings do not challenge infringement decisions.

Most of the appeals to the CAT concerned challenges to the level of the fine and arguments focused around the issue of unequal treatment between apparently differentially fined applicants. On the whole the CAT has demonstrated a significant and understandable lack of sympathy to most of the fine arguments made by appellants. For instance, in *Makers,*[9] the CAT demonstrated its lack of sympathy for the arguments of the appellants in relation to the Minimum Deterrence Threshold (MDT) which the OFT applied in the case. The MDT applies where the turnover in the relevant market is less than 15 per cent of its total turnover; in such case the OFT would calculate what the turnover would have been if 15 per cent of its turnover would have been achieved in the relevant market. This constitutes the MDT. However, the MDT is not even referred to in the OFT's penalty guidelines.[10] Nevertheless, the CAT took the view that this was a reasonable approach and let it stand, even though the contract was only worth £300,000 and the fine, with the MDT uplift, amounted to £526,000.

> "We therefore reject Makers' assertion that the uplift of £520,000 imposed at Step 3 of the calculation of its penalty was arbitrary or unjustified. The adoption of the Minimum Deterrent Threshold is, in our view, an appropriate way in which to ensure that the overall figure of the penalty meets the objective of deterrence referred to in the Guidance."[11]

Two further notable points arise from the appeals. First, underlining the (lack of) awareness of the unacceptability of price-fixing in parts of Corporate Britain and that price-fixing constitutes a serious offence for which heavy penalties will be imposed, is the lack of understanding amongst numerous undertakings within the construction industry that cover bids and any discussion of price in respect of a tender between bidders is likely to provide substantial evidence of an allegation of price-fixing. For example, in *Apex*, the defendant undertaking sought to characterise the action of the other

---

[8] *Football Shirts and Toys Appeal* [2006] EWCA Civ 1318.

[9] *Makers* v *OFT* [2007] CAT 11.

[10] *The OFT's Guidance as to the Appropriate Amount of a Penalty* (hereinafter *OFT Fine Guidance*) in OFT 423 (December 2004).

[11] *Makers,* para 134. The CAT does criticise the OFT for the oblique approach to calculation of the fine in the decision but sees no reason to reduce the fine.

tenderer, Briggs, as "unilateral" and rely on the fact that Briggs ultimately had not put in a tender. The CAT, after an extensive and detailed examination of the arguments, gave a robust response to the position taken by Apex, as follows:

> "We consider that the concept of a concerted practice relied on by Apex is self-serving. The principal object of the cooperation between Apex and Briggs was that Briggs would not win the contract. It was not that Briggs would put in a bid. We therefore accept the OFT's argument that it is immaterial that Briggs did not bid. Furthermore, that conclusion is consistent with the fact that once it is shown that the object of the concerted practice was anti-competitive, it is no longer necessary to show that it had an anti-competitive effect.
> We accept the submission of the OFT that the concerted practice is made out at a stage prior to consideration of whether the person receiving the price actually puts in a tender. We are satisfied that there was a concerted practice in place between Apex and Briggs to provide non-competitive prices such that Briggs would not win the FHH Contracts. The fact that in relation to the FHH Contracts Briggs did not put in a tender at all is not material to the question whether a concerted practice was in place. Likewise the reason for Briggs not putting in the tender is immaterial."[12]

The second notable feature of the case law is the discussion of trilateral price-fixing arrangements in respect of the *Football Shirts and Toys Appeal*. In the *Football Shirts* case, Umbro received complaints from JJB, one of its retailers, regarding undercutting by another retailer Sports Soccer. SS agreed to raise prices if other retailers did so. JJB, along with other retailers, agreed not to discount. There was no direct contact at any time between JJB and SS.

In the *Toys* case, Hasbro, the games manufacturer, held discussions with Argos, Littlewoods and other retailers. In those discussions the retailers would inform Hasbro of their future pricing intentions. Hasbro would brief retailers on the information it had gleaned on pricing from its prior discussions with other retailers. Hasbro also indicated to all retailers that it was seeking to ensure in relation to certain core games that pricing was maintained at the retail recommended price. Again there was no direct contact between the retailers, in this case Argos and Littlewoods.

There are a number of questions concerning the concept of trilateral price-fixing arrangements. One major question, which demonstrated differences in approach between the CAT and the Court of Appeal, was in relation to the standard of assessment of the evidence in trilateral price-fixing arrangements. The CAT suggested

---

[12] *Apex Asphalt & Paving Co Ltd* v *OFT* [2005] CAT 4, above, paras 235 and 236.

that an objective reasonably foreseeable test could apply. It argued that if,

> "a retailer (A) privately discloses to a supplier (B) its future pricing intentions 'in circumstances where it is reasonably foreseeable that B might make use of that information to influence market conditions' and B then passes that pricing information on to a competing retailer (C), that is sufficient basis for concluding, even if A did not in fact foresee what was reasonably foreseeable or C did not appreciate the basis on which A had provided the information, that A, B and C are all to be regarded as parties to a concerted practice having as its object or effect the prevention, restriction or distortion of competition."[13]

The Court of Appeal took the view that the CAT "may have gone too far" here.[14] However, the court accepted that this proposition did not have to be supported in such wide terms to determine the appeal.[15] It made the case for a more subjective test:

> "The proposition which, in our view, falls squarely within the *Bayer* judgment in the ECJ and which is sufficient to dispose of the point in the present appeal can be stated in more restricted terms: if (i) retailer A discloses to supplier B its future pricing intentions in circumstances where A may be taken to intend that B will make use of that information to influence market conditions by passing that information to other retailers (of whom C is or may be one), (ii) B does, in fact, pass that information to C in circumstances where C may be taken to know the circumstances in which the information was disclosed by A to B and (iii) C does, in fact, use the information in determining its own future pricing intentions, then A, B and C are all to be regarded as parties to a concerted practice having as its object the restriction or distortion of competition. The case is all the stronger where there is reciprocity: in the sense that C discloses to supplier B its future pricing intentions in circumstances where C may be taken to intend that B will make use of that information to influence market conditions by passing that information to (amongst others) A, and B does so."[16]

In practice, given the existence of substantial evidence of price-fixing via leniency applications and unannounced inspections, it is open to question how far the distinctions drawn by the Court of Appeal will really impact on the practical prosecution of price-fixing cases by the OFT.

One could take the view that the Court of Appeal has now provided a degree of legal security for the OFT to effectively prosecute trilateral arrangements. However, a second broader concern remains that the OFT and both courts have failed to stand

---

13 *Football Shirts and Toys Appeal*, n 7 above, para 140.

14 *Ibid*, para 91.

15 *Ibid*, para 140.

16 *Ibid*, para 141.

back and consider what is really going on in "trilateral price-fixing" arrangements. Essentially these arrangements have the effect of introducing or maintaining resale price maintenance. This is substantially different from hard-core price-fixing. Furthermore, the US Supreme Court in *Leegin* recently removed the almost century-old *per se* prohibition on resale price maintenance on the basis that modern economic analysis provides a considerable body of evidence and literature to the effect that resale price maintenance can have both pro- and anti-competitive effects. It is submitted therefore that the OFT should consider very carefully whether the "trilateral price-fixing" arrangement, in addition to being supported by substantial evidence of active participation by all parties, amounts to more than resale price maintenance and justifies a full cartel prosecution with the potential application of heavy financial penalties.[17]

The infringement decisions and case law, however, do not reflect the entire extent of the work of the OFT in respect of civil price-fixing. The "case closed" summaries published by the OFT since 2003 provide evidence of a number of additional price-fixing investigations. Some of these investigations found cause for concern and OFT intervention had the effect of prompt termination of what appeared to be a minor price-fixing issue in cases such as *Steel Dock Flooring Industry*,[18] *Sci-Net Lab Materials*[19] and *Calor Gas Price-Fixing in Shetland*.[20] In other cases, there were substantive allegations of price-fixing sufficient to launch unannounced inspections under s 27 in *Price-Fixing Corrugated Sheeting and Corrugated Boards*,[21] but not enough evidence was obtained to sustain an infringement decision. Equally, in *Scottish Milk*[22] there was sufficient evidence to issue a statement of objections but, on further representations and new evidence, again the conclusion was reached that there was insufficient evidence to sustain an infringement decision.

Dealing with minor price-fixing cases in this way appears to be an efficient and minimal resource method of terminating price-fixing. It is, however, noticeable that the application of this procedure in the last few years has significantly reduced, particularly in respect of price-fixing cases. This may be because the introduction of the criminal antitrust rules has made it more difficult to treat price-fixing in this light touch manner.

The OFT has also made use of early resolution agreements in

---

17 *Leegin Creative Leather Products Inc* v *PSKS, Inc* (2007) 551 US 877.
18 OFT, *Case Closed Summaries* (2003), 41.
19 OFT, *Case Closed Summaries* (2004), 13.
20 *Ibid*, 26.
21 OFT, *Case Closed Summaries* (2006), 16.
22 OFT, *Case Closed Summaries* (2007).

order to rapidly bring a case to a conclusion, although the actual infringement decision imposing the fines and cease and desist orders may take considerably longer to apply. This has the advantage for defendant undertakings of drawing a line under their behaviour and minimises reputational damage while allowing the OFT to limit use of staff resources on what otherwise would be a drawn-out contentious procedure. Early resolution agreements have been deployed recently in *Dairy Products*[23] and *Tobacco*,[24] both cases involving trilateral arrangements between supplier and retailers, and in both cases several firms were fined collectively over £100 million.[25] In August 2007 the OFT announced its largest individual fine to date in a civil case: British Airways agreed to pay £121.5 million in respect of the passenger fuel surcharge levy agreement with Virgin, in which Virgin played the part of the leniency applicant.[26] There is also an ongoing s 188 case against four BA employees.[27] Two other major ongoing investigations relate to big-rigging in the construction industry and loans provided to professional service firms.[28]

As argued above, this is a significant workload for a new anti-cartel regime in its first decade, particularly when, during that 10-year period, the regime, its law, practices and procedures had to be rapidly overhauled due to the enactment of s 188. The next three sections of this chapter look forward and consider how the anti-cartel regime can be improved to increase effectiveness and efficiency over the next decade.

2 LENIENCY

The OFT's latest statement on leniency, *Leniency and No Action: OFT's Guidance Note on the Handling of Applications*[29] provides an admirably clear and detailed account of the rules and policies of the OFT in relation to leniency and the operation of no action letters in a criminal antitrust context. In addition to clearly setting out the standards for Type A Immunity (available automatically in cases where an undertaking is the first to apply and the OFT has not yet opened an investigation), Type B Immunity (available at the

---

[23] http://www.oft.gov.uk/news/press/2007/170–07.

[24] http://www.oft.gov.uk/news/press/2008/82–08.

[25] Under early resolution agreements the fine is not paid until the infringement decision is actually made.

[26] http://www.oft.gov.uk/oft_at_work/enforcement_regulation/Cartels/fuel-surcharges.

[27] Three are now ex-employees.

[28] http://www.oft.gov.uk/oft_at_work/enforcement_regulation/Cartels/.

[29] OFT (hereinafter 803, December 2008). *OFT Leniency Guidance*. It should also be read with the outline of the Office's leniency programme provided for in the *OFT Fine Guidance*.

discretion of the OFT, where the OFT has opened an investigation and the applicant is first to apply), and Type B and C Leniency where fine reductions are available, the OFT has sought to maintain a high standard of clarity as to its attitude to different classes of applicants and the context in which they apply. This clarity is likely to provide leniency applicants with a significant degree of comfort in making use of the OFT's leniency procedure. This is reinforced by the clear willingness of the OFT in its Guidance to accept initial "no names' applications from legal advisers seeking to find out whether immunity is indeed available.[30]

While the Guidance does provide a substantial degree of clarity for leniency applicants, there are good grounds for arguing that the Guidance could be significantly sharpened to encourage more applicants to come forward. As Leslie has argued, in drafting a leniency notice the focus of regulators should be to make confession the dominant strategy of cartelists and that focus needs to be underpinned with as much certainty and clarity as to the availability of the offer.[31] Leslie makes a powerful case against the US Corporate Leniency Programme (and the *OFT Guidance*) in applying discretion as to whether immunity will be available to an applicant where the agency has already opened an investigation. He makes three convincing arguments as to why this discretion actually undermines the operation of the Programme.

First, he argues there is the question of lack of certainty undermining the incentive for potential applicants to confess:

> "If a cartel member needs to worry that it would not get immunity even if it confesses first, then this significantly changes the calculus of whether to confess. A firm may be willing to accept private liability in exchange for the certainty of amnesty if it is the first confessor. But it is less inclined to destroy the cartel and invite private lawsuits in exchange for the possibility of amnesty if it confesses first and the government decides that any investigation into the cartel was sufficiently early to warrant amnesty."[32]

Arguably the disincentive is greater under the *Guidance* than under the Corporate Leniency Programme (CLP). The *Guidance* envisages a balancing test based upon broader public interest criteria,[33] whereas it can be argued that the CLP's test does provide a degree of clarity and predictability by being based upon an evidential question

[30] *OFT Leniency Guidance*, para 3.20 *et seq*.

[31] C Leslie, "Antitrust Amnesty, Game Theory and Cartel Stability" (2006) Journal of Corporation Law 453.

[32] Leslie, "Cartel Stability", *ibid*, 481.

[33] *OFT Leniency Guidance*, n 29 above, para 4.2.

as to whether the prosecutor has sufficient evidence for a sustainable conviction.

Second, he argues that, even if an investigation is underway, rewarding the first leniency application with automatic leniency is a rational step for prosecutors. Evidence obtained from circumstantial evidence may not be as valuable a trial as initially thought. More powerfully, perhaps, Leslie makes the point that; "the first confession makes the investigation significantly more efficient; it can allow the government to secure search warrants in order to obtain incriminating evidence against non-confessing cartel members".[34] He makes a strong case that the first confession effectively terminates the cartel. Once that confession is in, the overwhelming incentive for other cartel members is to come in and make their peace with the regulators.

Third, abolishing the investigation-discretion rule actually increases the destabilising effect of any investigation by an agency into a cartel:

> "Once the firms in a cartelised market know that the government suspects price-fixing and is investigating the incentive to confess first increases significantly. The many disincentives to confessing first – the loss of cartel profits, private liability, and non-antitrust liability – no longer impose much deterrent to confession if the cartel is going to be exposed anyway."[35]

Leslie accepts that there are of course strong policy arguments for restricting immunity when a confession occurs during an investigation, but he argues that the government should give credit for such confessions, even if they are unnecessary in order to make confession the dominant strategy for cartelists.[36]

There is a real argument here for the OFT to consider. Abolishing the discretion rule would amount to creating a more radical leniency programme than that offered by the Antitrust Division. However, it is difficult to deny the potential benefits in terms of greater number of leniency applications, greater cartel destabilisation and greater efficiency in handling leniency applications.

A further question is raised by Griffin and Sullivan's analysis of the Commission's 2006 Leniency Notice in respect of the evidence standard required by the OFT.[37] Unlike the Commission's Notice, the OFT *Guidance* does not put such a premium on corporate state-

---

[34] Leslie, "Cartel Stability", n 31 above, 482.

[35] *Ibid*, 483.

[36] *Ibid*, 484.

[37] J Griffin and K Sullivan, "Recent Developments in Leniency Policies and Practices in Canada, the European Union and the United States' (2008) ABA Advanced Cartel Workshop, San Francisco.

ments or contemporaneous evidence, both of which come under Griffin and Sullivan's detailed and negative scrutiny.

However, they also raise considerable doubts as to the wisdom of the significant added value test applied by the Commission, as follows:

> "the requirements for a fine reduction inject uncertainty and ambiguity into the Leniency Program. Once again, the Commission has decreased the possible pool of self-reporters by requiring an applicant to provide 'significant added value' to the investigation and reward the applicant for 'compelling evidence.' The Commission understandably does not want to offer a fine reduction for an applicant that provides irrelevant or unhelpful information. However, by adding the qualifiers 'significant' and 'compelling,' the Commission unnecessarily raises the evidentiary bar. This standard also adds uncertainty to the leniency process and therefore threatens to decrease its viability."[38]

Unfortunately, the *Guidance* imposes not entirely dissimilar standards: in respect of both immunity and leniency it requires applicants to provide "added significant value"[39] and "significant value"[40] to the investigation. The particular concern here is the compounded disincentive of the "added significant value" requirement of Type B Immunity and its discretionary nature discussed above. Equally, the fact that for "second in" applicants under Type C a similar "significant value" test is applied, together with the additional disincentive that the maximum fine discount of 50 per cent is likely to deter applicants from coming forward.

There is ground here for the OFT to reconsider its evidentiary bar of "added significant value" or "significant value". As Griffin and Sullivan point out, the effect of a high evidentiary bar is to create uncertainty amongst potential applicants, reducing viability and ultimately limiting the number of applicants who are willing to come in.[41]

One further point is worth making. In the US system a high evidence standard is of less importance because of the impetus to come in and confess generated by the tiered discounts on offer. The tiered discount system is graphically illustrated in *Graphite Electrodes*, where the first in paid nothing, the second paid $32.5 million, the third $110 million and the fourth $135

---

[38] Griffin and Sullivan, n 37 above, 20–21.

[39] *OFT Leniency Guidance*, n 29 above, para 4.5.

[40] *Ibid*, para 5.2.

[41] Griffin and Sullivan, n 37 above, 19.

million.[42] The tiered discount system does encourage a "race to the authority", where evidence flows into the authority from applicants for fear of coming in too late and ending up facing very significant corporate and personal penalties.

Currently the OFT's *Guidance* actually eschews any notion of a tiered discount system.[43] However, a lower evidentiary bar, with a much simpler discount system which provides a significant discount for the second applicant in between 80 and 50 per cent, but which progressively leaves later applicants in an increasingly worse position; would encourage a race to the authority – and consequent flow of information. Furthermore, if, as argued below, civil personal financial sanctions and director disqualification were applied in parallel with civil corporate cases, they could reinforce the incentive to come in before personal sanctions were applied to corporate executives of tardy applicants.

It is also notable that, in the *Guidance*, not much is made of the British version of "Amnesty Plus" – "Leniency Plus". The *Guidance* indicates that only a relatively small discount will be granted for an applicant which comes in to report participation in one cartel and also is the first to report another cartel. The *Guidance* takes the view that the real benefit is the immunity itself.[44]

Given the impact Amnesty Plus has had in the United States in rolling up cartels across entire market sectors as cartelists come in and confess all, it does appear strange that the OFT does not want to make more of Leniency Plus. Furthermore, as Leslie has pointed out, Amnesty Plus plays a key role in destroying one of the major trust factors in building cartels, the existence of trustworthy cartelists.[45] A cartelist which has been involved in many cartels and has kept to the price-fix in different sectors is seen as a reliable non-cheating, respectable cartelist. However, for such a cartelist, Amnesty Plus is a boon as it allows the respectable cartelist to escape from the cartel under investigation by pleading all the other cartels in which the cartelist has been involved in order to escape heavy fines and potential personal sanctions in the first cartel. The existence of

---

[42] It should be noted that *Graphite Electrodes* provides a classic example in that the fines imposed reflect not only tiered discounts but also the volume of commerce. By contrast, in *Vitamins*, Hoffmann La Roche and BASF tied for second place, but, given their different turnover, Hoffmann paid $500 million after discounts, and BASF paid $225 million after discounts. The basic tiered discount point remains but the size of penalty for each undertaking may vary depending on corporate turnover.

[43] "Queue position in Type C cases is not decisive. It is possible that an applicant who is third in the queue may get a discount greater than an applicant who came second in the queue": *OFT Leniency Guidance*, above, n 29 para 5.7.

[44] *Ibid*, paras 9.8–9.9.

[45] C Leslie, "Trust, Distrust, Antitrust" (2004) Texas Law Review 515.

Amnesty Plus therefore undermines the credibility of respectable cartelists as a major trust factor in encouraging cartel formation and disrupts the operation of existing cartels. Furthermore, in the British context, given that the OFT cannot threaten Penalty Plus,[46] the flipside of Amnesty Plus, there is an even stronger argument in favour of an enhanced Leniency Plus to encourage applicants when they come in to report on other cartels.

The OFT has taken two steps connected to leniency which are worth briefly mentioning as they could be developed to help create a much more effective leniency regime. The first is the OFT's consultation paper on private rights to damages in competition cases.[47] One of the issues discussed in the paper is the idea of limiting the damages paid by leniency applicants. The OFT discusses a number of ways of limiting leniency damages.[48] Any of these options,[49] as argued by Griffin and Sullivan[50] and Leslie,[51] is likely significantly to enhance the effectiveness of any leniency programme. That is especially the case in a context where over the next few years more cartel damages claims are likely to reach the courts. In any reform of British leniency policy a limitation on damages would significantly enhance the effectiveness of the regime.

The second is the development of paid informants. Under this recently adopted scheme informants can be paid up to £100,000 for information which will assist the OFT in uncovering a cartel.[52] There is a strong argument here that, given the threat to an inform-

---

[46] If undertakings do not disclose all knowledge of cartels in which they have participated and the Division subsequently discovers evidence of such cartels, it will seek penalties at the higher end of the tariff range. The OFT cannot threaten penalty plus because to do so would breach the privilege against self-incrimination contained in Art 6 of the ECHR.

[47] OFT, *Private Actions in Competition Law: Effective Redress for Consumers and Business* (of the OFT 916, 2007).

[48] *Ibid*, para 717 *et seq.*

[49] One question concerns whether or not Community law permits any limitation on damages because of the concept of real and effective judicial protection of EC law rights. However, the author submits that this argument would never withstand the scrutiny of the ECJ. The very reason why damage claims are possible is because of the success of the leniency programmes. Limiting damages for leniency applicants allows cartels to be uncovered and for claims to be brought. The ECJ would be endangering the leniency goose that lays many golden cartel eggs. If the Community were to go down the road of protecting undertakings granted immunity from damages, this question would undoubtedly be raised before the ECJ. However, it could also be raised in a British context in a case where Community law is being applied by the OFT or post-*Bronner* where a purely domestic price-fixing case raised this issue. In any event, the author argues that the policy arguments are overwhelmingly in favour of limiting the rights of plaintiffs to ensure effective deterrence and the broader right of plaintiffs to recover damages.

[50] See n 37 above.

[51] Leslie, "Cartel Stability", n 31 above.

[52] http://www.oft.gov.uk/advice_and_resources/resource_base/cartels/rewards#named1.

ant's career, a £100,000 reward is not likely to provide a sufficient incentive for many informants to come forward.[53] However, an enhanced system of payments based on the sums available under the US Civil False Claims Act 1986[54] might well attract many more informants. In a British system, for instance, where the CAT imposed the fines, the CAT could, on application of the informant, supported by the OFT, make an additional award at the end of the case against the defendant undertakings, which would be paid directly to the informant.

If the OFT were to take these steps it would have the most radical leniency programme in the world. It is understandable that at first sight some officials may fear that this is a far too radical proposal. However, there are three compelling reasons for seeking a more effective leniency programme. First, for reasons to be discussed below, it is doubtful whether criminal price-fixing will add very much to the enforcement of British anti-cartel enforcement. Other measures are therefore required to undermine the incentive to form cartels. Greater fear of detection is one such incentive. Second, even a decade on from the coming into force of the Competition Act 1998 and over 35 years since Art 81(1) came into force in the United Kingdom, it is clear from the cases flowing through the OFT and the Commission that price-fixing is still a major feature of corporate life. A more efficient leniency programme would assist in undermining this feature of British corporate life. Third, unlike the United States with its open continental-wide economy, the United Kingdom has a much more closed business culture in which price-fixing is able to flourish. A more effective leniency programme would allow the OFT to cut deeply into this culture.

3 FINES

The current *OFT Fine Guidance*[55] was re-drafted in 2004 in order to bring it more into line with the Commission's then current Fines Notice[56] as part of the modernisation process. The Commission, however, subsequently considerably amended its Fines Notice in

---

[53] The only likely category of informant would be an LL.M. student taking a competition law module who had a cleaning job in the executive offices of, say, a classical cartel firm in the chemicals, steel or concrete sectors who cleaned but also kept his or her eye out for interesting papers.

[54] See the discussion on the operation of the CFCA in a European context in Riley, "Beyond Leniency: Enhancing the Enforcement of EC Antitrust Litigation" (2005) World Competition 377.

[55] *OFT Fine Guidance,* n 10 above.

[56] *Guidelines on the method of setting fines imposed pursuant to Article 15(2) of Regulation No 17 and Article 65(5) of the ECSC Treaty* 1998 OJ C9/3.

2006.[57] In the process, the Commission provided a basis for significantly increasing fines against cartels. This Notice has recently come under heavy criticism from Sir Jeremy Lever QC in his *Opinion* for the BDI.[58]

While the *OFT Fine Guidance* was not under examination by Lever, there are questions raised by the *Opinion* upon which the OFT should reflect. First, Lever raises the point regarding the appropriateness of the 10 per cent worldwide turnover threshold. He makes a strong argument:

> "that the turnover is only a reflection of the gross sales of the undertaking concerned, it cannot be said to reflect the size or financial position of that undertaking, or the deterrent effect of a fine of any given magnitude. In particular turnover does not adequately reflect the ability of an undertaking to pay a certain sum."[59]

Clearly this issue is more acute in the Community system given the scope the Fines Notice 2006 provides for the Commission to increase fines.[60] However, that does not mean that this issue will not eventually be raised in a British context. Whilst the application of a turnover threshold purely as a cap on the level of fine that can be imposed is not particularly objectionable, as Lever recognises.[61] The future application of turnover as an ingredient in the calculation of the fine may cause significant difficulties for the OFT. Here the relevancy of turnover, as Lever points out, is more open to question. For example, a price-fixing cartel may not in fact have had much impact on the market, as a result of cheating and new market entry, while another cartel may have been very profitable indeed. A focus on calculating the fine principally on the basis of turnover can produce sanctions which are likely to appear unfair and unjust. One solution for the future perhaps may be to place much greater focus on calculations that are based significantly more on the gains made by the defendant undertakings or the losses of the victims as under the US Sentencing Guidelines.[62] However, given the potential scale

---

[57] *Guidelines on the method of setting fines imposed pursuant to Article 23(2)(a) of Regulation No 1/2003* 2006 OJ C210/2 (hereinafter *2006 Fines Notice*).

[58] *Opinion* by Sir Jeremy Lever QC, "Whether and if so how, the EC Commission's 2006 guidelines on setting fines for infringements of Articles 81 and 82 of the EC are fairly subject to serious criticism" (2009) BDI Law and Public Procurement: see http://www.bdi.eu/103_1856.htm.

[59] *Ibid*, para 13.

[60] *2006 Fines Notice*, n 57 above.

[61] Lever, n 58 above, para 8.

[62] The sentencing guidelines were adopted in 1987 under the authority of the US Sentencing Commission. The statutory provision 18 U.S.C. §3571 [d] reads: "[if] any person derives pecuniary gain from the offense, or if the offense results in pecuniary loss to a person other than the defendant, the defendant may be fined not more than the

of profits from some cartels, fines could well be significantly higher as a consequence.[63]

Second, there is the question of an additional penalty for recidivism. Again, this is a particular issue in the Community context because of the possibility of a 100 per cent uplift in the fine under the 2006 Notice.[64] Clearly, given that the Competition Act 1998 came into force only on 1 March 2000, at least for domestic cases, the likelihood of a repeat offender coming to the attention of the OFT at this stage in the application of the Act is limited. However, recidivism is likely to become an issue in the future, especially as the *OFT Fine Guidance* does provide that repeat of an offence is an aggravating factor.[65] Lever takes the view that corporate persons are not capable of recidivism.[66] At the very least the OFT might consider whether any future guidance should include significantly more detail as to when a repeat offender penalty will be applied: for instance, setting out the required corporate and personal links between the two offenders and the indications as to what counts as a similar offence. As Nordlander also points out, consideration should also be given to instituting a time period after which repeat offences are spent.[67]

Third, there is the question of whether credit should be given for running compliance programmes in any fine calculation. The *OFT Fine Guidance* makes provision in this regard,[68] but the Commission *Fines Notice* does not. Lever argues that it should as there is a strong argument for distinguishing between an undertaking which made every effort to ensure compliance with the law, and undertakings which made no effort or which were complicit.

There is a connected argument here that does affect the OFT. It is argued later in this chapter that s 188 is unlikely to work effectively and, therefore, that civil penalties including the existing director disqualification penalty and civil fines should be applied to corporate executives. The connected argument is the link between the corporate fine and an individual civil sanction, where an undertaking has clearly complied with a rigorous compliance programme. If such an undertaking then discovers a rogue director has undertaken price-fixing there is a good argument, as long as the undertaking can demonstrate a prior rigorous compliance programme and provides full co-operation, that the fine

---

greater of twice the gross gain or twice the gross loss, unless imposition of a fine under this subsection would widely complicate or prolong the sentencing process".

63 J Connor, *Global Price-Fixing* (2nd edn, 2007, Springer Publishing), pp 424 and 447.

64 *2006 Fines Notice*, n 57 above, para 28.

65 *OFT Fine Guidance*, n 10 above, para 2.15.

66 See n 57 above, para 23 *et seq*.

67 K Nordlander, "The Commission's Policy on Recidivism: Legal Certainty for Repeat Offenders?" (2005) Comp L Rev 55.

68 *OFT Fine Guidance*, n 10 above, para 2.16.

on such an undertaking should be lighter than would otherwise be the case, and that heavy personal penalties should fall upon the rogue director. This approach would have the beneficial effect of removing a disincentive towards compliance with the civil regime under which a rogue director can profit from the operation of the cartel but only the defendant undertaking pays any penalty.[69]

It could be argued here that this approach would permit the defendant undertaking to avoid disgorging the profits it made from the price-fixing whatever the extent of personal liability of a rogue director, the good intent of its compliance programme and the lack of knowledge of the board. However, that argument overlooks the overall public policy interest in enhancing deterrence. Given the lack of effectiveness of s 188 there is little incentive for individual executives to comply with the prohibition on price-fixing where the fine falls solely on the undertaking. By the time the fine is imposed the complicit executive may have taken his additional bonuses based on the price-fixing and left the undertaking's employ. He is entirely unaffected by the price-fixing infringement decision. Individual civil sanctions which can actually be applied create a significant additional deterrent against such individuals and it is worth discounting the fines otherwise payable by responsible undertakings which run good compliance programmes and seek to comply with the law, even if they retain some cartel profits. In any event, at least some of the profits may well be disgorged as a result of civil action by plaintiffs.

Fourth, there is the connected issue of making damage claims more accessible. In his Opinion, Lever also raises the issue of taking into account the total cost of the case to the defendants, which will include damages to be awarded to victims. He makes an interesting suggestion that the Commission's contentious procedure should be divided into two stages. The first stage would be one where liability was established and fines levied. In stage two, defendants would come forward with their plans for compensating the victims.[70] Such a procedure could be adapted into the British model. However, as argued below, the existing contentious procedure should be abolished with the OFT bringing price-fixing cases directly before the CAT for decision. In such a system, the OFT would make a fine recommendation based on its *Fine Guidance* but the ultimate decision would be made by the CAT. It would then be for the CAT to look at the total assessment of the fines and damages to be paid by the defendant undertakings.

---

[69] Technically, of course, a rogue director could be prosecuted under s 188. However, there has only been one set of successful cartel prosecutions since June 2003 in *Marine Hose* and even that was as a result of an actual US criminal prosecution, as discussed by A MacCulloch, Chapter 11 below. For reasons discussed below, the author believes that there will be very few criminal prosecutions.

[70] *Opinion*, n 58 above, para 34.

The debate over very high European fines is likely to affect the OFT over the coming years as demands for greater transparency and targeting in fining policy impact on the Commission. Some issues such as recidivism will come on to the OFT's radar as the case law develops, and other questions such as individual sanctions may become pressing more quickly as the OFT finds it difficult to make much headway with criminal prosecutions.

4 PROCEDURE

The OFT's procedural model is drawn from the European Commission. It is not surprising that this model was adopted in the Competition Act 1998 given that British officials were familiar with it through the Advisory Committee. However, there are two very good reasons why this model should now be reconsidered as an effective procedure for prosecuting price-fixing cartels.

The first is the very success of the OFT in prosecuting cartels and generating more leniency applications, thereby creating an enormous resource burden for itself. It has to draft a detailed statement of objections, consider a reply, organise an oral hearing and then draft an infringement decision, which it may then have to defend before the CAT. If the OFT dealt with a cartel case only occasionally this procedure might be acceptable but it becomes very resource intensive when the OFT has to deal with several cartel cases at the same time. It is argued therefore that the OFT should seek to abolish the administrative procedure at least in cartel cases or whenever a significant penalty is to be levied. In such cases, the OFT would proceed by laying its statement of objections before the CAT. The case would then proceed through the CAT's procedure, with the CAT ultimately making the fine decision itself, taking account of the OFT's recommendation on fines. It could be argued that the OFT would be merely transferring its workload from one stage of the procedure to another in that it would still have to mount a major legal prosecution before the CAT in each case. This is unlikely because it overlooks the unwillingness of defendant undertakings to face prosecution in open court in front of the media, employees, shareholders and customers.[71] Most undertakings, caught red-handed by virtue of

[71] The author argues that this point has been overlooked in most commentary on European contentious procedures because when commentators look at the US model for comparison they assume the incentive for an undertaking to settle stems entirely from the existence of a jury and criminal sanctions. Clearly both those factors provide significant incentives to settle. However, there is a third factor: the prospect of defending a price-fixing case in open court where all issues of fact and law are in dispute in front of the media, employees, shareholders and consumers. This is no small disincentive. The author argues that by adopting

leniency evidence, would settle rather than fight. While the OFT would still face a handful of undertakings that would risk defending their position before the CAT, there would be a net reduction in the OFT's workload as a result of the shift to the CAT as the court of first instance in price-fixing cases.[72]

The second reason concerns the application of the case law of the ECtHR. There is a very extensive literature on the subject of the conflict of the case law of the ECtHR and Community law,[73] which raises a wide range of issues such as: the validity of the power to ask questions by decision under threat of the exercise of penal power; the overly narrow scope of judicial control over the power to undertake unannounced inspections; and the narrow scope given to legal professional privilege in Community law.

One particular issue which is key to the discussion of the appropriate procedure under which cartel cases should be conducted is the question of whether the existing administrative procedure or the subsequent judicial review complies with the case law of the ECtHR. Cases such as *Findlay*[74] indicate that the ECtHR is moving in the direction of the argument that where a serious penal charge has been laid it must be heard before an independent judge, an appeal at first instance to an independent judge not being sufficient for the purposes of the ECHR. In *Findlay* the ECtHR ruled that the requirement of an independent judge was required only where the serious criminal charge was formally part of the criminal law of the state in question. However, it is open to question how far that requirement will be maintained over time. The difficulty for the OFT is how best to grapple with changing perceptions in Europe over the last decade and a half, at least amongst regulators and courts, under significant American influence, as to the harm caused by price-fixing. These have significantly shifted from treating price-fixing as a form of administrative wrong to viewing it as an offence of considerable heinousness deserving of severe financial sanction. In such circumstances it is difficult to envisage how the OFT will be able to rely on the legal formalism of the *Findlay* ruling to sustain its right to continue operating the existing procedures without facing a successful legal challenge. The following in particular are likely to give the ECtHR very powerful reasons to apply *Findlay* to the OFT's

---

the Commission approach of closed administrative oral hearings, European regulators have removed a significant leverage on defendant undertakings to settle.

[72] In other words, while the caseload before the CAT would not change, the OFT would no longer face having to deal with replies, organise oral hearings and draft infringement decisions.

[73] The most notable and detailed recent contribution is A Andreangeli, *EU Competition Enforcement and Human Rights*, (2008, Edward Elgar, London).

[74] *Findlay* v *United Kingdom* (1997) 24 EHRR 221.

contentious procedures: the increasing size of the fines which makes price-fixing the most heavily fined non-criminal offence in the United Kingdom by a very significant margin; the condemnatory language used by senior OFT officials in respect of price-fixing, undermining the reputation of price-fixers and constituting an additional public condemnatory act; and the potential for actual parallel criminal proceedings (even though in practice they are unlikely).

Proceeding immediately before the CAT at first instance would minimise the potential for ECHR challenges, as well as reducing the OFT's work burden. It would also provide the OFT with the ability to levy civil personal sanctions directly in parallel with the case against the undertaking, which would permit an extremely efficient dispatch of business.[75] The discussion as to why civil sanctions are preferable to the application of s 188 follows below. The argument here is that the OFT is outgrowing its European-based administrative procedures, which are extremely burdensome for an agency with distinctly limited resources. Abolishing this procedure and seeking to prosecute directly before the CAT would result in a less resource-intensive process which would allow the OFT to resolve cases much more speedily.

5 ROLE OF THE CARTEL OFFENCE

At first sight the argument against s 188 looks as if it is clearly made out. There has been only one set of prosecutions in relation to a cartel, *Marine Hose*,[76] and that case was possible only because of a parallel US prosecution where as part of the plea agreement the three defendants agreed to return to the United Kingdom to surrender to the British authorities and plead guilty in an English court. However, one has to take account of the fact that s 188 only came into force in June 2003. It was always going to take time for any cases to arrive before a criminal court.

The author argues that it is not the flow, or rather the lack of flow, of criminal cases before the courts that is the core problem but the structural difficulties stemming from the "dishonesty test", the impact of the ruling of the House of Lords in *Norris*, judicial incomprehension and the lack of appreciation of the weaknesses of the American criminal antitrust model.[77]

First, it is open to very serious question whether, faced with a contested criminal case, the OFT will be able to sustain a prose-

---

[75] Again in most cases the individuals would be likely to plead guilty rather than face a day in court.

[76] *R* v *Whittle, Allison & Brammar* [2008] EWCA Crim 2560.

[77] For an alternative view, A MacCulloch, Chapter 11 below.

cution in an English criminal court. The high evidence standards of a criminal case, combined with the subjective nature of the dishonesty test, provide defendants with sufficient scope to obtain an acquittal. As Fisse has argued in the Australian context:

> "the approach ... is pre-occupied with making the element of dishonesty ... the prime distinguishing feature of criminal liability for cartel conduct. This pre-occupation is misguided. The concept of dishonesty is incapable of distinguishing serious from less serious forms of prohibited cartel conduct. Even very minor instances of deception or fraud are "dishonest"; the concept of "trivial" dishonesty is commonplace. It is a nonsense to suggest ... that dishonesty necessarily requires serious wrongdoing. The concept of dishonesty serves no useful purpose when defining a cartel offence, is uncertain in meaning, creates avenues for unmeritorious denials of liability and imprints a false and misleading label."[78]

It is not surprising, therefore, that the Australian legislature in drafting its criminal price-fixing statute has avoided a dishonesty test.

Second, *Norris* reinforces the impression that the dishonesty test is likely to prove a major stumbling block for prosecutors. Although in the context of a charge of conspiracy to defraud, the court held that in respect of a common law agreement in restraint of trade, unless there were aggravating features, "such as fraud, misrepresentation, violence, intimidation or inducement of a breach of such agreements were not actionable or indictable".[79]

While *Norris* applies to a common law charge of conspiracy to defraud in the context of a price-fixing case, any s 188 charge would now run the mill of defence lawyers seeking to argue on the authority of the highest court in the land that substantial aggravating features are required to be demonstrated. In effect, the dishonesty test would be assimilated to the aggravating features standard in *Norris*. Secrecy, it would be argued by defence counsel, would not be sufficient to demonstrate dishonesty. Instead, such aggravating features as fraud, violence or intimidation would be required, features usually whole absent from most price-fixing cartels.[80]

---

[78] B Fisse, "Defining the Australian Cartel Offence: Disaster Recovery", Competition Law Conference, Sydney, 24 May 2008 at www.brentfisse.com/../Fisse_Defining_the_Australian_Cartel_Offences_240608.pdf.

[79] *Norris Government of the United States of America* [2008] UKHL 16, at 17; n 6 above.

[80] One type of cartel which may find itself in some difficulty is the classic bid-rigging cartel where the cartelists have been required to sign tender documents which forswear collusion. Arguably, this act could count as an aggravating feature sufficient to satisfy the *Norris* test.

Third, there is concern regarding judicial incomprehension over the damage that price-fixing does to an economy. This incomprehension is noticeable in *Norris*. The judgment revealed significant judicial ignorance of a modern understanding of the damage caused by cartels on a modern economy in their discussion of the extant common law.[81] Whelan, for instance, points out that judicial hairsplitting based on the old case law did not recognise that: "[t]he distinction between maliciously injuring another and promoting one's own business interests is 'largely irrelevant' given what (economic) knowledge exists today concerning the damaging effects of cartel behaviour."[82]

Equally, in *Marine Hose*, on appeal the Criminal Division of the Court of Appeal significantly reduced the sentences of the defendants.[83] As MacCulloch points out, Hallett LJ was disconcerted by the US plea bargain, but she also did not appear to comprehend that, while the defendants may have been of previous good character, they had run an extremely serious international price-fixing ring.[84] But for the US plea bargain, it is possible that the Court of Appeal would have cut the defendants' sentences even more than it did.

Furthermore, it is far from clear that even the US success in bringing criminal price-fixing charges is as great as it seems. As Jacobs has pointed out, in most Federal cases where a defendant goes to trial, the conviction rate is 80 per cent, whereas in antitrust cases the conviction rate is 37 per cent.[85] Given that the number of cases where antitrust defendants decided to plead not guilty amounted to 60 out of 367 cases, where all other defendants pleaded guilty it could be argued that the plea-bargaining system was just effectively filleting out the weaker cases.[86]

However, Jacobs makes a strong case that the guilty pleas flow substantially from the enormous legal resources available to the Division in the prosecution of price-fixing cases. These include: a broadened notion of what constitutes a criminal conspiracy;[87]

---

[81] Which their Lordships recite and then indicate is still good law, see *Norris*, above n 17.

[82] P Whelan, "Resisting the Long Arm of Criminal Antitrust Laws: Norris v. United States" (2009) 72 MLR 272, 276.

[83] See n 76 above.

[84] A MacCulloch, Chapter 11 below.

[85] These figures are derived from a study by Jacobs of the Federal Justice Statistics from 1996 to 2005. See L Jacobs, "Criminal Enforcement of Antitrust Laws – Problems with the US Model" (2006) Fordham International Antitrust Law and Policy 25, 31. In fact, these statistics look worse for the Antitrust Division if defendant corporate entities are stripped out and only individuals are included. An earlier study (1992–1997) indicated that individuals escaped convictions approximately 80% of the time.

[86] *Ibid*, 31.

[87] *Ibid*, at 35–36.

the ability to produce evidence very late into a trial;[88] the ability to deploy the prospect of civil substantial damages to encourage criminal pleas;[89] the ratcheting up of criminal terms; and the prospect of additional parallel criminal charges if defendants do not plead guilty to the criminal price-fixing charge.[90]

As Jacobs stresses, "these unique features of US antitrust law have put the Antitrust Division in an enviable negotiating position that no other antitrust authority in the world can duplicate. The result is far more negotiated pleas than would be warranted on the merits".[91] There is a real danger of foreign antitrust agencies believing the American rhetoric and also that, even without the problem of a dishonesty test, US-scale criminal convictions are possible on foreign soil. This view overlooks the reality that, save with the advantages available to the Division, criminal price-fixing is inherently difficult to successfully prosecute. In price-fixing cases, evidence can often be given an alternative plausible explanation such as by reliance on oligopoly theory. Defendants can provide positive explanations as to their behaviour, such as the protection of the business and the maintenance of employment. These justifications are all made in the context of the criminal standard of proof and jury willingness to consider jail terms is normally reserved for significant crimes against the person. At the very least, to give s 188 a fighting chance, an amendment is required to remove the dishonesty test.

However, the author argues that considerably more could be achieved in terms of real deterrence and efficient prosecution if criminal price-fixing were abandoned and the OFT focused on civil corporate and personal penalties. First, the OFT would no longer have to comply with a higher standard of proof making it more difficult to obtain convictions against individuals and have such a high standard hampering civil prosecution.[92] Corporate and individual cases could run in parallel before the same court with the same OFT team dealing with the cases. This efficiency is underscored by the BA case, where the OFT agreed a fine of £121.5 million in August 2007 but the criminal trial against four BA executives does not open until January 2010. Personal financial sanctions and director disqualification would admittedly

---

[88] Normally the government is not required to identify its trial witnesses in advance: Jacobs, n 85 above, 36.

[89] *Ibid*, 44.

[90] *Ibid*, 45.

[91] *Ibid*.

[92] The practical consequence of the existence of s 188 is to raise the standard of proof and the procedural standards that the OFT has to comply with in all civil price-fixing cases in case there is a later criminal charge, again increasing the administrative burden on the OFT.

have limitations in deterrence terms, unlike jail sentences; however, they would be achievable, and clearly would have a deterrent effect in relation to rogue directors. There is currently little incentive for such officials to comply with rules against price-fixing, as if anyone is sanctioned it is the undertaking itself, the criminal law or the civil sanction rarely being applied to individuals. Individual financial sanctions and director disqualification could also further underpin the operation of the leniency regime by creating additional incentives for undertakings to enter into the programme earlier by punishing later applicants with individual sanctions.

It is argued that the choice for the OFT is between a real deterrent, though limited in its impact, that has a genuine effect, and a phantom deterrent effect of a criminal sanction than can rarely be applied in practice, which in addition slows down the prosecution process, adds administrative burdens and raises the standard of proof.

6 CONCLUSION: CLEARING THE WAY TO A MODERNISED ANTI-CARTEL REGIME

The OFT has made a considerable degree of headway in the development of its anti-cartel regime in its first decade. The essential case law has been established and cartel procedures such as the leniency programme successfully put into place. Infringement decisions have been adopted and appeals in price-fixing cases have been successfully defended before the CAT and the Court of Appeal.

The OFT now has the opportunity to take stock and look to prepare its price-fixing regime for the next decade. There are compelling arguments, made above, favouring the streamlining of the leniency regime and the procedural system to encourage more applicants to come forward and then the rapid prosecution of the new flow of cartel cases directly before the CAT. This could be reinforced by introducing a more attractive informant regime, offering innocent parties with knowledge of a cartel incentives to come forward and ultimately receive a very significant reward from the CAT. Equally, providing a degree of immunity for leniency applicants would significantly increase the incentive to come forward.

Most fundamentally of all, a major review of EA 2002, s 188 is required in which the OFT needs to consider whether the Cartel Offence can really be made to function effectively or whether it should seek personal civil financial sanction powers against individuals combined with greater use of the existing director disqualification power, and then apply both in parallel with its civil powers against undertakings.

Clearly some of these proposals will require further legislation. However, given the damage that cartels do to the British economy and the prospect of a new government in 2010, new competition legislation to enhance the OFT's ability to discover and prosecute cartels may well be on the political agenda of an incoming administration.

CHAPTER 11

THE CARTEL OFFENCE: IS HONESTY THE BEST POLICY?

*Angus MacCulloch**

Contributing to a retrospective work such as this is not an easy task when one is asked to pen a contribution on the topic which was the last to the "reform party", and by definition has the least practice to examine. That problem is exacerbated when that reform – the introduction of criminal penalties for certain "hard-core" cartel practices – was one of the most significant departures from the traditional model of competition law enforcement. The new cartel offence, as introduced by ss 188–189 of the Enterprise Act 2002, came into force in relation to conduct occurring after 20 June 2003. The key elements of the offence are found in s 188. Subsection (1) set outs that an individual commits an offence if he "dishonestly agrees with one of more other persons to make or implement" certain arrangements. Subsection (2) limits the type of "arrangement" which can result in liability. Those are arrangements which, "if operating as the parties to the agreement intend", would (a) fix prices, (b) limit supply, (c) limit production, (d) divide supply, (e) divide customers, or (f) bid-rig. Section 189 further limits liability to horizontal arrangements, where the parties operate at the same level of the market.

While the offence is now 6 years old, there is relatively little activity to speak of. There has been one, successful, prosecution,[1] and there is one high-profile case at the beginning of the criminal

---

* Senior Lecturer, Law School, Lancaster University. The author would like to thank Caron Beaton-Wells, particularly for her incredible help with the new Australian offences, Barry Rodger, and Andreas Stephan for their comments on the draft of this chapter; any errors, of course, remain entirely the author's.

[1] *R* v *Whittle, Allison & Brammar* [2008] EWCA Crim 2560.

process.[2] Such a slow start is almost inevitable in relation to criminal cartel investigations where cartel behaviour is usually the result of a relationship measured in years rather than in months and the avoidance of retroactive punishment is a fundamental concern, but it is also clear that while the cartel offence may not have had a particularly difficult birth, its formative years have not proven to be easy.

This chapter intends to outline the introduction of the offence and the limited practice to date. This context sets out our limited current understanding of the offence. The text moves on to consider what has become the most controversial element of the cartel offence – the place of dishonesty as one of its fundamental elements. The issue of the dishonesty test was a matter of some contention at the time of the introduction of the offence; and the judgment of the House of Lords in *Norris* v *Government of the United States of America*,[3] while not directly involving the cartel offence, raised further questions as to its use within cartel cases. The position of dishonesty in relation to the UK cartel offence is particularly difficult to assess given that the jurisdiction has not yet witnessed a full trial. The only prosecution was the result of a guilty plea acquired through a foreign plea bargain. Only after a number of full jury trials will its practical impact be fully understood.

While the debate surrounding dishonesty was ongoing in the UK there was an intriguing counterpoint in Australia. Since 2003 two Australian Governments have considered the criminalisation of some cartel activity.[4] The Australian cartel offences were passed by both houses of the Australian Parliament in June 2009. From a UK context it is particularly interesting to note that early versions of the Australian offences contained a dishonesty element but, following strong criticism, it was dropped in favour of an alternate mechanism. The Australian model will be examined and compared with the UK offence.

In summary, this chapter seeks to set out the limited practice to date and examine if the issues surrounding dishonesty are a significant problem for the maturation of the UK's cartel offence.

---

[2] Four BA executives have been charged in relation to the airline fuel surcharges cartel. See OFT Press Release 93-08, "OFT announces criminal charges in airline fuel surcharges cartel case", 7 August 2008. The men appeared in court on 12 November 2008, but were not required to enter a plea. The case was transferred to Southwark Crown Court for a jury trial.

[3] [2008] UKHL 16, [2008] 1 AC 920.

[4] Although the ACCC had been campaigning for some time, the recommendations of the Dawson Committee, Trade Practices Review Committee, "Review of the Competition Provisions of the Trade Practices Act", January 2003, http://www.tpareview.treasury.gov.au/content/report.asp, probably began the formal debate.

Will it become a fully fledged part of the UK competition regime or will it require further reform in order to play a more significant role alongside its civil law relations?

1 THE PRE-HISTORY OF THE CARTEL OFFENCE

The Parliamentary debate which led to the introduction of the cartel offence was of very mixed quality; many politicians seemed to struggle with some of the complex issues in contemporary competition policy. The Government's position, as set out in the White Paper, was quite clear. The introduction of the cartel offence was primarily designed to increase the deterrent effect of the competition regime; to bolster the corporate penalties available in s 2 of the Competition Act 1998 and Art 81 EC.[5] The Under Secretary of State made it clear that:

> "there is an important relationship between an offence on the statute book and a deterrent. The current measures do not have that deterrent effect, as they do not deal with individuals, but allow them to hide behind companies. There are commercial trade-offs for companies between fines that they may receive for entering into such arrangements and any commercial gain that, as we all accept, they may receive from cartels".[6]

But it was also made clear that the Government did not expect to see a wave of cases coming before the courts:

> "The point is not about how many people we send to prison. We do not want to have any cause to send anyone to prison for anything. However, if people break the law and the law states that a prison sentence is necessary, that is what they will receive. We would rather that people did not end up operating cartels, but it is important if they do that we send a message, both to the individual and to society, that it is unacceptable and a serious offence."[7]

While the number of prosecutions may not be key, for the cartel offence to have any real deterrent effect there must be a *real* threat of successful prosecution. If that threat is not active in the minds of individuals who may be tempted by the potential profits of a cartel at the time they are tempted there is no real deterrence. It was also made clear by the Government that they envisaged the threat of imprisonment as a key part of that threat; it being a much greater

---

[5] See *Productivity and Enterprise: A World Class Competition Regime* (Cm 5233, July 2001), Chap 7.

[6] *Hansard*, HC, Standing Committee B, Enterprise Bill, Fifth Sitting, col 169 (23 April, 2002).

[7] *Ibid*, col 162.

deterrent than a mere fine – notwithstanding that fines are also available in relation to the offence.[8]

This focus on deterrence very much fits in with the academic literature which addresses the question of cartel criminalisation[9] – and much of the debate which surrounds the relationships between criminalisation and other developments in the wider regulation of cartel activity through traditional administrative competition law prohibitions, enforcement mechanisms, and private actions.[10]

2 THE CARTEL OFFENCE SHOWS ITS TEETH

Prosecutions are crucially important in providing a real deterrent threat. Unfortunately the only case to date, *R* v *Whittle, Allison & Brammar*,[11] is highly unusual, its peculiarity reducing its wider impact, and the judgment of Hallett LJ in the Court of Appeal sends out a rather mixed message. This first UK prosecution had its genesis in Texas, where three UK nationals, associated with a UK company, were arrested at a Marine Hose cartel meeting, which also involved representatives of companies from Japan, Italy and France, held during the annual Offshore Technology Conference.[12] The cartel was responsible for price-fixing and bid-rigging. After being arrested in relation to breaches of US antitrust law, all three UK nationals confessed to their involvement and agreed to co-operate with the US Department of Justice. After a few days in custody and 7½ months of co-operation, under strict supervision,[13] all three entered into a plea bargain with the Department of Justice which would allow them to return to the

[8] Enterprise Act 2002, s 190.

[9] See W P J Wils, "Is Criminalization of EU Competition Law the Answer?" (2005) 28 World Comp 117 and P Whelan, "A Principled Argument for Personal Criminal Sanctions as Punishment under EC Cartel Law" (2007) 4(1) CompLRev.

[10] See C R Leslie, "Trust, Distrust and Antitrust" (2004) 82 Texas LRev 515, J M Connor and R H Lande, "The Size of Cartel Overcharges: Implications for US and EU Fining Policies" (2006) 51(4) Antitrust Bul 983, W P J Wils, "Optimal Antitrust Fines: Theory and Practice" (2006) 29(2) World Comp 183, C R Leslie, "Cartels, Agency Costs, and Finding Virtue in Faithless Agents" (2008) 49 William & Mary LRev 1621, W P J Wils, "The Use of Settlements in Public Antitrust Enforcement: Objectives and Principles" (2008) 31(3) World Comp 335, and P Nebbia, "Damages actions for the infringement of EC competition law: Compensation or deterrence?" (2008) 33 ELRev 23.

[11] [2008] EWCA Crim 2560.

[12] It is interesting to note that before the clandestine meeting in Texas one of the participants joked about checking for listening devices; unfortunately for them they did not check thoroughly or they might have found the US authorities' covert equipment that was about to record events.

[13] Including electronic tagging.

United Kingdom if they pled guilty to a charge under the UK's cartel offence. Part of the plea bargain sought to ensure that, should the sentences imposed by the UK courts be below a certain level, they would return to the United States to serve the remaining time there. Initial interviews with officials from the OFT began when the three were still in the United States. On their return to the United Kingdom all three co-operated and pled guilty at the earliest opportunity.

From the sentencing comments by the Honorary Recorder of Westminster Judge Rivlin it does not appear, should it have been necessary, that the prosecution would have struggled to prove the dishonesty of the three individuals involved. The highest level of condemnation was directed at Peter Whittle. He had begun his career with Dunlop Oil and Marine Ltd, but left in 2000 to set up a number of consulting companies. Those companies were effectively used to co-ordinate the cartel. It should be noted that this occurred before the cartel offence came into force, but Judge Rivlin, while noting the activities had been in place for some years, also made it clear that from June 2003, "until May 2007, when you were arrested, you were engaged in crime, and you knew it".[14] The clandestine nature of the cartel and Whittle's efforts to disguise its activity were indicated by the use of code names, covert meetings, and e-mail accounts with no connection to their companies. Whittle was paid $50,000 by each member of the cartel as remuneration for his efforts, but he also supplemented that income by receiving "commission", what can perhaps be better termed as "kick-backs", from cartel members who wished to circumvent the normal bid-rigging process and secure contracts of particular interest. It would be difficult to characterise these forms of behaviour as anything other than dishonest. In the case of David Brammar, the Sales and Marketing Director of Dunlop, there was also clear evidence of involvement in the clandestine day-to-day running of the cartel as co-ordinated by Whittle. Brammar also supplemented his normal salary with payments made by the cartel into a Swiss bank account. Presumably this account was not designed to be highly visible. The situation of Bryan Allison, the Managing Director of Dunlop, is perhaps more difficult. While he was not involved in the day-to-day running of the cartel, he was certainly aware of its activity and attended the meeting in Texas. In his sentencing remarks, Judge Rivlin considered Allison's involvement to be worse than that of Brammar; largely because Allison was more senior within the company and as Managing

---

[14] *R* v *Whittle, Brammar & Allison*, Sentencing Remarks, Crown Court at Southwark, 11 June 2008.

Director his task was to ensure the company was run honestly – in that he had "signally failed".[15]

In his final consideration of the sentence, Judge Rivlin listed a number of aggravating and mitigating factors. The aggravating factors were: (1) it was a "carefully planned and executed cartel fraud",[16] (2) the prolonged nature of the activity, (3) the sums of money involved, and (4) the damaging effect on business confidence and the integrity of the bidding process. The mitigating factors were: (1) the good character of the accused, (2) the dishonest conduct was entrenched at the time the act came into force and did not affect the quality of the goods, (3) that, in relation to Dunlop, the cartel was seen as necessary, by those involved, to secure the future of the company, and (4) all had been open, frank and co-operative and pled guilty at the earliest opportunity. Although Judge Rivlin was aware of the US plea bargain, saying it was "in the back of my mind",[17] it did not govern the decisions made.

The sentences imposed at trial were 3 years' imprisonment for Whittle, 2½ years' imprisonment for Brammar, and 3 years' imprisonment for Allison.[18] The terms of imprisonment were also bolstered with lengthy periods of director disqualification. The disqualifications were for 7 years, 5 years and 7 years respectively. Judge Rivlin also issued a stern warning in relation to future cases. While he had accepted that the entrenched nature of the cartel, before the offence came into effect, was a mitigating factor, he stressed: "Anyone minded to commit an offence of this nature now must understand that that will not be a feature of the mitigation open to them, and the likely sentence for any serious offence of this nature will be higher than imposed in this case."[19]

Further sanctions were imposed on Whittle and Brammar in a subsequent confiscation hearing. As they had received direct payments from the cartel they were found to have directly benefited from their criminal activity and were ordered to repay £1 million.[20]

One of the key concerns regarding the criminalisation of cartels, a concern shared with many other "white collar" offences, was the (un)willingness of the courts to impose lengthy terms of impris-

---

[15] *R* v *Whittle, Brammar & Allison*, n 14 above.

[16] *Ibid.*

[17] *Ibid.*

[18] The author understands that all three defendants served their sentences in Ford Open Prison.

[19] *Ibid.*

[20] See <http://business.timesonline.co.uk/tol/business/law/article4249992.ece>. Allison had not received direct payments and therefore was not subject to an order.

onment. Following Judge Rivlin's comments one could almost hear a collective sigh of relief among interested commentators. Notwithstanding the age, good character and co-operation of the defendants,[21] significant jail terms were imposed. This is particularly important in cartel cases given that those involved are not normally career criminals. They are invariably successful business persons of a certain age who, if required, could call on a number of highly respected character referees. The UK's standard reduction in sentence for those who plead guilty at the earliest opportunity is one-third.[22] The sentences imposed in this case were therefore at the top end of the spectrum with little reduction made for previous good character. Discounts for early pleas may well have an impact in many cartel offence cases, as the majority of prosecutions will probably follow some form of corporate or personal leniency application. In the face of a deluge of information coming to light in a leniency "race" between corporations seeking to limit their exposure, an early guilty plea may well be the most sensible option for those potentially facing a criminal charge in the UK.

The optimism following the sentences in the first UK case was rather short lived. The Court of Appeal, in November 2008, significantly reduced the sentences.[23] Hallet LJ was clearly uncomfortable with the impact of the US plea bargain in the UK case. While it may have been at the back of Judge Rivlin's mind, it was at the forefront of hers. One of the key factors that made the case difficult for the Court of Appeal was the element of the US plea bargain whereby the three men had agreed not to "seek from the UK court a sentence of imprisonment less than that" agreed in the US.[24] The sentences agreed to in that plea bargain were 2½ years for Whittle,[25] 20 months for Brammar,[26] and 2 years for Allison.[27] The Court of Appeal did not, therefore, hear full argument from counsel with regard to mitigation – their clients had an understandable desire not to be required to return to the United States. Although the court did not hear a full plea in mitigation it did outline, generally, the issues it took into account: the parties' otherwise good character; the assistance given to the authorities; the evidence given by Whittle in US proceedings, which

[21] In the face of overwhelming evidence against them.

[22] Sentencing Guidelines Council, *Reduction in Sentence for a Guilty Plea* (2004). The discount falls to 10% for a change of plea at the courthouse door.

[23] *R* v *Whittle, Allison & Brammar* [2008] EWCA Crim 2560.

[24] *Ibid*, at para 25.

[25] With a fine of $100,000.

[26] With a fine of $75,000.

[27] With a fine of $100,000.

was afforded special recognition; the fact they pled guilty at the first opportunity; and, the loss of livelihood and consequences to their families. Arguments were made, on behalf of the three, that the case was not "conceivably" one of the worst of its kind.[28] It is interesting to ponder how you could measure what would be the "worst" cartel in a situation such as this. In traditional administrative proceedings it would make sense to look at the value of affected market and the duration of the agreement, but when one is looking at the culpability of an individual's actions is the value of the affected market the only matter of import? The UK overcharge as a result of Dunlop's activities was referred to at trial and on appeal, but, surely, as the dishonest making or implementing of the arrangement is the heart of the offence, the individual culpability of those responsible for that particular arrangement must be key? This cartel was an international cartel covering an entire industry using sophisticated systems and techniques to hide its operation for a lengthy period. Is there a worse type of cartel? It is uncertain which criteria Hallet LJ adopted to decide the matter, but it is clear that the view was taken that the starting point adopted at first instance, which must have been very close to the maximum in Whittle and Allison's cases, was too high.[29] The second issue concerned mitigation. The Court of Appeal made it clear that had full arguments been heard they may have reduced the sentences much further had they been invited to do so.[30] Notwithstanding those comments, and their stated misgivings, the court considered it had no alternative to reduce the sentences to the level agreed in the US plea bargain.[31]

The willingness of the Court of Appeal to reduce the sentences considerably appears to reduce the deterrent threat of sentences for those convicted under the cartel offence. While that may be the case there are some reasons not to be too disheartened at this early stage. There may be three reasons for cautious optimism:

(1) The Court of Appeal made it very clear that they were not laying down any guidance in this case; presumably because of the unhelpful influence of the US plea bargain. It will be interesting to note what influence the judgment has on subsequent sentencing decisions.
(2) It is far more important that jail terms *are* imposed; rather than *lengthy* jail terms being imposed. The deterrent effect

---

[28] [2008] EWCA Crim 2560, at para 30.
[29] *Ibid*, para 30.
[30] *Ibid*, para 31.
[31] *Ibid*, para 32.

of the cartel offence, given the nature of the likely offenders, is based on the possibility of jail at all. Aging "white-collar" offenders are unlikely to take the view that 6 months' imprisonment is worth the risk, whereas 18 months is not. The individuals involved are likely to be successful and well respected. The threat of imprisonment is not only the loss of liberty for a period, but also the harm to their reputation in both business and social circles.[32] The appeal indicates the appellants' clear desire to minimise the pain of jail time, but no attempt was made to reduce the length of the director disqualifications. That choice suggests that CDOs constitute a much less effective deterrent; perhaps because imprisonment would effectively end a career, or it may be that CDOs are not, in reality, a significant hindrance to future earnings.

(3) The sentences imposed in the Marine Hose cartel did result in a limited, but useful, level of publicity. While the case may not have caused much of a ripple in the mainstream media, it did cause a flurry of press releases and discussion in the legal community.[33] It is this sort of publicity which is vital in creating a real deterrent threat. While the Marine Hose cartel did not prick the public consciousness, it is likely that the trial of the BA executives in the airline fuel surcharge cartel will be much more high profile.[34] While publicity before and during a trial is problematic it is important that the OFT uses high-profile cases to ensure that the business community is made aware of the real threat the cartel offence poses.

Any attempt to draw conclusions from one, rather unique, case is always fraught with difficulties. It was never envisaged that there would be a large number of prosecutions, but the lack of activity, in particular the fact that there has not yet been a full trial, is disappointing. Hopefully the upcoming trial in the airline fuel surcharge cartel may help us to understand many of the outstanding questions, but there is always a risk that high-profile acquittals could be counterproductive. The corporate settlements in the United Kingdom and United States in that case suggest that there is strong evidence of

---

[32] The impact of prosecution and conviction on a cartelist's family and friends is highlighted in G Geis, "The Heavy Electrical Equipment Antitrust Cases of 1961" in G Geis, R F Meir and L M Salinger (eds), *White Collar Crime* (3rd edn, 1995, NY, Free Press), at pp 153 and 161.

[33] See, Cobbetts, "'Banged Up' – Imprisonment for breach of competition law in the UK now a reality", and Wragge & Co, "Prison sentences for marine hose cartelists".

[34] The case was transferred to Southwark Crown Court for jury trial on 12 November 2008.

the existence of the cartel.[35] It would appear, then, that the trial will, rightly, focus on the culpability of the individuals involved.[36]

3 A QUESTION OF DISHONESTY – THE IMPORTANCE OF *NORRIS*?

The issue of dishonesty is likely to be central to the future development of the cartel offence. While there has been limited opportunity to examine the issue in cartel offence cases to date, an opportunity did arise for the House of Lords to examine the concept of dishonesty in another cartel context in *Norris* v *Government of the United States of America*.[37] While the situation in *Norris* was only indirectly related to the cartel offence, the events in *Norris* occurring before the offence came into force, the discussion of dishonesty in that case may have an impact on future developments

Ian Norris retired from his position as CEO of Morgan Crucible in 2002 after 29 years with the company. While the parent company was based in the United Kingdom, it had subsidiaries in the United States of America. In 1999 the US authorities began an investigation into price-fixing in the carbon industry in which the US subsidiaries of Morgan were involved. Many of Morgan's US directors, officers and employees were granted immunity from prosecution in a plea bargain, the companies paying fines. Mr Norris was not part of the plea bargain and in 2004 a grand jury returned an indictment with regard to Norris. The United States then sought to extradite Mr Norris on four counts in the indictment. The first count related to price-fixing in the carbon industry with agreements being made outside the United States, in Europe, Mexico and Canada, but implemented within the US between 1989 and 2000. Counts 2, 3 and 4 of the indictment related to various forms of obstruction of justice. Much of the discussion in the case was in relation to count 1, which

---

[35] See OFT Press Release 113/07, "British Airways to pay record £121.5m penalty in price fixing investigation", 1 August 2007, and Department of Justice Press Release, "British Airways plc and Korean Air Lines Co. Ltd. agree to plead guilty and pay criminal fines totaling $600 million for fixing prices on passenger and cargo flights", 1 August 2007. It is also interesting to note that a former BA executive has agreed to serve 8 months in a US jail for his part in the Air Cargo Shipments cartel: DoJ Press Release, "Former British Airways executive agrees to plead guilty to participating in price-fixing conspiracy on air cargo shipments", 30 September 2008.

[36] It is interesting to note that Martin George, the former BA Commercial Director, noted in his resignation letter that "inappropriate conversations" may have occurred in his office, but he stressed that, "the board have not found that I have behaved in a dishonest way". The wording used in that statement was no doubt influenced by the existence of the offence. See BBC News Online, "BA pair quit amid surcharge probe", http://news.bbc.co.uk/1/hi/business/6032975.stm.

[37] [2008] UKHL 16, [2008] 1 AC 92.

the Crown Prosecution Service had translated into English offences as conspiracy to defraud. The question that their Lordships had to answer was whether, at the material time between 1989 and 2000, the price-fixing behaviour would have constituted a criminal offence at common law. The Extradition Act 2003 requires that the conduct should be criminal in both the requesting and requested states.

The Appellate Committee, in a composite opinion, surveyed the historic position of price fixing at common law. It noted seminal cases such as *Jones* v *North*,[38] *Mogul Steamship Co Ltd* v *McGregor, Gow & Co*,[39] and *AG of the Commonwealth of Australia* v *Adelaide Steamship Co Ltd*.[40] The Committee summarised the position thus:

> "The common law recognised that an agreement in restraint of trade might be unreasonable in the public interest, and in such cases the agreement would be held to be void and unenforceable. But unless there were aggravating features such as fraud, misrepresentation, violence, intimidation or inducement of a breach of contract, such agreements were not actionable or indictable."[41]

It later went on to state:

> "Considering the matter as at the 1990s, the period covered by count 1, the consistent message which had been conveyed both by Parliament, through legislation enacted between 1948 and 1976, and by the judiciary, through cases decided from 1875 through to 1984, was that price-fixing was not of itself capable of constituting a crime. This message was reinforced by ministerial statements, even into this century, and in textbooks. There was no reported case, indeed, it would appear, no unreported case, no textbook, no article which suggested otherwise. Further, the legislation indicated that cartel operating was a matter for regulation, and the cases indicated that it did not even constitute a civil wrong."[42]

On the basis that there was nothing in the US indictment to suggest that any of the "aggravating features" mentioned above were present in Mr Norris's case their Lordships found that there was no extradition offence in count 1. The position was not as clear for the remaining counts, as obstructing an investigation would have been an offence in the UK, and the matter was remitted to the Divisional Court for further evidence to be heard.[43]

---

[38] (1875) LR 19 Eq 426.

[39] (1881) 21 QBD 544.

[40] [1913] AC 781.

[41] *Norris*, n 37 above, at para 17.

[42] *Ibid*, para 55.

[43] The Divisional Court ruled against Mr Norris and the Secretary of State ordered Mr Norris's extradition in September 2008. An appeal was lodged in the High Court, but

While the final judgment of the House of Lords was not entirely a surprise,[44] some of its statements can be read in a way which potentially causes difficulties for the prosecutions under the 2002 Act. The potential problem was indicated by Whelan as follows:[45]

> "The Law Lords essentially held that even with the inevitable secrecy that it entails, price-fixing cannot amount to a dishonest practice in law prior to 20 June 2003. But what happened on 20 June 2003? Did the entry into force of the Cartel Offence automatically establish that price-fixing is dishonest? And if so, how exactly did it do that? If not, then the judgment of the Lords may be persuasive enough authority to convince the Office of Fair Trading or the Serious Fraud Office not to go forward with a prosecution where "aggravating features" do not exist."[46]

Joshua and Fisse have expressed similar concerns[47] which, if accurate, would mean that the introduction of the cartel offence in 2003 simply narrowed the existing common law in that it cannot apply to corporations – only to individuals – and it reduced the maximum sentence to 5 years, as opposed to 10 for conspiracy to defraud. That surely cannot have been Parliament's intention? It also does not accord with the tenor of debate in the House when the cartel offence was introduced; as the Law Lords clearly indicate in *Norris*, the offence was not simply introduced to sit alongside the existing criminal law, but to create a new offence and criminalise behaviour that was not seen as being criminal before. It seems contradictory that the position at common law before the offence's creation, the position that the cartel offence explicitly sought to depart from, should be used to explain one of its constituent parts thereafter. The other confusing aspect of the Lords' position, if read forward into cartel offence cases, is that the dishonesty test is, essentially, one of morality; it is not a "legal" test. It is a matter for the jury to decide whether the behaviour of the individuals charged was contrary to standards of "ordinary and honest people".[48] As a moral question,

---

was dismissed: *Ian Norris* v *Government of the USA & Secretary of State for the Home Department* [2009] EWHC 995.

[44] As the author of a competition law text during the relevant period, the present author cannot claim to have suggested that cartel activity was criminal before the Enterprise Act 2002 came into force.

[45] P Whelan, "Resisting the Long Arm of Criminal Antitrust Laws: *Norris* v *The United States*" (2009) 72(2) MLR 272.

[46] *Ibid*, at 281–282.

[47] J Joshua, "Dishonesty after Norris" (2008) 7(4) Competition Law Insight 13, and B Fisse, "Price fixing and the cremation of dishonesty by the House of Lords", 14 November 2008, <www.brentfisse.com>.

[48] *Ghosh* [1982] QB 1053, [1982] 3 WLR 110, [1982] 2 All ER 689 (CA), at 696. The approach to dishonesty in this case has been held to be of general application, even outside the Theft Acts: *Lockwood* [1986] Crim LR 244 (CA).

it is clear that standards will change through time; behaviour that in the time of *Jones* v *North* may have been seen as "very honest"[49] may well not be considered as honest today.[50] The only empirical test of the British public's view of cartel activity was undertaken in 2007 by Andreas Stephan.[51] In that study he discovered that 63 per cent of Britons believed price-fixing to be dishonest.[52] That can be compared with 73 per cent who believed that price-fixing is harmful and should be punished. In an earlier study[53] there was also an indication that the views of the public hardened after they were educated as to the nature of cartel arrangements; presumably a trial would provide a useful education for those jurors who must decide on dishonesty. The author supports the view expressed by Lever and Pike, in 2005, that secrecy in a cartel should, in itself, denote dishonesty in that the cartelists, by hiding the truth, implicitly represented that "offers are being made competitively".[54] Harding and Joshua, in discussing the hardening of attitudes to cartel in the post-war era, described the process where cartels members are driven to ever greater efforts to hide their unlawful activity as a "spiral of delinquency".[55] It is arguable that in an increasingly harsh legal environment, which forces cartels into greater levels of subterfuge in order to avoid detection, it will be very difficult for many cartelists to convince a jury that what they were doing was honest and legitimate commercial practice. The first prosecutors will have an important task in painting a convincing picture for their juries.

4 AN ALTERNATIVE TO DISHONESTY IN AUSTRALIA

The Trade Practices (Cartel Conduct and Other Measures) Bill 2008 was passed by both Houses of the Australian Parliament on 16 June 2009; it became law 28 days after it received Royal Assent on 26 June 2009. One of the most important elements of that legislation was the introduction of cartel offences with a maximum jail term of 10 years for individuals. The offences also apply to corpora-

---

49 *Jones* v *North*, n 38 above, at p 429.

50 On the importance of morality to the cartel offence, see A MacCulloch, "Honesty, Morality and the Cartel Offence" [2007] ECLR 355.

51 See A Stephan, "Survey of Public Attitudes to Price-Fixing and Cartel Enforcement in Britain" (2008) 5(1) CompLRev 123.

52 Only one in four held that view strongly.

53 A Stephan, "No Worse than Shoplifting: Public Perceptions of Collusion at the 2006 BA Festival of Science" (2006) 11 CCP Newsletter 8. This was a much smaller study with less rigorous methodology.

54 J Lever and J Pike, "Cartel Agreements, Criminal Conspiracy and the Statutory 'Cartel Offence'", Part I, [2005] ECLR 90, 95; Part II [2005] ECLR 164.

55 C Harding and J Joshua, *Regulating Cartels in Europe* (2003, OUP, Oxford), p 51.

tions. The Australian offences are different from the UK offence, under the Enterprise Act 2002, in various respects. This chapter cannot undertake a comprehensive review of all the aspects of the legislation,[56] but there are a number of important areas of difference which act as an interesting counterpoint to the UK position; particularly as the Australian legislature, and commentators, had the benefit of the early UK experience to inform them.

The first official move towards the criminalisation of cartels in Australia was the report of the Dawson Committee in 2003.[57] There was a long wait, and a change of government, before the first Exposure Draft Bill was published in 2008.[58] One of the most controversial elements of that Exposure Draft Bill was to be found in ss 44ZZRF and 44ZZRG, where the two offences were set out:

> "**44ZZRF Making a contract etc. containing a cartel provision**
> Offence
> (1) A corporation commits an offence if:
> (a) the corporation makes a contract or arrangement, or arrives at an understanding, with the intention of dishonestly obtaining a benefit; and
> (b) the contract, arrangement or understanding contains a cartel provision.
>
> ...
> **44ZZRG Giving effect to a cartel provision**
> Offence
> (1) A corporation commits an offence if:
> (a) a contract, arrangement or understanding contains a cartel provision; and
> (b) the corporation gives effect to the cartel provision with the intention of dishonestly obtaining a benefit."

While the offences refer to corporations, they also create individual liability.[59] The introduction of the requirement of intention to

[56] For a comprehensive examination of the provisions, see C Beaton-Wells and B Fisse, "The Cartel Offences: An Elemental Pathology", LCA-FCA Workshop, Adelaide, 4 April 2009. Much of this section of the chapter relies heavily on this detailed study. See also C Beaton-Wells and B Fisse, Criminalising Serious Cartel Conduct: Issues of Law and Policy (2008) 36 Australian Business Law Review 166.

[57] Trade Practices Review Committee, "Review of the Competition Provisions of the Trade Practices Act" (January 2003) <http://www.tpareview.treasury.gov.au/content/report.asp>.

[58] Exposure Draft, Trade Practices Amendment (Cartel Conduct and Other Measures) Bill 2008, <http://www.treasury.gov.au/documents/1330/PDF/Attachment_A_cartels_Exposure_draft_bill.pdf>. For a critique of the Exposure Draft, see B Fisse, "Defining the Australian Cartel Offences: Disaster Recovery", Competition Law Conference, Sydney, 24 May 2008, available at <www.brentfisse.com>.

[59] Caron Beaton-Wells explained, in correspondence, the position as follows: "As the Australian *Trade Practices Act* is a federal law that regulates corporations in accordance with the federal constitutional powers, primary liability for contraventions of the Act

dishonestly obtain a benefit went even further than the UK offence. It was justified in the Press Release announcing the Government's intention to legislate in the following manner:

> "The Dawson Review put the view that using an element of dishonesty to identify criminal cartel conduct could cause difficulties to a jury. However, dishonesty is an established concept in Australian Criminal Law and is widely used in corporations and fraud offences. Further, dishonesty appropriately captures the genuinely criminal nature of serious cartel conduct."[60]

This addition was subject to a significant degree of criticism, most notably, but not exclusively, from Fisse.[61] His criticisms were numerous, but some of the most important were as follows:

- Dishonesty does not denote serious harm or culpability.
- The *Ghosh* test is "an undefined and undefinable populist notion"[62] which will cause problems in practice.[63]
- Dishonesty is a subjective test that may allow well funded defendants to escape liability.
- There are better ways of limiting the offence to serious cartel conduct.

The tone of the criticisms is summed up in the following:

> "the approach taken in EDB and the accompanying Discussion Paper is pre-occupied with making the element of dishonesty ... the prime distinguishing feature of criminal liability for cartel conduct. This pre-occupation is misguided. The concept of dishonesty is incapable of distinguishing serious from less serious forms of

---

rests with corporations, and this is reflected in the terms of ss 44ZZRF and 44ZZRG. For the purposes of this liability, the conduct and mental state of directors, employees or agents is imputed to the corporation provided they were acting within actual or ostensible authority. Individuals or non-corporate entities such as unincorporated associations or partnerships may attract primary liability under the application legislation of the States and Territories (the Competition Code) if they breach any of the prohibitions in that legislation. However, individuals may also attract ancillary (accessorial) liability in relation to the conduct of the corporation of which they are a director, employee or agent (see s 79). Ancillary liability arises, for example, where an individual aids, abets, induces or is knowingly concerned in contravening conduct. The standard for such liability is knowledge of the essential facts."

[60] Peter Costello, Treasurer of the Commonwealth of Australia, "Criminal Penalties for Serious Cartel Behaviour", 2 February 2005.

[61] See B Fisse, "The Cartel Offence: Dishonesty?" (2007) 35 ABLR 235, and B Fisse, "The Australian Cartel Criminalisation Proposals: An Overview and Critique" (2007) 4(1) CompLRev 51.

[62] B Fisse, "The Australian Cartel Criminalisation Proposals: An Overview and Critique" n 61 above, at p 53.

[63] The *Ghosh* test is used for all types of dishonesty within the Australian Criminal Code: Criminal Code Act 1995 (Cth), Chapter 7, 130.3–130.4.

prohibited cartel conduct. Even very minor instances of deception or fraud are 'dishonest'; the concept of 'trivial dishonesty' is commonplace. It is nonsense to suggest (as the EDB and the Discussion Paper seem to imply) that dishonesty necessarily requires serious wrongdoing. The concept of dishonesty serves no useful purpose when defining a cartel offence, is uncertain in meaning, creates avenues for unmeritorious denials of liability and imprints a false and misleading label."[64]

4.1 The new offences

The Australian Government appears to have taken heed of the criticisms made with regard to dishonesty, although many other issues remain unresolved, and revised the Bill to remove the "dishonestly obtaining a benefit" requirement. The version that eventually was passed in both Houses reads:

"**44ZZRF Making a contract etc. containing a cartel provision**
Offence
(1) A corporation commits an offence if:
    (a) the corporation makes a contract or arrangement, or arrives at an understanding; and
    (b) the contract, arrangement or understanding contains a cartel provision.
Note: Chapter 2 of the Criminal Code sets out the general principles of criminal responsibility.
(2) The fault element for paragraph (1)(b) is knowledge or belief.
...
44ZZRG Giving effect to a cartel provision
Offence
(1) A corporation commits an offence if:
    (a) a contract, arrangement or understanding contains a cartel provision; and
    (b) the corporation gives effect to the cartel provision.
Note: Chapter 2 of the Criminal Code sets out the general principles of criminal responsibility.
(2) The fault element for paragraph (1)(a) is knowledge or belief."

Before going on to look in more detail at how criminal responsibility and the fault elements operate, it is useful to consider the meaning of "cartel provision" and the relationship between the criminal provisions and the new forms of *per se* civil liability under ss 44ZZRJ and 44ZZRK of the Act. The concept of a "cartel provision" is common to both forms of liability and is defined in the

[64] B Fisse, "Defining the Australian Cartel Offences: Disaster Recovery", Competition Law Conference, Sydney, 24 May 2008, p 8 (footnotes omitted).

lengthy s 44ZZRD.[65] There are two basic elements to the concept. First, there is a purpose/effect condition, in price-fixing cases, or a purpose condition, in relation to output restriction, market allocation, and bid-rigging cases. The second element is the competition condition in subs (4). The competition condition requires that at least two of the parties be in competition, or would be in competition with each other without the offending behaviour. As the concept of cartel provision covers both civil and criminal liability it is wider than the behaviour covered by the UK offence, which is more narrowly defined in ss 188–189 of the Enterprise Act 2002. It has been argued that the definitions in the new parts of the TPA have considerable "overreach":

> "The definitions are too far-reaching for per se liability generally and for criminal liability, in particular. They capture conduct that is either not anti-competitive or may be positive in terms of consumer welfare. They do not seek to capture the essence of what is "serious", in economic terms, about cartel conduct, that is conduct that is intended by a firm to lessen competition between it and an actual or potential competitor or competitors."[66]

The fact that the same definitions are shared between the *per se* civil liability and the criminal liability raises interesting questions. Is the definition too broad because the two, arguably very different, forms of liability have been defined concurrently?[67] Would it have been better to allow for separate definitions to indicate the criminal liability falls only for particularly "serious" forms of cartel activity, or is it better to take the view that there is no such thing as a "trivial" cartel? Or is this simply another occasion where parliamentary draftsmen have struggled to deal with the complex economic reality of competition in the wild?[68] Whatever the reason for the concurrent

---

[65] As Beaton-Wells and Fisse note, in Beaton-Wells and Fisse, n 56 above, at fn 14, "Typical of the highly convoluted style of drafting the TPA generally, the definition of "cartel provision" in s 44ZZRD comprises 11 subsections and 36 paragraphs and runs for six pages."

[66] *Ibid*, at section 2.3 (footnotes omitted). Note also the lack of an ancillary restraints doctrine: see C Beaton-Wells, "Australia's Criminalization of Cartels – Will it be Contagious?", paper delivered at 4th ASCOLA Conference, 16–17 June 2009.

[67] It should also be remembered that the TPA retains other provisions that can be used against anti-competitive conduct in s 45(2): "(2) A corporation shall not: (a) make a contract or arrangement, or arrive at an understanding, if: (i) the proposed contract, arrangement or understanding contains an exclusionary provision; or (ii) a provision of the proposed contract, arrangement or understanding has the purpose, or would have or be likely to have the effect, of substantially lessening competition."

[68] See the author's comments with regard to the drafting in the Enterprise Act: A MacCulloch, "The Cartel Offence and the Criminalisation of United Kingdom Competition Law" [2003] JBL 616, 619.

definition of the "physical elements" of the offence, it does mean that considerable emphasis falls upon the "fault elements" to identify what is intrinsically criminal about the conduct and separate it from the per se civil liability.[69]

By virtue of the default application of the *Criminal Code* (Cth) to physical elements involving conduct,[70] the fault element of intention applies to making a contract or arrangement or arriving at an understanding under s 44ZZRF and giving effect to a cartel provision in s 44ZZRG. Both sections also require "knowledge or belief" in relation to their additional respective physical elements; that the contract, arrangement or understanding contains a cartel provision. Thus, in s 44ZZRF there must be an intention to make a contract, arrangement or understanding, and knowledge or belief that it contains a cartel provision. In s 44ZZRG there must be an intention to give effect to the cartel provision, and knowledge or belief that the contract, arrangement or understanding contains a cartel provision. The *Criminal Code* defines several of these terms. Intention has the meaning prescribed in s 5.2(1): "A person has intention with respect to conduct if he or she means to engage in that conduct." Knowledge has the meaning prescribed in s 5.3: "A person has knowledge of a circumstance or a result of he or she is aware that it exists or will exist in the ordinary course of events." Belief is not defined in the Code, and bears its ordinary meaning.[71] After criticism of the Draft Bill, recklessness will not be sufficient in relation to any physical element of the offence. The requisite fault elements must be present at the same time as the physical elements and can be proved by inference from circumstances or by direct evidence.[72]

4.2 Does this create a clear difference between civil and criminal liability?

The addition of the intention and knowledge or belief requirements is the key difference between the different forms of liability in the legislation, but it has been suggested that the true distinction between civil and criminal liability is the specific fault element in subs (2) of both sections – knowledge or belief. Beaton-Wells and Fisse argue that the "consensus and commitment" elements

---

[69] The concepts of "physical element" and "fault element" are central to the Criminal Code Act 1995 (Cth).

[70] A particular form of physical element, see *Criminal Code* (Cth), s 4.1; s 5.6(1).

[71] Attorney-General's Department, *The Commonwealth Criminal Code: a Guide for Practitioners*, (2002), p 69.

[72] See *R* v *Saengsai-Or* (2004) 61 NSWLR 135; and *Cao* v *The Queen* [2006] NSWCCA 89.

required for a contract, arrangement or understanding are "tantamount to an intention to agree".[73] As intention is implicit within the physical element of the offences, proof of knowledge or belief is effectively the only additional requirement for criminal liability. This appears to limit the offences to situations where the parties to the contract, arrangement or understanding are aware of and understand the basic nature of the cartel provision at the time they make a contract, arrangement or understanding, or give effect to the provision contained in the contract, arrangement or understanding. The main recipients of the protection then appear to be those who give effect to agreements, made by others, but who are not aware of, or do not appreciate, their true nature. It is more difficult to foresee circumstances in which a party makes a contract, arrangement or understanding but is not aware of its purpose.[74]

It is also important to remember that both civil and criminal forms of cartel liability in the TPA apply to both corporations and individuals.[75] If the criminal sanctions of the Act are to be applied to a corporation, intention and knowledge or belief must be imputed to the company from individuals within it. It should, however, be noted that such intention and knowledge or belief can come from a director, employee or agent of the body corporate.[76] It is thus vicarious rather than fault-based responsibility.

From the summary above it appears that the differences between the civil and criminal liability under the new Australian provisions are relatively limited. The definition of the physical elements of liability must be broad enough to catch all forms of "cartel provision" that should attract *per se* civil liability, and the only further hurdle from that wide starting point is the addition of a separate fault element, of knowledge or belief, for criminal liability. Due to the overlapping nature of the separate forms of liability in the legislation there is an important role for prosecutorial discretion to limit the use of criminal liability to the more deserving cases. A Memorandum of Understanding between the ACCC and DPP has been issued which sets out factors which would be taken into account in deciding whether a case should be referred by the ACCC for prosecution by the DPP.[77] The ACCC will consider whether: the

---

[73] Beaton-Wells and Fisse, n 56 above, p 54.

[74] However, see the discussion of the purpose element, "wilful blindness" and the impact of exceptions and authorisations in Beaton-Wells and Fisse, n 56 above, p 55 et seq.

[75] See the explanation in n 59 above.

[76] See the revised s 84.

[77] Memorandum of Understanding between the Commonwealth Director of Public Prosecutions and the Australian Competition and Consumer Commission regarding Serious Cartel Conduct, December 2008. A Memorandum of Understanding has also been

conduct was longstanding or had a significant impact on the market in which the conduct occurred; or, the conduct caused significant detriment to the public, or caused significant loss or damage to one or more customers of the alleged participants; or, one or more of the alleged participants has previously been found by a court to have participated in cartel conduct either criminal or civil; and, the value of the affected commerce would exceed $1 million within a 12-month period. It would therefore appear that the scale and impact of the cartel, along with recidivism, are the key drivers for prosecution. Is it satisfactory to leave such an important question outside the legislation itself, and in effect pass it to enforcement agencies? Prosecutorial discretion will always play an important role in offences such as these, but the present author would be more satisfied with a much clearer indication, on the face of the legislation, as to what forms of conduct and fault, or physical and mental elements, make behaviour criminal rather than simply unlawful.

4.3 Comparison with the UK cartel offence

The new Australian cartel offences act as a useful counterpoint to the UK offence, but are not a good comparator; the two offences are very different in many respects. Some of the key differences, relevant to this chapter, can be summarised as follows: the dual definition of civil and criminal liability in Australia, the availability of corporate and individual criminal liability in Australia, and the different indicators of fault or culpability in the UK and Australian offences.

Dual definition

In the revised TPA the same physical elements are required for both civil and criminal liability for cartels, although there is provision in s 45(2) for a wider form of civil liability based on a substantial lessening of competition test. This can be compared with the very different forms of liability in the UK under Art 101 TFEU/Chapter I of the 1998 Act and the cartel offence under the Enterprise Act 2002. Looking only at the wording of the statutory provisions, as there is relatively little practice outside Art 101 TFEU/Chapter I, it appears that the dual definition in the revised TPA is potentially problematic. One of the most obvious differences is the distinction between the drafting of Art 101 TFEU and the drafting in the statutory definitions in both the Enterprise Act 2002 and the TPA. It appears that contemporary statutory draftsmen tie themselves in knots trying

---

issued by the DPP and ACCC in relation to Immunity Policy: see ACCC, "Revised ACCC immunity policy for cartel conduct", 26 June 2009.

to capture the essence of the competition problem, but largely fall short of the mark.[78] Older competition law provisions, which would include the Treaty on the Functioning of the EU and the Sherman Act, were drafted in a very different style; which has allowed a better understanding of their extent to develop over time. While it is arguable that deliberately drafting a vague provision that can be honed over time is a dereliction of responsibility, it does have the benefit of flexibility. Such flexibility is, however, potentially desirable only in relation to civil liability. There is little good to be said for flexibility of definitions in the criminal law. In such circumstances it is important to be able to clearly indicate what form of behaviour and state of mind are required for criminal liability to attach.

It is suggested that any attempt to draft a fully worded definition of cartel activity for civil liability, where the main concern is catching behaviour which has an effect harming consumer welfare, is a near impossible task. The indications are that the revised TPA definition is problematic in that it may be both over- and under-inclusive in different ways.[79] While the drafting in Art 101 TFEU is in no way perfect, it has shown that it is capable of adaptation to reflect the changing economic thinking of the times and be interpreted to catch new, and previously unconsidered, forms of anti-competitive behaviour. The drafting of the ss 188–189 of the Enterprise Act 2002 shares many issues with s 44ZZRD, in that it struggles to get to the heart of the problem that the offence seeks to address; rather than simply describing the obvious topographical features of cartel behaviour. The Enterprise Act 2002 may have a slight advantage in that it is somewhat narrower: only describing the relationships between individuals in certain "hard-core" cartels.[80] However, it struggles to do even that.

Corporate and individual liability

While the new Australian offences allow for both corporate and individual liability, the UK offence provides only for individual liability; corporate responsibility is dealt with by Art 101 TFEU/ Chapter I of the 1998 Act. There are strong arguments for corporate criminal liability in the regulation scholarship,[81] but there is little chance of such a development in the current European context. Since the settlement between the European Commission and the

[78] The draftsmen of the Chapter I and II prohibitions in the 1998 Act made a very wise decision to avoid drafting difficulties by simply copying the relevant parts of the EC Treaty.

[79] See, in particular, Beaton-Wells and Fisse, n 56 above.

[80] Perhaps that is the only reason it is a little shorter.

[81] Interestingly much of that scholarship comes from Australian academics: see, eg, B Fisse and J Braithwaite, *Corporations, Crime and Accountability* (1993, CUP, Cambridge).

Member States in Art 3 of Regulation 1/2003[82] it is quite clear that the United Kingdom could not effectively put in place, or certainly not effectively enforce, a separate and different national provision in addition to Art 101 TFEU.[83] Recital 8 of Regulation 1 makes it clear that criminal sanctions against individuals do not impinge upon the EU prohibition. The author has previously argued that the clear distinction between Art 101 TFEU and the cartel offence is beneficial; and still holds that view.[84] The fact that the two provisions try to achieve different things in different ways is helpful in giving each provision a clear role within the overall regime; that clarity of purpose is an aid to their separate and unique development and, hopefully, future success.

Indicators of fault or culpability

How properly to impute criminal responsibility for cartel activity is still one of the most difficult issues for cartel criminalisation. The Australian approach, requiring intention to make an agreement and knowledge or belief as to its nature, resolves some of the difficulties of proof and uncertainty that have haunted the discussion of the dishonesty test. While it is accepted, in many jurisdictions, that cartel behaviour is damaging, and therefore wrong, it is a separate question as to whether it is generally accepted that those involved should be criminally culpable. The Law Lords' view, in *Norris*, that pre-2002 cartel behaviour in the United Kingdom was not dishonest only goes to demonstrate that ongoing difficulty. The Australian test removes some of that difficulty, as it is no longer necessary to prove that the behaviour is dishonest to the standard of "ordinary and honest people", but it puts a much greater burden on the correct definition of the physical elements of the offence. If culpability is not defined through the mental element, the act in itself must be such as to indicate culpability. The definitions of the culpable act are not particularly satisfactory in either the TPA or the Enterprise Act 2002. It seems that the TPA may simply be replacing one set of problems with another. The much wider TPA could be seen as criminalising acts which the wider public do not intrinsically consider to be "real crime".

To avoid the criminalisation of trivial, i.e. not serious, cartels the TPA will rely on prosecutorial discretion as set out in the Memorandum of Understanding between the ACCC and the DPP.[85]

---

[82] [2003] OJ L1/1. See also Recitals 8 and 9.

[83] Criminality alone would not be an issue, as the unique constitutional position of the Republic of Ireland indicates, but applying a separate standard or test alongside Art 81 would raise difficult questions.

[84] See MacCulloch, n 68 above.

[85] See n 77 above.

That Memorandum highlights another potential distinction between the approaches in Australia and the UK. It defines seriousness, first, through the effect of the behaviour, a significant impact or detriment. The second element is a very narrow form of moral culpability – recidivism – and that is subject to a *de minimis* test based on the value of commerce. The author has argued that the UK offence, through the use of the dishonesty test, moves away from defining culpability through effects. Article 101 TFEU enforcement and fines are the mechanisms to deal with the effects of collusion.[86] The UK offence, as currently constituted, looks much more closely at the intention and manner of the individual's behaviour to define the criminality of the act. That is not to say that the impact or detriment caused by the behaviour is irrelevant to that culpability, as was shown in the *Marine Hose* case, but that it is only one of the issues that could indicate the nature and extent of the individual's culpability. Behaviour may be more culpable when it has a great impact, but is not only culpable when it does so.

5 CONCLUSIONS

The UK cartel offence's report card at this early stage in its development should probably read: "qualified success, but could try harder". It has general support across the legal community and the significant jail terms in the Marine Hose cartel suggest that the judiciary is willing to impose real sanctions. The only important group of people that may remain to be convinced of the importance of the cartel offence is the general public. The public still has relatively little awareness of the cartel problem but will have a vitally important role to play in the future development of the offence.

The public's view of the honesty, or dishonesty, of cartel behaviour remains the most controversial – and most unpredictable – issue. The judgment in *Norris* was unhelpful in many regards,[87] but the author does not believe that it will pose an insurmountable problem. The Law Lords were required to address a legal question of a historical nature. The jury in the airline fuel surcharge cartel trial will not be looking at legal history; they will be focusing on the moral culpability of an individual's involvement in a particular series of events. The continued debate surrounding dishonesty has dominated this chapter. No apology is made for that as, at this point in time, we are faced with the uncertainty of a "Chicken/Egg" debate. As *Norris* made clear, cartel activity was not considered to be wrongful in the

[86] See MacCulloch, n 50 above.

[87] *Norris* v *Government of the USA*, n 3 above.

early part of the 20th century, but attitudes have been consistently hardening in the post-war era.[88] Which came first, dishonesty or the offence? Have attitudes simply hardened over time so that the increasingly delinquent behaviour of cartelists is considered more harshly, or has the creation of the offence tipped the balance and made it clear that the cartel behaviour set out is clearly wrong, and therefore it is more likely that a jury will see it as dishonest? We will probably never get an answer to the question of how that change came about, but it is hoped that we see, in the context of a trial, that the change has definitely occurred.

If dishonesty is such a problem should the UK follow Australia's example and look for an alternative to indicate culpability? It is understandable why there was strong pressure applied to drop the original suggestion of a "dishonestly obtaining a benefit" test from the revised TPA. The early history of the UK's cartel offence has hardly shown that the dishonesty issue is easily resolved. From a first reading of the new Australian provisions it seems clear that they are not without their own difficulties and complications. The use of intention and knowledge or belief will be easier to establish at trial and explain to a jury, but they do very little to explain why cartel behaviour is criminally culpable and deserving of serious punishment. As an offence moves to a stricter form of liability, more and more importance is placed on the correct delineation of truly culpable acts or conduct. The author is not convinced that either jurisdiction has such a definition. In consumer law there has been a move away from strict liability criminal offences towards other forms of regulation. Part of that shift may be explained by the attitude taken to such offences by the courts; they were not seen as "real" crimes. This sort of attitude is typified by Lord Scarman in *Wings Ltd* v *Ellis* stating that the Trade Descriptions Act: "is not truly a criminal statute. Its purpose is not the enforcement of criminal law but the maintenance of trading standards. Trading standards, not criminal behaviour, are its concern".[89]

The dishonesty element brings the cartel offence clearly into a group of offences that are truly criminal in nature. The removal of the dishonesty element may jeopardise that position and risk the offence being demoted to a mere "regulatory offence" of a lesser nature. As the threat of imprisonment is key to the success of the cartel offence as a real deterrent, the author would urge caution before embarking on such a risky development.

---

[88] For a comprehensive history of that hardening attitude, see Harding and Joshua, n 55 above, Chaps 3–5.

[89] [1984] 3 All ER 577, at p 587. For a fuller discussion, see G Howells and S Weatherill, *Consumer Protection Law* (2nd edn, 2005, Ashgate, Aldershot), Chap 11.

It would be preferable that a great deal of care be taken to prosecute only the truly delinquent behaviour of the worst cartelists, where the individual's behaviour looks most suspect, to ensure that there are small number of high-profile jail sentences. The other option might be easier, in the sense of making successful prosecutions more likely, but it is arguable that the defendant will not be seen as being a true criminal and the courts may choose not to punish them as such. The author is keen to see the cartel offence take its place as part of criminal law; not merely to be the guarantor of good "business standards".

INDEX